THE COMPLETE BOOK OF
THE GREENHOUSE

THE COMPLETE BOOK OF
THE GREENHOUSE

IAN G. WALLS

With contributions from

A. G. Channon, R. A. Martin & J. W. Newbold

First published in the United Kingdom in 1973 by
Ward Lock

Reprinted 1974, 1976, 1977
2nd edition 1979
3rd edition 1983
4th edition 1988
Reprinted 1991 (twice), 1992, 1997, 1998, 2000, 2004, 2005

Copyright © Ian G. Walls & Cassell & Co
1973, 1979, 1983, 1988, 1996

This paperback edition first published in 2001 by
Cassell Paperback,
This edition published in
Great Britain in 2004 by Cassell Illustrated,
a division of Octopus Publishing Group Limited
2-4 Heron Quays, London E14 4JP

Copyright © Ian G. Walls
& Octopus Publishing
Group Limited 2004

Distributed in the United States of America by
Sterling Publishing Co., Inc.
387 Park Avenue South,
New York, NY 10016-8810

A CIP catalogue record for this book is available
from the British Library

ISBN-10 1-84188-145-7
ISBN-13 978-1-841881-45-4

Printed in Slovenia by DELO Tiskarna

Contents

Preface

Recent years have seen a tremendous increase in greenhouse gardening among non-professionals. It has been due partly to the now ready availability of factory-built greenhouse units, partly to the flood of automatic aids to environmental control which are so necessary for the part-timer, and also to the plant breeders who have produced heavy cropping and disease-resistant varieties of many popular crops. Many new growing aids such as special composts and growbags help to stimulate interest. High unemployment and early retiral have also played a vital part.

The secret of success in this as in most aspects of gardening is attention to detail, and the detail necessary for satisfying and rewarding greenhouse cultivation in temperate latitudes is what this book sets out to provide. It takes into account the findings of recent horticultural research and the development of new cultural techniques, and attempts some reconciliation between amateur and commercial practice.

The author gratefully acknowledges the invaluable assistance he has received from numerous individuals, companies and research bodies in the preparation of the book. In particular he wishes to thank A. G. Channon B.Sc. Ph.D. and J. W. Newbold B.Sc. for the tables on the pests, diseases and physiological disorders of greenhouse plants; R. A. Martin B.Sc. for the chapter on composts for greenhouse plants; J. R. Woodhams (Supervisor of the Fern Collection at the Royal Botanic Gardens Kew) for his assistance in preparing the chapter on the cultivation of ferns under glass; Susan Phillips for the chapter on the cultivation of cacti, and the late Charles Simpson for his contribution on the cultivation of orchids in the greenhouse. He would also like to record his gratitude to Suttons Seeds Ltd, Hele Road, Torquay, Devon; Robinsons of Winchester Ltd, Chilcomb Lane, Chilcomb, Winchester, Hampshire. Clovis Lande Associates Ltd, Branbridges Road, East Peckham, Tonbridge, Kent; "Garden Rewards" 104 Branbridges Road, East Peckham, Tonbridge, Kent; National Chrysanthemum Society, 2 Lucas House, Craven Road, Rugby, Warwicks; Greenock Telegraph, Crawfurd St, Greenock, Strathclyde.

The author also gratefully acknowledges the many individuals and firms who have supplied pictures, product or plant information and helped generally with the production of this edition, in particular to David Gannicott, Senior Advertisement Manager of *Amateur Gardening*, ICI Agrochemicals and Alan Wright of ADAS for their assistance with the Pests and disorders section.

His sincere thanks are also due to the editorial staff of Ward Lock Ltd and in particular to Denis Ingram and Jenny Hopkins. In addition thanks are also due to Frank Hardy for his line drawings.

I.G.W.

Publisher's Notes

1. Readers are requested to note that, in order to make the text intelligible in both hemispheres, timings are generally described in terms of seasons not months. In some instances, e.g. in some tables, it is not practicable to use seasons and the months cited are for the northern hemisphere. However, by using the following table the reader can easily translate timings of seasons or months from one hemisphere to another.

NORTHERN HEMISPHERE				SOUTHERN HEMISPHERE
Mid-winter	=	January	=	Mid-summer
Late winter	=	February	=	Late summer
Early spring	=	March	=	Early autumn
Mid-spring	=	April	=	Mid-autumn
Late spring	=	May	=	Late autumn
Early summer	=	June	=	Early winter
Mid-summer	=	July	=	Mid-winter
Late summer	=	August	=	Late winter
Early autumn	=	September	=	Early spring
Mid-autumn	=	October	=	Mid-spring
Late autumn	=	November	=	Late spring
Early winter	=	December	=	Early summer

2. Readers are also requested to note that new legislation has been introduced for pesticide availability and use. You are recommended to consult a current copy of *Pesticides*, published by the Ministry of Agriculture, Fisheries and Food or *Garden Chemicals* (see page 259).

PART I

On the Design and Running of Greenhouses

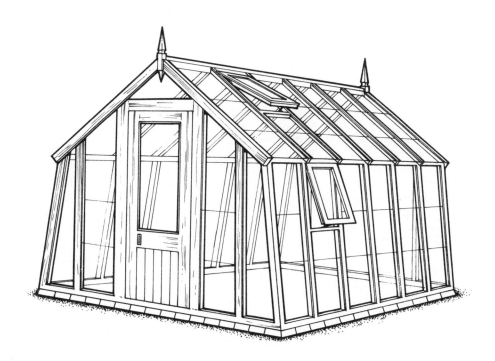

CHAPTER 1
The Historical Perspective

The growing of plants in covered houses, whether they be greenhouses, conservatories or orangeries, is essentially a northern hemisphere phenomenon. It is not, however, a new phenomenon, and the first attempts at growing plants under artificial conditions go back to at least early classical times. For countless generations much use has also been made of 'shade houses' or natural cover to allow the cultivation of many plants which are affected by excess sunlight. Shade houses have in recent years become very widely used for crop protection in warm or tropical countries.

The Greeks with their 'gardens of Adonis' appear to have had forcing houses in miniature. Plato in his *Phaedo* says that 'a grain, a seed or a branch of a tree placed in or introduced to these gardens acquired in eight days a development which could not be obtained in as many months in the open air'. Columella, a Roman writer on rural matters, speaks of Rome possessing 'within the precincts of her walls, fragrant trees, trees of precious perfumes such as grow in the open air in India or Arabia'. The implication of this is that they were not grown in the open air in Rome. It was Caesar Tiberius, however, who introduced a utilitarian note to these early attempts at covered gardening. Told by his doctor that he needed a cucumber a day to cure an illness, he instructed his gardener to produce a cucumber a day or else! The gardener succeeded in growing cucumbers *fere toto anno* by cultivating them in pits filled with fermenting dung and covered with frames or lights of talc or mica.

In later Roman times forcing was done by means of *specularia*, buildings covered with sheets of mica, thinly split, and it was mainly fruits, cucumbers and peaches among them, that were grown in this way; the epigrammatist Martial refers to peaches in *specularia*. Among the ruins of Pompeii a building of this kind has been discovered, with masonry staging for displaying plants and hot air flues in the walls; it was apparently originally glazed with talc or rough glass.

With the decline of the Roman empire the practice of forcing fruit in artificial conditions seems to have been abandoned in Europe, and not until the thirteenth century do we hear of any attempt to revive it. In 1295 Albert Magnus, a Paduan, is said to have entertained William of Holland, king of the Romans, in a garden maintained in flower and fruit by artificial heat. The wealthy merchants of Venice and Genoa, importers of many luxurious fruits, were probably the next to attempt glasshouse construction.

Farther north, the earliest development of the greenhouse appears to have taken place in France; the lead was subsequently taken by the Dutch when at the height of their maritime empire, and it passed ultimately to Britain. The first covered gardens were orangeries, normally without heat, built for sheltering citrus fruits during the winter months, but by the seventeenth century these had reached a fair degree of perfection. In 1685 Jules Mansard (or Mansart) built the noblest orangery in Europe for Louis XIV at Versailles. It had three arcaded galleries, the central portion of which was 154m (508ft) long, 13m (42ft) wide and 14m (45ft) high. In 1693 Fagon, Superintendent of the Jardin Royal, constructed the famous hothouse which he warmed with 'stoves and furnaces' for the preservation of tender plants, including the tea plant. The first successful attempt in Britain at greenhouse gardening was made at the Physic Garden at Oxford where the buildings were of wooden construction, very little better than cold frames.

In general, orangeries, which were unheated, came first; these were followed by conservatories, essentially houses for conserving tender plants; the stovehouse, which was heated to a high degree, came later. The credit for coining the word greenhouse (a house for conserving tender "greens") goes to the diarist, Englishman John Evelyn.

In the early days the greatest problems related to heating, and all sorts of fantastic methods were used. The Dutch first used free-standing stoves which had to be fuelled from inside the greenhouse. It was fairly soon realized, however, that fumes from the stoves were destroying the plants, and quite a number of gardeners also appear to have been choked to death by these early furnaces. Even more primitive was the portable brazier, filled with burning coals and wheeled to and fro, used to heat the first greenhouses at the Oxford Physic Garden. Subsequent developments involved moving the stove outside and heating the back wall of the greenhouse by means of complicated flues.

At this time the only people who had greenhouses were the very wealthy. In Britain there was no real progress made in glasshouse development until the tax on glass was repealed in 1845. At that time when a gardener's day rate was 1s 6d (7½p) and a tradesman's 2s (10p), crown glass sections were 9d (4p) each and measured 23cm × 50cm (9 × 20in) approximately. Before 1845 a crate of crown glass cost £12, but by 1865 the price had dropped to £2 8s (£2.40). With such a reduction in the price of glass, development was rapid and greenhouses sprang up everywhere. Every gentleman with any self-respect had to have a greenhouse. The aristocracy really became enthusiastic and a number of structures similar to the Palm House at Kew were erected, perhaps the most famous being the huge conservatory built by Paxton for the Duke of Devonshire at Chatsworth.

Another major breakthrough occurred when hot water heating for greenhouses was invented. Incredible though it may seem, until 1818 nobody realized that hot

The great conservatory at Chatsworth House built by Paxton, one of the indefatigable pioneers of greenhouses. He was also one of the moving forces behind the Crystal Palace built for the Great Exhibition.

THE GREAT CHATSWORTH CONSERVATORY.

THE EXTERIOR, FROM THE ITALIAN TERRACE.

water circulated naturally. Once this principle had been understood all manner of boilers were invented, the manufacturers of each one claiming invariably that their boiler presented a larger area of water to the fire than anyone else's and was therefore a more efficient heat exchanger. One wonders what the proud possessors of the first boilers would have thought of a modern small bore, or mini-bore, heating system! The next problem, of course, was how to ventilate the heated greenhouse efficiently, while keeping it at an acceptable temperature to the plants being raised.

Once electricity became available, fur-

ther advances followed in greenhouse development, and while it was cheap many greenhouses used it for heating to high levels. Today electricity is used mainly for heating to moderate levels, but is essential for the operating of almost everything in greenhouse mechanics. It is also used for artificial illumination, both so that one can see in the greenhouse after dark and to encourage the growth of plants generally or those with long-day requirements: for automatic ventilation and shading and for air circulation.

Thus, although greenhouses have developed rapidly and have come a long way

An interior view of Paxton's great conservatory at Chatsworth House. This was one of the great 'sights' of its day.

from the earliest attempts by the Romans in classical antiquity, the basic problems faced by greenhouse designers and engineers today are still the same as they were in those days, and indeed throughout the whole history of the development of greenhouses, including the heyday of the Victorians. The giant conservatories such as that built by Paxton at Chatsworth House faced precisely the same problems as the 2.4 × 3.6m (8 × 12ft) greenhouse found so frequently in private gardens today. The difficulty has always been to find an effective balance between heating and ventilating, and between light and shade. Too much heat and the plants boil to death in their own condensation; too much ventilation and it becomes almost impossible to raise the temperature to the desired level; too much light and the greenhouse overheats in summer; too much shade and the plants become drawn and leggy. However, with modern electric and other largely automatic aids it is now possible to overcome all these problems and to have a greenhouse that is not only more efficiently heated, ventilated, lit and shaded than ever before, but also to have these elements in proper balance and so automatic in their running that the greenhouse can virtually be left to run itself at a reasonably economic price. Indeed, all the modern greenhouse gardener need do is enjoy his plants in theory at any rate.

Recent years have also seen the introduction of many different kinds of plastic materials such as polythene, PVC and others, and these have brought a new dimension to protected gardening. Greenhouse prices are also highly competitive.

Nowadays conservatories or garden rooms have become extremely popular for a wide range of gardening activities, including plant raising during the early part of the year. They take the form of sophisticated greenhouses of various shapes, either built into the original design of the home or built on to a wall of favourable aspect and linked to the living quarters by patio doors or other form of access doors. Gardeners are increasingly keen to have a section of their homes where they can relax in the sun and enjoy being surrounded by plants.

In a more practical vein, gardeners are anxious to link what is generally a highly efficient house heating system to the conservatory or garden room. It is always wise to take professional advice regarding heating and ventilation. Quality conservatories are not cheap and it is important to look for designs which have a superior trouble-free glazing system and adequate ventilation facilities. Propagators or mini-greenhouses in their various forms can provide a congenial propagating and growing temperature at low running costs. It is also of note that newer types of polythene are effective in trapping heat and can provide growing conditions very similar to a greenhouse in terms of light values and running costs for heating.

CHAPTER 2
Site Selection & Preparation

Some climatic factors in greenhouse siting

Careful consideration of terrain and climate is important in siting the commercial greenhouse if it is to be economically viable in face of competition from more favoured countries. The non-professional greenhouse gardener, though he may have no choice but to stay where he is, ought at least to be aware of basic climatic principles and their significance.

Latitude The nearer a country is to the equator the nearer it is to the sun; the farther one journeys away from the equator, broadly speaking, the colder it gets.

Effect of large areas of water Water like glass has reflective properties and large bulks of it add to the total amount of illumination available.

The thermal warmth of large areas of water is also of great significance, as heat is stored in the water and radiated back to the air (see Fig. 1). The influence of the Gulf Stream or Mid-Atlantic Drift on the whole western and southern coast of Britain is considerable in the raising of air temperatures and the reduction of winter frost.

Prevailing winds The prevailing wind for the whole of Britain is a south-westerly, coming from warm areas, and this, combined with the Gulf Stream, makes the whole western part of the country milder and wetter than the east.

Humidity Areas near large bulks of water and areas of high rainfall have high humidity; so do densely planted areas due to transpiration of water through the leaves of the trees. A high moisture content in the air not only affects the growth of plants but also the incidence of disease.

Many gardeners erect a greenhouse and expect it to be (in terms of horticultural capabilities) the exact image of any other greenhouse. Such is not the case. An

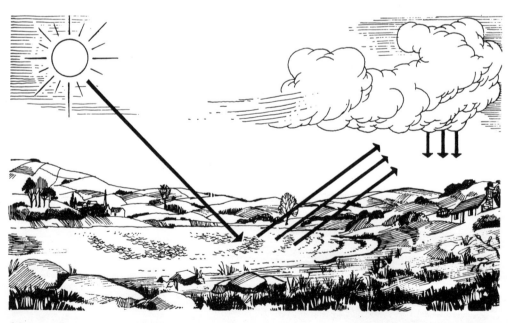

Fig. 1 The reflection of light from large bulks of water is considerable—especially where the land lies to the north (in the northern hemisphere). Thermal warmth is also derived from large water areas.

accurate assessment of weather patterns is an invaluable exercise which should under no circumstances be neglected, the paramount issues most certainly being light intensities and exposure.

Good light

While a dwelling house could conceivably be designed around a well-sited greenhouse or conservatory, it is more usual to design a dwelling house primarily for the living facilities it offers, and to relegate the greenhouse or conservatory to a position of less importance. There is, however, much to be said for incorporating the greenhouse or conservatory as a special feature in the home, both for aesthetic and practical reasons. It offers a pleasant adjunct to the home and is also an economical way of greenhouse gardening since the heating can be linked to the domestic system.

These considerations, however, do not affect the fundamental importance of siting the structure where it will receive good light, though obviously if a conservatory is to be used mainly for leisure and pleasure one will wish to avoid having the temperature raised to an unacceptable level by the midday sun and will prefer a west orientation enjoying the evening sun.

Good light is highly desirable for many horticultural activities, especially the propagation and growing of light-loving plants during the winter months. It is therefore elementary to choose a situation for the greenhouse which is as ideal as possible for light reception, *especially* during the winter months. A site which lies in brilliant sunshine most of the day from March to October may be in real gloom for most of the winter when light is at a premium. Check with a sighting angle. This will indicate whether buildings or dense trees are likely to be a real problem (Fig. 2).

Is shelter necessary?

Questions of light and shelter are obviously closely related. A greenhouse can be erected in a garden closely surrounded by tall hedges or fences and enjoy the very best of shelter yet the poorest of light as a result.

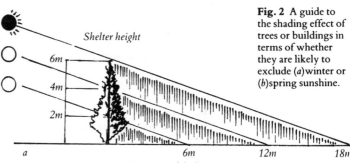

Shelter height

6m
4m
2m

a 6m 12m 18m

Distance of shadow at noon (December & January)

Fig. 2 A guide to the shading effect of trees or buildings in terms of whether they are likely to exclude (*a*) winter or (*b*) spring sunshine.

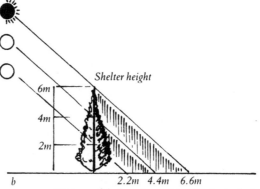

Shelter height

6m
4m
2m

b 2.2m 4.4m 6.6m

Distance of shadow at noon (April & September)

It is in some locations impossible to garden effectively or have a greenhouse without shelter.

In many gardens shelter is in fact of no real consequence, as the whole general area does not have an exposure problem. There is no better natural guide to this than the 'shaping' of trees in the neighbourhood — better even than the advice of local gardeners, though this should not be discounted.

Wind can play many unpredictable tricks by bouncing off building and hills or creating areas of extreme turbulence on the lee side of walls and fences.

Providing shelter

Providing shelter is usually more concerned with the garden as a whole than specifically for a greenhouse. The same general rules apply for both.

Solid wind barriers are now frowned upon. They do not 'stop' the wind at all. All they do is deflect it upwards, to descend

---

Footnote: Remarks generally apply to northern hemisphere. The converse is true for the southern hemisphere.

Fig. 3 Shelter for the greenhouse also means shelter for the garden and the house.

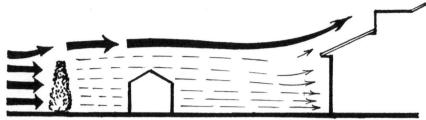

Distance of effect = 10 × height of hedge.

later with some force, sometimes creating a considerable degree of turbulence immediately behind the barrier. All the evidence of recent research shows clearly that media about 50% permeable are ideal for slowing the speed of the winds, thus avoiding both deflection and turbulence.

Windbreaks are effective for a distance of approximately ten to twelve times the height of the barrier itself, which means that in practical terms a hedge 2.4m (8ft) tall will provide shelter for 24—30m (80—100ft). The area of maximum shelter is in the region of five to six times the barrier

height, or 12—15m (40—50ft) in the case of a hedge 2.4m (8ft) high, a distance which raises no shade problems (see Fig. 3). A tall hedge of densely planted poplars, on the other hand, would provide excellent protection for a large area but could pose considerable shade problems in summer.

The directional placement of the shelter in relation to the greenhouse will depend, as we have said, on the prevailing wind and aspect. The ideal arrangement in most areas of Britain is shown in Fig. 4, a formula which can be fairly well adhered to in many gardens with a little planning.

Fig. 4 Shelter and shade. How they affect siting of a greenhouse in a garden. The dark shaded area is shade created in spring, and this is a 'no-go' area for siting glass. If winter sunshine is required then the central area only is suitable for siting the greenhouse.

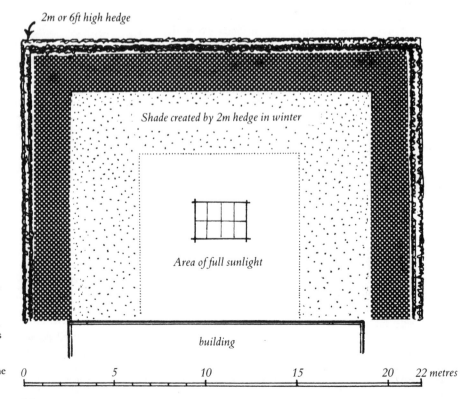

2m or 6ft high hedge

Shade created by 2m hedge in winter

Area of full sunlight

building

0   5   10   15   20   22 metres

Some natural shelter media

Hedges
  Beech
  Holly (common)
  Hornbeam
  Myrobalan (*Prunus cerasifera*)
  Privet
  Prunus cerasifera 'Nigra'
  Quickthorn (common hawthorn)
  Willow (trimmed as hedge)
  Yew, and many others

Will make thick impenetrable hedges 1.8−2.4m (6−8ft) in height. Should be cut regularly to avoid loss of light. Good planning is essential with regard to these key issues.

Conifer hedges
  Chaemaecyparis lawsoniana
  Cupressocyparis leylandii
  Thuja plicata

Grow fairly quickly to around 3−4.5m (10−15ft)

Trees
  Larch
  Limes
  Mountain ash
  Poplars (*Populus nigra* 'Italica'; *P. alba*)
  Scots pine (*Pinus sylvestris*)
  Silver birch
  Spruce (*Picea abies/excelsa; P. sitchensis*)
  and a great many others

Provide effective shelter belts but require sufficient room for development and are suitable only for the larger garden; seldom applicable to suburbia

Artificial shelter media on strong supports
  Interwoven fencing
  Rustic fencing
  Plastic trellis
  Wood trellis
  Hollow blocks (as a wall)
  Alternate offset slats
  Horizontal canes
  Vertical canes
  Netlon
  Nicofence *
  Lobrene
  Weldmesh
  Wire netting and straw
  Vertical laths
  Horizontal laths
  Single layer slats
  Polypropylene
  Rokoline
  Paraweb (ICI)

These are examples of materials in current use; all have their virtues and failings according to conditions. In all cases strong support is essential

Tree roots
Roots of trees or hedges situated adjacent to a greenhouse can be a problem particularly where the greenhouse border is used for crops, taking away moisture and nutrients and also disturbing foundations, poplars being notorious in this respect.

Drainage
Water shed from the roof of a greenhouse is best collected in a gutter and conveyed by a downpipe to a drain. With greenhouses of newer design and smaller size, rainwater is frequently allowed to run off into the soil, but only if natural drainage is sufficiently good, otherwise a rubble, tile or plastic drain must be run along the outside of the greenhouse to collect this rainwater and prevent seepage into the greenhouse. Drains should always have an effective outlet.

Site levelling and soil conditions
Since the physical and nutritional characteristics of soil and the whole question of soil analysis will be examined in detail in a later chapter, it is sufficient at this stage merely to draw attention to the importance of having a good soil, of even depth and good drainage, when growing plants in the greenhouse border. This matter is often airily dismissed as being of little significance in the small amateur greenhouse, yet in fact even a moderately sized structure 5.4 × 3.6m (18 × 12ft) will require 20m²

* (Garden Rewards/Clovis Lande−see Appendix)

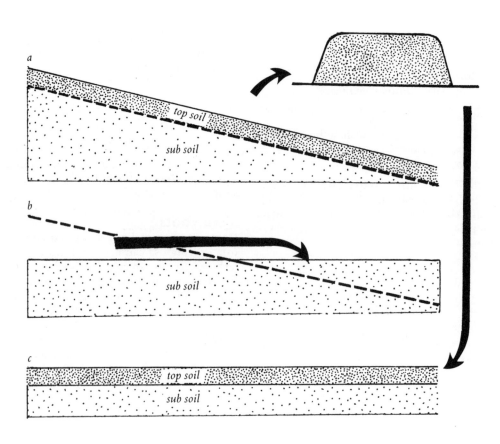

Fig. 5 Soil levelling by cut and fill. (*a*) Remove top soil and stack (*b*) Halve area and cut & fill sub soil (*c*) Replace top soil on levelled land.

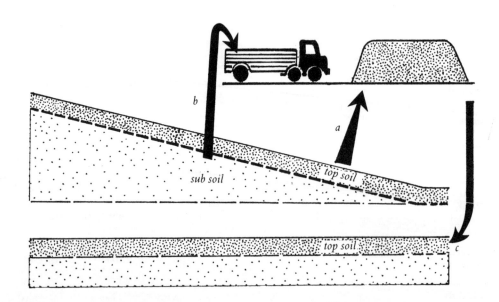

Fig. 6 Soil levelling to the lowest point. (*a*) Remove top soil and stack (*b*) Remove sub soil from site (*c*) Replace top soil on levelled land.

(24 sq yd) of soil 30 cm (1ft) deep or, to put it another way, 6m³ (8cu yd) of soil – not the sort of soil bulk readily come across or physically easy to handle. For a benched greenhouse or for container or bed systems of culture, the importance of good soil diminishes. The popularity of growbags today is a typical instance where soil quality in borders is of no concern, although drainage is still important.

Every attempt should be made to preserve the top layer of fertile soil and to replace it after levelling. Failure to do this will result in an intermingling of poor quality subsoil and top soil, with decidedly deleterious effects on any border grown crops. Soil in its natural state has a porous structure due to the activity of micro-organisms, earthworms, and the action of plant roots. Subject this to pressure with heavy mechanical levelling equipment and much of the natural structure is destroyed by the breaking down of porous crumb formation and the compression of air and moisture channels.

Levelling methods currently used are as follows:

1 Cut and fill (Fig. 5)   After stripping off the top soil, the difference in level is made up by splitting the difference between the lower and higher levels by movement of subsoil, avoiding compaction. The top soil is replaced carefully. A banking is left and a retaining wall with a catchment drain may be necessary.

2 Levelling to lowest point (Fig. 6)   In this method the top soil is first removed and then the sub-soil is excavated to allow a level to be made at the lowest point. This will undoubtedly result in a much steeper banking than with the 'cut and fill' method, and this can give rise to proportionately greater drainage problems. Alternatively a retaining wall with a drain behind it may be necessary.

3 Levelling to highest point (Fig. 7)   In this method, soil or ballast is used to bring up the level to the highest point. The advantages of this system are roughly counter-balanced by its disadvantages. While it avoids disturbing the existing soil structure it does, on the other hand, leave the greenhouse sitting proud of the natural levels and this can lead to over-effective drainage.

With all the above methods, a suitable period of time must be allowed for subsidence before the building of the greenhouse can commence. Alternatively, deeper foundations which allow contact with existing soil levels can be made, though this of course adds to the erection cost.

The disturbance of soil structure is of less importance where a slab floor is to be laid down and the greenhouse permanently benched, or where growbags or similar growing systems are to be employed. There should, however, still be adequate provision for drainage, and sufficient time for subsidence should be allowed before building.

Weeds

Little account is usually taken of weeds when building a greenhouse, yet they can be a serious nuisance. There are several highly obnoxious weeds such as *Polygonum cuspidatum* (Japanese bamboo), *Equisetum* (horsetail), and *Agropyron repens* (couch grass) – to mention but a few – which are very difficult to control. If the site is infested with weeds of this character, mere physical levelling or the building of foundations will do nothing to control them. The presence of bad weeds in the periphery of a greenhouse will always be a hazard and a nuisance.

Many weed-controlling chemicals are extremely potent, but when used out of doors they are in time leached out by the rain; this will not be the case in a green-

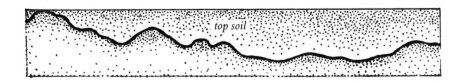

Fig. 7 Soil levelling to the highest point. Import top soil to fill in hollows.

house so obviously it would be a much better practice to carry out a general weed-control programme some time before building the greenhouse, treating a sufficiently wide area to prevent the weeds from rapidly recolonizing the greenhouse site. It is wise to consult official literature on the subject, strictly following instructions issued with the chemicals.

Services—water

Supplies of water and electricity are essential for the modern greenhouse. The volume and pressure of water required will depend on a number of cirumstances best taken up with the appropriate water board. Normally a 2cm ($\frac{3}{4}$ in) supply pipe will suffice for small greenhouses on an amateur scale, although if spraylines and mist irrigation are to be used then a larger pipe is desirable, it being remembered that the smaller the bore of the pipe, the greater the friction, which reduces pressure. Gardeners frequently make temporary connections to a tap at the rear of the dwelling house or garage, using long lengths of small-bore hose, and wonder why they get only a trickle at the greenhouse. This is of course the result of friction.

When *permanent* pipes are laid into a greenhouse they must be at sufficient depth to avoid freezing. The take-off from a main *must* be approved by the water board (who will usually make a charge) and invariably must be connected by a qualified plumber.

A compromise arrangement using a semi-permanent supply pipeline underground, but with a detachable connection to a tap, may be favoured and this may avoid the charges and complications of a permanent supply. Note that there should be facilities for draining this pipe in winter, especially if it is of steel. More usually these days pipes are of alkathene, and this tough material is not so badly affected by frost, but it can nevertheless be damaged.

The methods used to distribute the water within the greenhouse can vary considerably, problems of freezing being of importance once again. On the other hand, a deeply laid pipe and a standpipe in a correctly built and well-heated greenhouse will present few problems.

Electricity

The load necessary for a greenhouse will depend on its size and the range of equipment to be used. If an all-electric greenhouse is planned, the load can be quite heavy. The average small greenhouse of 3×2.4m (10×8ft) will normally require a $2\frac{1}{2}$kW heater, plus lighting, fan ventilation and possibly soil warming, adding up to a total of $3\frac{1}{2}$–4kW. Later in this book the formula for working out the loading will be dealt with. Qualified installation with waterproof fittings is essential.

Access

There should always be ready, unobstructed access to any greenhouse, preferably a hard path of sufficient width to allow the use of a trolley or barrow. Tool stores, potting sheds and supplies of soil should also be in reasonable proximity. There is a lot to be said for a greenhouse being attached to or as near the dwelling-house as possible, for the obvious reason that walking to and fro takes time and can be wet and unpleasant in bad weather.

Planning permission

It is usually wise to seek planning permission before embarking on any work connected with the erection of the greenhouse. For commercial greenhouses under a certain size and over a permitted distance from a main road, planning permission may be completely unnecessary, but it is always advisable to check the situation with the authority or council involved. For amateur greenhouses under a certain size, planning permission may also not be needed, but here again it is better to make sure by approaching the planning body. Procedure differs under different authorities, but in most areas when making planning application it is obligatory to provide:

1 A location plan showing the exact siting of the greenhouse in relation to home, roads, and neighbouring buildings on a plan taken from the ordnance map of the area. The siting of the greenhouse can then be drawn in accurately and to scale in red ink, making sure that there is strict adherence to boundary lines (information on this should be requested beforehand from the planning body, and you should find out at the same time whether there are any local building regulations about the type of greenhouse allowed).

2 Full details of the greenhouse, its foundations (if any), side and end elevations to scale, details of materials and dimensions of the main structural members. Most greenhouse manufacturers have the necessary plans ready and in a form acceptable to the planning authority. Do-it-yourself enthusiasts could draw plans for themselves.

3 Notes on any drainage necessary, especially if this involves linking up to an existing drainage system.

4 A completed application form, with the signatures of adjoining neighbours or their landlords or ground superiors certifying that they have no objection to the erection of the greenhouse. Permission may also be necessary from your own landlord or ground superior in the case of lets or feus, unless of course the ground is self-owned. A point of some interest is that where there is a building society involved with either land or house or both, they certainly must be told of your plans, especially if the greenhouse is to be attached to the house.

Regulations for erecting greenhouses, conservatories, porches and home extensions generally have been relaxed in most areas in recent years—but it is always better to check and be safe rather than sorry!

The erection of small plastic greenhouses, frames or cloches requires no planning permission. *With conservatories or garden rooms the same general procedures apply as for greenhouses and it is essential to conform with local planning regulations, especially building control.*

CHAPTER 3
Greenhouse Selection

Preliminary considerations
(Fig. 8)

Before embarking on the erection of a greenhouse the following highly specific questions should be considered:

1 Is the district concerned well served with natural light, sheltered or exposed, and free from industrial pollution? In the same vein, is the area a very dry one, raising maintenance problems with wooden houses?

2 Does the proposed site receive the maximum amount of sunlight?

3 Is the greenhouse intended for use the whole year round or only for spring/summer?

4 What plants are to be grown and when – eg pot plants only, or general propagation followed by tomatoes and late chrysanthemums?

5 To what level is the greenhouse to be heated – fully, partly or not at all? A minimum of 13–16°C all the year round, or merely to provide frost protection regardless of how cold it is out of doors?

6 What facilities are available for heat, with particular reference to the possibility of

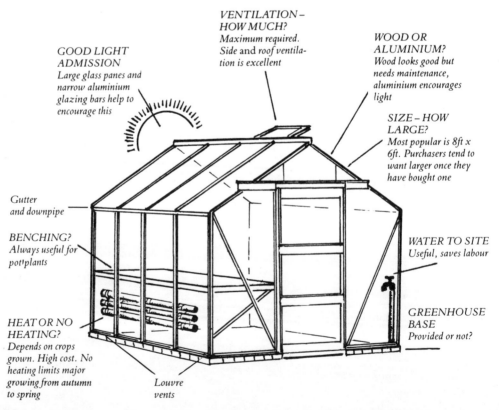

VENTILATION –
HOW MUCH?
Maximum required.
Side and roof ventilation is excellent

WOOD OR
ALUMINIUM?
Wood looks good but needs maintenance, aluminium encourages light

GOOD LIGHT
ADMISSION
Large glass panes and narrow aluminium glazing bars help to encourage this

SIZE – HOW
LARGE?
Most popular is 8ft x 6ft. Purchasers tend to want larger once they have bought one

Gutter
and downpipe

BENCHING?
Always useful for pot plants

WATER TO SITE
Useful, saves labour

GREENHOUSE
BASE
Provided or not?

HEAT OR NO
HEATING?
Depends on crops grown. High cost. No heating limits major growing from autumn to spring

Louvre
vents

Fig. 8 Features to consider in selection of a greenhouse.

linking the greenhouse system with that of the dwelling house?

7 Is the greenhouse intended primarily as a room to relax in, or primarily for the growing of plants?

8 What size and shape of greenhouse is contemplated? Is money no object, or is there a strict budget involved? Might it in practice be better to consider a combined shed and greenhouse, or even a porch or conservatory?

9 What constructional materials are considered suitable – wood, treated metal or alloy?

10 Must allowance be made for occasional absences from home, with vents, heating and perhaps watering and feeding being carried out in a semi-automatic manner?

11 Has any thought been given as to whether the greenhouse is to be fixed or mobile to allow a system of crop rotation?

12 Would a low cost, plastic greenhouse or frame achieve all that is required?

13 Type of glazing system, whether nailed, clip or sealed, the last named being highly desirable.

These are all issues which arise in more detail later.

District

The level of natural illumination in any district varies not only according to latitudinal placement, but also with nearness to large bulks of water, the presence of industrial pollution and in relation to several other factors. A garden may be situated at the top of a hill and so receive good light, yet be exposed to strong winds, making the maintenance of a high temperature all the year round both difficult and costly. Poor winter light makes the growing of light-demanding early tomatoes and winter lettuce, for example, extremely difficult in many northern districts, and in industrial areas atmospheric pollution detracts still further from the available light. While deficits in heat levels can be made good relatively easily, deficits in light intensity cannot so easily be remedied. The gardener receiving poor winter light and often gardening under conditions of extreme exposure and winter cold may be better advised to have a permanently benched base-wall type of greenhouse instead of an all-glass type, which will not only reduce heat loss and keep fuel bills down, but serve better for spring propagation or year-round pot plant growing activities, followed by some later cropping. It is unfortunate that base wall type greenhouses are not now so readily available. On the other hand, in an area of good light with no exposure problem, an all-glass greenhouse could be used successfully for a completely unrestricted production programme over the full year.

Desirable temperature levels

The amount of heating required in any greenhouse is usually determined with regard to the minimum *winter* temperature to be maintained. The following are the four normally accepted levels for greenhouse heating.

Cool greenhouse

This provides frost protection only, keeping the temperatures between 7–10°C in winter. Type of greenhouse is not critical apart from winter light issues, other than that a base wall reduces heat loss.

The use of a separately heated propagating frame in the cool greenhouse is becoming very popular as it allows an intensive propagation programme at very low cost within the cooler atmosphere of the greenhouse.

Intermediate, or moderately warm, greenhouse

In this heat range a minimum temperature of between 13–16°C (55–60°F) is maintained continuously throughout the year. Such a temperature range is suitable for the great majority of greenhouse plants, and a wide variety of propagating activities can be carried on in the greenhouse itself (as opposed to within a separate propagating frame). It costs money to keep a greenhouse at these minimum temperatures, yet on the other hand there are great benefits in having a twelve-month gardening calendar. The culture of light-sensitive crops such as early tomatoes or early lettuce should be avoided in poor light areas, irrespective of the heat level which can be achieved, unless one is prepared to invest in artificial lighting and the operating costs of this (see Chapter 10).

'Stovehouse'

This rather frightening title refers to a greenhouse for the culture of extremely heat-demanding plants such as some orchids, ferns and other epiphytes, in which the minimum temperature range is 18°C (65°F) or above. Few amateur gardeners think in these terms for very obvious economic reasons. A more localized concentration of heat such as that provided by the larger types of propagating case may be an acceptable compromise on grounds of cost. The well-heated home is now being used more and more for heat-demanding growing activities.

Cold greenhouse

No artificial heat is involved at all, all heat being derived from the sun. The gardener in a very mild situation can derive great value from a completely cold greenhouse; in colder areas it is normally useless over many of the winter months for anything other than hardy shrubs or plants.

The real limitation is, in fact, one of cost: it is perfectly possible to heat what started as a cold greenhouse up to stovehouse level, but it would be very expensive to do so, because, ideally, the design and materials used in a greenhouse intended to be run at stove temperatures would be different from those used in a greenhouse intended to remain unheated. Because of the higher temperature required in a stovehouse, one would tend to go in for double-glazing or polycarbonate sheeting and a house with brick half walls in order to minimize heat losses, whereas the greenhouse one might have purchased originally as a cold house might well have been of glass-to-ground design which would have a very high heat loss. One would really do better to scrap the old greenhouse and start afresh with one better designed to do the job required.

A compromise may occasionally be reached, though this is really only practicable in fairly large greenhouses. This is a system that is sometimes adopted in the greenhouse of botanic gardens and other horticultural institutions, whereby the greenhouse is divided into two or more sections, each heated to a different temperature level, or bought as such. Alternatively heavy gauge translucent polythene can be used to create a curtain-type division, though this is not entirely satisfactory.

Value for money

The cost of a proposed greenhouse is perhaps the most pertinent question of all. Value for money should always be sought after, and there can be an immense variation between different greenhouses, not so much in price but in respect of serviceability, lack of maintenance and other related matters. More sophisticated types of wooden houses constructed of Western Red Cedar or pressure-treated wood are excellent buys for general greenhouse activities at low cost (particularly if glazing systems avoid the use of putty and nails). Alloy and treated metal houses in their more sophisticated forms are generally more expensive than wooden houses, although there are a lot of highly competitively priced alloy houses now available.

Intensity of use

What has so far been said gives fairly clear guidance concerning the year-round use of a greenhouse. To think in terms of natural illumination only and disregard temperature would be wrong. In the more southerly latitudes a completely unheated greenhouse can be reasonably effective in winter, allowing overwintering of pelargoniums, storage of dahlias, and the housing of quite a range of pot plants that are fully hardy, like some hardy fuchsias, primulas and many half-hardy bedding plants. The situation can be very different in more northerly latitudes where, unless the winter is exceptionally mild, a completely cold greenhouse is virtually useless over the coldest winter months, with the possible exception of a few very mild coastal areas exposed to warm ocean currents, and even then winter dampness can be a real problem. Lining with bubble or plain polythene can reduce heat losses considerably in a *heated* greenhouse.

CHAPTER 4
Design, Materials, Construction

Does shape matter?

A little research around the world, both into the past and the present, would no doubt bring to light greenhouses of every conceivable size and shape. Certainly with many of the earlier 'Botanic Garden' types of greenhouse, architects went to extremes; in modern idom the same may be said of some new plant houses.

Such diversity provokes the question: does shape or design really matter anyway? For most greenhouse gardening purposes what matters most is stability coupled with light transmission. Only where the absolute maximum light is sought for certain commercial crops, especially during the duller winter months, and when earliness of cropping or the quality of bloom is crucial, does glasshouse design become a critical matter.

Light is of two basic forms: the total illumination of the whole sky from all directions and the direct light transmitted by the sun as solar rays. The translucent material of a greenhouse will transmit about 90% of the total illumination of the whole sky through the roof and sides of the greenhouse with almost equal efficiency. Direct radiation from the sun is only transmitted at maximum efficiency when the sun's angle is at 90° (normal) to the glass. Each degree away from normal results in a greater amount of deflection. A little thought along these lines shows the extreme difficulty of designing and erecting a greenhouse so that it will enjoy maximum light transmission at all times. The situation is, however, not quite so bad as it looks, since during the summer months the total radiation from the sun is usually far in excess of the requirements of many plants;

Important note: Remarks generally apply to the northern hemisphere. The converse is true for the southern hemisphere.

it is only during the winter months that maximum light transmission is vital.

As the sun is never in the same position for long, any conventionally shaped greenhouse receives the maximum amount of light only for the very short period when the sun's rays penetrate the glass at 90°. Curved greenhouses were quite popular in earlier days, especially the all-important centre planthouse of the greenhouse range in the private estate garden; these offered a varied surface, part of which would always be at around 90° to the sun's rays. Modern types of round or geodesic greenhouses have been designed expressly to allow maximum light transmission over a period.

Much research has recently been concerned, however, with the conventionally shaped greenhouse. Assuming a roof pitch of approximately 30°, it can be seen that with a winter sun angle of approximately 15°, the angle of incidence at best is 180° − 45° = 135° (Fig. 9a). The vertical side of the greenhouse is better placed to transmit light with an angle of presentation of 75°. The higher the vertical side wall, the greater the amount of light transmitted, which in a single span house of normal width will reach the rear of the house easily. If the side wall is slightly angled off the vertical it is possible for the low-angled winter sun to have a 90° angle of incidence. Recent experiments have aimed at making the roof pitch steeper on the side facing south, to transmit instead of deflecting the low-angled winter sun (Fig. 9b). A roof pitch of 60°, for example, gives an angle of incidence of 105° which is much more efficient in light transmission than the 135° achieved with the normal roof pitch (Fig. 9c).

Obviously there is more than winter to consider, and the normal roof pitch of 25−35° (Dutch light houses are often 15−25°) is much more efficient for light transmission in the spring and summer months than the 60° pitch, although as light transmission is

Fig. 9 Shape and orientation of a greenhouse greatly affects light (and heat) transmission into the greenhouse, especially in winter when sun angle is low in sky.

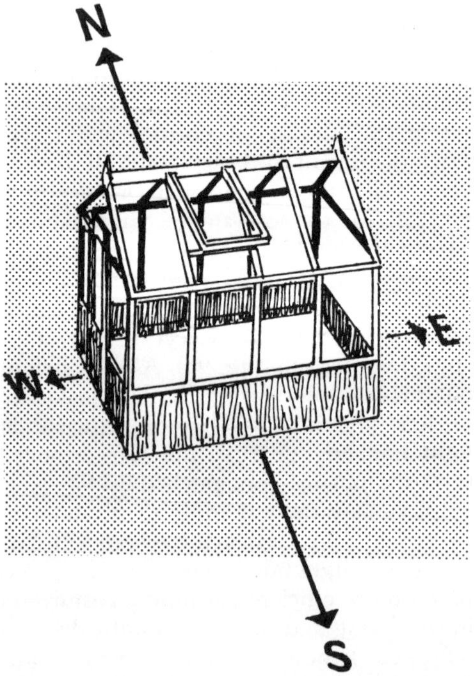

Fig. 10 (*Right*) To derive maximum winter/spring light, site a conventionally shaped greenhouse with the ridge running east/west.

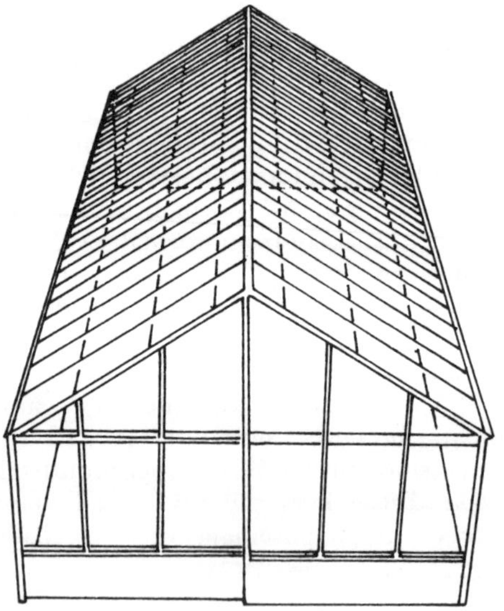

Fig. 11 (*Far right*) The 'lattice blind' effect produced by the roof spars of a greenhouse sited north/south when the sun is at a low angle in winter.

so often in excess of the plants' needs, the steep roof pitch is not necessarily detrimental (Fig. 9d).

It becomes apparent that if a conventionally shaped greenhouse is to derive maximum winter light it must be sited with the ridge running east-west (Fig. 10); to have it running north-south would present only the south-facing gable end favourably for winter light, the sides and roof deriving very little owing to the very acute angle of incidence presented on two planes. The glazing bars or astragals also create a lattice blind effect (Fig. 11).

Summary
1 The ideal greenhouse for light transmission would be completely rounded, but these have some drawbacks in respect of size, cropping, etc.
2 The ideal greenhouse of otherwise conventional shape would have its roof pitched more steeply on the south-facing side. A greenhouse of such a design is available, but can be somewhat impractical unless as a conservatory.
3 For maximum light transmission in winter the conventional greenhouse should be orientated east-west to present its long axis to the south.
4 Where summer cropping only is concerned, north-south orientation is acceptable and indeed allows for a more equable distribution of light on both sides of the greenhouse and perhaps better ventilation.

Wooden greenhouses

The last ten years have seen rapid transition from wood to alloy as constructional material for greenhouses. Aluminium alloy has many advantages. It is strong (where extruded), light and extremely resistant to corrosion without any painting or other treatment. Superior or properly pressure-treated wood cannot, however, be discounted and is still viewed with much favour, since a tightly glazed wooden greenhouse is considerably 'warmer' than an alloy one, which means in effect that wooden houses cost less to heat. There are usually fewer condensation problems in a wooden greenhouse.

Main timbers available

The four timbers mainly used are Baltic redwood *(Pinus sylvestris)*, British Columbian pine *(Pseudotsuga menzieii taxifolia)*, Western red cedar *(Thuja plicata)*, and Norway spruce *(Picea abies/excelsa)*. Hardwoods such as oak and teak are only used to a limited extent on account of their far higher cost.

Baltic redwood Strength/bulk ratio is good, being $497kg/m^3$ (31lb/cu ft) and it does not split badly when being nailed. It is readily impregnated with preservative.

British Columbian pine Similar in many ways to Baltic redwood, it can be obtained in long lengths. It is difficult to impregnate with preservative. It has a strength/bulk ratio of $529kg/m^3$ (33lb/cu ft) and is therefore broadly similar to Baltic redwood.

Western red cedar This is an excellent wood for amateur greenhouse work when it is not used in long lengths, as it has a poor strength/bulk ratio of $384kg/m^3$ (24lb/cu ft); for this reason larger-sized members may have to be used, particularly for astragals and ridge boards in exposed areas or where heavy snowfalls are frequent. Its chief virtues are inherent resistance to decay and excellent appearance, which makes it highly acceptable aesthetically for porches or conservatories adjoining the home. Western red cedar lends itself to treatment with oil.

Norway spruce Quite widely used for cheaper greenhouses on account of low cost, but to achieve reasonably long life it must be treated or painted, preferably both. Being soft it is very easy to work and it does not split readily in the process. It has a strength/bulk ratio roughly similar to redwood.

Teak and oak Both of these are specialized woods of very high durability, having bulk/strength ratios of around $721kg/m^3$ (40—41lb/cu ft). Easy to work, they are excellent where a greenhouse extremely resistant to varying climatic conditions is wanted, but when used in smaller sections they will make the greenhouse very expensive.

A greenhouse may be constructed of one type of timber, a variety of timbers, or a mixture of steel and timber.

Preservation of timber

This is a task best left to the timber or greenhouse supplier, but it is useful to know something about preservative treatment. Assessing the quality of timber is work for a specialist, but even the uninitiated can judge whether timber is free from small knots, large knots which may be loose, and 'splits', or whether it is too sappy (new). Many defects can be covered up with a coat of priming paint. Ideally timber should be both pressure treated and painted, unless of superior quality, although either will suffice in part. Paint protects the wood from the entry of moisture, which in turn protects it from decay, provided a perfect cover of paint is maintained. Preservatives impregnate the wood and immunize it against both the entry of moisture and decay, but obviously a painted greenhouse is more attractive than one which is merely preservative treated.

Western red cedar is usually treated with linseed oil or special paints which is simply brushed on when the wood is dry.

It should be realized that hand painting as a method of applying preservatives only results in penetration of the skin of the wood, which means that this will require fairly regular treatment.

Painting of timber

The painting of greenhouses is rather a boring task. Some manufacturers send their wooden greenhouses out either flat coated or fully painted, and the latter is to be preferred.

Newer paints based on organic oils and synthetic resin with pigments other than lead, have considerably better light reflective qualities than those based on lead. They are also longer lasting and do not powder or dissolve. They must, however, be applied to *dry* timber, otherwise they will soon blister or flake off.

When painting wood it is usual to apply a priming coat to timber which has not previously been painted. This should be wire brushed before applying the primer if necessary. If you are erecting the greenhouse yourself, it is important to put on the priming coat before erection, otherwise joint surfaces are left unprotected. Next comes the undercoat, which may be put on after erection *but before glazing*. The final coat is put on after glazing.

Repainting will be necessary every three or four years on untreated or poor quality timber, perhaps more frequently in industrial areas. It is largely because they do not need painting that aluminium alloy, superior or preservative treated timber, and treated metal houses are now so popular.

Whatever type of paint is used, it is better not to bring plants into a newly painted greenhouse for a few days after painting, since they could be damaged by fumes.

Steel greenhouses

The high tensile strength of steel and its high strength/bulk ratio make it an ideal structural material for all buildings, and greenhouses are no exception. Many commercial greenhouses now use steel for the gutters (now often alloy) and the supports, for purlin posts and rails, side and end supports, roof trusses and pitch frames whether they are cladded (the astragals holding the glass) with wood, steel or alloy.

The main problem with many steel frame glazing bars lies in the fact that steel of sufficient thickness, unlike aluminium alloy or expanded metal, cannot readily be pressed into a shape to allow a glazing method which secures the glass effectively without the use of a putty or bitumen type of glazing system.

Steel must of course be properly treated against corrosion, otherwise it will quickly rust, and hot dip galvanizing is essential *after* the steel has been cut to size, shaped and all holes bored. Aluminium paint is also very effective as a rust preventive for steel, provided the steel is reasonably clean before the aluminium paint is applied. Enamel is also used for painting over galvanized steel. Stainless steel can also be used with a coat of enamel.

Personal experience over many years with the steel components of commercial and amateur greenhouses has shown the inadequacy in many cases of the metal galvanizing treatment. A further problem with steel, especially if used in conjunction with aluminium alloy, is the bi-metallic corrosion caused by electrolytic action. Even the water running from alloy glazing bars on to galvanized steel gutters can give problems. All manufacturers now ensure that a plastic seal prevents the actual contact of the two metals, although nothing can be done about the shed water. Fortunately this is a problem which does not usually occur with amateur-sized greenhouses, as gutters on alloy greenhouses are also invariably of alloy.

Aluminium alloy

Earlier types of alloy were subject to corrosion, especially in areas of salty air or industrial pollution. Even now considerable powder deposit may form on the alloy, but this need not give rise to concern. Aluminium alloy has an excellent strength/bulk ratio and, being a light metal, it can readily be extruded into sections of various shapes, the sections all being designed to give additional strength. It can also be shaped into complicated sections to form drip channels and to allow either clip or groove glazing, this latter being a system which has gained considerable favour in recent years since it gives a really tight seal and prevents air losses.

Direct contact with steel should be avoided, and where this is impossible it is most important that the steel should be protected with bitumen paint. Where aluminium alloy gutters are used, drip channels should be provided underneath to prevent the condensation droplets damaging crops, the condensation occurring owing to the high thermal conductivity of alloy. With commercial greenhouses it is advisable to use gutter support braces to ensure that the alloy gutter in a long section house does not sag, which can happen with snow load or under a worker's weight when doing repairs.

Construction standards

Commercial greenhouses are manufactured to a code of practice based on the minimum acceptable standards. This takes into account (1) the structure as a whole, (2) individual structural elements such as trusses, stanchions, purlins, joints, fixing, foundations, (3) cladding elements (glazing bars, etc). Amateur greenhouse manufacturers have not perhaps given such detailed study to their designs as these products are not subject to government approval for grants, but minimum construction standards should ensure that all greenhouses are stable enough to withstand very strong winds, snow load *and* crop weight, this last being of particular importance; greenhouses can, for example, easily be damaged by a very heavy crop of tomatoes suspended from the roof or from wires stretched between the ends of the greenhouse (p. 34).

To lay down section sizes for the component parts of a greenhouse poses problems, owing to the differing bulk/weight ratios involved; astragal bars of Western red cedar 5 × 5cm (2 × 2in) will not be as strong as similar sections of Baltic redwood, for instance. Nor is it easy to give exact roof angles, height to ridge, height to eaves, size of doors, and all the other relevant measurements. A minimum *eaves height* of about 1.5m (5ft) gives adequate headroom but is not really sufficient; 1.65 to 1.8m (5ft 6in to 6ft) is better. The ridge height is commensurate with eaves height to give a roof pitch of from about 14—18° for Dutch light houses with no glass overlap, up to 35° for overlapped glass, with an average of 25.5°. Teething troubles can occur with a new model of motor car, and similarly with a new design of greenhouse, especially over mechanical items such as vents.

Do-it-yourself greenhouses
For the do-it-yourself enthusiast wishing to build a greenhouse there is a fairly wide margin of tolerance in design and, most amateur joiners tend to err on the side of safety by using heavier timber than is really necessary.

All nails used in timber greenhouses should be galvanized, and screws and bolts in all alloy structures should be of alloy or brass.

Glazing systems

The type of glass used for greenhouses in Britain is drawn glass weighing 3mm/240oz per sq ft (was called 24oz horticultural glass) with a stress factor of up to 470n/m^2 (10lb per sq ft). Continental types of glass are also used and these are slightly heavier. A still heavier type of glass 4mm (32oz per sq ft), is used for certain large-paned greenhouses, generally of commercial design. Commercially, and in some amateur greenhouses, the standard size of pane is 60 × 60cm (24 × 24in), while many amateur houses are 50 × 45 cm (20 × 18in), or alternatively Dutch-size glass measuring 14 × 73cm (56 × 28¾in) and 3mm thick. Venlo sized glass, which is widely used in commercial structures is 142 × 73cm (4ft 6in × 2ft 4in), or 165 × 73cm (5ft 4in × 2ft 4in), and is 4mm thick. There is certainly virtue in having larger pane sizes, as it increases the ratio of translucent to opaque material, which in turn ensures maximum transmission of light, provided the greenhouse is orientated to the best possible advantage. The main drawback in having a large ratio of glass to structural materials, and in particular no base wall is, as stated earlier, the increased heating costs. Replacement costs after breakages are another drawback with large panes.

Alternatives to glass

Various forms of rigid plastics are available and can be used in lieu of glass in conventional greenhouses. Fibreglass sheets can also be used, especially in warm climates. They can readily be used in curved sections, which is a distinct advantage as far as light transmission is concerned. They perform the same function as glass, although it is claimed that in some respects they are more efficient in transmitting light. The most interesting of these are the range of acrylic and polycarbonate twin- or triple-walled sheetings. These are not only easy to cut and fit, but very resistant to breakage. They also give much better (30–40%) heat retention than glass. Newer forms of PVC are also available, such as Biolex 2000.

Several forms of clear polythene are available. The light gauge (38mu) is mainly used for 'double-glazing' to reduce heat loss. For plastic greenhouses or polythene tunnels, polythene 150mu (600 gauge) and polythene 180mu (720 gauge) are best used. Anti-fog 'Thermic' 720 film is now available as is 4-year AD 200 thermic film

(Clovis Lande). Double skinning using a 600g inner and a 720g outer cover or two sheets of 720g – kept apart by a small fan – is now very popular in commercial circles, resulting in *very* considerable savings in heat with minimal light loss.

PVC film is also available and is clearer than polythene but tends to be more expensive. A range of other plastics is available (e.g. woven materials) especially in the U.S.A. Also of interest is the Serac system involving PVF (TEDLAR) outer skin and Melinex 071 inner skin (see Appendix), which provides a combination of excellent light transmission and conservation.

Polythene is efficient in transmitting short-wave solar radiation, the light being all diffused and not directly admitted as in the case of glass. But normal grades of polythene, unlike glass, do not at present trap the long-wave radiation from heated objects within the greenhouse, but new types of polythene are available which are more effective in trapping solar heat and reducing condensation problems. Polythene destruction also occurs constantly, due to ultraviolet rays (which tend to be stronger in areas of unpolluted air), but a large degree of ultra-violet proofing is now incorporated into polythene, which makes it last longer. The build-up of static electricity to which dust clings tends to cloud polythene and detract from its light transmission efficiency and general appearance.

The 'U' value or thermal coefficient of polythene is basically higher than that of glass, which results in a great deal of condensation unless the polythene has been treated or designed to disperse moisture.

The problem of how to secure and tension without tearing has been successfully overcome in many of the latest designs: loose flapping polythene quickly deteriorates whereas tightly stretched polythene, even if of thinner grade, remains undamaged. Aluminium channel ('Grip Strip' from Clovis Lande Associates – See Appendix) is ideal for securing and tensioning the plastics.

Glazing methods for glass

The simplest method of glazing is the use of putty and nails, as carried out on wooden

Fig. 12 Conventional glazing with putty and nails (now largely outdated) in timber greenhouses.

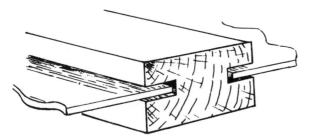

Fig. 13 Conventional dry glazing in the wooden grooves of a Dutch light's timber (now outdated).

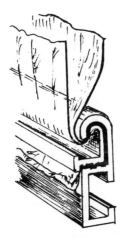

Fig. 14 Double skin polythene tunnels are best held by an alloy 'grip' system.

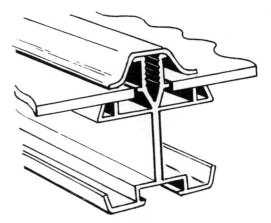

Fig. 15 Bar cap or sealed glazing system used in exposed areas for securing glass tightly, which avoids damage and air leaks. PVC is often used for bar caps.

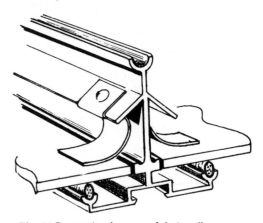

Fig. 16 Conventional system of glazing alloy greenhouses with clips on a plastic or mastic strip.

Fig. 17 Future glazing may well be in clear polycarbonate materials (a double glazing system) held by a simple 'T' & bar system.

glazing bars. Linseed oil putty is bedded in the channel of the glazing bar and the glass laid on this. The panes nearest the eaves in each section are laid first and the glazier then works upwards to the crest of the roof. Six brass sprigs are required per sheet of 60 × 60cm (24 × 24in) or 20 × 45cm (20 × 18in), two at the bottom of the lap, two 2.5−5cm (1−2in) from the bottom of the pane, and two in the middle of each side. The next sheet of glass is laid on with a .62−1.25cm ($\frac{1}{4}$−$\frac{1}{2}$in) overlap (see Fig. 12).

When necessary, glass is cut with a good straight edge and a sharp glass cutter, working on a flat wooden surface such as the top of a table. This system of glazing has been in use for a great many years and is still occasionally used for the conventional wooden house construction. In time putty tends to crack and allow the entry of moisture.

The use of aluminium covered sealing strips has much to commend it on a new structure, to prevent rapid deterioration of the putty. They are often used after the glazing has already deteriorated, as a first-aid measure to avoid re-glazing. A modification of conventional glazing which is quick and effective is to use strips of non-hardening mastic put down the grooves in the glazing bar, tacking the glass with *brass nails* — not sprigs.

Dry glazing is practised with Dutch light greenhouses, the glass being held in a groove and consequently supported on all four sides. It might seem that this is a highly inefficient method of glazing since the glass rattles and the air space allows loss of heat, besides admitting water. In fact dry glazing is reasonably efficient, especially when the glass is held tightly. Vigorously blown rain *can* find its way into the structure but many gardeners have, after many years of experience, a high regard for the maintenance-free character of dry glazing and on balance the disadvantages are more than cancelled out by the advantages. Dutch greenhouses, if well constructed, seldom suffer any serious damage from gales or hurricanes (Fig. 13).

Dry glazing systems are by no means confined to wooden houses. In recent years they have been adapted in alloy greenhouses in many forms, the glass being retained in an alloy glazing bar extruded to form a groove which retains the glass in a similar manner to the Dutch light system with or without plastic seals (Fig. 14).

Mastic and clips The more usual way of glass retention with alloy glazing bars is to bed the glass on a strip of mastic and retain it with a stainless steel or alloy clip (see Fig. 15). 'Barcaps' of alloy or PVC can also be fitted over the clips to provide a tight seal and thereby avoid a convenient lodgement area for moss growth. More sophisticated forms of glazing depend on a continuous bar-cap arrangement (see Fig. 16). Steel houses are also usually glazed on the same system of non-hardening mastic and clips, although one commercial system used non-hardening bitumen and plastic clips. It is obviously more difficult to bar-cap a steel bar than one of extruded alloy.

In very exposed districts something more sophisticated than the simple glazing clip system employed in many amateur structures would be advisable, owing to the degree of vibration of the glass which can be caused by persistent high winds. It needs merely one pane to loosen and slip for the wind to gain entry and rip out glass wholesale. Most glasshouse manufacturers will, I feel, be prepared to provide bar-capping as a not-too-expensive extra where this is not standard.

Future trends in greenhouse design

While research in greenhouse design, and the materials from which they are made, is constant, the rising cost of all materials will undoubtedly accelerate matters greatly.

The great interest in the use of plastics primarily resulted because of their cheapness. Yet the world rise in oil prices which has occurred will tend to make oil derivative materials such as polythene and PVC suspect in the long term, although polythene structures are still very competitive in price. It seems likely that for the foreseeable future conventional greenhouses will hold their place and any changes which occur will be simple refinements of existing designs (Fig. 17). Double-glazed systems to reduce heating costs, even if only for ends and sides of greenhouses (in view of weight problems for roof structure) will undoubtedly become as popular in amateur circles as they are in commercial growing spheres. Of special interest is the new Biolex 2000 PVC, rigid sheeting, with its high tensile strength, excellent light transmission and a thermal transmission (U value) about 30–40% less than glass. There are other PVC sheets with broadly similar characteristics. The Serac system is also forward looking (see Appendix).

Many gardeners have, in the last year or so, found that the use of corrugated PVC, or fibreglass sheeting nailed to a wooden framework, has made a reasonably satisfactory greenhouse. Rigid, reasonably priced, translucent sheeting of some form is now being widely used, and will get still more popular among those looking for cheapness.

SUMMARY OF GREENHOUSE MATERIALS

Material	Type	Strength/bulk ratio	Further comments
TIMBER On the whole 'warmer' greenhouses with less condensation provided glazing system is 'tight'	Baltic Redwood	Good	Good durable wood. Easy to work with. Readily impregnated with preservative
	British Columbian Pine	Good	Very similar in nature to Baltic Redwood. More difficult to impregnate with preservative
	Western Red Cedar	Poor but satisfatory in short lengths	Excellent appearance and resists decay. A most desirable wood for amateur structures unless in very exposed situations
	Teak and Oak	Very high	Excellent woods with many qualities. Exposure is no deterrent to their use
STEEL Makes very strong greenhouses. Exellent for internal structure	Must be well galvanized or enamelled	Very high	Excellent material but corrosion is a constant problem. Difficult to 'shape' for glazing purposes, (unlike alloy)
ALLOYS Light enough to work with and resists corrosion	Various types	Low	Good appearance (when new). Possibly the best material to use

Glazing systems

	Description	Comments
Putty and Nails On wood or metal houses	The conventional system still favoured by many gardeners	If well maintained gives a remarkably 'tight' greenhouse. Will in time deteriorate if not well maintained
Glazing Strips	The glass is laid on glazing strips instead of putty	A good system, the value of which is not yet fully appreciated. Very quick and simple
Dry Glazing	The glass is held supported in grooves in either wood or metal	Excellent maintenance free system even if it does allow a certain heat loss
Mastic and Clip	Clips are used to hold the glass on to strips of mastic or plastic	Most systems now satisfactory but additional 'Barcaps' necessary in exposed areas (alloy or PVC)

Light transmitting materials

Glass Clear	3–4mm (24/26-32 oz). (thinner glass can be used but not advised)	Glass is still the most effective transmitter of solar light and heat
Translucent	Cloudy glass which breaks up direct sunlight	Good for propagation activities and especially useful in very sunny climates
Plastic Rigid, including fibreglass	In various forms in flat, curved and corrugated sheets	Apart from expense makes excellent greenhouses. Cheaper forms of corrugated sheeting can quickly make a useful structure (see pages 33 and 44)

Description	Comments
Polythene & PVC	In various gauges. 150mu, 180mu	Deteriorates gradually but has a very useful role. Condensation still a major problem (see page 30). Best used in double skin and operate a small fan to separate the two sheets if heat is to be used

NOTE: For conservatories the use of either polycarbonate or safety glass is strongly advised to avoid accidents caused by falling objects.

Constructional standards for greenhouses

There are accepted standards for commercial greenhouses in the UK. These vary according to regional location. Standards for amateur-sized greenhouses are less stringent but basic principles are the same.

Snow load

This is to building design standards as shown in BS 6399 Part 3 1988. It varies from 0.3 KN/m^2 (30 Kg/m^2) in parts of southern England to 1.0 KN/m^2 (98 Kg/m^2) in parts of the Scottish highlands. Conversion from 'snow on ground' to 'snow on roof' depends on the shape factor but a good average for a single span greenhouse is 0.8 KN/m^2 imposed load on roof.

Many 'run of the mill' greenhouses can only withstand 0.5 KN/m^2 and 'cheapies' even less which shows their vulnerability in the wrong situation.

Wind load

Depends on dynamic pressures and on height and shape. Requirements for UK are given in BS CP3 Chapter V Pt 2. In parts of southern England 38 m/sec (82 mph) is acceptable, while in most of Scotland it is 52 m/sec (113 mph). An accepted standard for domestic greenhouses is a dynamic pressure range of 0.6 to 1.0 KN/m^2 but this can be affected much by building shape.

Many 'cheapies' can only stand 25 m/sec (54 mph). Well-constructed greenhouses can stand up to 52 m/sec (113 mph).

Crop loads

BS 5502 requires that commercial greenhouses withstand a crop load of 0.150 KN/m^2 (15 Kg/m^2). Amateur or domestic greenhouses are seldom likely to require this level of crop load. Very cheap greenhouses may, however, not stand much crop load at all.

Overall stability

Standards for overall stability of greenhouses tend to be couched in broad terms as they much depend on shape, height and various other factors. It is, however, a relatively simple matter to check the general stability of a greenhouse by exerting sideways pressure at gutter height or in the middle of glazing bars or astragals. Excessive movement in any greenhouse will predispose the structure to glass slippage, glass breakage, ventilator damage etc. The need to consider these issues and pay accordingly has already been stressed elsewhere.

Standards and specifications for plastic greenhouses

There has, in recent years, been considerable upgrading of the standards required for plastic greenhouses. Reputable companies have carried out considerable research into plastic greenhouse design and have banks of information on computer when, by referring to various wind speeds across the country, a plastic greenhouse can be designed for virtually any conditions. The critical issues for the structure itself relate to tube diameter, tube wall thickness, spacing of hoops, roof and end stress bars etc. Companies such as Clovis Lande Associates Ltd rigidly follow this procedure and their structures vary from 30 m/sec (67 mph) and a snow load of 460 N/m for the 14 ft wide model up to structures such as the crossbrace Highlande 21 which can stand a wind speed of 63 m/sec (141 mph) and a snow load of 745 N/m. It is important to note that these figures refer to the structure itself and not the coverings which themselves vary considerably in ability to withstand wind stress and snow load according to thickness, age and other factors. In extremely exposed areas such as the Western Isles of Scotland it may be necessary to resort to strengthened covers rather than standard grade polythenes. This is a matter to be taken up with the suppliers of the structure as listed in the Appendix.

CHAPTER 5
Types of Greenhouse

We turn now from the actual structural materials and their inherent strengths and design points to consider the basic forms of greenhouse. Before discussing them in detail there are a number of criteria for selection to be taken into account. These may be summarized as follows:

1 Maximum light transmission compatible with heat loss, bearing in mind the main purpose. Whether double-glazed or not. e.g. polycarbonate.

2 Freedom from maintenance, taking into account not only the structural materials, but also the glazing system.

3 Easy access to, and within, the greenhouse. Doors should be wide enough to permit entry of a barrow.

4 Reasonably easy and simple erection.

5 Cost. A relative matter. There is an excellent choice of structures to suit everyone's pocket.

6 Adequate ventilation, a really important issue which will be referred to in detail later.

7 Adaptability for automation, ie for ventilation, watering, heating, thermal screens etc.

Span-roofed greenhouses

This is the conventional shape with straight sides and a sloping roof, fairly standard heights for amateur houses being about 2.1–2.25m (7–7½ft) to the ridge and 1.65m (5ft 6in) to eaves. Most alloy greenhouses are glass-to-ground type. The length and breadth of the greenhouse varies from approximately 2.4m (8ft) long by 1.8m (6ft) wide, up to 3.6 × 2.4m (12 × 8ft), which is an ideal width module as it allows two good sized widths of border or benches. There is a very wide range of sizes available and most are readily extendable in length.

Mobile greenhouses

A most interesting type of greenhouse for the amateur is the single-span Dutch light greenhouse constructed of interlocking Dutch light frames. The interlocking principle involving male and female lights fitting snugly into each other gives rigidity and avoids drip. It also lends itself admirably to being mobilized by the fitting of pulley wheels to the bottom of the lights and running them on angle iron rails. If the ends of the greenhouse are hinged so that they can be raised clear of a crop the whole house can be moved *en bloc* and a system of crop rotation practised.

Mobile greenhouses need not, of course, be of Dutch light design, indeed many of those in Britain, Holland and Germany are not. Plastic structures with their cheaper capital costs, coupled with newer cropping techniques, have tended to oust mobile greenhouses to a great extent.

Commercial greenhouses

There is a vast range of sizes and types, and in this highly competitive business much experimentation. It is interesting to note that the massive ultrawide-span houses erected in Britain in the sixties have given way recently under pressure of Continental competition to less costly narrower span structures and layouts designed to achieve maximum light transmission. In Europe, however, the popular Venlo type (improved Dutch light) 3.2m (10ft 6in) houses are being superseded in many cases by a width module of 6.4m (21ft), again with economy of production in mind although double and triple supported or 'floating' gutter venlos are still very popular.

Mansard and curvilinear greenhouses

Mansard or curvilinear design simply sets out to provide a range of angles so that at any sun angle on the vertical plane there is a surface area of the glasshouse near the 'normal' angle (90°) for maximum solar

A typical commercial block of Venlo glasshouses, of which there are countless acres in the U.K. and continental Europe. In many cases this particular design has been superseded by supported or 'floating' gutter structures.

radiation distribution if orientated east-west. This can give rise to problems in summer, necessitating shading, since variable-pitch roofs give more headroom for less air volume, and the increased solar radiation heats the air more than would be the case with a conventional greenhouse.

Mansard and curvilinear greenhouses have not found a great deal of favour in commercial circles, being more costly to build than span-roofed houses and not so amenable to multi-span erection. For private gardens or parks' nurseries, however, the extra cost may be justified, especially when there is a lot of light-demanding winter work.

Greenhouses of this kind are available as glass-to-ground structures, or on a base block or wood or brick based wall. The Mansard roof is also suitable for the lean-to greenhouse.

Lean-to greenhouses

The lean-to greenhouse was much favoured by earlier gardeners on account of the heat-reflecting and heat-storing qualities of the wall on which it was constructed. In recent years, lean-to greenhouses have fallen out of favour, largely because they pose tremendous ventilation problems in very hot weather, sited as they are invariably on a south-facing wall. But in the last year or so the high costs of fuel and the universal installation of central heating in the home have revived interest in the lean-to or conservatory, since heating can possibly be linked to the domestic system and run very economically.

Lean-to greenhouses, or conservatories, can take three forms:

1 The three-quarter span, where it is preferable to extend the ridge of the greenhouse above the top of the wall and gain the full benefit of two-sided ridge ventilation.
2 The single pitch lean-to glass-to-ground, or on a base wall.
3 The curvilinear- and Mansard-shaped lean-to, variable pitch.

There has been sufficient discussion on light transmission for the finer points of configuration to be appreciated. The variable pitch roofed structure is obviously best

for good light transmission throughout the year, although excessively hot in summer. But both the three-quarter span and single-pitch types, if facing towards the sun, suffer from excessive summer heating. Shading can be carried out, both outside and inside, or a fan ventilation system installed to moderate temperatures.

Circular and geodesic greenhouses

Not a great deal can be said about circular greenhouses other than to extol their obvious advantages for light and solar heat transmission. They are more expensive to manufacture than conventional shaped houses offering comparable growing space. Nevertheless, the circular bench arrangement necessary with a circular greenhouse allows a high percentage of bench for pot plants or propagation under conditions of excellent light transmission and easy management. Effective ventilation can be a problem; fan ventilation or air conditioning is more or less essential if temperatures are

to be kept to an acceptable level in very hot weather.

Plastic greenhouses

Plastic greenhouses made their enthusiastic debut in kit form in the early 1950s, and followed the basic design of a rigid tubular steel or wood structure of conventional shape over which the plastic was stretched. At that time, however, plastic deteriorated very quickly due to the dual effects of ultraviolet rays and cold. It was particularly vulnerable when in contact with structural members due to heat build-up. Modern experience has shown, however, that provided a good quality polythene or PVC is used and treated as being reasonably expendable (three years on average), such greenhouses can be cheap and efficient for crop production. A basic fault is the condensation of moisture which occurs, necessitating very efficient ventilation if it is to be prevented. Double skin polythene helps in this respect, especially if the skins are kept apart with air, using a small fan. This arrangement has excellent heat conser-

A four-acre block of Solardome (Clovis Lande) plastic structures which, with their lower capital investment compared to glasshouses, are an attractive form of crop protection for growers.

37

vation properties but results in the loss of a small percentage of light.

Various types of polythene greenhouses can be bought ready to erect and the more successful designs tension the polythene effectively. Recent recommendations indicate the need to orientate plastic greenhouses so that the prevailing wind can assist ventilation and the need to keep the polythene tightly tensioned. Aluminium "Grip Strip" is available to help in this direction (see Appendix). Disease incidence should be no greater than in a glass greenhouse if correct ventilation is achieved. A recent criticism of plastic greenhouses is that carbon dioxide starvation occurs due to lack of air change when ventilation is poor. Water requirements in a properly ventilated plastic structure will be basically the same as those in an ordinary well ventilated greenhouse.

While the majority of polythene greenhouses are of simple curved roof design, they can also be obtained in more conventional multi-span form. In do-it-yourself designs, where wood is used for the structural members, it is essential to use a wrap-round system of securing the polythene so that it does not tear at local stress points which occur when nails are used (or use "Grip Strip"). Much can be done by using polythene roofs and netting using "Grip Strip" to join them.

While a modicum of ventilation can be obtained in the polythene greenhouse by leaving doors or flaps open, orientating the house to catch the prevailing wind, or using vents, really effective ventilation can be ensured by the installation of a suitably sized fan, and here of course is where the cost of the total structure starts to rise. Alternatively a strip of Nicofence, Lobrene or similar 'net'-like material helps greatly with ventilation (see Fig. 18).

One of the most interesting types of polythene greenhouse is the 'bubble'. Here the polythene is kept inflated by a fan, ventilation being effected by an ancillary extractor fan, which brings a counterbalanced ventilator into use in an inlet.

Fig. 18 Diagram showing ventilation of a plastic tunnel greenhouse by means of a woven plastic netting, such as Nicofence, and the use of double channel 'Grip Strip' (Clovis Lande). Wind-up flaps are now very popular.

Variations in span-roofed greenhouses

Type	Design detail	Comments
1 Straight-sided span roof	Glass to ground level on very low base wall or base blocks or with "kick" board	Good light transmission. Heating costs high in winter due to rapid heat loss
2 Slightly curved roof and sloping sides—several variations	Glass to ground on low base wall or base blocks	Better light transmission overall strength but tends to be more costly
3 Sloping-sided span roof	As above but with sloping sides	Loss of headroom if side slope acute; orientate east–west for winter sun; stable
4 Span roof, sloping sides	Constructed of interlocking Dutch lights	Easy to erect; dry glazed; but can lose heat and be draughty

Variations in span-roofed greenhouses – *continued*

Type	Design detail	Comments
5 Conventional span roof, vertical or slightly sloping sides	Base wall 75–85cm (30–34in) high	Best type for cold exposed areas, especially for propagation; very stable
6 Span roof and vertical sides	Base wall of wood, plastic or metal	No great advantage in respect of heat loss unless fibreglass lined over base wall
7 Span roof and vertical sides	Roof half glass, half wood. Best done longitudinally	Dual purpose greenhouse/shed at low cost; keep shed to north side or end

Summary of greenhouse types and their use

Greenhouse type	Special features	Range of activities
SPAN-ROOFED (wood, alloy, steel)	Brick base wall	Pot plants, propagation chrysanthemums in pots. General use for heated crops.
	Weatherboard base wall	Not so advantageous as brick in respect of heat retention, but base wall can be lined with insulation materials such as fibreglass.
	Glass to ground level or "kick board"	More costly to heat, but better light transmission makes them ideal for ground grown crops. "Kick" board avoids glass breakage at ground level
LEAN-TO (single pitch, $\frac{3}{4}$ span or variable pitch)	With or without base wall	Will grow most crops. Ventilation and overheating problem unless extractor fans or air conditioning systems installed. Light distribution unequal. Excellent for peaches etc against wall
DUTCH LIGHT of simple design (including some of Mansard design)	Static	Ideal for summer crops. Frequently used for lettuce and tomatoes. Heat loss occasioned by loose glazing system in some cases
	Mobile	Allows a system of crop rotation which can be highly advantageous
CURVILINEAR or MANSARD	On small base wall	Ideal for most activities, as in the case of glass-to-ground-level types. Heat loss higher with the latter
CIRCULAR	Several different designs	Good for pot plants and propagation. Fan ventilation or air 'conditioning' desirable
PLASTIC (see next page)	Do-it-yourself type	Will grow most crops well if crop support system adequate. Fan ventilation desirable.
	Sophisticated type	Excellent for all activities with added advantages of mobility. Fan or side ventilation highly desirable.
	Bubble	Has great potential for professional and amateur. Continuous running electric motor for inflation

Summary of plastic greenhouses

Type	Design detail	Comments
DO-IT-YOURSELF types of various designs	Conventional span-roofed shaped	As efficient a production unit as a conventional greenhouse, provided they are fan ventilated, although wear and tear of polythene or PVC is inevitable, necessitating fairly regular renewal. Cooler than a conventional greenhouse, especially at night.
	Tunnels	Reasonably stable in design and will suffer little damage by tearing until polythene weakens by ultra-violet deterioration. Ventilation problems still exist unless fans are used or there is a base strip of permeable material (see Fig 18). Double skinned if to be heated or use Thermic plastic.
	Conventional shaped multi-span structures.	More sophisticated forms are also stable and efficient. Crop supports require special consideration. Effective ventilation in all types may be a problem unless side or fan ventilated. Double skinning for heated crops
BUBBLE HOUSES	Either total or part inflated	Likely to be developed to a greater degree in the passage of time.
RIGID PLASTICS	Acrylics Rigid PVC Polycarbonate Fibreglass	Will obviously be developed a great deal in the next few years, especially double- or triple wall types for heat conservation. 'Biolex 2000' sheeting of special interest (see Appendix — Clovis Lande)
SERAC	Double skin panel system	Good light transmission with excellent heat conservation (see Appendix)

CHAPTER 6
Buying & Erecting Greenhouses

It is logical to think about the selection of a greenhouse before considering erection procedures, heating, ventilation, and other related matters, but it is imperative to understand the rudiments of these important matters before actually confirming the greenhouse order in precise detail. It happens far too often that people innocently buy greenhouses only to find out that they are insufficiently ventilated, not wide enough, or have other deficiencies.

Greenhouse buying can be approached in a variety of ways – you may send off for a catalogue you have seen advertised, or you may come across a greenhouse display at a flower show or garden centre. The information contained in greenhouse catalogues varies greatly: some are detailed in the extreme, some frustratingly imprecise. On the whole, however, they provide sufficient detail to enable one to make a selection even if technical issues such as stress and strain factors and general stability are seldom referred to.

Points to note when ordering
1 Structural materials Select for stability, lack of maintenance and aesthetic appearance. *Glazing system is most important.*
2 Size and dimensions Largely a question of suiting the greenhouse to the site, its size to intensity of use, and cost to money available. A frequent mistake is to purchase too small a greenhouse and soon find it bursting at the seams. Comparatively speaking, a larger greenhouse is a better investment than a smaller one on a sq m (or ft) basis, this being readily ascertained by dividing the sq unit area obtained into the total price. There is not a great difference in price between some alloys and conventional wooden structures, especially if the latter are of superior wood.
3 Ventilation There is a distinct lack of reference in many catalogues to the actual ventilation area in relation to the actual area of the greenhouse, and this information is necessary in order to work out whether or not the design gives a satisfactory rate of air change. Methods of calculating ventilation requirements are given elsewhere and these should be studied before specifying the number of vents required. Very little reference is made in many amateur greenhouse catalogues to fan ventilation, although it is the most positive way of achieving air change, provided one does not mind paying for electricity.
4 Number of doors One door is standard in amateur greenhouses. Two doors would only be necessary where a greenhouse is large enough to merit them. Sliding doors are now almost standard, and these have great advantages.
5 Constructional base blocks These are frequently offered, particularly with wooden greenhouses, and they are worth purchasing as they not only ensure a tight seal between the sill plate and the foundations, but make sure that the greenhouse is firmly secured to the ground. They also assist in simple, quick erection. Base blocks can be a hazard around the door. Securing cleats are now popular.
6 Benching This is usually available from manufacturers if required, there being merit in the fact that their benching will fit precisely into the greenhouse purchased.
7 Other extras Autovents, heaters, gutters and downpipes (if not standard), shades and other items can usually be ordered along with the greenhouse, and there is much to be said for buying them at the outset.
IMPORTANT NOTE Always double check the order, seeking the advice of a horticultural consultant or knowledgeable friend if in doubt on any important details. The cost of delivery should also be checked; some firms make a charge for delivery in

certain areas, others include it in the basic price.

Delivery

Greenhouses are delivered in various forms, from the fully complete sections of prefabricated wooden greenhouses, glazed or unglazed, to the alloy structures neatly packed in a container. Where bulky and heavy sections are involved, some care should be taken to ensure that they are off-loaded from the delivery lorry relatively convenient to the erection site without impinging on it. These sections should be carefully stacked and adequately supported so that they are not likely to topple over in a gale; if in doubt lay them flat, but keep an eye on damage to a lawn!

Checking to see that everything is delivered undamaged and that no parts are missing is not always easy, but if at all possible it should be done, although this is not practical with alloy sections packed in boxes. The delivery note should be signed appropriately if there is any obvious damage, and the supplier informed immediately. Most reliable firms double check everything when it leaves the factory, as non-delivery of parts can cause a great deal of annoyance. Mistakes do occur however; new designs being particularly prone to missing parts, and in some instances sections do not fit properly together.

Plans and problems

Erection plans, in some cases very detailed indeed, and coded, should always be sent by the manufacturer, and they may in fact arrive before the greenhouse, which is a better arrangement as it allows the site and foundations to be prepared and the erection instructions and plans to be carefully studied. Note precisely whether centre to centre, outside to outside, or inside to inside measurements are quoted; outside to outside measurements are the most usual.

Consideration should be given to intended orientation for the greenhouse when making the actual purchase and most certainly if seeking planning permission. It can happen, however, that a different orientation seems preferable when the actual erection is in hand. It would then be better to delay work until the matter is corrected and I would imagine that most planning authorities would be fairly sympathetic to an alteration involving, in many cases, only a small distance one way or another with an amateur sized greenhouse. To ignore the tremendous implications of correct orientation would be folly.

Marking out the site

To peg out the position of the greenhouse on the ground, accurately cut pointed pegs 2.5 × 2.5cm (1 × 1in) and at least 30cm (12in) in length. Knock in the first peg lightly at the appropriate distance from some fixed line such as a fence, path or building, and by the use of a steel measuring tape tap in another peg to mark the length of the greenhouse, *using centre to centre* measurements for each peg. Check that the line of the pegs is in line with the fence or building making sure at the same time that it follows the desired orientation. Note that it is the length of the greenhouse, the line of the ridge, which must conform to east-west or north-south orientation. A few degrees off the intended orientation one way or another is not vital, it being better, however, to err to the north (for the U.K.) for an east-west ridge orientation and to the east for a north-south orientation.

With a reasonably square greenhouse it is, on balance, marginally better to have the ridge running east-west for transmission of winter and spring light. Where, by necessity, the greenhouse has to be erected with an orientation between east-west and north-south to maintain a tidy line, there is not much one can do about it: the full implications of light transmission must, however, be appreciated.

The levels of the two pegs should now be set accurately, knocking them into the ground sufficiently to make them stable. With the average amateur sized greenhouse up to about 3–3.6m (10–12ft) in length, a long straight unwarped board and a spirit-level should suffice for level checking. For a longer greenhouse an intermediate peg or pegs is advisable, checking their line by the use of a light piece of cord or string which should always be set tautly between the two end pegs. If a Cowley or similar level can be borrowed, set up and properly used, this helps to get the top of the pegs exactly level, although final checking with a spirit-level is always desirable.

Smaller greenhouses are usually erected dead level; a large type with a gutter may have a slight fall in one direction, as advised by the manufacturer, to facilitate the run of water. With commercial greenhouses, especially in multi-bay form, a run is essential to ensure that the water moves quickly along the gutter and does not flow back through the glass. A fall of about 15–30cm (6–12in) per 30m (100ft) length of greenhouse is usual.

Now tap a 5cm (2in) nail *lightly* into the *centre* of each peg. Forming the right angle necessary to measure up the width of the greenhouse can be tricky and should never be guessed. A triangle carefully made up with pieces of straight unwarped wood 90cm (3ft), 1.2m (4ft) and 1.5m (5ft) in length may be used, checking that the right angle formed is exact by using a joiner's square. The triangle should be put exactly *to the nail* on one corner peg and one leg should be supported with bricks along the taut line between the two end pegs. After supporting the other right-angle leg, put a line along it and tie this to a peg set outside the width of the greenhouse. Then measure along the line and insert a peg at the exact width required. Repeat this procedure at the other corner and then check the two pegs longitudinally, also checking that the diagonals are equal. One usually finds it necessary to make slight adjustments so that everything tallies. (This task can also be undertaken with a site square, which is not perhaps the easiest instrument to use as it must itself be very carefully set up *dead level* over both of the first inserted corner pegs in turn.) Now level up the corner pegs and tap nails into their centres. Finally set taut good-quality lines on each corner peg to make the outline of the house by using short pieces of wood, or more pegs, 60–90cm (2–3ft) outside the house outline so that work can proceed on the foundations of the greenhouse without impediment by moving the corner pegs and lines out of the way as necessary (see Fig. 19).

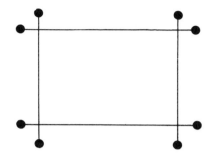

Fig. 19 When erecting a greenhouse, foundations should be marked by lines set on pegs *outside* the actual greenhouse area which remains undisturbed. These lines can be removed to allow unimpeded working and replaced, if necessary, to check alignments.

Foundations

With certain types of Dutch light greenhouses it is merely necessary to set down base blocks on levelled soil, though this is not a very satisfactory long-term arrangement either in the interests of stability or to prevent lateral movement of soil moisture. It is a practice adopted frequently by those taking short cuts in the interests of economy, or where a greenhouse site is being treated as temporary. A foundation of one kind or another is highly desirable to keep the greenhouse completely level and entirely stable in spite of the destructive forces of such things as gales and hurricanes. The precise nature of the foundation, if any, depends on a number of factors, and more specifically on the actual design of the greenhouse being erected. Study very closely the erection plans or booklet applicable to the greenhouse. Base blocks may be provided with the greenhouse if specially ordered; alternatively it may be necessary to build a brick base wall or run in concrete with fixing pegs. For most amateur greenhouses a half-brick 11.25cm (4½in) wall will be adequate, and this is usually exactly the width of any special base blocks provided. In this case, after determining the exact centre line of the greenhouse base, take out a trench 20–23cm (8–9in) wide and 18–20cm (7–8in) deep, or deeper if the soil has recently been levelled in order to make contact with undisturbed soil. This may not always be practical. Using a mixture of 3 parts finely broken brick, 2 parts rough sand, and 1 part cement, run in a layer about 8–10cm (3–4in) deep and 'dump' this as level as possible by the use of a fairly heavy straight board, using a spirit-level on top of this to check levels regularly. Where a full brick foundation wall of 23cm (9in) is necessary, as could be the case on a sloping site, or for a large greenhouse, the trench should be 30—35cm (12—14in) wide and again 12.5—15cm (5—6in) deep, although in many cases a half-brick wall would suffice if suitably reinforced with piles. Greenhouses can in certain circumstances be laid directly on the foundations without the base blocks, in which case any securing bolts will need to be inserted into the foundations at the appropriate points. Alternatively anchor cleats may be used. Special base blocks invariably have an in-built system of anchorage for the green-house. Always allow the foundations to harden sufficiently before starting building. In all cases it will be necessary to put the line back in position and keep this suitably taut when necessary to check that there is precise adherence to the stated outside measurement. Before building opposite walls, it is advisable to check the widths and length, as bricks tend to get out of alignment, especially if laid by someone who is not an experienced bricklayer.

Perusal of greenhouse catalogues fre-quently shows a complete perimeter wall with no allowance for doors, which in-volves an awkward step up unless there is a suitable ramp. Base blocks, when supplied, ideally should leave the door flush with ground-level, a much more sensible arrangement, provided there is a concrete step.

It may seem that these items are trivial, yet they make a great deal of difference over the years to the easy management of a greenhouse, especially when wheeling barrows full of soil or debris. It is advisable to have a slight rise *up* to the door to avoid rain running into the greenhouse, which may happen if the ground slopes the other way.

Skill in building even a low wall varies, but by using a 3:1 sand/cement mixture and checking the line and level of each brick or block carefully, it should be pos-sible for even the rawest amateur builder to make a reasonably accurate job of it, failing which call in a builder or handyman. Note that if using faced bricks the faced side should be to the outside, otherwise they will quickly weather.

Building procedures

Where the type of greenhouse being built demands a low base wall of 75cm (30in) or thereabouts, this must be carefully built, otherwise there can be erection problems. Very few prefabricated greenhouses in-tended for base walls now seem to be about, but they can be obtained if required and may be necessary on very exposed sites. Do-it-yourself enthusiasts frequently use the base-wall method of building a greenhouse, following conventional de-signs of sill plates on top of the wall to bear the astragals (see Fig. 20). Second-hand ex-commercial structural material is bought for the purpose of cutting down to build an amateur greenhouse, which is not usually a difficult job, provided care is taken to clean all the wood properly, giving it a good coat of paint before building commences, especially as the ends of the old astragal bars are generally removed. Galvanized nails should be used throughout, as steel nails can quickly rust.

There are seldom any problems in build-ing a prefabricated greenhouse, particularly if time is taken to study erection plans. Some of the instruction booklets are de-tailed in the extreme, every part being marked and identified by a diagram, there being explicit erection diagrams bearing part numbers in addition. With alloy structures it is normal to build up the gable ends and one side on the ground; then, after

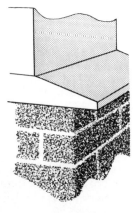

Fig. 20 Sill plates set on top of base walls should overlap the base wall to allow water to be shed.

putting up one gable end, proceed first with one side and then the other before putting up the other gable end. The roof and ventilators are generally left until last.

The completely glazed sections of a pre-fabricated wooden grenhouse are erected in similar order, but it will be necessary to obtain help as the sections are often heavy. If building a greenhouse with wood on a do-it-yourself basis, it is a case of building the main framework first before putting in the astragals. When glazing, although procedures vary, it is often preferable to do the roof first, followed by the gable ends, leaving the sides until last so that if there should be a high wind it will blow *through* the structure. A very important point when building any type of greenhouse is to tie down loose vents at night, particularly if they are glazed, otherwise they can flap about and cause a lot of damage.

The need to anchor greenhouses securely cannot be emphasized too strongly, allowing cement to harden before fully erecting a valuable structure.

Glazing should take place only during dry weather, as neither putty nor strips of mastic seal properly if the glazing bars are wet, in addition to which wet glass is very dangerous to work with. With alloy greenhouses all joins in gutters or main members should be properly sealed with mastic or other material.

Where there is a gutter the downpipe should be taken to an appropriate outlet or soakaway, and where the greenhouse is built on a slope it may be necessary to install a drain along the higher side to stop rain seeping into the greenhouse.

Installation of water

The installation of water has already been mentioned in connection with site preparation. If a supply pipe at low level is taken into the greenhouse, care should be taken not to damage the foundations. Ideally the water pipe should be laid before the greenhouse is built. The precise arrangements for water will depend on a number of circumstances, but a screw type tap is more or less a standard fitment. The most convenient place for the tap will again vary, but in the majority of cases the end opposite the door is most satisfactory. For mist irrigation, capillary benches, spraylines, heating systems and other water-demanding equipment, special arrangements will be necessary, all readily accomplished with alkathene pipe and patent screw fittings.

Installation of electricity

Because greenhouses are damp places, *and with alloy greenhouses in particular*, plastic covered cable, preferably PVC conduit or PCP sheathed cable, must be used along with waterproof fittings for the installation of electricity. The complete installation should be supervised by a qualified electrician or someone with a sound knowledge of electrical installations, and properly earthed. An alloy greenhouse can frequently 'go live' because of the nearness of an open connection to the structure. With a wooden greenhouse, while the same care is not perhaps as necessary, the installation should be carried out to rigid standards of safety. Whether to bring power in overhead or by underground cable is a matter best decided by a qualified electrician who will also ensure that the supply cable is adequate for the load demanded by the equipment, and taken right back to a suitably placed junction box and *not* a convenient plug.

Main path and greenhouse flooring

There should be a good slabbed path, or one of concrete or asphalt, to the greenhouse door or doors, there being nothing worse than a dirty wet path which, apart from being dangerous, constantly carries dirt and possible disease into the greenhouse.

The nature of the flooring in a greenhouse will usually be dependent on the cropping arrangements. With a permanently benched greenhouse with a bench on each side, a slab path at least 60cm (2ft) wide is the general rule. The area under each bench is usually left 'rough', covered with a larger of gravel, although the fastidious gardener may well wish to slab the whole floor, Slabs can be laid on a bed of sand, ashes or rubble, this last allowing the slabs to be held at the corners by cement.

Alternatively a concrete path can be run in using a 5:3:2 mixture and shuttering boards, making the concrete at least 5cm (2in) thick.

When the borders are used for cropping purposes, a wooden 'cat walk' may be used instead of a slabbed centre path as it can be removed to allow complete soil sterilization and cultivation. Where ring culture of tomatoes is practised, slabs are simply laid down the centre of the aggregate, unless some more permanent arrangement is preferred.

Maintenance of greenhouses

The painting procedure for greenhouses has already been referred to, as also have types of paint and frequency of painting. The current theme of erecting a greenhouse of materials and of a design which require little or no maintenance is founded on sound common sense, as there can be nothing more troublesome than constantly attending to the upkeep of buildings.

One of the main chores with any type of greenhouse is the cleaning of the glass, especially in industrial areas. Dust adheres to sticky deposits and in time a skin of dust develops on the glass, restricting light transmission very considerably. Moss and algae grow at any overlaps and on the glazing bars unless a carefully sealed barcap glazing system is used. Even then moss and algae can develop under the bar-cap if moisture gains access, which it usually does. The build-up of moss and algae, especially the former, can be extremely destructive and will literally push the glass out of position, causing leaks.

Glass cleaning can be carried out by using a proprietary glass cleaner or oxalic acid crystals dissolved in water, 100g to 1 litre (1lb to 1 gallon) sprayed on and then washed off, the latter being especially necessary when a metal greenhouse is involved. The oxalic acid also burns off a fair proportion of the moss, the remainder being freely dislodged by a good strong jet from a hose pipe. Moss and algae also grow inside a greenhouse and the removal of these is better undertaken when the greenhouse is empty. The cleaning operation usually demands the wearing of protective clothing, including a waterproof hat. Cresylic or carbolic acid (or Jeyes Fluid) used in a solution of 1 part to 39 parts of water is useful for cleaning down the inside as it burns off moss and algae very effectively. Moss and algae in glass overlaps may have to be removed with a piece of metal and a jet of water.

Base walls should be cleaned annually with a wire brush; if necessary paint them with whitewash or emulsion paint.

The maintenance of heating systems will be dealt with in another chapter.

CHAPTER 7
Heating Greenhouses

To study in depth the full implications of heat is well beyond the scope of this book. It will suffice to translate the three methods of heat distribution, ie conduction, convection and radiation, into practical terms in relation to greenhouse heating. Briefly, **conduction** is the transmission of heat through a substance from molecule to molecule, **convection** the transference of heat through a liquid or gas by circulation of the heated portion, and **radiation** the transference of heat energy by electro-magnetic waves from heat source to absorbing object, and between objects.

Solar radiation

The short wave radiation from the sun passes through the glass of the greenhouse, warming everything it contacts, floor, soil, bench, plants, pots, and so on. These in turn re-radiate the heat back into the greenhouse on long waves which cannot pass through the glass. The heat trapped within the greenhouse sets up convection currents, establishing in effect a convection cycle of warmed air.

Artificial heating systems

Where an artificial heating system is introduced into the greenhouse it will operate independently of solar radiation, and more generally and preferably when solar radiation falls below an effective level. There are several forms of artificial heating available. Hot water pipes are a good method of heating greenhouses: the metal is a good conductor of heat and in turn transmits radiation heat; and both pipes and objects warmed by radiation set up convection currents. Hot pipes also transmit heat by conduction when they are in actual contact with the soil. Electric tubular heaters are another frequently used method of greenhouse heating and operate in the same way as water heated pipes. Direct or indirect

warm air heaters, free discharge or fan assisted, are becoming increasingly popular for greenhouse heating. The air on discharge sets up convection currents. Fans push the heated air out more quickly, though convection currents still subsequently develop.

Soil warming cables, used mainly for propagation benches, become warm by conduction, then transmit this heat by conduction and radiation to the soil or sand. Mineral insulated cables can also be used for warming the air.

Some variable factors in greenhouse heating

One important point which should be stressed is that these heating processes can readily be upset or disturbed. For example, one side of a greenhouse may be much colder than the other, despite a well-designed perimeter system of warm pipes, because a very cold wind blowing along that side is causing very rapid heat loss through the glass. Similarly, a fan heater may fail to direct warm air to all parts of the greenhouse, because a cold wind outside has produced an internal curtain of cold air.

Lack of uniformity in temperature throughout a greenhouse can be checked by the use of integrating jars or, less accurately, with a number of ordinary thermometers. These integrating jars, which are silver-foil-covered, water-filled bottles containing thermometers, are left in different areas of the greenhouse long enough for the water content in the jar to achieve uniform temperature (there may be difficulty in this respect during short summer nights). On inspection at 7−8 am the temperatures recorded may be found to vary considerably (Fig. 21).

The particular problems of greenhouse heating centre around the unavoidable rapid loss of heat through the glass by

Fig. 21 (*Right*)
Temperature bottles
are easily made and
will measure air
temperature, ideally
overnight when they
are not affected by
solar radiation.

Fig. 22 (*Far right*)
Convection currents
will be set up by
evenly distributed
warm pipes.

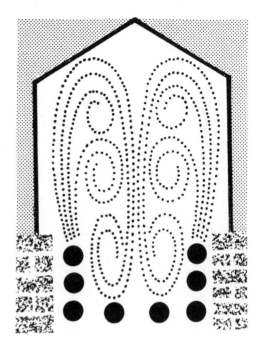

conduction, and inevitably also through leaks in the structure. There is therefore great need of a constant high output and uniform source of heat sufficient to overcome this rapid heat loss. A central source of heat, such as an oil heater or an electric fan or convector heater, will not warm a greenhouse as uniformly as it would the room of a solid building. Ideally a greenhouse should have a complete ring of warm pipes to give off radiation heat and initiate convection currents, and in the centre there should be further radiation heat from pipes, which would also set up smaller convection currents (see Fig. 22). Where there are benches there should be allowance for convection currents between the bench and the outside of the greenhouse (frequently this is prevented) in addition to radiation heat to plants on the bench by individual pipes. The diagrams referred to show the greenhouse longitudinally, but the ends of the greenhouse should develop similar convection currents, it being good practice to complete the circuit of pipes under the door by containing them in a grille.

Although a centrally sited unit heater is unable to achieve uniform heat distribution, this matters less as the season progresses and outside temperatures rise. Warm air fan heaters are slightly better than natural convector heaters (electrical, oil or gas), as they do move the air positively which assists with the mixing of warm and cold air, though there are inevitable cold spots. Warm air heaters, however, can be as efficient as warm pipe systems if the air is distributed in polythene ducts.

Calculating heat losses

It is essential to make exact measurements of the greenhouse so that the heat loss through all external surface areas can be calculated accurately. The areas of glass (including glazing bars) and the areas of base walls of brick or wood or other material should be measured separately since each will lose heat at different rates (Fig. 23). Heat loss is calculated by the rate of thermal transmission (loss of heat by conduction) or μ value; different materials have different μ values. These are, despite metrication, usually still quoted in British thermal units, one unit being the amount of heat needed to raise the temperature of 1lb of water 1°F The metric term is $w/m^2 °C$. The following are the accepted μ values for various materials and, in keeping with modern practice,

The Robinsons professional range for keen amateurs starts with the Regent model at 1980cm (6ft 6in) x 2590cm (8ft 6in).

A Royale 8–10, one of the smaller of the Robinson range. Of traditional sturdy design, it has good headroom, double doors and excellent working space.

For those who like traditional wooden structures the Alton Cedar with vertical sides from Banbury is a good choice. Various sizes are available with vertical or sloping sides and side ventilation as standard. There is adequate working space inside and maintenance is negligible.

The Robinson Rosette 10/20 of traditional shape, double doors and five vents is ideal for the more serious minded gardener.

The Cambridge plant house with continuous ridge ventilation is available in a range of sizes and has a block infill base.

A roomy design of plastic structure of particular interest to the gardener who expects snow, is the 'Sungrow' from Garden Rewards.

Of revolutionary design, the Serac 'Northern Light' solar greenhouse combines maximum solar transmission with a patented double glazing system for maximum heat conservation. Other designs are available.

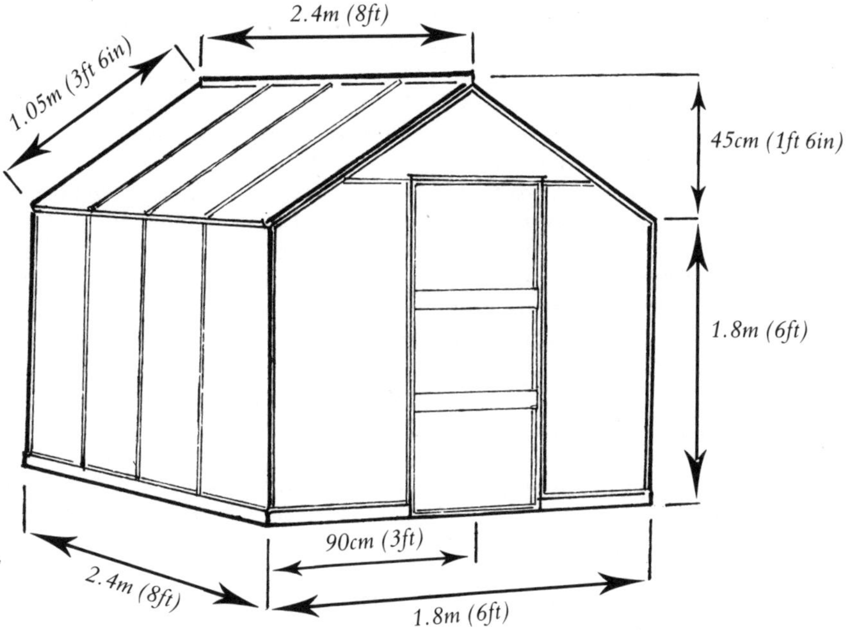

Fig. 23 Measuring your greenhouse for heat loss calculations.

they are quoted in slightly higher figures to allow for inadvertent heat loss. Note also that heat losses will be higher in exposed situations, lower in sheltered ones.

Average thermal transmission coefficients for different materials in w/m²/°C (Btu/ft²/hour/°F).
Btu/FT²/hour/°F = 5.678 w/m²/°C
w/m²/°C = 0.176 Btu/ft²/hour/°F

Glass including glazing bars	
W/m²/°C	Btu/ft²/hour/°F
7.94	1.4
Brickwork 11.2cm (4½in)	
3.63	0.64
Brickwork 22.5cm (9in)	
2.66	0.47
Concrete 10cm (4in)	
9.9	1.75
Concrete 15cm (6in)	
3.46	0.61
Wood 2.5cm (1in)	
2.83	0.5

Fibreglass and rigid PVC
Broadly similar to glass with the exception of PVC materials such as Biolex 2000 sheeting, which has a heat loss 30–40% less than glass. Polythene of various grades, usually 150 mu or 180 mu, for practical purposes taken as
7.94   1.4

PVC and new thermic films
Usually slightly less than basic polythene, between 10–20%

Bi- or triple-walled acrylics and polycarbonates 30–50% less than glass. The same is true for twin-skinned polythene structures with a fan system to keep the skins apart.

Technically there is also a heat loss through concrete or earth floors, but this is so small it can be ignored. In actual fact the floor can often serve as a considerable store of heat for re-radiation, but any heat loss is allowed for in the higher figures quoted above. It is now a relatively simple matter to calculate the total surface area of the greenhouse.

Sides 2 × 2.4m (8ft) × 1.8m (6ft)	= 8.64 m² (96 sq ft)
Ends 2 × 1.8m (6ft) × 1.8m (6ft) × 1.8m (6ft)	= 6.48 m² (72 sq ft)
Roof 2 × 2.4m (8ft) × 1.05m (3ft 6in)	= 5.04 m² (56 sq ft)
Gable ends 2 × 90cm × 45cm (3ft × 1ft 6in)	= 0.81 m² (9 sq ft)
TOTAL	20.97 m² (233 sq ft)

As this is an all-glass greenhouse the total heat loss is 20.97 × 7.94 = 166w/m²/°C

(233 × 1.4 = 326Btu) This figure is the difference per degree C or degree F between inside and outside temperatures and it is then necessary to calculate for the heat lift required; this is done by multiplying the 166 (326) by the selected heat lift: an 11°C (20°F) lift is adequate for frost protection and normal temperatures in spring; a 22°C (40°F) lift will ensure a reasonable level of temperature throughout the year, even when it is 6.7°C (20°F) out of doors; the 16°C (30°F) lift is a compromise between the two. Thus the figures to be aimed at

166 w/m²/°C × 11 (20) = 1826 watts (6520 Btu) = approx 1.8 kW
166 w/m²/°C × 16 (30) = 2656 watts (9780 Btu) = approx 2.6 kW
166 w/m²/°C × 21 (40) = 3486 watts (13040 Btu) = approx 3.4 kW

give the respective heat losses for the various lifts. These figures represent the actual heat requirements from the heating system, no matter what type or design this may be. Note that exact conversion from metric to imperial terms is not practical.

It is usual to have a slightly larger heat production unit than necessary to allow quick response and to cope with periods of excessively low temperatures. Where a hot pipe system has the boiler sited away from

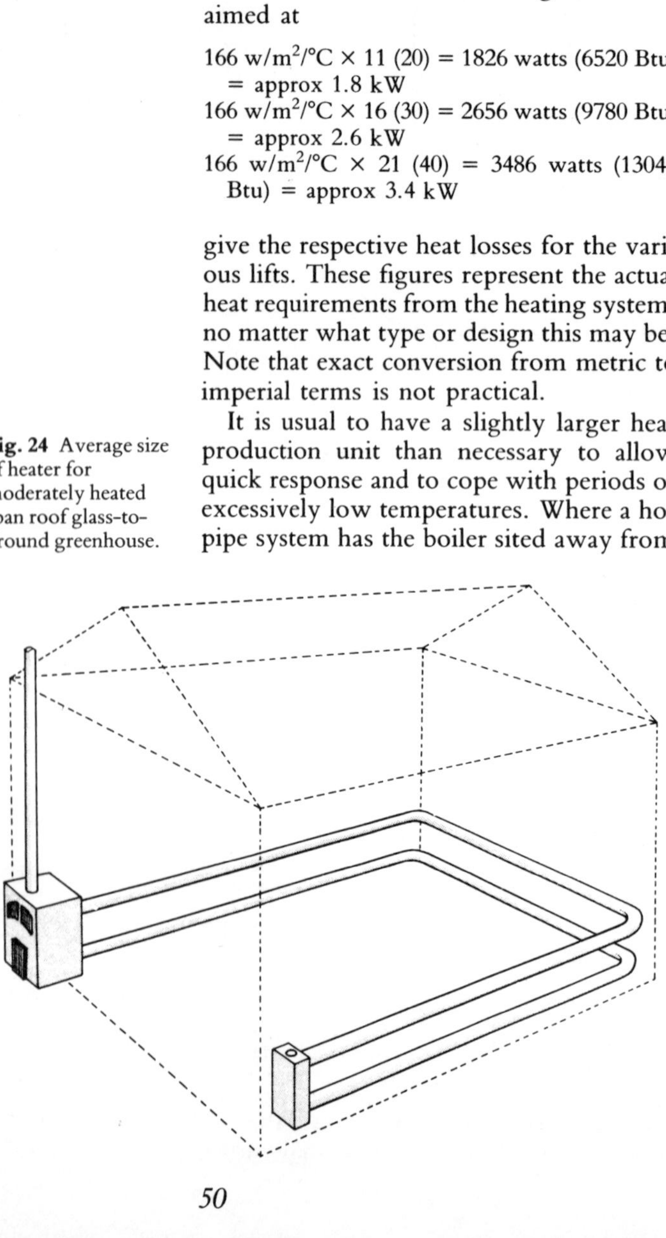

Fig. 24 Average size of heater for moderately heated span roof glass-to-ground greenhouse.

the greenhouse (perhaps in a shed or garage), there will be some loss of heat en route to the greenhouse, a quarter to a third being the usual allowance for this loss. Allowance may also have to be made for an exposed situation.

Designing a heating system around the calculated heat requirement will depend on the type of crop to be raised and practical matters such as the availability of electricity, oil or gas, and the possibility of linking the system to an existing one in the home.

Hot water systems
Large bore pipes
These were once normal installation for all greenhouses, but are not now considered economical for large units. Pipes are usually of 10cm (4in) diameter and the water circulated by gravity, provided there is a gradual rise from the boiler to the highest point in the unit and a gradual fall-back to the boiler. There are design problems here, in avoiding obstruction to doors and in siting the boiler or heat source at a sufficiently low point—often below ground-level unless the heating pipes in the greenhouse are fairly high (see Fig 24).

It is a slow and costly operation to heat up large volumes of water, but once hot it retains and radiates its heat for a considerable period. This, however, in combination with solar radiation often causes the temperature of the air in the greenhouse to rise excessively, which is not only wasteful but may be injurious to the plants, although it can help to encourage air currents through a crop. Once solar radiation ceases there may be a quick demand once again for heat, and the whole process of re-heating the now cool large volume of water has to be begun again.

Advantages of small bore pipes
Smaller bore pipe systems of 2.5—5cm (1—2in) diameter are invariably installed now in greenhouses: there is much less water to heat, and thus the total bulk cools more rapidly. A further advantage of small bore pipes is that as they take up less room they can be readily taken to the crop and spread over the cropping area or under benches, between plants, and placed on the

soil — especially important for plants such as early tomatoes which must be planted in warm soil.

Accelerated hot water systems

The main disadvantage of small bore pipe systems is that as the diameter of the pipe decreases the friction increases, and it may be found that the hot water does not circulate rapidly enough or may not be capable of completing its circuit back to the heat source again. This can be overcome by the use of an accelerator pump — a matter for consultation with a heating engineer. Existing gravity systems can, in many cases, be greatly improved by the fitting of such a pump, although this will seldom be necessary on smaller installations.

High speed hot water system

Accelerator pumps merely *assist* the circulation of the water but still alllow some natural circulation; high speed hot water systems, usually of small bore design, depend entirely on pumps for the circulation of the water, allowing no natural circulation. They include alkathene soil warming pipes underground, and 'minibore' bench warming systems. Problems do exist with high speed water systems unless an entirely automatic system of firing is involved. The temperature of the greenhouse is usually controlled by a thermostat which operates the pumps and if a non-automatic solid fuel boiler is being used and the pump is shut off by the thermostat (due to a rise above the desirable temperature in the greenhouse) there can be serious overheating of the boiler. With automatically fired boilers, especially with oil or gas where there is no great residual heat involved, this situation does not arise. The problem can be overcome by using a non-return valve on a bypass which opens when the pump is non-operative.

In high speed hot water systems, and to a limited degree with accelerated systems also, it is important to ensure that the pump is the correct size for the system. An inadequate size of pump would fail to overcome the frictional resistance of the pipes, but too powerful a pump would not only circulate the water, but could force it out of the system through the header tank. The design of pumps and accelerators and their selection for a specific task is a highly technical matter best taken up with a specialist supplier who will specify a particular size for the heating system involved after taking into account the length of pipe, its diameter, the calorific rating of the system, the acceptable temperature drop between flow and return pipes, and the design of the whole system.

Formulae exist which allow the ready calculation of pump sizes which are rated on what is called their 'circulating head' *and it should be repeated that a pump with a larger circulation head than is necessary may give rise to problems.* There are several ways of overcoming this, such as fitting it on the flow pipe instead of, as is normal, on the return, or ensuring that the header tank is on the suction side of the pump, or alternatively raising the height of the header tank. Pumps with variable circulating heads which allow some adjustment are available and may be the answer for smaller domestic greenhouse systems.

Types of piping

Cast iron piping is now seldom used for greenhouse heating, although there are still some older systems in existence. Steel pipes are invariably used and this has the distinct advantage of allowing screwed couplings or alternatively welding to be readily carried out — not possible with cast iron pipes. Pipes rust readily and while it was stated for a while that aluminium based paint should not be used as this reduced heat output, research has shown the reduction in heat transmission to be insignificant. Aluminium paint is therefore advised to reduce external rusting and general deterioration. Bitumastic paint should not be used as this gives off fumes when the pipes are warm. Newer types of vegetable oil paint have also been developed.

Transmission of heat from different pipe sizes

The transmission of heat from pipes varies according to their diameter, the temperature of the water in them, and the external temperature of the air surrounding them.

Fig. 25 Heat output: Approximate heat output from different pipe diameters.

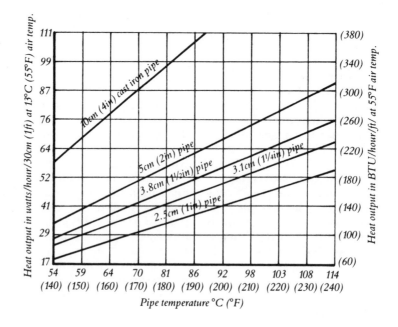

The above chart shows the respective output of pipes of different diameters at an air temperature of 13°C (55°F), the variation of output for different air temperatures being shown in the accompanying table (see Fig. 25). To use this chart read upwards from the base to the line indicating pipe size, then move left to ascertain the output per 30cm (12in) of pipe. As the temperature of the water in a heating system varies, as indeed does the air temperature, it is necessary to accept a workable figure for design purposes. It can be seen, however, from the figure that the output from pipes can be considerably greater with a higher water temperature, especially when the water temperature rises above boiling point (see note under pressurized hot water systems). With smaller greenhouse systems one must be realistic and, considering the difference between the flow and return temperatures, the following figures are reasonably workable. Pipe emission at 37°C (100°F) temperature difference to nearest round figures per 30 cm (12in).

2.5cm (1in)	23 w/hour/°C	(80	Btu)
3.1cm (1¼in)	29 w/hour/°C	(100	Btu)
3.8cm (1½in)	32 w/hour/°C	(110	Btu)
5cm (2in)	38 w/hour/°C	(130	Btu)
10cm (4in)	67 w/hour/°C	(230	Btu)

Gilled pipes are available and these permit a much greater heat emission according to the design (up to four or five times as much as plain pipes) (see Fig. 26).

Fig. 26 Gilled piping—this encourages distribution of heat into air.

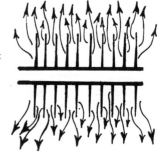

Designing a hot water heating system
To design a pipe heating system the first stage is to determine the heat loss of the greenhouse and thereafter to calculate the length of pipe needed to supply the necessary heat in a form which will conveniently fit in with the type of cropping being practised. To return to the 2.4 × 1.8m (8 × 6ft) greenhouse, and assuming a 22°C (40°F) lift, we are concerned with the supply of some 3810 watts (13,000 Btu) The respective lengths of piping of different diameters will be, to quote two examples,

3.1cm ($1\frac{1}{4}$in) piping

$\dfrac{3810 \text{ (watts)}}{29 \ \ (3.1\text{cm})} = 131 \times 30\text{cm} = $ approximately 39.30m

$\dfrac{13000 \text{ (Btu)}}{100 \ \ (1\frac{1}{4}\text{in pipe size})} = 130 \text{ ft of } 1\frac{1}{4}\text{in pipe}$

10cm (4in) piping

$\dfrac{3810 \text{ (watts)}}{67 \ \ (10\text{cm pipes})} = 56 \times 30\text{cm} = 17\text{m}$

$\dfrac{13000 \text{ (Btu)}}{230 \ \ (4\text{in pipe size})} = 56 \text{ ft of 4in pipe}$

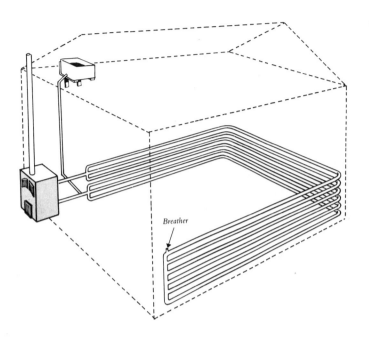

Breather

If a 10cm (4in) system was selected the normal arrangement of pipes will be a double run of pipe along each side and across the end, which comes to 13m (44ft), some 3.3m (12ft) short of the calculated figure. Assuming slightly hotter pipes in view of the nearness of the boiler, it is fair to assume that the required input of heat could be supplied, bearing in mind that this allows for 16°C (60°F) in the greenhouse at −7°C (20°F) outside temperature. If, however, it is decided to use 3cm ($1\frac{1}{4}$in) pipes, the required 39m (130ft) will necessitate either spreading or banking on the sides requiring six lines of pipes along each side and across the end (see Fig. 27). There is virtue, therefore, for greenhouses of this small size, in using larger bore pipe, especially as to do this would also facilitate circulation without the fairly costly installation of a pump. As a compromise 28m (approx 90ft) of 5cm (2in) pipe would be required — four lines on the sides and at the end.

It will be noted that no provision has been made in this instance for heating in the region of the door and it would be difficult to allow for this where circulation depends entirely on gravity. Where a pump and small bore pipes are being used, these could conveniently be taken either below or above the door. Pipes can all be installed at high level and this has virtues for flower crops. Where larger greenhouses are concerned and spread heat is desirable for an early tomato crop, the pipes should be spaced out over the greenhouse. Commercially much use is made of flexible rubber couplings to allow the pipes to be raised or lowered as desired. When the soil is to be heated prior to planting tomatoes, the pipes are allowed to actually lie on the ground, and subsequently when the soil is warm and more convection heat is necessary to warm the air, the pipes can be raised on bricks. On the Continent, and increasingly in the U.K., much use is made of underplant alkathene pipes. A frequent practice in smaller houses is to install benches for the earlier part of the year for intensive propagation, removing these in the spring to make way for a groundgrown crop of tomatoes or chrysanthemums. In this case rubber coupled pipes capable of movement could be kept up a short distance below the bench to provide local heat for propagation, then dropped down to the ground to warm the soil for tomatoes or other crops (see Fig. 28).

Low pressure steam heating systems
These have little place in small installations, a steam boiler being an expensive item, only economical between about 363−454kg (800−1,000lb) of steam per hour, this being capable of supplying heat for a greenhouse of about 1000m² (one−quarter of an acre). As with medium pressure hot water systems less heating pipe is required.

Fig. 27 Designing a small diameter pipe system can mean using considerable lengths of piping to give the required heat input which can be much reduced by using gilled piping (see Fig. 26).

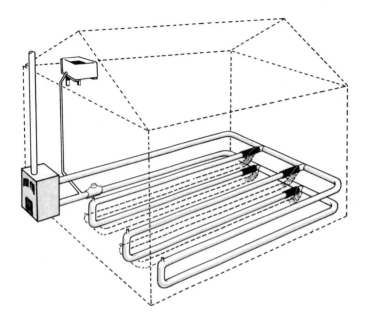

Fig. 28 The use of flexible hose connections not only allows movement of the heating pipes but means easier installation.

Medium pressure hot water systems

In these systems hot water can be circulated through the heating pipes, if necessary above boiling point, the water being prevented from boiling because it is under pressure. The pressure is provided either by an ancillary unit or by a steam 'pad' in the boiler. Hot water boilers can be used where an ancillary unit is to be used, whereas with the pad system a steam boiler is necessary. As water temperatures in the pipes can be as high as 110–121°C (230–250°F), less radiation surface is needed in the greenhouse, so reducing the total length of pipe required, although the pipe layout will follow a similar pattern to a hot water system. A circulating pump is required to move the water round quickly. One advantage of the steam pad boiler system, where the heated water is taken off well below the steam level, is that steam for sterilization is available simultaneously with the output of pressurized water for heating. Such systems have little place in smaller installations.

Low pressure steam systems (using steam boiler)

A problem with low pressure steam heat-

ing systems is how to achieve good control of pipe temperature. The flow of steam into the pipe, while generally controlled by an electrically operated motorized valve, merely allows for the heat being either 'on' or 'off'. Temperature gradients are also liable to develop, as it is warmer nearer the boiler, though this can be overcome if the length of heating pipe is kept short on each line and there is a large reserve of steam. It is also best to keep the diameter of the pipe as small as possible to keep the thermal inertia low. The steam condenses and is allowed to flow back to a condenser tank for pumping back into the boiler. Steam is of course also available for sterilization purposes.

Other systems centre round the injection of steam into water contained in 4in pipes, somewhat noisy but nevertheless quite effective.

Calorifiers or heat exchanger systems can also be used whereby steam is put through the calorifier, which in turn heats the water which is then pumped round the heating circuit. Low pressure steam injection systems have also been developed in recent years and have proved fairly efficient.

Systems linked to domestic heating

There are many instances where it is possible to combine home and greenhouse or conservatory heating, especially when the home system is of the small or mini bore type. A normal pipe system may be designed in the greenhouse or conservatory served by the domestic system, although home-type radiators may be used. Provision must be made for night operation when domestic systems are frequently shut off and this is a matter best taken up with the heating contractor.

Warm air heating systems

There are a great many types of heaters suitable for greenhouse use. The advantages of warm air heating can be weighed against the disadvantages. Compared with pipe systems, installation costs are low; heaters are easily moved and so do not obstruct soil cultivation or sterilization; they provide positive air movement, especially if fan-assisted; there can be a quicker response to changing temperatures than with a pipe system, especially where the latter has a high thermal inertia.

Some disadvantages of warm air heaters are as follows: temperature variations can be much greater over the greenhouse area than with a well-designed pipe system, especially when heaters are of the free-discharge type; there is not the same ability to warm soil by radiation as with a well-designed pipe system (although recent experimental work has shown that a well-designed ducted system can give almost comparable results to a pipe system and also give positive air movement); where a number of warm air heating units are necessary, this adds considerably to the cost, but total cost may still be considerably less than a boiler and pipe system; running costs can be higher than with a well-designed pipe system, taking into account that warm air heaters are either on or off and there is no residual heat such as that contained in the water of a pipe system. Technically speaking, however, the lack of residual heat could be considered desirable in respect of achieving even temperatures.

Solid fuel units

Solid fuel warm air units take the form of a boiler with external flue and a heat exchange unit, the air being pulled in at the base of the unit and discharged through the top, either freely into the atmosphere or through ducts. Smaller types of these are hand-fired and are reasonably efficient but suffer from the disadvantage of inaccurate temperature control. While the combustion of the fuel can be controlled to a certain extent by the damper, it is obvious that this will leave much to be desired in the interests of accuracy.

Steam/air heat exchangers

Live steam passes through a heat exchanger, and warm air is discharged by a fan. These have little application in smaller units.

Oil-fired units

Many oil-fired warm air units are available, fired either by natural draught or pressure jet burners and of various sizes. The smallest economic size of pressure jet burner is in the 14.65–17.5kW (50,000–60,000Btu) range-but they go up to 30kW (100,000 Btu) or more, and this is capable of heating a fairly large greenhouse of 73–83m² (800–900sq ft). They lend themselves admirably to automatic control.

Small oil- or gas-fired warm air units

The smallest type of natural draught oil burner is a simple oil stove of which there are many types, which is in effect a warm air heater. It should be noted that the products of combustion are discharged into the atmosphere, and while the CO_2 (carbon dioxide) content of combustion could be useful as a means of CO_2 enrichment, the sulphur content of oil could be damaging to crops. These small paraffin burning stoves are suitable for small greenhouses and are in the range of 2.1–6kW (7,500–20,000Btu) output per hour and must of course have their burning rate manually adjusted to meet needs. Recent designs of oil heating units with very accurate heat control are available. They are generally placed centrally in the greenhouse, which has disadvantages for providing an even temperature throughout the greenhouse although some have 'arms' and other devices for more effective heat dispersal. In recent years gas-fired warm air units have become available, using propane. (Town gas, with its damaging effects on plant growth, is now no longer available in the U.K.)

Electric warm air heaters

These are becoming increasingly popular for the heating of small greenhouses. They are fairly cheap to purchase, operate on a thermostat, and are reasonably efficient in use. They are available in different sizes, popular models being the 1,250 watt, 2,500 watt, and 3,000 watt (3kW). As 1kW is equal to 3,412Btu, the respective Btu values are:

1,250W model	4,262Btu
2,500W model	8,530Btu
3,000W model	10,236Btu

A range of much larger models is also available.

It has been stated that the main disadvantage of unducted fan heater units is the fact that they must be sited at some central point, and this inevitably results in temperature gradients over the greenhouse. A further disadvantage is that the direct blowing of warm air on to plants immediately it is discharged by the heater should be avoided, as plants could be damaged. Nevertheless, the high efficiency of the small fan-assisted heaters and the advantages of built-in thermostats with which most of them are fitted can result in very efficient heating at low initial cost. Fan unit heaters are extremely useful for the cool greenhouse where frost protection is the aim. Large types of fan heater are available which have polythene ducts for distributing the warmed air, which largely overcomes the problem of even air distribution. With the increasing use of warm air heating units in the home, it could be possible to arrange for a duct to serve the lean-to greenhouse or conservatory built on to the house. This should be taken up with a qualified heating engineer, a basic problem being one of control (as with small or mini bore heating systems) as the home heating system may be designed to shut off at night when there would be the biggest demand in the greenhouse or conservatory.

A thermostatically controlled Jemp electric heater is a popular way of heating smaller greenhouses — especially when frost protection is all that is required.

Electric convector heaters

These are generally fitted with thermostats and operate on the lines of taking air in at the base where it passes over a hot element and is discharged as warm air at the top of the heater. The warm air sets up convection currents and displaces the colder air, but it does this over a narrower zone than warm pipes distributed round the greenhouse. As with fan heaters, therefore, convectors have their limitations in respect of warming the greenhouse air uniformly and cold zones may frequently exist. Whether their shortcomings are acceptable depends largely on the range of crops being grown and whether these are particularly sensitive to temperature differences. The biggest drawback of convector heaters is the gentle movement of air compared to the positive distribution achieved by fan heaters, which encourages movement of both cold and warm air and minimizes 'dead' pockets.

Storage heaters

Storage heaters operating on off-peak power can be fitted with fans which operate on a thermostat and push out the warm air. So far there has been little use of storage heaters for greenhouse heating, as they offer temperature control problems; research work has been carried out on the feasibility of heating concrete paths, but it is likely that they would also offer temperature control problems. They would seem to have a useful role in conservatories.

Electric tubular heaters

Mains voltage waterproof tubular heaters are a very useful means of heating greenhouses, as they can readily be distributed round the perimeter. Of approximately 5cm (2in) diameter they can be installed standing 15cm (6in) from soil-level, either singly or in banks of two or three. Special fixing brackets are generally supplied with them. For metal houses they are best put on the base wall, if any, or on a wooden support. Electricity loading is usually 60W per 30cm (12in) which involves calculation of the exact kW requirement, remembering that 3,412Btu−1kW (1,000W), which means just under 5.1m (17ft) for 1kW (3,412Btu). For calculating the length needed, the heat loss of the greenhouse is worked out and the length of tubular heaters readily follows. Tubular heaters give off a fair amount of radiant heat which could scorch plants in the near vicinity, and this should be taken into account. Their operation should preferably be controlled through a thermostat. Mineral insulated (MI) cables have a useful application where thermal requirement is relatively low. They consist of a heating wire encased in an inert mineral material and protected by a copper sheath. Of only pencil thickness, the cables are secured to the sides of the greenhouse (as for tubular heaters) in porcelain holders, and are available in packaged units of 2, 3.3 and 5.2kW. MI cables cost less than tubular heaters of similar loading, but they cost more to install as this is invariably a task for an experienced electrician. Plastic-covered mains voltage heating cables are also available. Infra-red heaters are becoming more widely used in greenhouse heating. They transmit heat of a wavelength absorbed by plant leaves.

Heat production units for pipe systems

A very wide range of 'boilers' exists, extending from simple sectional boilers to sophisticated steel-packaged units complete with controls. The basic purpose of any boiler is to burn the selected fuel and then transfer the heat to the water contained in it. This is achieved with widely varying efficiency, resulting in a combustion loss in all cases, except where an electric boiler or immersion heater is used, as electricity operates at 100 per cent efficiency. To bring about combustion of oil, gas or solid fuel of various types, air is necessary, but this must be supplied in the correct amount to bring about efficient combustion. Where solid fuel is burned, a great deal of the generated heat will be transferred to the water contained in the jacket of the boiler by radiation and conduction. In addition the hot gases given off by the burning fuel pass through the flueways en route to the chimney and in doing so further warm the water by the process of conduction. It is obvious that the more heat which can be 'extracted' from the hot gas before it

reaches the chimney, the greater the efficiency, although too much extraction of heat and the discharge of too cool gases below around 204°C (400°F) can result in condensation in the chimney, especially if an unlagged metal chimney is involved. Combustion results in the production of the gas carbon dioxide (CO_2) and the efficiency of the combustion is directly related to the percentage of CO_2 contained in the flue gas. When this is measured with special instruments, in conjunction with flue temperature, it is a means of determining the percentage efficiency of any boiler or appliance. With the high cost of fuel the various modern types of boilers take this into account and are designed accordingly with balanced flues. A simple and cheap boiler equipped merely with a grate for burning fuel allows the gases to pass directly into the flue at high temperature and can obviously never be as efficient as a boiler in which the flue gas must travel as far as possible within the limit of design, often through tubes jacketed by water. This is applicable no matter what fuel is being burned, although there is little radiant heat where oil or gas are used (see Figs. 29 and 30).

Where there is an excessive 'pull' or draught in a chimney because it is of too large a diameter or too high, this can also be a frequent cause of excessive heat loss and low efficiency, as the gases are pulled out before their heat can be passed on.

Fig. 29 (*Below left*) Excessive heat loss and lower boiler efficiency will result in hot gases being discharged directly into the flue or chimney before they have transferred their heat to the water in the boiler.

Fig. 30 (*Below right*) Much higher efficiency is achieved on a sophisticated boiler where the flueways of the boiler are able to extract much of the heat from hot gases before they reach the flue or chimney.

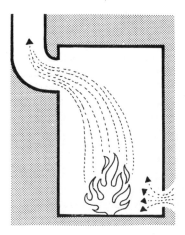

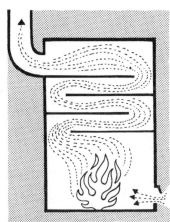

There can be no overall formula for setting up a boiler for maximum heat transfer and combustion efficiency, as this depends on the precise requirements of each boiler. The same is true of chimney height; the outlet should of course be above the ridge height of the greenhouse. It is also advisable to site the boiler so that the prevailing wind takes flue gases away from the greenhouse. *Draught diverters* or flue balancers are essential particularly for oil- or gas-fired boilers as they break the solid column of air in the chimney and enable a stable draught or chimney 'pull' irrespective of wind speed out of doors.

Solid fuel boilers
These are available for hand-firing or automatic firing in a wide range of forms. The smaller inexpensive types used for smaller greenhouses are not noted for their high efficiency, being of very simple design. More expensive boilers are of course available which have a hopper feed and shaker grate and are remarkably efficient and reduce stoking and maintenance labour to the minimum. All solid fuel boilers are available in a very wide range of sizes and forms.

Natural draught oil burners installed in boilers
There are different ways of achieving 'automatic' heating in small heating units to avoid the constant necessity of hand-firing and cleaning. Natural draught burners are frequently installed in boilers intended for solid fuel burning with the fire grates removed, but the boiler can of course be bought complete with the burner. Natural draught burners are exceedingly simple in design and take several different forms, all of which rely on the natural intake of air for combustion. The burner must be installed completely level and the level of the oil control valve must be such that it cannot be over-filled. The simplest types must be manually lit and the level of heating controlled by a hand operated valve. For high efficiencies the flames should be baffled on to the sides of the boiler and a draught diverter must be fitted to reduce draught, as any excessive chimney 'pull' will extract

the hot gases before they have effected heat transfer to the boiler surface. Natural draught burners are available in a range of sizes to suit the smaller boiler unit for heating small greenhouses, ie 3—9kW (10,000—30,000Btu).

Pressure jet and wall flame oil-fired burners
A wide range of these exists and generally speaking the design of boiler is more sophisticated, as a pressure jet burner injects oil vapour and air under pressure which, on combustion, results in a surge of hot gases. Wall flame burners operate on a rotating system and are very efficient. Unless these hot gases can be directed through an efficient heat exchanging system they are expelled before they have given off a high proportion of their heat.

All oil-fired burners must be correctly installed with no air leaks and they must be set up so that the correct quantity of air is used for efficient combustion. Simultaneously there should be correct adjustment of the flue draught — both matters for heating engineers or fuel consultants with the correct instruments. Pressure jet burners are of course fully automatic, which is a great boon to the busy gardener. Systems of control for boilers will be discussed in a later chapter.

Waste oil burners
There are several types of burners for using waste car engine oil, and one made in Scotland of 3,682 watts burns for 24 hours on 13.6 litres and has a rating of 3,682 watts heating 21m (69ft) of 10cm (4in) pipes. These burners do not require any electricity which is a point in their favour. The only real draw-back is handling the oil, which can be messy, and cleaning the burner which can also be dirty operation, but is essential since this type of waste fuel has a high waste-matter content and builds up carbon fairly quickly.

Gas boilers
Basically gas boilers are similar in design to oil-fired boilers. Indeed the same design formula is frequently used for both, with the obvious difference that the gas requires a different burner. The availability of

natural gas in many areas has led to an increased interest in gas firing for greenhouse heating, especially with the rise in oil prices over the years. Bulk gas is now readily available. Automatic control is more or less standard on all gas-fired boilers.

Solar heating

Solar panels are now available for domestic use in homes, installed on the sunny slope of the roof. They consist of a number of gilled pipes backed by reflectors. Their principal use is to provide domestic hot water. Several prototype solar units have been produced for greenhouses, but so far nothing impressive has appeared at an acceptable price for use in temperate zones. Basically speaking all solar heating units aim to heat water from direct solar radiation, the water then being stored in insulated tanks for recirculation through a pipe system when solar heat input is low or non-existent and the air temperature in the greenhouse drops sufficiently to demand the input of heat. Large diameter, black, water-filled polythene pipes and PVC mattresses have been used a great deal in France for absorbing the sun's heat during the day to be radiated back into the greenhouse or plastic structure in the evening and night (Fig. 31). In temperate zones, including the U.K., the weakness so far of all solar heating units lies in the low level of solar radiation from autumn to spring when there is likely to be most demand on a heating system for the greenhouse. Research into ways of transmitting solar radiation more effectively by microwaves from afar is still in the very early stages of development. At the moment such solar heating units which do exist are likely to be far too costly for small-type greenhouses and the more successful uses of solar radiation have combined the heating of living quarters and greenhouse-growing quarters, so justifying the high cost.

'Waste' heat

Heat from a wide range of domestic and industrial processes, which is normally allowed to 'escape' into the atmosphere, has been effectively collected and distributed and has a vital role in greenhouse

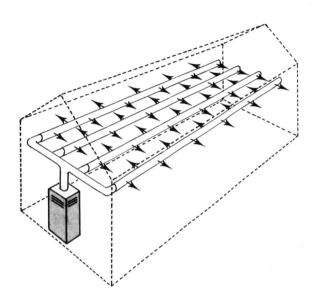

heating. With the ever increasing cost of fuels, many temperate climate zones have started to look very closely at methods of utilizing waste energy. This involves a number of different approaches, including the use of flue gases and the installation of heat exchangers to 'catch' the heat, waste warm water from industrial processes and other techniques, many of which are of little interest to the average amateur gardener but which could in future years have a profound application on all forms of glasshouse growing. Several large commercial units have already been set up using waste industrial energy and more will undoubtedly follow.

Wind and water power

There is also considerable interest in using electrical power generated by wind or water. While at present the interest largely centres around larger installations suitable for the commercial grower, here again there will undoubtedly be application for smaller greenhouses before many years have passed.

Heat pumps

Heat pumps are also being used for greenhouse heating, preferably and ideally when there is a fairly warm source of base heat available eg subterranean water, waste industrial heat etc.

Fig. 31 Warm air heaters: Transmission of heat is through polythene ducts either at high or low levels.

Low temperature corrosion of boilers

The problem of low temperature corrosion of boilers caused by the sulphur and possible chlorine content of fuels in conjunction with the temperature of the boiler heating surface is a major one. In essence what happens is that acids are formed which corrode the boiler surface, this occurring at operating temperatures below about 65°C (150°F), and there will, in greenhouse heating, be many occasions when pipes are required no hotter than this. A simple way of overcoming this, and at the same time enabling the pipe to be regulated to give a range of temperatures, is to install a "mixing valve". This allows a close loop of heat to circulate through the boiler in a ratio dependent on the heat demand as called for by thermostat or by manual adjustment.

Note that a pump is required for circulation before close loop systems will operate. Mixing valves are frequently installed in domestic systems not only to keep the boiler at a high operating temperature, but to ensure a constantly warm domestic hot water supply and supply heat as required for home heating.

Cost of heating greenhouses

Estimating the cost of heating a greenhouse is always open to some conjecture, although it is possible to arrive at a reasonably accurate figure. It is obvious that the prevailing outside temperature patterns for any country will greatly affect heating costs. Some reconciliation of the regional implications can be reached by checking on the degree day tables published by the Meteorological Office. These tables give estimates for average months, but variations are bound to occur seasonally and locally.

A 'degree hour' is the sum of the temperature difference between the inside and outside temperatures of the greenhouse (when it is cooler outside) multiplied by the time in hours which each temperature difference lasts. To keep the figures to a reasonable size they are divided by 24, and called 'degree days'. This tends to be a little complicated but should offer no difficulties to the competent mathematician. A more basic approach is to consult a table of costs which takes into account the varying opera-

tional efficiency of different equipment and different fuels.

It is thus relatively easy to calculate the running cost on a 24 hour basis assuming a 50–60% demand overall, although it should be pointed out that this is assumption and nothing more and demand depends on exposure, region, tightness of greenhouse and other issues. If, for example, one has a greenhouse with a calculated heat loss of 2.3kW (8,000Btu), working on a 13°C (55°F) minimum, then using a 2½kW (8,530Btu) fan heater, the cost of heating will be 50–60% of the actual cost per hour, which is the cost of about 1¼–1½ units per hour, as electricity is 100% efficient, there being no combustion heat loss. When calculating the cost of electrical heating it is usual to discount the primary unit rate, which tends to be used up in the home, and simply calculate on the basis of a *flat average rate* unless there is a separate meter to give "off peak" power. Where frost protection only is desired, i.e. 4–7°C (40–45°F) maximum, then there will obviously be a much lower demand than 50–60%, as low as 10–12% in some cases. Relating this to solid fuel with a calorific value of 32MJ/kg (12,500Btu/lb) and 60% boiler efficiency, you only get 60% of 32MJ (12,500Btu) which is 19.2MJ (7,500Btu) for every kg/lb of fuel you burn, so by relating this to fuel cost you can roughly calculate what your fuel bill is likely to be. It is of course again necessary to assume a figure for percentage loss of efficiency on combustion. In the absence of a properly carried out efficiency test, help is given in this direction by taking into account the calorific output of the boiler. With small boilers of around 4.3kW (15,000Btu) capacity it is fair to assume an operational efficiency of about 60%, when it will require 1kg (2.2lb) of coal per hour on rapid burning, which would be 21kg (48lb) per 24 hours. Rapid burning is seldom a constant necessity, however, and 9kg (20lb) per day or 63kg (140lb) per week is a fair average.

With an oil-fired boiler or oil stove the same calculations can be made assuming 75% efficiency and 50–60% demand.

It can perhaps now be appreciated that while it is possible to *estimate* running costs,

Table of Costs

Type of system	Average operational efficiency	Approx running cost per 29kW (100,000Btu (therm)) at fuel prices as stated		
Simple solid fuel boiler	50%	Based on coal at 32MJ/kg (approx. 12,500/Btu/lb)		
		Cost of fuel/50kg (cwt)	£4 or 53p/therm	
			£5 or 66p/therm	
			£6 or 80p/therm	
			£7 or 93p/therm	
Refined solid fuel boiler (smokeless fuel)	60%	Based on value of 32MJ/kg (approx. 12,000/Btu/lb)		
		Cost of fuel/50kg (cwt)	£4 or 50p/therm	
			£5 or 62$\frac{1}{2}$p/therm	
			£6 or 75p/therm	
			£7 or 87$\frac{1}{2}$p/therm	
Purpose-made oil-fired boiler	75%	Based on oil at 42MJ/kg (approx. 162,000/Btu/gal)		
			200p/gal or 160p/therm	
			150p/gal or 120p/therm	
			100p/gal or 80p/therm	
Purpose-made gas fired boiler	75–80%	Based on cost of gas per therm, varies according to district, plus 20–25% loss of efficiency		
All electrical heaters (storage heaters not considered here)	100%	Based on normal tariff		
		Cost per unit	5p or 120p/therm	
		1kW (3412Btus)	4p or 96p/therm	
			3p or 72p/therm	

so much depends on the temperature range desired in the greenhouse and, more important, on the outside temperature.

Linked systems
Where linked systems are involved there is no basic difference in calculation, it being a case of working out the heat loss for the greenhouse and, provided this is efficiently linked by small bore pipes or ducts, it should be possible to calculate the heating costs in the same way as for an independent system. A distinct advantage is likely to be the higher operational efficiency of the more expensive and sophisticated type of domestic heating units invariably used. In certain instances it may of course be possible to site the domestic boiler inside the greenhouse or conservatory, the greenhouse then being kept heated by the radiant heat from the boiler, which could be completely lost if the boiler is sited out of doors. While there

could be temperature control problems, these are not likely to be any greater than the control problems which can arise with linked systems.

Boiler siting for greenhouses

In most instances where larger type solid fuel or oil-fired boilers are being used for a pipe heating system, space does not often permit the siting of the boiler in the actual greenhouse, although this is a highly practical course of action because of the radiation heat obtained from the boiler which will, as stated above, be lost if the boiler is sited separately. With smaller installations it is ideal if the boiler can be sited in the actual greenhouse. When sited elsewhere it should be protected from the elements and from wind which will interfere with the combustion rate. Care should always be taken to lag any exposed pipes running between the boiler and the greenhouse to avoid wasteful heat loss. Boilers and their housings should not shade the greenhouse; keep them to the north side if possible. As flue gases are carried away by prevailing winds, north siting is doubly preferable.

All smaller self-contained heating units, including fan heaters of larger size, should be sited in the actual greenhouse, the flue pipes, if any, being taken through the roof by the fitting of a special waterproof gland. Free-discharge heaters are best sited centrally, but when polythene ducting is to be used it is better to keep the heater to the north end, if possible, and run the ducting out from this point.

CHAPTER 8
Environmental Control

The ventilation of greenhouses is one of the most important facets of environmental control. It is necessary for the following reasons:

> to limit undue rise in temperature,
> to replace exhausted air with fresh,
> to maintain humidity at the required level.

Control of temperature

This is the most important consideration with many gardeners, as solar radiation between spring and autumn is very frequently in excess of needs on bright sunny days, necessitating frequent air changes to keep the greenhouse air temperature at an acceptable level for plants. When solar short-wave radiation reaches the plants in a greenhouse about three-quarters of it is absorbed by the leaves and the remaining quarter reflected back to the greenhouse as long-wave radiation. As all other objects in the greenhouse reflect back the radiation, absorbing only a small proportion, the net effect is therefore to cause a rise in temperature of the plants' leaves and the surrounding area. The rise is reduced to a certain extent by the loss of heat by evaporation, caused by the process of transpiration. The total amount of foliage in any greenhouse varies considerably, and this in turn greatly affects the percentage of radiation absorbed and reflected, and in turn the amount of transpiration which takes place.

As air, when warm, becomes less dense and rises, an exit is ideally allowed for it at the highest point in the greenhouse along the ridge. Cool air also gains entry into the greenhouse through the same 'exit' by a complicated interchange mechanism, provided there is enough air movement out of doors to give sufficient impetus for this interchange. If, however, cool air is allowed entry through lower vents this speeds up the whole process of interchange (Fig. 32).

Ventilator size and position

The size of ventilator on the ridge is obviously critical and an actual ventilation area of at least one-fifth to one-sixth of the actual floor area (irrespective of lower vents) is the accepted commercial norm, although if a greater area can be provided this is better still. Lower vents or louvres should be proportionate in size with ridge vents. It helps greatly if ridge ventilators are capable of opening to an angle of 55° — in line with the slope of the opposite roof (Fig. 33) and well above the horizontal — as in this position they scoop in the wind while also allowing easier exit for warm air.

Correct provision of ridge vents is a critical point. For greenhouses of a width module of over 6m (20ft) it is advisable to have continuous ventilation on both sides of the ridge (see Fig. 34) which allows effective air change under a wide range of conditions. On smaller greenhouses (which will include most amateur sized structures) continuous ridge ventilation is seldom fitted, it being usual to rely on alternate ridge ventilators, with fixed glazing opposite each vent. In this case, when a wind is blowing, air comes in on one side and is discharged out the other. It is important to

Fig. 32 (*Below left*) A combination of side and top ventilation provides ideal ventilation.

Fig. 33 (*Below right*) Where top ventilation only is provided, the ventilators must be of adequate size if they are to be effective.

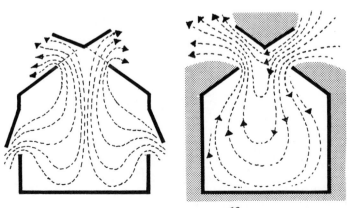

Fig. 34 Two types of ventilation—continuous ventilation (*a*)is ideal but not available in small greenhouses. Alternate ventilation (*b*)is used for most small structures.

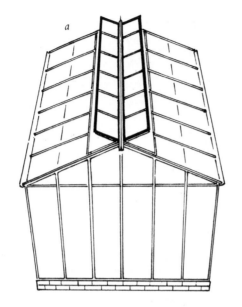

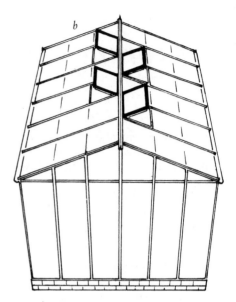

Fig. 35 Louvre type ventilators are useful for sides or doors of greenhouses.

Fig. 36 Rack and pinion mechanism for operating ventilators is frequently installed on larger conventional greenhouses.

remember that the total area of these should still be at least one-fifth to one-sixth of the floor area. For a 3×2.4m (10×8ft) greenhouse with a ground area of 7.44m^2 (80sq ft), one-fifth is 1.48m^2 (16sq ft). This would allow for four 60×60cm (2×2ft) ridge vents, provided they are capable of opening fully to that area. Most manufacturers are quite happy to provide additional ventilation up to the required ratio. Amateur greenhouses do, in fact, because of a higher glass/ground ratio, need a higher ventilation percentage than commercial greenhouses, possibly up to 30–40% of the ground area. Some manufactures take the door into account to provide satisfactory ventilation.

With simple opening type vents on roofs, sides or doors, draughts are unavoidable. Louvred types, frequently used in sides or ends, are less liable to allow entry of draughts but it is doubtful whether any system of ventilation depending on the opening of a flap or louvre can be 100% draught proof (Fig. 35). Attempts at air-conditioning to allow 'perfect' ventilation without draughts will be referred to later.

Operation of ventilators

Ventilators can be operated by simple levers or by pulley and cord. In recent years rack and pinion operation for commercial glasshouses has become almost standard (Fig.

A plastic structure of the Clovis Lande Highlande range showing additional crop support bars to give tremendous added strength for windy sites.

Greenhouse benching is very important and allows better space utilization. This is aluminium benching with a lower shelf for pots.

In the right setting, a conservatory can add a new dimension to living, as this Banbury curved eaved model shows, fitted into a convenient corner.

A Crittall Warmlife 'Limelight' square eaved conservatory is a handsome addition to any home. This popular unit measures 3035 cm (9ft $11\frac{1}{2}$in) × 2240 cm (7ft $4\frac{1}{4}$in) with an eaves height of 1956 cm (6ft 5in).

A Solardome III geodesic, sun-admitting structure from Rosedale Engineers Ltd with a diameter of 5.95 m ($19\frac{1}{2}$ feet) gives plenty of scope for growing and leisure.

Building a plastic greenhouse: not too difficult a task for the 'Do-it-Yourself' enthusiast. It is important to get the hoops square to the axis and accurately spaced.

An autovent is more or less an essential feature on any greenhouse to avoid inadvertent 'cooking' of plants. This is the Alton (Banbury) 'vent opener' in a cedar house.

Electric propagators are available in many shapes and forms. They provide local warmth at low cost and are ideal for all aspects of propagation.

The use of supplementary light for plant growth is a technique which has advanced considerably in recent years. Sungro-Lites with their special reflectors are ideal in this role.

36). To ensure as accurate a temperature regime as possible ventilators should operate automatically, either by electric motor or, on an amateur scale, by expansion type lifts which are cheap to purchase yet highly dependable in practice.

The mechanism for automatic ventilators is varied in design and depends much on the type of greenhouse and all the various design factors involved. Step control to give a quarter, one-third, three-quarter and full opening is available, the most sophisticated types of ventilator being linked to a proportional or modulating controller which sets the position of the vents according to the rate of change required in the greenhouse temperature. In addition there can be a wind gauge to open or shut vents in one direction to avoid draughts and a rain gauge to shut vents up when it rains. The whole system can be integrated with computers.

Fan ventilation

Although this is still not widely used in amateur greenhouses, fan ventilation is widely accepted in commercial spheres. When designing a fan ventilation system it must be remembered that most plants dislike rapid air movement which, like excessive wind out of doors, causes them to transpire too rapidly. It would be easy to fit a high output fan in a greenhouse to move the air at high speed, but this would inevitably cause turbulence and air movement to the detriment of the plants. Research work over many years has shown quite clearly that plants will tolerate an air flow rate of 0.1982 m^3/s (7cu ft per sq ft) maximum. On a practical level this involves using relatively slow speed fans which are capable of moving a large volume of air slowly, rather than high speed fans which suck air rapidly over a fairly localized area.

The basic design of an extractor fan ventilation system is to extract the air at one end or side of a greenhouse and provide for the entry of air at the opposite end or side. Where large units of greenhouses are involved, several fans are required, spaced to allow even, complete air extraction with no stagnant areas. With large

commercial type greenhouses it is usual to have 1.2m (4ft) fans operating at 360–470rpm spaced evenly along the north or east side wall of the block, allowing for 5.58m^2 (60sq ft) per fan of inlet area on the opposite wall. This results in air movement which is achieved whenever the fans are in operation, irrespective of wind speed or weather conditions out of doors, generally maintaining a satisfactory air flow. The inlet can either be manually or automatically operated, it being important to ensure that the fans cannot operate until the vents are open. Fans are best operated from an aspirated sensor or thermostats which can either operate all the fans simultaneously or in batches to come on at different temperatures. Time clocks or computers are considered necessary on commercial holdings to give short periods of night ventilation, otherwise humidity can build up to a dangerous level, although fan operation can also be controlled by a humidistat. Variable speed fans are also available, worked by thermostatically operated variable speed controllers, but special types of 3 phase fan motors are necessary, along with the sophisticated control gear for the inlet vents, which adds considerably to the cost of the installation.

While the installation height of a 1.2m (4ft) fan offers little difficulty as it invariably rests on the foundation wall, choosing the height for small fans is not entirely straightforward. Experience has shown that with high set 60cm (24in) fans on the side wall of smaller blocks of commercial greenhouses, the inlet being provided on the opposite wall, there is a tendency for the air to move *over* a dense crop such as tomatoes, rather than through it.

Amateur gardeners will almost certainly be using the smaller type fans, the specification for which must be carefully calculated by a firm specializing in fan ventilation of greenhouses, many domestic type fans being incapable of giving the requisite number of air changes. All fans should ideally be louvred so that unwanted air cannot gain entry when the fans are not operating. It is convenient to install these fans fairly high in the greenhouse, a usual location being above the door.

Inlet for fans

The position of the inlet for fans has proved to be critical, experience showing that vents on the side wall rather than the roof are better for blocks of greenhouses. This allows the incoming air to make a quick loop before moving across the greenhouse. Single greenhouses lend themselves to the fitting of the fan in the gable end, either at both sides of the door if two are used, or above the door for one only. A further advantage in having side vent entry for fans is that heating pipes can partially warm the incoming air, a distinct advantage in cold weather as it tends to prevent any cold shock to the plants. Damp pads can also be used to wet incoming air, a technique practised in very hot, *dry* countries, and gaining some favour in Britain for certain crops.

The temperature gradient which can exist between inlet and outlet in fan-ventilated greenhouses causes concern in certain quarters, the exact difference in temperature depending on length of travel of the air. In practice this seems to be of negligible proportions, certainly if compared to the temperature gradients which exist in greenhouses where conventional ventilators are fitted.

The positive air movement induced by fans ensures that humidity is kept at a low level and stagnant pockets avoided, there being ample experimental and practical cropping evidence to support this. The positive intake of air, especially in hot, still conditions when conventional vents cannot induce a sufficient number of air changes, results in a constant supply of carbon dioxide being brought to the plants. The form of air intake can vary from top-hinge ventilators to louvres, in both cases ensuring that there is sufficient inlet to cope with the fan capacity. Use has been made of mesh material, which allows entry of small amounts of air all the time and, with the suction developed when fans are in operation, acts as an efficient inlet. Flap arrangements are also possible, using sheets of plastic dropped down over the back of an inlet, which lifts up when the fans are in operation but prevents draughts when the fans are not in operation. Collapsible poly-

thene tubes may also be used as inlets. A more recent development is polythene ducted fan in-takes to try and minimize temperature gradient between intake and fans.

Air conditioning

In addition to conventional ventilation and extractor fans, a more recent aspect of environmental control is "air conditioning". This can take several forms, the most elementary of which is to pull air *into* the greenhouse thus pressuring it to a limited degree. The air is exhausted out of counterbalanced louvres. Such systems, although not complex, have proved effective, although temperature gradients in the greenhouse can be excessive if the design is not correct. Warm air can be introduced by the same basic system and humidity control can also be effected to a certain degree by using a humidistat to inject water into the moving air stream when necessary. These matters are, however, better taken up with specialist suppliers of equipment, as most systems need to be designed specially for each individual greenhouse.

Desirability of environment control

Plants have their own inbuilt requirements in respect of leaf temperature, air temperature, humidity, carbon dioxide and light required for photosynthesis. While a greenhouse creates an artificial environment, it is necessary to try to control this within reasonable limits in sympathy with the needs of the plants being grown in it. Under commercial growing conditions, where only one specialist cropping system may be involved, every attempt is made to conform to a "blue-print" in respect of environment, level of water and feeding requirement. This is now done by computer. The object of this is to ensure the maximum production of quality crops or plants on what can be a very tight schedule. Amateur or professional gardeners are not perhaps so deeply concerned with their greenhouse gardening, but there is still considerable virtue in calling on modern aids to control the environment automatically as far as this is possible, simply to ease the load of looking after plants and at the same time help to ensure quality despite enforced absence at business or elsewhere.

The full control of the greenhouse environment is a complex matter with a great many inter-related factors to be taken into account. Much research is still likely to take place over the next decade to try to discover what exactly constitutes the ideal environment for different plants and thereafter set out to achieve this effectively without too much complicated and expensive equipment.

Control of heating systems

With simple solid fuel hand-fired boilers and large diameter pipes, where the water circulates entirely by gravity or thermosyphon, there is no real place for automatic control, and the usual control of temperature is to rely on the boiler damper and the level of firing in association with regulating air entry at the fire door. It may be possible to restrict the flow from the boiler by the use of a check valve situated on the flow pipe, although this could be dangerous and lead to overheating of the boiler. Solenoid valves electrically operated by thermostat can also be used, but suffer the same drawbacks. In practice and with experience a fair degree of control of actual temperature can be exercised, but only with constant vigilance, this showing the defects of such systems where strict environmental control is sought.

Where circulation of the water relies *largely* on an accelerator pump, good temperature control can be achieved by linking the accelerator to an on/off thermostat set in the greenhouse, the amount of control which can be exercised varying according to the degree of dependence on pump circulation. Where the circulation of water depends *entirely* on the pump, there can be excellent temperature control, especially if the boiler is automatically fired by oil or gas.

Ideally there should be an independent on/off thermostat to control the boiler at a pre-set temperature (generally above 71°C/160°F) and an on/off or multi-step control (a combination of two or more on/off units arranged to operate in stages) sited in the greenhouse to call for heat. This operates the pump and sends water round the system. There are definite drawbacks to this system when large bore pipes are concerned, especially if these are of cast iron with cemented joints. Unless there can be arrangements to 'bleed' a small quantity of water into the pipes to keep them warm, especially adjacent to the boiler, the sudden rush of hot water when the pump is set in motion can split the pipes or loosen the cement joints. Arrangements to bleed in a small quantity of water usually consist of a pipe-fitted on/off thermostat, adjacent to the boiler on the greenhouse side of the pump and set to override the greenhouse thermostat when the temperature of the pipes falls below about 27°C (80°F).

Pump control is ideal for small mini bore systems of heating with their low thermal inertia and lack of complications from pipe damage. The methods of arranging a by-pass to ensure a continuously warm boiler and simultaneously give a range of temperatures in the pipes, have been referred to earlier but an electrically operated modulating valve would ideally then require to be linked to a modulating controller. Modulating controllers can of course also be linked directly to pumps. Like proportional controllers they operate on the principle that the amount of heat supplied is related to the variance of the greenhouse air temperature from the previous level, rather than by successive periods of full heat input followed by no heat, as dictated by on/off control. Night setback of temperature can also be manipulated according to average day temperatures.

A still further development is the use of integrating photometers or light sensors which control the input of heat according to the prevailing light intensity and, still more sophisticated, relate this to the prevailing weather pattern in order to avoid sudden shocks to the plants' physiology. Night setbacks according to light intensity and temperature can also be incorporated.

Ventilators or fans can conveniently be operated on the same range of instruments as heating systems—independently but perfectly integrated by computer.

What has been said about hot water

heating systems applies equally well to other heating systems, whether these are steam or warm air supplied by direct firing or through heat exchange units. Reference has been made earlier to the complications of steam heating with regard to its on/off qualities, but in essence the same basic principles of automatic control apply.

Carbon dioxide enrichment and humidity control

The dispensing of carbon dioxide can be as simple as on/off and the shutting down of vents during the enrichment period to avoid wastage. In any case supplies of extra CO_2 are now invariably provided by direct fired gas or paraffin heaters. Preferably, however, there must be integration between the two factors, so that ventilators are automatically closed and fans out of action when CO_2 is being dispensed. The amount of CO_2 supplied can also be related to light intensity.

Humidity control is not straightforward. When a rise in humidity is called for by a humidity sensor something of a dilemma may result, there being a choice of bringing into operation spraylines or mist jets and shutting the vents. Conversely, for lowering the humidity, are the vents to be opened, or the fans operated, or the heating called on to raise the temperature (warm air holding more moisture than cold air)?

It has previously been stated that allowance must be made in really sophisticated systems for damage to open vents caused by sudden winds, demanding a wind sensor, and a rain sensor to shut down the vents when it is raining heavily.

Automatic feeding and watering control

The supply of water and liquid feeding of plants and crops is also carried out automatically with sequence controllers operating solenoid valves, and this will be referred to in a later chapter.

Measuring and recording instruments

An accurate thermometer is an essential piece of equipment and these can take several forms, but undoubtedly the most useful is a maximum/minimum model, especially a push button reset type. A humidity gauge or hygrometer is also a useful item. Ideally these instruments should be in an aspirated screen, failing which a metal foil shield is reasonably effective in shading them from direct sun.

However no instrument that is exposed freely to solar radiation, draughts, or radiation loss can be considered accurate. Solar radiation absorbed by the body of a thermometer or the case of a thermostat will result in a variance between the recorded and the actual conditions. For this reason the only way of ensuring accurate sensing is to use an aspirated screen for housing all instruments. This is an insulated box or section of large diameter PVC tubing fitted with a constantly operating small fan which pulls air gently through the box or tube over the thermostat or other instrument housed in the screen. This ensures that the actual air temperature or humidity is accurately recorded. Far more popular these days is the use of an electronic sensor, which gives highly accurate temperature control and is relatively unaffected by solar radiation and draughts.

Aspirated screens are usually provided with the instrument installed, and the unit generally sited in the centre of the greenhouse; for greater accuracy it can be placed in the actual area of crop growth.

Control equipment and the amateur

The above items of control equipment in one form or another, and in various degrees of refinement and sophistication, are fully operational in many commercial and local authority units. Their application in amateur spheres is obviously more limited, and gardeners should confine their horizons to reasonable levels, seeking perhaps the automatic control of ventilation and heating on a simple on/off basis and little more. In recent years, however, mist and drip watering systems on automatic control have made a big impact in amateur circles.

Electric heating units of all types readily lend themselves to thermostatic control and it would be foolish not to take advantage of this. Manually operated appliances of any kind, and similarly hand-operated heaters, require constant regulation and, more important, the presence of the gardener. One cannot, however, always get good results by relying entirely on manual management; many have achieved excellent results, especially those blessed with intuition and a good growing sense.

Environmental control survey

Factor to be controlled	Manual	Type of Control		Automated
		Automatic		
		without feedback	*with feedback*	
Vents or fans	By handle, lever, or switch reference to thermometer	Thermostat or sensor opens vents fully and vice versa. Pulse control can be introduced. Fans operated until temperature drops. Time clock control for fans	Thermostat or thermister in conjunction with monotronic control, but vents open only a certain amount as controller knows position of vents. Same with fans	Solar radiation measured and applied, by light meter. Integrated control for all aspects using computers.
Heat	By reference to thermometer control valve or stoking	Thermostat + solenoid valve. Motorized or pump with no knowledge of conditions	Same as above with reference to actual temperature and conditions	As above
Irrigation Overhead and mist	Hoses, watering cans, trickle and spraylines in manual form or from taps. Light meter can be used at this level	Time clocks + sequence controller but no relation to actual crop state. Electronic "leaf" is also used at this level but can give rise to problems	Systems not yet designed which will give details on actual state of crop	Solar energy related to exact crop needs by means of light meter. Can be computer controlled.
CO_2	Not used a great deal in 'manual' form	Time clock control, possibly over-ridden by switch when vents open. No real knowledge of CO_2 level in greenhouse	Monitor which measures CO_2 content of atmosphere and controls input	Solar light intensity related to level of enrichment

CHAPTER 9
Additional Equipment

Benching

The provision of benching or staging for a range of activities is invariably necessary, except when a greenhouse is being used exclusively for ground-grown crops. Even then propagation space is invariably demanded for a limited period of the year. Benching must be strong as it has frequently to bear a considerable weight. Fixed benching is not so popular as it was owing to management problems, but it certainly allows better presentation and utilizes space especially if tiered.

Conventional benching employs slatted wood of 10–12cm (4–5in) and approximately 1.75–2cm ($\frac{5}{8}$–$\frac{3}{4}$in) section, set on bearers with approximately 2.5cm (1in) between the slats. Ideally the wood for the slats should be of good quality such as Western red cedar, although preservative treated redwood would suffice. Benches from about 67cm (2ft 3in) wide up to about 1.2m (4ft) permit ease of access, although centrally sited benches with both sides accessible can be much wider – up to about 1.5 or 1.8m (5 or 6ft). A height of 75cm (30in) (average table height) was previously thought to be ideal, but there is now commercial interest in knee-high benches of about 50cm (20in). These allow a much closer surveillance of the plants and their watering needs, a vital issue with the widespread use of plastic pots.

Wider spaced slats can be used where stock plants are being maintained so that there is no contact or run of moisture between the plants, so cutting down the risk of infection. Wood slats can also be inserted into angle iron or alternatively patent angle steel with a mesh top used. Much more popular in recent years is aluminium benching, especially tailored to fit respective sizes of greenhouse. These generally incorporate aluminium gravel trays, which can be filled with gravel, sand or capillary matting if desired. Modular shelving is also available. Solid benches can be made by using corrugated iron or wood; they are considered to be more suitable for certain types of pot plants by some gardeners, though a difference of opinion exists. Solid benches are essential for mist propagation units or for the construction of capillary benches. Where solid benches are used there should always be a space between the bench and side of the greenhouse to allow the passage of air. The usual arrangement is to have benches on both sides of a central path. With a greenhouse 2.4m (8ft) wide, two benches each 75cm (2ft 6in) wide would allow a 90cm (3ft) path. In narrower houses one 90cm (3ft) bench might be preferable, although two very narrow benches are possible but not always practical. Greenhouses 36m (12ft) in width could accommodate two side benches each 75cm (2ft 6in) wide and a central bench does not restrict access through the door or doors. The free opening or entry from the door must also be taken into account when deciding on the width of the side benches. A sensible width of central path is always advisable to allow the entry of a barrow or trolley.

Benches may be supplemented with shelving at higher levels, useful for ensuring maximum light for plants and utilizing space. On vertical wooden-wall greenhouses they can be fitted with galvanized shelf brackets, while on alloy or metal houses manufactures offer special shelf fittings.

Capillary benches

These involve the use of a completely level solid bench with 8–10cm (3–4in) sides which is lined with inert washed sand of acceptable capillarity: a coarse gravelly sand to a depth of 2.5–4cm (1–1$\frac{1}{2}$in) to give a free water zone is topped by 2.5cm (1in) of finer sand. A perforated hose is laid

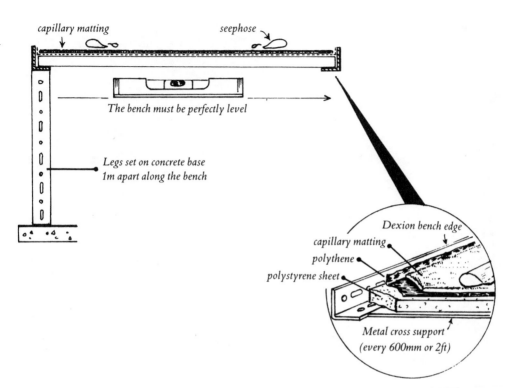

capillary matting

seephose

The bench must be perfectly level

Legs set on concrete base
1m apart along the bench

Dexion bench edge

capillary matting

polythene

polystyrene sheet

Metal cross support
(every 600mm or 2ft)

Fig. 37 Home-made capillary bench, made by using angle iron (or Dexion), polystyrene sheets (2.5 cm (1in) thick), polythene, capillary matting and seephose.

down the centre of the bench before or during filling with sand, preferably under broken sections of drainage tiles so that water can pass through the perforations in the hose without restriction into the free water zone, or sections of curved asbestos can be used. Water can in fact be led in almost as satisfactorily at a single point in the free water zone, when it will spread effectively, although care should be taken to ensure that sand does not block the outlet. To control the level of water a plastic fish tank fitted with a ball and cock can be used so that the water level is held constantly 2.5–4cm (1–1½in) below the top of the sand. Alternatively a float control unit can be used connected to a storage tank, adjusting the supply of water to the necessary level by adjustment of the control unit. More simply a slowly dripping hose or bleed-type irrigation units can be used to supply the water to the bench, or it can merely be kept topped up at regular intervals, although neither of the two latter methods is entirely satisfactory, owing to the varying degree of solar heat (Fig. 37).

Plants in pots spaced out on a capillary bench extract water by capillary pull, plastic pots being rather better in this instance than clay pots. Plants can also be fed with liquid nutrients by this method, although there can be problems of local build-up of salts, causing chemical damage to plants. In recent years individual drip systems have tended to supersede capillary watering, one reason being that roots from the pots develop into the sand on capillary action, especially if the sand is too dry, resulting in severance and checks to growth when the plants are moved. Fibre glass mats can replace sand, ideally covered with perforated black polythene to prevent growth of algae, which will grow on either sand or bare matting.

Bench and soil warming

The escalating cost of all fuels has thrown new emphasis on the highly efficient localized application of heat directly to the propagating material. The use of alkathene pipe at 23–30cm (9–12in) depth and 1.2–

Mains-voltage, soil-warming cables are an excellent method of bench warming, using a thermostat to control the temperature accurately.

Mains-voltage, soil-warming cables are an excellent method of bench warming, using a thermostat to control the temperature accurately.

1.5m (4–5ft) apart linked to a pump-circulated hot water system has achieved certain favour in continental European countries for the production of early crops such as very early tomatoes or strawberries demanding soil warmth. Similar systems are now used in conjunction with rock-wool or perlite methods of crop production using indented polystyrene slabs. These can also be used for benches. (see respective chapters).

Electric soil warming using 2.5mm (12 gauge) wire of known electrical resistance at 6–30 volts through a transformer at 23–25m (9–10in) depth and 8–23cm (3–9in) apart, to give a loading of 55–110w/m² (5–10 watts/sq ft), has also received little attention since the 1950s, possibly because of the high cost of electricity when used on the scale necessary to heat large bulks of growing media such as tomato borders. Such systems do, however, have an application for smaller border areas in many cases, using sheathed mains voltage cables.

The use of soil warming cables for bench application is, however, an entirely dif-ferent matter, as the loading necessary at 86–130w/m² (8–12 watts/ft) ensures that the level necessary (approximately 1kW per 10m²/ 100sq ft) is a highly efficient and economic operation. The cables are laid on a shallow bed of sand and covered to the depth of 5cm (2in) with more sand. Control of the soil warming cable temperature can be achieved by several methods: (1) at off peak tariff by time clock operation (8 hours in 24), (2) according to the weather, by inspection with a soil thermometer, or (3) the best method, and essential for the higher temperatures necessary for mist propagation, by the use of phial and capillary tube thermostats set across the run of the wires below the sand surface. It helps to induce warmth if spaces between pots or boxes on the bench are filled up with moist peat.

The local application of heat to either borders or benches (or plants or cuttings in pots) has little effect on the air temperature of the greenhouse, but such locally applied warmth to the media in which the plants are growing generally allows a lowering of the air temperature in the greenhouse,

Propagators come in all shapes and sizes. This Jemp '3−in−1' unit is ideal for the gardener who works to a smaller scale.

which has tremendous economic benefits. Indeed the success of mist propagation or white polythene "tents" (see next section) with the necessary attendant warmth in the actual rooting media has revolutionized propagation of many previously difficult-to-root plants. Germination of seed benefits too.

Propagation cases and mist propagation units

Vegetative propagation is the production of young plants by inducing the formation of roots on sections of vegetative tissue removed from the parent plant. The more quickly this can be achieved the better, and it is therefore important to maintain the tissue in good condition. Soft tissue is particularly prone to rapid wilting when removed from the parent plant, simply because the leaves lose their moisture by rapid transpiration, which cannot be entirely replaced by the usual uptake of moisture because the water-absorbing tissue has been severed. While a certain amount of moisture can be obtained

through the exposed xylem, the condition of all the tissue quickly deteriorates, which inevitably holds up the complicated process of forming new root tissue. If the air around the vegetative tissue (leaves, cuttings or other sections of plant) can be maintained in a very humid state, transpiration is considerably reduced and the tissue cells remain turgid. This can be achieved in several ways such as the use of a heated propagation case, by polythene drapes, or on a smaller scale in a porch or conservatory by the use of polythene bags. Alternatively it can also be achieved by maintaining a fine film of moisture over the young plant sections, as achieved by mist propagation. Seed germinates better too.

Propagating cases and polythene drapes both have the advantage of providing an environment which can be maintained independently of, and generally higher than, the greenhouse temperature, which offers considerable fuel savings. It is desirable also to have bottom heat which can either be provided by a pipe heating system beneath the bench on which the propagating case is placed or by the use of soil warming cables.

Propagating cases can be of any convenient size and can be purchased complete, the larger sizes with soil warming cables and the smaller sizes with an electric bulb providing the warmth. Any handyman can make a propagating case with a sheet of glass and some wood, or even glass, for the sides, a convenient depth being about 25—30cm (10—12in). A distinct disadvantage of a propagating case is that condensation builds up on the underside of the glass, causing drips, but a good slope will encourage these to run to one end. Adequate ventilation will help.

Plastic domes and germinating cabinets
Plastic dome cases for plastic seed trays have in many ways tended to replace propagating cases because of their cheapness and mobility, and if they are placed on a soil-warmed bench they achieve the same basic purpose as a propagating case.

Considerable heat build-up can, however, occur in propagating cases, polythene drapes and plastic domes unless ventilated, which can be detrimental to young plants; damage can usually be avoided because of the extremely high humidity but it is generally safer to shade the greenhouse with coloured polythene or other material.

Propagating cases and domes can of course be used for all other aspects of propagation, including seed germination. Germinating cabinets have, however, in recent years become popular for seed germination, and these are merely highly insulated, unlit, shelved compartments fitted with a humidifier and heater, or on a less sophisticated scale merely a heater, the floor being maintained in wet condition to give the necessary humidity.

Mist propagation
This technique, invented in the U.K. but developed in the U.S.A., aims at overcoming many of the disadvantages of closed propagating cases by maintaining a constant fine film of water on the propagating material, so keeping the tissue cool by restricting the elementary process of loss of heat by evaporation and simultaneously preventing rapid transpiration. To be effective it must be used in conjunction with

high level soil warming 160w/m² (15 watts per sq ft) to achieve 24°C (75°F), keeping the atmosphere moist by constant applications of water. A series of vertical mist nozzles 38—60cm (15—24in) high are spaced 90cm—1.2m (3—4ft) apart (or according to water pressure available). Overhead mist lines can also be used.

It is highly important that the drainage in the bench is perfect to avoid saturation, which could have highly detrimental results. The film of moisture is maintained in relation to air temperature and solar radiation by using either a selenium cell light sensor, electrode-type 'leaf', or absorbent pad controller, all of which operate a solenoid valve to control water flow. Various types of 'leaf' are obtainable and it is necessary to obtain advice on which is the best for the particular type of water involved. A good pressure of water, say 2.7—4bar (40—60psi), is necessary to operate the mist nozzles effectively, and if this is not available from the mains, a pressure tank will be necessary. In most areas, however, water pressure is adequate provided the supply pipe is of sufficient diameter.

Weaning mist-rooted plants to become accustomed to growing naturally involves ideally a period of less frequent watering, and this can be achieved either by moving the 'leaf' nearer the nozzle, adjusting the particular type of leaf, or by a time control unit. Root temperatures should also be reduced gradually by altering the thermostat setting.

Shading equipment
The provision of shade restricts solar radiation very considerably and this in turn reduces air temperature. It may be necessary for propagating activities or for certain groups of plants, or crops such as tomatoes suffering from wilt diseases. The simplest method of shading is to apply proprietary shading material, usually green tinted, to the outside of the glass, or alternatively lime plus water which is less permanent. Much diluted emulsion paint is also useful but can be too persistent. All materials will invariably wash off by the end of the season, although some assistance with a long-handled brush may be necessary to ensure

maximum light transmission in winter. A shading material, Varishade, obtainable from Clovis Lande Ltd or 'Garden Rewards' (see Appendix) which is transparent when wet and white when dry, is available to apply to the outside of glass. Blinds can be fitted both outside and inside, and green polythene blinds, fitted at the ridge inside the greenhouse, are extremely useful. Slatted blinds can also be used for special plants such as orchids. It is important to ensure that the shading equipment purchased is suitable for the size of the greenhouse. As a temporary measure green polythene or plastic netting can be used, supported on wires, canes or any other rigid stiffeners.

Polythene lining (see also page 80)

Double glazing, which has become very popular in domestic circles, involves the use of two sheets of glass hermetically sealed so that a layer of air is trapped, the net effect of which is to reduce heat loss considerably. This is not always considered practical for greenhouses on account of weight and cost, and such attempts as have been made by simply using two panes of glass on either side of wooden or metal glazing bars have not always been too successful, as it is difficult to ensure a tight enough seal to prevent the entry of dirt and moisture. Much more practical is the use of twin or treble walled polycarbonate sheeting, which is readily available and widely used for conservatory roofs, and is also highly efficient for reducing heat loss. New designs of PVC sheeting are also more effective than glass for reducing heat loss. Both polycarbonate and PVC are, however, more expensive than glass to purchase. Polythene lining is frequently used as a simple form of double glazing, ideally using 'bubble' polythene, which can be tacked on to the inside of wooden glazing bars, using paper pads and drawing pins or staples. With metal houses a piece of wood inlaid into the groove in alloy glazing bars is possible, failing which a wooden framework can be used. Special clips are available for securing polythene (Fig. 38). Approximately a 25% reduction in heat loss can be expected when all but the vent areas are covered. Problems of excess humidity can develop for some crops, although this high humidity can be an advantage for propagating activities. Probably one of the main advantages of polythene lining is to prevent draughts and drips in older type greenhouses in poor repair. Light transmission is only slighthy reduced by the polythene lining. Thermal screens of various materials pulled across above head height or as rollups on outside of structure overnight are now much used commercially to reduce heat loss.

Fig. 38 A system for attaching polythene to the interior of an aluminium glasshouse.

Carbon dioxide (CO_2) enrichment

The natural complement of the gas carbon dioxide in the atmosphere is 300 parts per million, and this is normally a sufficient concentration for the photosynthetic needs of plants. Research has shown, however, that under conditions of good light intensity and compatible temperatures, the growth rate of greenhouse plants may be restricted by lack of sufficient carbon dioxide. When the atmosphere is enriched up to approximately 600–900 parts per million (two- to threefold) the velocity of photosynthesis increases.

The breakdown of organic matter in the soil results in the production of CO_2, and this takes place in the soil continuously. Where cultural methods involve the use of large quantities of organic matter, such as 'hot' beds or straw bale culture of tomatoes or cucumbers, a considerable quantity of carbon dioxide is produced which enriches the air in the vicinity of the growing plants. Plants vary in their response to additional CO_2 and even certain varieties of the same species respond better than others.

The artificial enrichment of the atmosphere can be achieved in a variety of ways. The burning of paraffin heaters results in carbon dioxide in quantity, but unfortunately impurities such as sulphur are also produced and this can be harmful to plants if it reaches too high a concentration. The burning of propane gas in special burners is an efficient way of achieving carbon dioxide enrichment, propane gas being relatively pure. Natural gas greenhouse heaters would also produce CO_2 without any of the complications of sulphur production. Liquid CO_2 piped into the greenhouse from bulk supply tanks is a commercial technique still practised, as is the use of dry ice.

One of the problems of supplying extra carbon dioxide is checking the level of enrichment, this requiring specialized testing equipment. Ventilation should not proceed simultaneously with CO_2 enrichment for obvious reasons.

Watering and feeding equipment

The application of water and soluble nutrients is an essential part of greenhouse gardening. Watering methods may be as simple as a watering can filled directly from a tap or barrel or tank topped up by a hose, and liquid fertilizer used for each watering can application. Alternatively liquid fertilizer can be dissolved in barrels or tanks, but great care should be taken to measure both water and liquid fertilizer accurately.

Few modern commercial holdings are without some form of automatic or semi-automatic watering device, with the complementary use of dilutors for liquid fertilizer application. Amateur gardeners are fast catching on to the fact that there is great scope here, not only for reducing labour, but for ensuring greater accuracy in the realm of water and liquid fertilizer application, using dilutors at hose ends.

Taps

A greenhouse should have a good tap supplying water at a fair volume and pressure. Screwed taps or 'plug' types are preferable to plain types as they allow hose couplings with no leaks. Meters for fitting to taps are now available.

Watering cans

These are available in tough plastic ranging from 2.25 litres ($\frac{1}{2}$gal) capacity upwards, the most popular being the 4.5 litres (1gal) size, both for weight and for ease of measuring up liquid fertilizers. Enamelled metal cans are still very popular, although more expensive, and range from 1.7–9 litres (3–16pt). Diminutive copper watering cans are useful for house plants and are generally 0.5–1.1 litre (1–2pt) capacity. A selection of roses is available to give fine or coarse droplets of water.

Containers for water

Old sinks or wooden barrels are frequently used as reservoirs for water, though modern plastic water baths holding from 112–180 litres (25–40gal) are available and are much more hygienic as they can readily be washed out. This is essential for all forms of water storage, as algae and scum can quickly grow on still water, a further problem being contamination with bacterial and fungal diseases. It helps if containers are shaded.

Sprinkler lines

These provide large droplets of water from revolving nozzles spaced approximately 2.4–4.5m (8–15ft) apart. They are installed at a height of 1.8–2.4m (6–8ft) according to headroom available, and if sufficient volume and pressure of water is available, will dispense droplets over an area within a distance of approximately 6m(20ft) at a water pressure of between 1.3–2.6bar (20–40psi). Their main role is for the damping down of crops such as tomatoes, to shake the plants and assist with pollination, and they have therefore little general application. They are available generally in alloy with quick release couplings.

Spraylines

These can take several different forms and are available in both alloy or plastic, the latter tending to sag a little unless adequately supported. They can be used either at high or low level and are available with nozzle sprays spaced approximately 1.5 to 2.25m (5ft to 7ft 6in) apart with different sized jets for operating at different pressures. Typical output of 2.3mm ($\frac{3}{32}$ in) jets ranges from 81 litres (18gal) per hour at 0.6bar (10psi) up to 240litres (53gal) per hour at 2.6bar (40psi) pressure. For larger jets of 5.5mm ($\frac{7}{64}$ in) the outputs are nearly doubled and range from 136litres (30gal) per hour at 0.6bar (10psi) to 363litres (80gal) per hour at 2.6bar (40psi). The specification for spraylines varies according to manufacturer, as do the trajectories of the nozzles or jets. Fine atomization is generally achieved at good working pressure, which saturates the whole growing area. The details given apply merely to commercial equipment, which of course can be utilized for large amateur greenhouses. For small amateur greenhouses spraylines of various types are available with much closer nozzle sprays, generally 1m (3–4ft), for operating a 3m (10ft) sprayline from a 1.5cm ($\frac{1}{2}$in) hosepipe, and usually require a water pressure of 2.4bar (35psi). The output per hour of these units will obviously vary greatly according to the specification, and it is a matter which must be taken up with the supplier.

Control of spraylines can be effected either on a time basis with a solenoid valve through a sequence controller on a large scale or more simply with a hand-operated tap on a small scale. 'Automatic' waterers are also available which operate either on the saturation of a moisture sensitive pad or by a selenium light cell or other methods similar to those used to control mist irrigation units. The main drawback of spraylines lies in their inability to spray water into containers protected by foliage. Spraylines are therefore more useful for crops such as tomatoes, used at a high level until the plants reach 1.5m (5ft) then at low level generally at 30cm (12in) on wire supports, and covering a smaller area. Lettuce crops and other bordergrown plants are successfully watered with spraylines.

Damping down is effectively carried out with spraylines, increasing the humidity and reducing water needs, which is valuable for the gardener absent during the day, particularly when the spraylines are linked to an automatic device. A fair quantity of water can reach the pots in many instances. Liquid fertilizers can also be applied through spraylines in a form which makes them readily acceptable to the plants, either through their leaves or in the soil.

Trickle systems

These take several forms, all having in common the precise placement of droplets of water in a pot, container or growing border. The ability of water deposited in droplet form at a specific point to move through the growing medium varies within the type of medium. It has been found in certain free-draining light soils that trickle systems do not adequately water a sufficiently wide zone, although this can be overcome by moving the position of the nozzle at regular intervals. There are two basic forms: those where plastic nozzles are used in a rubber hose, or 'spaghetti' systems where capillary tubes lead out to each plant and are held in position by a peg. Trickle systems can be used for either border-grown, container-grown, grow bags or bench-grown plants and can be either manually operated or by a timing device operating a solenoid valve, or by a light cell.

This older style trickle irrigation system has been largely replaced by 'spaghetti' systems, but the basic principle is the same — individual supply of water and liquid nutrients to each plant.

Low-level watering systems

Perforated 'lay-flat' polythene tubing of 5cm (2in) width throws out fine jets of water on expansion with a sufficient volume of water and is a useful system for border-grown plants. It is not so suitable for container-grown plants. Round PVC tubing with small holes operates in a similar way, but is not usually so efficient as a trickle system. More recently bi-wall tubing has been introduced to even up emission of water from small holes. Overhead gantry watering systems are now used commercially.

Hosepipes

These are still indispensable for watering on a small scale, but care must be taken to avoid damage to soil structure by allowing an open-ended hose to splash on to the soil with force. Soil thus splashed on to tomato fruit is a frequent cause of fruit rotting. A rose or other attachment on the end of the hose can do much to avoid indiscriminate water dispersal, even a paraquat weedkiller dispenser being useful *(but used only for water application)* especially for tomatoes and other border-grown crops. Damping down is frequently practised with a hosepipe by pinching in the end, or by using a fine rose. Trigger lances are now popular.

Dilutors

While, as stated earlier, liquid fertilizers can be mixed as required in small quantities or prepared in bulk, a much more satisfactory arrangement is to use a dilutor into which the stock or concentrated solution of fertilizer is placed, the dilutor then being set at the correct dilution rate and placed in the supply line for spraylines or irrigation nozzles. Bottle dilutors are now used almost entirely on the displacement principle, although other systems work on a capillary tube system. Problems arise where water pressures are erratic, as this can both damage the dilutor and alter the dilution rate. In addition, although now available, it is not generally permitted to connect dilutors direct to a mains supply. Proprietary liquid fertilizers are usually colour dyed so that a quick visual check on dilution is possible, although on a large scale the concentration check of the liquid fertilizer should be regularly carried out with a salt meter. Self-formulated feeds should also be colour dyed for visual checking. Note that a bottle of correctly diluted liquid feed should be available for colour comparison purposes. The quantities of water and soluble feed required by various plants is dealt with under cultural notes referring to each crop.

Assessing the water requirement of crops
In addition to controlling the application of water by solenoid valves, sequence controllers and other apparatus, various methods are used actually to determine the *needs* of the crop. The simplest of these is a tensiometer, a device which consists largely of a ceramic pot connected to a vacuum gauge, graduated in centimetres or inches of mercury. This instrument indicates the suction necessary to extract water and can be related to the water requirement of the crop. The evaporimeter consists of sand in a thistle funnel connected to a graduated tube, so that the evaporation of water can be calculated and related to crop needs. More recently simple, sensitive, tipped water meters, which state whether soil in pots or borders is 'wet', 'medium' or 'dry', have been available. Solarimeters are installed regionally at research stations and record the solar radiation, so that water requirements can be issued to the commercial horticulture industry.

Frames—cold and heated

With the advent of fan ventilation the greenhouse temperature can in fact be lowered to such an effective degree that acclimatization can take place *in situ* without recourse to the frame. But although acclimatization is the main role of a frame, it can also be used very effectively as a production unit in its own right, like a small greenhouse—especially the elevated form with hessian sides used by specialist flower growers. Sophisticated types of frames, some of which are on rollers and capable of easy movement, can in fact achieve results commensurate in many ways with a greenhouse. In design, shape and orientation the same basic principles apply. Ventilation and watering are two problems, the former being achieved by lifting the sashes and the latter either by hand or by the use of low level spraylines. Heating can be by any of the methods already discussed, the heat loss being calculated in a similar manner to that for greenhouses, although with a brick base wall. For all practical purposes the square area in metres or feet of the frame sashes multiplied by 7.94 (w/m^2 °C) or 1.4 (Btu 2h°F) and ignoring the sides will give a fairly accurate figure. It is very easy to put the required amount of piping, mineral insulated cable or tubular heaters into the frame. Soil warming cables are also used at a loading of 80watt/m^2 (7$\frac{1}{2}$ watts per sq ft), either by a mains voltage cable led in at 20−23cm (8−9 in) depth or by low voltage lines through a transformer.

Types and construction of frames
For many years the 1.8 × 1.2m (6 × 4ft) light sashes were standard items, but their weight plus their upkeep has made them a thing of the past. The Dutch light sash measuring approximately 75 × 150cm (2ft 6in × 5ft) is ideal for frame construction. This has a single sheet of 3mm (24oz) horticultural glass 1.42 × 73cm (56 × 28$\frac{3}{4}$in) and is simple and light to handle, being virtually maintenance-free if constructed in pressure treated wood. Bases for frames can be brick, concrete or breeze block, or wood (old railway sleepers serving on a large scale). The front of the frames should be approximately 23−25cm (9−10in) high and the rear 30−35cm (12−14in) to give a reasonable 'run'.

Frames can also be constructed against the base wall of a greenhouse, an ideal arrangement when the heating system is to be linked, a sun-facing orientation usually being preferable. Metal or alloy types come with directions, but there are no precise designs otherwise; many gardeners simply adapt what materials they have to the best advantage. Polythene sashes can readily be made up by using the wrap-round principle of construction in any convenient size. Wood should be preservative treated, this including both the sash spars and the groundwork. It is important to ensure that sashes are secure, otherwise they may be blown off in a high wind.

Of special interest is the range of alloy frames now available with ingenious ventilation facilities. Many types of polythene cloches have also reached an advanced stage of design. Very significant also is the perforated polythene film which can be put over a crop in spring and expands as the crop grows (Floating mulches).

Potting sheds

Whether or not a special shed is desirable for compost mixing, potting and other activities will depend on the scale of operations, but a shed is certainly very useful for the storing of pots, tools, equipment and raw material for compost making. If work is to be carried out there, a good stout, level, well-placed bench, preferably with a window adjacent, is highly desirable.

The combined shed/greenhouse, either longitudinally or centrally, has its value, but the shade factor must invariably limit the scope of the greenhouse section, which may be undesirable.

Heat conservation for greenhouses

In recent years, commercial growers in temperate zones have increasingly incorporated heat-saving methods into greenhouse design as a standard feature. These methods include the use of polycarbonate sheeting for ends and side walls – and in some cases for the roof also – and, in addition, the use of thermal screens of various materials which are automatically pulled over the crops above head height at night. Full details of these heat-conservation measures are available from commercial greenhouse manufacturers (see Appendix).

CHAPTER 10
Lighting Greenhouses

Any discussion on illumination must be prefaced by the reminder of the precise role of light in plant growth. The intensity or level of light has a vital effect in the velocity of the photosynthesis process which is essential to all green plants; the duration of light, or day length, also has profound photoperiodic influences; and sources of artificial light, as distinct from sunlight, have differing stimulative effects on plants.

Types of artificial lighting
Tungsten filament lamps
These lamps (the type frequently used for home lighting) produce light from a super-heated filament which contains a good deal of the far red in its spectrum and this will, in many plants, produce intense elongation. The intensity of light they produce is low but is sufficient to produce photoperiodic and photosynthetic reaction in extremely sensitive plants such as chrysanthemums, pelargoniums and many others. Tungsten filament lamps are also satisfactory for bringing many bulbs into flower.

The introduction of Sungro-Lites has brought a new dimension to the use of artificial lights for plant growth in the home and greenhouse. With their low heat emission and excellent light spectrum, with specially designed fittings, they can now be used at relatively low cost for both supplementary and replacement units in convenient places. Other lights of this type are available.

Discharge lamps
These produce light by the discharge of electricity through a gas, and the colour varies according to the gas employed. Neon gives a largely red light, vaporized sodium a yellow light, and mercury a greeny blue. Neon is at present not thought to be a great deal of use for horticultural purposes, but sodium (SOX) has proved very ef-

fective. Mercury vapour lamps (MB) on the other hand are excellent for the production of high intensity lighting and are therefore used to supplement natural daylight where this is too low for optimum photosynthesis activity. The spectrum of light supplied by mercury vapour lamps appears to be adequately balanced for most plants, although their use is not recommended for growing room cultivation entirely under artificial light as they produce a lot of heat. A 400W mercury vapour lamp is usually suspended at least 90cm (3ft) above the bench or floor area being illuminated, to give a high level of illumination compatible with maximum coverage of plants.

Fluorescent lamps
Types MBF or HLRG have a larger enclosed glass area than mercury vapour lamps and are coated entirely with fluorescent powder, so that some of the ultra-violet radiation is converted to visible light. This is an extremely useful light source for a wide variety of activities, including night-break or growing room techniques.

Tubular fluorescent lights (MCF) operate with mercury vapour at a much lower pressure than fluorescent lamps, and much of the ultra-violet radiation is successfully extracted and converted to useful light by the use of powders. By varying the powder coating, white, natural or warm white light is produced, the warm white being most suitable for horticultural purposes. A further advantage is that they do not produce much heat, having a low surface temperature.

Reflectors
Effective reflection ensures that the maximum amount of light is concentrated on the plants being treated, without at the

same time directing too much heat upon them. Reflectors should not unduly restrict the entry of natural light, unless of course under growing room conditions.

Aluminium foil plates are used for tungsten filament lamps, whereas mercury vapour lamps need large reflectors. MBFR/U fluorescent lamps have a coating of reflective titanium oxide, and special fluorescent tubes with a small reflector so that maximum illumination is concentrated through a 130° arc.

Four main roles for lighting in greenhouses

1 To allow working on short winter days or in the evenings tungsten filament (the domestic type) lights or fluorescent strip lighting can be used, care being taken to position the lights so that standing at the potting or working bench on dull days or in the evening does not cast a shadow. Light fittings and control switches should be of waterproofed design.
2 To provide day-length manipulation or night-break techniques by the use of low intensity tungsten filament lights, suspended above the plants.
3 To supplement the natural daylight when it falls below a level sufficient to maintain optimum photosynthetic activity, and to improve vegetative development and flower truss initiation a high intensity light source is used. This was mainly supplied by mercury vapour lamps in the early days, but fluorescent tubes are now widely used, for a set number of hours per day over a limited period when the plants are at an early stage of development. Recently, however, more prolonged use of supplementary lighting has been made on more mature plants, with spectacular results in poor light areas. Reference to the precise use of supplementary lighting will be given in the respective crop notes.
4 To illuminate growing rooms.

Growing rooms

The term applies to a variety of techniques whereby artificial lighting supplants natural light. In most cases the waste heat generated by the lighting is used to provide a heat source. Low-intensity lights at 100 watts for every square metre of growing areas are used in a building or cupboard of high thermal insulation. This is particularly suitable for bringing bulbs into flower: the tungsten filament lamps are kept suspended about 45cm (18in) above the leaf tips of the bulbs, light being given for 12 out of 24 hours, preferably by time switch. In a well-insulated building, heat from the lamps may be sufficient to keep the temperature sufficiently high, while during dark periods electric heaters are used (see Fig. 39).

Details of the construction of a growing room can be obtained by application to local electricity boards who have plans of standard growing rooms, although many different and varied designs of growing rooms are now in use, the basic objective being to increase the actual area available for the plants and at the same time reduce capital costs. The basic formula is a chamber within a building of high thermal insulation. The sides of the chamber are of pegboard to allow the passage of fan—circulated air, which avoids the local build-up of heat from the lights. A thermostatically operated ventilation vane allows entry of cooler air from outside when the temperature rises above the desirable level; when heat falls below the desirable level, a heating bank then comes into operation. These have in many cases now been superseded by linear growing rigs in commercial spheres.

Some very rudimentary growing rooms involving banks of fluorescent lamps above benches have been installed, surrounded by black/white polythene, with suitable air outlets, in basements or rooms in older buildings and have been used successfully for many years. Here again Sungro-Lites and similar types have a useful application at low cost and without complicated installation. More recently growing rooms have been developed in black (insulated) plastic greenhouses. The basis of the technique is the utilization of light and heat in combination with low heat loss, thus avoiding the cost of heating a traditional greenhouse with its high heat loss.

The many technical issues which surround the construction of growing rooms and their use are beyond the scope of this

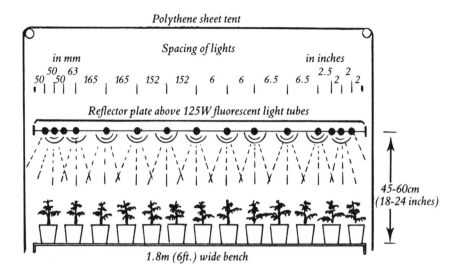

Polythene sheet tent

Spacing of lights

in mm

in inches

50 50 63 165 165 152 152 6 6 6.5 6.5 2.5 2 2 2

Reflector plate above 125W fluorescent light tubes

45-60cm
(18-24 inches)

1.8m (6ft.) wide bench

Fig. 39 Ligh rigs using fluorescent lights.

book and are best taken up either directly with the Electricity Council or the agricultural/horticultural officers of the respective electricity boards, although reference will be made to their use in connection with crops such as tomatoes and bedding plants, which lend themselves admirably to growing room production.

It would be wrong to make a special issue of the physiological aspects surrounding plants being grown in a greenhouse, as the mechanics of growth and all the associated facets are common to all green-leaved growing plants. The only special case which could be made for greenhouse plants is that they will, in most cases, be growing a lot quicker than they would out of doors, so that everything will generally happen faster. On the other hand it is possible to control the environment of a greenhouse to fairly fine limits, which is a distinct advantage, compared to the resigned acceptance of conditions as they occur out of doors. Perhaps then, taking all things into account, there does exist the need for a nore complete understanding of basic physiological processes if greenhouse gardening is to be entirely successful.

Basic requirements

All green plants, given air and moisture in the absence of any inhibiting or restricting factor, will grow at a rate commensurate with the light level and temperatures to which that particular species or cultivar of plant is attuned. This rather complicated sentence perhaps requires some explanation. A tomato plant, a native of South America originally, has an inherent need for high light intensity and warmth. For it to grow, flower and produce fruit successfully, it is therefore incumbent on the gardener to provide for these conditions as far as possible. Plant a tomato plant outside in Britain during the month of March, instead of in the greenhouse, and if it does not die fairly quickly it will certainly not grow to any great degree, but will tend to debilitate. Conversely, plant a cabbage, a native of Europe, outside in March and, provided it has been suitably acclimatized, it will grow quite happily and in time produce a heart. Put the cabbage into the warm greenhouse environment suitable for the tomato and it will certainly grow at great speed, but it is unlikely that a heart will be produced, the plant developing vegetatively and showing elongated growth.

These rather elementary examples by no means explain why the tomato and the cabbage must have an environmental regime compatible with their metabolism. One point, however, which does clearly emerge is that the velocity of growth of plants is invariably increased when they are put into an environment warmer than that to which they are attuned by inheritance. It is highly important to remember this elementary issue and to think of it categorically: the completely *hardy plant* which will survive out of doors all year in Europe in category I; *half-hardy plants* such as the pelargonium in category 2; the tender tomato in category 3; and the very tender melon in category 4.

Basic plant processes

Any attempt to understand plant physiology must be prefaced by some discussion of the basic plant processes common to all green plants. While these will be grouped for convenience under separate headings, it should be appreciated that all processes are closely inter-related, each having a bearing on the other.

Respiration

Breathing is a function essential for all living organisms. In the case of green plants air is taken in through the pores on the leaves (and to a lesser extent through the stems and roots), its oxygen content extracted as energy for various chemical processes, and carbon dioxide gas expelled as a waste product—in a similar way to a fuel being burned by a fire or an internal combustion engine. The speed of respiration varies according to the age of the

84

plant, the temperature of the atmosphere, and the rate of growth, this last activity not always being completely in keeping with temperature, as a combination of other factors may have a bearing on the growth rate irrespective of age or temperature.

Respiration is a continuous destructive process as compared with other functions such as photosynthesis which are carried out only during daylight hours. The destructive nature of respiration therefore draws on the reserves of the plant night and day, which means that food manufactured by the process of photosynthesis is utilized at night, a fact that has considerable significance in relation to day and night temperatures. If, for example, a warm bright day when a great deal of carbohydrate is manufactured in the plant leaves is followed by a cold night, there will usually be a surplus of carbohydrate, which in the case of the tomato plant will result in starch filled curled leaves. The converse is also true, and cool dull days with limited photosynthesis, followed by warm nights, will in fact dissipate the reserves of carbohydrate resulting in drawn spindly plants.

Process of respiration

Air taken in through pores in leaves, stem and roots	→	energy extracted for chemical processes	→	carbon dioxide expelled through pores

Photosynthesis
This is the process whereby the air taken in through the pores in the leaves has the carbon dioxide gas contained in it extracted (at approximately 300 volumes/parts per million) and the oxygen content of the air expelled, more or less the converse of respiration. Carbon dioxide is the vital source of carbon needed for the build-up of carbohydrates, which are synthesized with the aid of the catalyst chlorophyll, the green pigment present in all green plants. The supply of water and nutrients taken up by the plant roots (which will be discussed shortly) is also closely involved with photosynthesis.

Research has shown that there is a direct relationship between the rate of photosynthesis and the prevailing light intensity, provided that temperature is sufficiently high and there is no restriction in water and nutrient supply. Adding to the natural complement of carbon dioxide, up to three-fold enrichment, by various means under conditions of high light and temperature levels can, in certain cases, increase the rate of photosynthesis, which has various benefits largely centring round the increased supply of carbohydrates for the plant's vital processes.

No research has yet shown precisely what physiological processes are brought into play by carbon dioxide enrichment but it is quite clear that photosynthesis is an extremely complex function. The practical implication for greenhouse gardening is to ensure that there is no light restriction for light-demanding crops except when there is excess sunlight, and that all other environmental factors must simultaneously be given strictest attention.

Process of photosynthesis

Air taken in by plant	→	carbon dioxide content extracted	→	oxygen expelled

Transpiration
Water absorbed by the plant roots and other parts of the plant passes up through the xylem tissue in the stem, and into the leaves where quantities in excess of requirements for various chemical processes are expelled as water vapour through the pores in leaves and stems, and to a limited degree through the epidermis or plant 'skin'. Apart from helping to keep the plant 'cool' by loss of heat through evaporation, a transpiration stream is created, this being essential for the movement of dissolved foodstuffs throughout the growing plant. Transpiration rate is controlled in an interesting way, as the pores or stomata are opened and closed by the activity of guard cells which close the stomata when flaccid and open it when turgid (see Fig. 40). Thus the rate of water loss is directly related to the temperature and humidity of the air. Once again it would be wrong to consider transpiration in strict isolation, as there are in addition many other interrelated issues: (1) the healthy state of the roots and their ability to absorb sufficient water, (2) free-

Fig. 40 Stomata. (*Top*) Hot and dry – open (*Lower*) Cold and humid – closed.

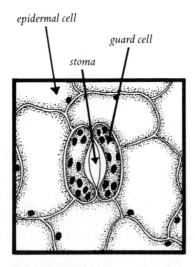

epidermal cell

guard cell

stoma

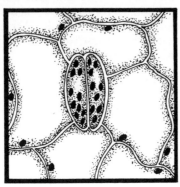

Osmosis

This is undoubtedly not only one of the most important physiological processes, but an activity over which the gardener can exert considerable control. Any botany book will state that osmosis is the process whereby a higher concentration of salts in solution on one side of a semi-permeable membrane will absorb the *water* of a less concentrated solution by pulling it through the semi-permeable membrane. Relating this to plants, the stronger solution contained in the cell of the root (or other tissue) absorbs the water from the less concentrated solution of salts in the soil or growing medium, the net result of which is to set up suction pressures which are always endeavouring to equalize.

Botanists make much of the fact that only water is absorbed by osmosis and that soluble plant nutrients move in by diffusion and absorption, as few semi-permeable membranes are perfect; but for all practical purposes the two processes are so closely related that they can be considered simultaneously. Once the salt solution is contained in the cell of root or other tissue a chain reaction process goes on, as the cell receiving water has its concentration lowered, altering the osmotic pressure, which allows the more concentrated solution in the next cell to pull in the now less concentrated solution to even up the pressure, and so on.

The rate at which osmosis proceeds depends on many factors such as transpiration rate and the speed of other processes, but undoubtedly the salt concentration of the soil water is of paramount importance. When concentrated and soluble chemicals (some weedkillers and many fertilizers) are applied to the soil or growing medium, they alter the salt concentration. Where near equilibrium exists there can only be limited osmotic activity, if indeed there is any at all, whereas should the salt solution in the growing medium become more concentrated than that of the plant cell, osmosis in reverse can and will take place. The importance of salt concentration in the growing medium and successful osmosis on the part of the growing plant cannot be divorced from the availability of water

dom from disease or restriction on the part of the xylem and other conducting tissue, (3) the age and size of the plant with particular emphasis on the leaf area, (4) the respective osmotic pressures of both soil and plant which will greatly affect the ability of the plant to take up moisture and nutrients in the first case (see below), (5) the species of plant involved and whether it is botanically adapted to moisture conservation, as indeed is the case with most cacti when the leaves are modified to 'needles'.

Process of transpiration Water taken in through the process of osmosis passes up through the xylem and a proportion is given off as water vapour at a rate dependent on temperature, humidity, the osmotic pressures of plant and soil and other related issues.

supplies, as when water supplies diminish, salt solutions will become more concentrated and vice versa. This is a factor of considerable importance in greenhouse culture where the majority of plants will be growing in limited quantities of media. The sensitivity of plants to salt concentrations varies very considerably. Reference will be made to salt solution measurement in a later chapter when some scale of susceptibility for various plants will be stated. It must be further appreciated that some measure of growth control can be achieved by adjustment of the salt concentration of the growing medium, by applying either solid or liquid fertilizers, something which intuitive gardeners have been unconsciously carrying out for years.

Process of osmosis The stronger solution of salts in the plant cell pulls in the water from the weaker solution of the soil or growing medium and simultaneously there is absorption of liquid nutrients. A measure of growth control can be achieved by paying strict attention to the salt concentration of the growing medium.

Translocation

This function relates to the transport of elaborated foodstuffs throughout the plant tissue, the main conducting tissue being the phloem. Many gardeners fail to realize that the food synthesized in the leaves is moved into the flower or swelling fruit as required, there often being the allusion that leaves and flowers or fruit have a separate unrelated existence. Further credence is given to this philosophy by the various feeding formulae prepared for the swelling of fruits or the size and colour of flowers. Neither flower, fruit nor leaf of the plant exists in limbo, and it is the successful culmination of all processes in which translocation is merely one vital part which results in good flowers, fruits, or for that matter foliage.

Disruptions of any kind such as irregular watering, unsuitable or variable temperatures, or the wrong dilution of liquid feeding, can frequently affect the usual movement of elaborated foodstuffs around the plant, resulting in physiological trouble such as blotchy ripening or black bottoms of tomatoes, flower drop in many pot plants, lack of hearting in greenhouse lettuce, to mention only a few malfunctions which are closely linked to faulty circulation of elaborated foodstuffs or the direction of simple elements into their respective roles. Here again is a case, however, for emphasizing that there is a very close relationship between all physiological factors and that compartmentalized thinking can be confusing.

Pollination and fertilization

Sexual reproduction is a feature of most flowering plants and is a process which depends on the minute pollen grain or male sperm successfully and in good condition reaching the ovary of the same or other flower of similar species, and thereafter germinating, producing a pollen tube through which fusion between male gamete (sperm) and female gamete (egg or ovum) can take place, resulting in fertilization and the production of new cells which form the fruit. Flowers which contain both male and female organs producing pollen capable of reaching and acceptable to the ovary are said to be self-fertile. When the pollen from another flower of the same species is necessary, a flower is said to be self-sterile; where male and female organs are produced on separate flowers, the flower is unisexual. Both of these factors can give rise to problems when the fruit of the plant being grown is important. In some cases, however, fertilization is not desirable and before it happens the flowers of male blooms are generally removed. There are many cases where fertilization is unsuccessful, either because the pollen is not fertile or it dried out before germination, a frequent state of affairs in tomato growing due either to poor environmental conditions or the production of infertile pollen under conditions of poor light. Fertilization of tomatoes can be aided by damping down frequently. In the case of peaches and nectarines pollination is assisted by collecting the pollen on a rabbit's tail or cotton wool and transferring this to open flowers, whereas with melons the male flower is removed and inserted into the female flower.

By contrast, it is inadvisable to allow fertilization of cucumber flowers, as this

Fig. 41 Some
aspects of plant
growth.

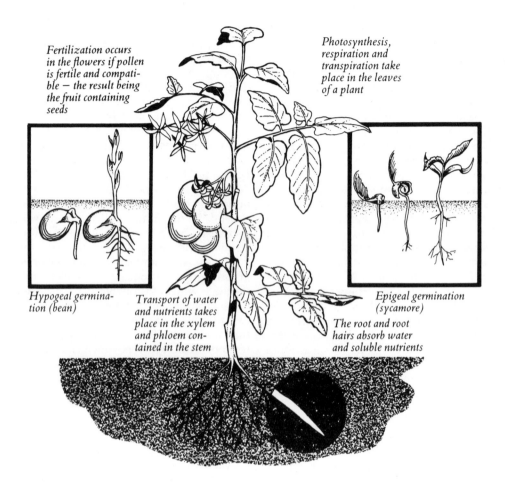

*Fertilization occurs
in the flowers if pollen
is fertile and compati-
ble – the result being
the fruit containing
seeds*

*Photosynthesis,
respiration and
transpiration take
place in the leaves
of a plant*

*Hypogeal germina-
tion (bean)*

*Transport of water
and nutrients takes
place in the xylem
and phloem con-
tained in the stem*

*Epigeal germination
(sycamore)*

*The root and root
hairs absorb water
and soluble nutrients*

results in the production of bitter fruit.
Modern breeding programmes have now
produced 'all female' cucumbers.

Germination of seeds
A seed contains a new plant in an embryonic state, and given suitable conditions
the young plant will develop into an adult
plant. The initial awakening of the embryonic plant is called germination, which
will occur when moisture has penetrated
through the protective seed coat or testa to
trigger it off. Air, moisture and suitable
temperature are the prerequisites for successful germination, but these must be
balanced to the particular inherent requirements of each species. Primed seed is now
available.

Most seeds have a dormancy period during which they cannot be readily induced

to germinate and this period varies according to species. Various ways and means
are practised to break this dormancy period,
for example by subjecting the seed to
periods of low or high temperature. The
time taken for a seed actually to germinate
will vary with the species, and also the age
of the seed. Seeds vary considerably in their
viability or ability to germinate, and reference to both these facts will be made in
the respective cultural notes where applicable, it being worth noting that the particular germinating procedure which has
evolved for a particular type of seed has
probably come partly by usage and partly
by research over many years. Some seeds
germinate below the compost surface
(hypogeal), others above (epigeal) (Fig.
41).

CHAPTER 12
Greenhouse Plant Nutrition

The subject of plant nutrition is very complex and it is not possible here to give more than an elementary background to it. In a great deal of what is written about plant nutrition, assumption rather than fact plays a very large part. As with the physiological aspects of plant growth, it is convenient to consider nutrition in a sectional manner. Here again there is such a complex relationship between all the nutritional elements and chemical processes that the ability of one chemical element to fulfil a role depends a great deal on the activity and presence of all the others. It could be said that each chemical element is a cog in a large wheel, and should a cog be missing some malfunction or complete breakdown of vital processes is likely. It is, however, true to say that the greenhouse gardener has matters under his control to a much greater extent than the gardener out of doors. He also has the ability to meter the quantity of each particular chemical element supplied to the plant.

All living organisms require a range of essential chemical elements if they are to generate the energy to carry out all the various processes concerned with their growth and development. Animals can take in food and drink in either solid or liquid form and digest the chemical elements in them, but living plants take their 'food' only in soluble or gaseous form, this being true even of insectivorous plants which 'digest' their prey. The majority of elements are assimilated by the roots, and carbon and oxygen are absorbed through the leaves. A plant nutrient is therefore a chemical which has a precise function in the plant's growth and a vital part to play in the plant's further development.

Soil types
Mineral soils are derived from the long-term chemical and mechanical breakdown of the earth's crust, a process which has been going on for millions of years. The size of particle to which the rock has been reduced varies greatly, from coarse gravel, through sand, down to silt and clay. Few mineral soils are, however, 'pure', having become interlaced with the organic remains of plants and animals, in addition to a vast population of micro and macro-organisms such as bacteria, fungi, worms, and other forms of life. All these living organisms have differing functions and in the course of satisfying their own nutrient needs they decompose or chemically change a great many of the contents of the soil, rendering complex chemicals into a soluble form suitable for absorption by the living plant.

Mineral soils are classified largely according to their mineral particle size and are broadly divided into sandy soils or loams, which have a predominance of large particles; heavy clay loams, which consist of a large percentage of fine particles; and medium soils or loams, which have a reasonable proportion of all particle sizes. Size of particles in different soils is as follows:

	Particle size in mm
Coarse sand	2.000–0.200
Fine sand	0.200–0.020
Silt	0.020–0.002
Clay	less than 0.002

Particle size has a profound effect on the ability of air and moisture to penetrate freely through a soil, the sandy soil allowing free movement of air and moisture through the large pore spaces, the clay soil tending to lock up moisture and air because the particles adhere very closely together. Without movement of water, plants are unable to extract it for their needs and when there is a lack of air the chemical cycle is restricted, with profound effects on the availability of plant nutrients. This is why the leaves of overwatered plants in pots frequently go yellow.

The organic matter content of the soil, coupled with chemicals, micro- and macro-organisms and worm activity can, however, greatly influence the behaviour of a soil, especially if of a clay type, by causing the particles to adhere together in a crumb formation instead of existing separately. This is due both to the adhesive effect of humic gums and to the electolytic effect of positively and negatively charged chemical elements. When this can be encouraged to happen to a high degree, a soil is said to have a good structure. Conversely, when soil is badly lacking in organic matter, or where micro-organism activity is reduced to a low level due to waterlogging or other factors, a soil may lose structure and become inhospitable to desirable plants. Organic as opposed to mineral soils are derived from plant and animal remains, fen or peat soils being classic examples, although few, if any, soils are 100% organic.

It would be wrong to make too large an issue of the ideal soil or loam consisting of a good distribution of mineral particle size, organic matter in reasonable quantity, an excellent crumb structure, and a supply of both immediately available and long-term nutrients. While such soils do exist and are capable of growing excellent plants, research work and practical growing experience in recent years have shown that plants are grown highly successfully in a very wide range of soil types, from sandy soil with negligible organic matter content, to pure peat with barely any mineral content at all, provided there is a constant supply of readily available plant nutrients. It would be more correct to say that the nearer 'ideal' a soil is, the better the results from plants without so much attention and without recourse to additional nutrients. For greenhouse culture of border-grown plants, or culture in pots using soil-containing media, the same principles will apply.

The range of essential nutrients

The nutrient content of a mineral soil will vary according to the constituents of the native rock from which the soils were originally derived, the treatment which the soil has received over the years and the weather pattern. One could scarcely expect a cultivated light sandy soil in a very wet district to be rich in nutrients; these would tend to be washed or leached out. On the other hand, a light sandy soil which had supported a good cover of growth in a dry area could be surprisingly rich in plant nutrients. Clay soils tend to be richer in plant nutrients than light sandy soils, being invariably richer initially in plant nutrients which are not leached out so rapidly.

The range of mineral elements or plant nutrients varies from soil to soil in different regions, but they invariably contain the macro-elements phosphorus, potassium, calcium and magnesium, along with the micro-elements silicon, aluminium, sulphur, boron, manganese, copper, zinc, iron, molybdenum, chlorine, sodium, iodine, cobalt, selenium, and others less well known. In addition, the major element nitrogen is supplied by the breakdown of organic matter and by fixation (synthesis from the atmosphere), and hydrogen and oxygen are supplied 90–95% by water and carbon in gaseous form from the atmosphere.

While the natural complement of these elements may well suffice to sustain a plant growing naturally out of doors, this is not the case in realms of intensive greenhouse culture, which means resorting to the application or addition of these nutrients, particularly those of the macro category which are used in large quantities by most actively growing plants.

Macro-elements

Nitrogen (N)
The element nitrogen is a constituent of all forms of plant material, and is essential for the formation of proteins. It is taken up by the plant largely in the form of nitrate, but can also be absorbed as ammonia. The effect of nitrogen on plants is to cause an increase in total bulk, which in practical terms generally means larger leaves and larger plants, although they may not necessarily be more productive of fruit and flowers; in fact, the reverse is often the case. Too much nitrogen in relation to other nutrients can also induce a lateness in flower or fruit formation. With tomatoes, a

gross excess of nitrogen can, in the early part of the year when light intensity is low, induce such lush, soft vegetative growth that the plant fails to develop flower trusses, and, even if it does, these can 'miss' completely. The amount of nitrogen present naturally in soil can vary greatly, and soils rich in organic matter can contain up to 1% or more, whereas an infertile soil will contain only 0.05%. A usual figure would be in the order of 0.10 to 0.30%.

The total nitrogen figure in the soil is no real guide to its availability to the plant, a lot depending on the rate of bacterial activity, which in turn depends on temperature, lack of competition from competing organisms such as protozoa, waterlogging, lack of air, excess consolidation and other factors. Partial soil sterilization or pasteurization by means of heat will result in a flood of available nitrogen because the pasteurization heat kills off pests and diseases and destroys competing organisms, leaving the thick-walled spore-forming nitrogen bacteria free to carry on with their activities. The breakdown of organic matter in the soil results in the production of CO_2 (carbon dioxide) which will form a weak carbonic acid solution which is one of the main dissolving agents for nitrogen and other plant nutrients. As nitrate is highly soluble it can quickly be leached out of the soil by overwatering, which shows the folly of over-watering greenhouse plants. At the same time, flooding out of excess nitrogen can be a useful technique when there is known excess, as is the case following soil sterilization methods which rely on heat. Ammonia is also washed out by flooding. While an excess of nitrogen generally results in lush unproductive growth, prone to disease, shortage is quite clearly exhibited by pale sickly yellow leaves. Plants can also assimilate nitrogen as ammonium compounds, which can result in problems, a typical example being associated with black bottoms in tomato fruit.

Breakdown of nitrogen When a fertilizer such as hoof and horn meal is added to a *soil*, it is necessary for soil bacteria to attack the hoof and horn meal particles and break them down first into nitrite and then into soluble nitrate before the plant can utilize the hoof and horn's nitrogen content. Soil-less media are initially fairly sterile, containing few bacteria, and it takes time before the hoof and horn can be converted to nitrate. If, on the other hand, nitrogen is applied in the form of nitrate (e.g. potassium nitrate) the plant can absorb it almost immediately.

Nitrogen summary Required for all plants, especially those of a leafy nature. Taken up largely in the form of nitrate, but also as ammonia. Induces lush soft growth in many plants if applied in excess, especially tomatoes and other leafy crops early in the year when light intensity is low. Can also reduce flowering and fruiting potential of plants if over-applied. If in short supply, this results in small and often yellow leaves, along with a general lack of vigour.

Phosphorus (P and P_2O_5)
Phosphorous is associated with all life and is a constituent of every living cell in plants and animals. It might therefore be expected that large quantities are required by growing plants, but this is not the case; while it is constantly needed, the actual amount required is relatively small in proportion to the nitrogen and potash required.

Natural supplies of phosphorus are in most types of soil, a percentage of 0.15 being the amount present in an average loamy soil (a medium soil with a good proportion of organic matter). In chalky soil areas the amount present rises considerably to the order of 0.2−0.3%, whereas in some types of infertile soil its presence may be minimal.

Phosphorus is frequently associated with successful root growth and early maturity, yet the need for it persists right through to flowering and subsequent fruit formation and ripening, where this is applicable. On the other hand many soils are heavily overloaded with phosphorus, indicating that its actual uptake by the plant can be relatively small. The surplus phosphorus remains in the soil because of its low solubility. Its availability to the plant is in the form of a weak phosphoric acid dissolved in a weak acid solution produced by micro-organism activity. In a very acid soil, phosphorus combines with iron and aluminium to form even less soluble components. The particular role of calcium in relation to phosphorus is by no means fully understood, as phosphorus would appear to be quite readily available to plants under the acid conditions of a soilless media (pH 5.5). The way in which phosphorus actually becomes available to plants is thought to be linked to the process through which previously insoluble phosphorus becomes available to the plant when more phosphorus is added, but, to confuse the issue still further, plants seem to exist quite happily in soils shown on analysis to have a high phosphorus content *without* the addition of any additional phosphorus.

The temperature of the soil or growing medium and the temperature of the air seem to be closely associated with the availability of phosphorus and the ability of the plant to assimilate it, this being illustrated quite clearly by the bluish coloration which results when many tender plants are subjected to cold. General lack of vigour and a distinct tendency towards poor rooting and late flowering are further symptoms of phosphorus shortage.

The effect of excess phosphorus on the plant is extremely difficult to define, no doubt because any excess phosphorus applied is rendered insoluble or is possibly lost by drainage in a free draining soil or growing medium.

Fertilizers are stated as having a percentage of soluble and insoluble phosphoric acid, a somewhat confusing statement; it is better if the percentage is stated as phosphorus (P) only.

Phosphorus summary Required by all plants in relatively small quantities. Has an effect on root development and early maturity. Shortage results in blue coloration; excess difficult to define.

Potassium (K and K_2O)

Potassium is required in very large amounts, particularly by flower and fruit producing plants. It is present initially in many soils in larger quantities than either nitrogen or phosphorus (1% or more), although only a small proportion of the total quantity may be actually available to the growing plant.

Excess results in hard stunted growth, whereas shortage gives rise to marginal leaf scorch and further encourages the soft lush growth typical of nitrogen surplus. There is therefore a very close relationship between the effects of nitrogen and those of potassium, and successful cultivation of most plants relies on the correct ratio of nitrogen to potash, phosphorus playing little part provided it is present in sufficient quantity.

Potassium is said to afford disease resistance qualities to plants, yet this is invariably associated merely with a hard or balanced growth which, apart from ensuring a good protection, has no surplus of carbohydrates for the disease organisms to plunder readily. Colour pigments develop well in the presence of adequate potash, which means clearer expression of colour in flowers, or better colour in fruit. An excess of soluble potash in the soil can also give rise to soluble salt problems, which can affect the osmotic process adversely, or burn the roots physically.

Potash summary Required in large amounts for most plants. Shortage is indicated by marginal leaf scorch. Excess results in stunted dark blue tinted growth, and in some cases burning of the leaf tips, no doubt because an excess in the growing medium results in a high soluble salt content.

Magnesium

The importance of magnesium varies according to the species of plant involved, but is essential for the photosynthesis process and the translocation of elaborated foodstuffs round the plant. Where this element is either in short supply or rendered insoluble, browny-orange areas appear *between* the veins, especially in older leaves. For those plants which make large demands on magnesium, this element is added regularly to the growing medium, often along with lime.

Excess of magnesium will create a salt problem in the growing media before its toxic effects, if any, are exhibited by the actual plant. The unavailability of magnesium to the plant is a complex subject, centred around the quantities of potassium

and nitrogen in the growing media, and possibly other factors. Often when there is an excess of potash, or potash is used copiously, as with tomato soils, magnesium deficiency is at its worst. On soils of poor physical structure, potassium seems to be taken up in preference to magnesium, or alternatively the magnesium is rendered insoluble in some way. Magnesium deficiency is also worse in areas of strong light: in the case of tomatoes those along the outside areas nearest the glass seem to be the first to show deficiency symptoms.
Magnesium summary Required by all plants and in large amounts by some. Shortage results in interveinal chlorosis, with a yellowing or bronzing of the chlorotic area. Areas most exposed to strong light are usually first affected in a greenhouse. Plants in light soil heavily dressed with potassium are usually prone to magnesium deficiency. Excess is difficult to define, although excess salt concentration with all its side effects will usually result when it is over-supplied.

Calcium

Many authorities do not discuss calcium under plant nutrients, preferring to give this element a special consideration as a neutralizing agent. Calcium is, however, an element needed by plants, especially for the cell walls, apart from its other functions – which are best pursued in a work on chemistry.

The exact causes of acidity in the soil or growing media have been studied for many years and are still not completely understood, but the gardener need merely think in terms of the amount of free lime available to the plants enabling the base exchange mechanism to operate whereby plants obtain their nutrients. A soil or growing medium may contain considerable amounts of calcium, but this may be 'held' by the organic content or humus content of the soil, a situation by no means unique in greenhouse culture, especially with soilless media.

A growing medium not supplied with lime will become considerably more acid, due to the acid-forming activities of micro-organisms and chemical activity.

pH scale The measure of exchangeable calcium in the soil or other media (including of course liquids) is recorded on the well-known pH scale which, for the technically minded, is a logarithm of the calcium ion concentration. The pH scale runs from 1 to 14, most plants falling between about 4.5 and 7 for their particular preferences. However, matters have been further complicated by the lower pH range at which plants, in many cases, seem capable of growing satisfactorily in soilless media, no doubt because of the use of nutrients which are available to the plants without recourse to micro-organism activity. Unfortunately the amount of exchangeable calcium can greatly affect the availability of other nutrients and vice versa. Ammonium and potassium can, for example, immobilize the calcium if present in large quantities, whereas too much calcium can result in insolubility of manganese and iron, and too little can produce calcium toxicity of the same elements. It can be seen therefore that what might appear to be, on the surface, a simple question of acidity and alkalinity with calcium acting as the neutralizing agent, is far from the case. At the same time there is much to be said for ignoring the complexities and pursuing the more simple course of relying on the pH figure, although deeper consideration will be given to the whole matter in a later chapter.
Calcium summary Required in varied amounts by most plants, especially for cell wall formation. Amounts needed vary and this translates itself into adjusting the soil or growing media to a suitable pH figure. Actual shortage of calcium in the plant will result in yellowing of leaves, rather typical of nitrogen shortage, or in extreme cases a whitening of the growing points. It is difficult to consider calcium shortage by itself, as there are so many associated issues involved, the same being true of an excess of calcium of which the yellow-white leaf coloration of iron deficiency is so typical.

Lesser or micro-elements
Sulphur
This element has a general role in plant nutrition, it being difficult to explain its exact function. Sulphur is present initially

in most soils and in addition in many fertilizers used, so its shortage is seldom, if ever, a problem.

Iron

This is an important element in greenhouse culture and is greatly concerned with photosynthesis. It is very insoluble and is rendered still more so by *high* pH figures. Symptoms of shortage are yellowing of the whole leaf, although in extreme cases the leaf can turn white, the older leaves usually being more affected than the younger ones. Deficiency usually arises from an excess of exchangeable calcium in the soil or growing medium. Excess is difficult to detect, no doubt because excess iron combines with phosphorus to form insoluble compounds, but excessive iron application is not to be recommended.

Manganese

Like iron, this is much concerned with photosynthetic activity, which is why any shortage invariably produces a leaf-mottling effect. High pH figures usually spark off any deficiency of this element, although the mottling of the leaves of young plants caused by the invariably high pH figure of many growing composts usually disappears as the pH figure drops. Toxicity of manganese is a much more common problem, particularly in older tomato borders which are steam sterilized. Here a blue–black coloration develops on leaf tips, in addition to a general drooping.

Boron

Much more has been heard of boron in recent years, largely because its importance in tomato culture has been highlighted. It would appear to have a multifarious role to play in plant growth, as its shortage in many plants causes shrivelling of leaf tips and a blueing of stems and petioles. Tomato fruits develop a corky brown layer beneath the skin. In the majority of cases, and with properly formulated growing media, boron deficiency should not arise, although it is obviously an element which can cause considerable trouble. Care should be taken not to use boron to excess, as the efficiency of boron-based weedkillers is well known.

Other elements

The other elements referred to earlier do not usually give cause for great concern unless present in excess, or rendered so by general soil imbalance. There can also be a degree of substitution where the microelement replaces the macro-element, resulting in deficiency symptoms of the latter in some cases, although they may serve admirably; eg silicon can replace phosphorus, and sodium can substitute for potash.

The changing fertilizer scene

The fertilizer scene has changed a great deal in recent years as gardeners have become more knowledgable on the vital issues surrounding plant nutrition. In addition there is increasing enthusiasm for organic growing methods. Addresses to obtain detailed information on organic growing methods are given in the Appendix, as also are some of the firms supplying the chemicals which both organic and conventional gardeners are likely to use. Most well stocked garden centres these days carry a reasonable range of products. It cannot be stressed too strongly, however, to avoid becoming caught up in what could be called a "chemical syndrome" — when every nuance exhibited by the growing plant sets off a warning bell — and the gardener rushes to try and alleviate the trouble by applying another chemical. Variance in plant performance can be due to many circumstances, of which chemical imbalance is merely one, and there must always be some compromise.

Fertilizers for greenhouse culture

The main types of fertilizers and other nutrients for greenhouse culture are shown on the following pages (pp. 95–100). Most fertilizers are now sold in kilograms (kg). In *round* figures, 50kg = 1cwt. Other equivalents the reader may find useful are:

$$1oz/sq\ yd = 28g/sq\ yd$$
$$= 34g/sq\ metre\ (m^2)$$

Main types of fertilizers for greenhouse culture (for additional types see

Fertilizer	N	P_2O_5	K_2O	Other elements	
Hoof and horn meal	12–14%				in tomato ... release of ammonia ... complete release of nitrogen co... over a period. Now expensive. Use up to 136g/m² (4oz per sq yd).
Dried blood	7–12%	1–2%	1%		Organic, a 'safe' top dressing for tomatoes, bulbs and other plants at 34–68g/m² (1–2oz per sq yd) as a quick-acting source of nitrogen. Also useful diluted at up to 13g/l (2oz per gallon) of water as a quick-acting stimulant.
Nitro-Chalk Nitro 26	26%			carbonate of lime in varying amounts.	Inorganic quick-acting sources of nitrogen. Used for border-grown plants requiring an urgent 'boost'. Use cautiously.
Nitra-Shell Nitram	34% 34.5%				Useful where virus check occurs in tomatoes. Use at 17–33g/m² ($\frac{1}{2}$–1oz per sq yd).
Ammonium nitrate	35%				Inorganic. Used as a constituent of liquid fertilizers.
Nitrate of potash or potassium nitrate	13%	44–46%			Inorganic. excellent source of readily available nitrogen. Used as liquid fertilizer—not dry.
Urea	46%				Organic. Main use as a constituent of liquid feeds. Can be used dry at 17g/m² ($\frac{1}{2}$oz per sq yd) as an organic source of nitrogen. The more sophisticated form is urea formaldehyde which releases nitrogen over a period.
Ammonium phosphate	11%	61%			Inorganic. Used mainly in slow-release type fertilizers and seldom as a separate fertilizer.
Bonemeal	1–5%	15–32%			Organic. Not used greatly in greenhouse culture, but would be useful in a soil very low in phosphates, applied in addition to base feed. Use at 100–135g/m² (3–4oz per sq yd). Now expensive.
Superphosphates of lime		18–21% (other forms available)			Inorganic. Best form of phosphates used generally as a constituent of base feeds and in composts. Can be used at up to 135g/m² (4oz per sq yd).

of fertilizers for greenhouse culture—continued

	N	P_2O_5	K_2O	Other elements	Comments & rate of use★
phate of potash			50%		Inorganic. Use dry at 17−34g/m² (1−2) oz per sq yd as quick source of potash. Diluted in water at 6g/litre (1oz per gallon) it is very quick acting.
Epsom salts				magnesium oxide 9%	Inorganic. Use at up to 100–200g/m² (3–6oz per sq yd) for tomatoes Also used as foliar feed at 20g/litre (2lb per 10gal) with a spreader.
Lime (hydrated) ground				calcium oxide analysis variable	The main form of lime used for tomato culture is *ground limestone*, a relatively slow-acting form of calcium. *Magnesian* or *dolomitic limestone* is frequently used for tomato growing as it contains maganesium. Both forms are used according to soil analysis.

★ 1 oz/sq yd = 28g/sq yd or 34g/sq m.

Liquid feeds

These are either in liquid form or for dissolving. A very varied range is available but generally in the following regions:

	Nitrogen N_2	Sol. phos. acid P_2O_5	Potash K_2O	
Chempak (High N)	25	15	15	
Chempak (balanced)	20	20	20	Plus
Chempak (High K)	15	15	30	trace
Chempak (Low N)	12.5	25	25	elements

Important note: There are many proprietary liquid feeds. Use as directed. It is important to check up on the levels of nitrogen, phosphorus and potash, and the balance of these elements to each other in relation to the crop being grown. Tomatoes, for example, relish high potash feeds for the early part of the season, whereas cucumbers require higher nitrogen. Reference is made to this in the respective cropping notes.

Natural or artificial?

There is often a dilemma in gardeners' minds whether they are using natural or artificial chemicals — especially if they are of the organic turn of mind. Organic gardeners do, of course, lay much stress on the use of organically derived materials such as animal manures and garden composts, along with seaweed in natural, meal or calcified form. Then, of course, there are the well known materials such as Bone Meal, Dried Blood, Fish Meal, Hoof and Horn Meal, plus less well known chemicals such as Rock Phosphates and Rock Potash — which are all natural materials — provided they are not contaminated in any way. There are also materials like wood ash, soot, sewage sludge, municipal compost, and of these there can be doubts about sewage sludge (from the disease angle) and municipal compost (for its heavy metal content). Lime is, of course, readily available as ground limestone and is a matural material.

Compound fertilizers

There are many different types of proprietary compound fertilizers available. Typical analysis figures are as follows; it being stressed that these will vary (see Chapter 15).

N	P_2O_5 soluble	insoluble	K_2O	Comments
				(see cultural notes in Part II for rates of application)
12%	5.5%	0.5%	6%	High nitrogen base dressing for crops demanding a 'boost', e.g. lettuce or end-of-season tomatoes
6%	10%	0.5%	17.5%	High potash for tomatoes in heat sterilized soil
9.5%	9%	0.5%	13.2%	More balanced crop dressing for established crops
10.5%	7.5%	0.5%	10.5%	For plants such as chrysanthemums demanding a balanced level of nutrients

N	P_2O_5 soluble	insoluble	K_2O	Magnesium
John Innes Base Fertilizer				
5.2%	7%	0.5%	10%	For John Innes composts see chapter on composts. Also as a base dressing for many crops

Enmag (SAI) – a mixture of magnesium, ammonium phosphate, sulphate of potash

5%	0.5%	17%	9%	8%	Slow-release general base dressing

Q4 (Vitax)

5.3%	6.8%	0.7%	10%	1.75%	Manganese 30.36 mg/litre (ppm)★
					Iron 58.81 mg/litre (ppm)★
					Zinc 42.50 mg/litre (ppm)★
					Copper 30.36 mg/litre (ppm)★
					Boron 15.13 mg/litre (ppm)★
					Molybdenum .41 mg/litre (ppm)★

(★in chelated form) A widely used slow-release dressing especially useful as it contains trace elements. Much used for composts.
Other forms available.

Footnote: mg/litre = parts per million (ppm)

Bulky organics used in crop culture

Precise recommendations regarding use are given in cultural notes, in Part II. Most of these organics contain trace elements in addition to those stated.

Type	Average moisture %	Dry matter %	Approx % in fresh manures			Comments
			Nitrogen (N)	Phosphorus (P)	Potash (K)	
Farmyard manure (FYM)	81	15	0.43	0.19	0.44	Farmyard manure varies. Should be well decomposed. Contains reasonably balanced quantities of the main nutrients. Can be very weedy!
Poultry manure	53	30	2.1	1.21	0.60	High nitrogen content, which can give rise to problems when used too liberally.
Sewage sludge	40–75	65	2.32	1.29	0.25	More useful for crops grown out of doors. Nitrogen content may not be in such an available form as in FYM.
Composted wood bark						This is extremely variable in analysis, especially nitrogen. It is used increasingly in composts (see Ch. 15).
Seaweed	70–80	10–20	0.4–0.8	0.1–0.2	1–2	A useful form of organic matter fairly rich in potash. Use fresh or composted.
Peat*	40–60	97	0.7–3	0.1–0.2	0.1–0.3	Used mainly to 'condition' soils intended for crop cultivation, also as top dressing or mulch, and as the main or sole ingredient of soilless composts. The pH of peat is in the 3.5–4.5 range; sedge peats have a higher pH.

* Peat is now sold entirely by bulk:

1 bushel = 8 gallons = 36 litres

21 bushels = 1 cu yd

27 bushels = 1 cu metre

Important Note. As the use of peat for horticultural purposes is increasingly under pressure from environmentalists, many alternative forms of organic matter are coming onto the market. These include coconut pith (coir), composted timber waste, composted forest bark, composted paper etc. See Chapter 15 for more details.

Small propagators are very useful — this 40 watt thermostatically controlled unit taking two standard sized seed trays.

Pelargoniums are one of the most popular plants grown and they produce a wealth of growth ideal for taking cuttings.

Liquid organics—seaweed

The use of liquefied seaweed offers an excellent organic source of macro- and micro- elements in readily available form. One such is marketed by Maxicrop, and is very popular with organic gardeners. It has a wide range of uses, including straw bale treatment for tomatoes and cucumbers. A special feature of seaweed-based liquid feeds is that they contain the complete spectrum of nutrient content. An increase in pest and disease resistance is thought to be an important feature of seaweed-based fertilizers.

Liquid Feeds Supplying Nitrogen, Phosphorus and Potassium Fertilizers

Liquid feed nutrient ratio $N:P_2O_5:K_2O$	Oz/gal and g per litre of stock solution						ppm (mg/litre) in 1/200 dilution		
	Nitrate of potash		Mono-ammonium phosphate		Ammonium nitrate				
	oz/gal	g/l	oz/gal	g/l	oz/gal	g/l	N	P_2O_5	K_2O
2:1:1	10	65	7	48	20	131	300	150	150
2:1:2	17	110	6	41	14	91	250	125	250
2:1:3	24	155	6	39	10	66	240	120	360
2:1:4	29	186	5	35	6	42	215	108	430
2:1:5	31	198	4	30	3	21	180	90	450
1:1:1	17	110	13	8	12	76	250	250	250
1:1:2	29	183	10	68	4	29	210	210	420
1:1:3	38	241	9	60	—	0	195	185	555

Liquid Feeds with Nitrogen and Potassium Fertilizers

Liquid feed $N:K_2O$	Oz/gal and + g per litre of stock solution				ppm (mg/litre) in 1/200 dilution	
	Nitrate of potash		Ammonium nitrate			
	oz/gal	g/l	oz/gal	g/l	N	K_2O
2:1	10	65	23	149	300	250
1:1	18	114	17	109	260	260
1:1.5	24	156	12	80	240	360
1:2	28	179	8	52	205	410
1:2.5	31	176	4	31	180	450
1:3	35	224	2	15	170	515
1:3.5	41	261	—	0	170	600

+ g per litre = 1g in 1,000g which equals 1lb per 100 gallons (1,000lb)

CHAPTER 13

Soil & Compost Analysis

Most soil analysis procedures are based on the extraction of nutrients with an extractant which attempts to estimate the quantity of nutrient that the plant itself can extract from the soil or growing media. Whether the results of the analysis truly reflect the quantities of nutrients *actually available* to the plants is a matter of some conjecture.

This does not mean that soil analysis procedures can be set aside lightly, as they do have considerable value if interpreted correctly and linked to practical growing experience.

Testing 'kits'

Several different types of 'kits' are available: (a) litmus papers which indicate alkalinity or acidity when dipped into wet soil; (b) a series of litmus papers which indicate the approximate pH of the soil; (c) indicator fluids which, when used either separately with a solution of soil and water or with barium sulphate as a precipitant, give a remarkably accurate pH figure by comparison with a colour chart; (d) complete testing outfits which, by use of indicator fluids and colour comparison give, in addition to the pH figure, the relative availability or percentage deficiency of the three main elements — nitrogen, phosphorus and potash; in some cases magnesium, too, is indicated; (e) pH and 'salt' meters.

The value of these kits and meters is that they give a fairly accurate indication of the fertility of a soil or growing medium without the inevitable wait associated with laboratory analysis. It should be pointed out, however, that the kits and meters do not work entirely on the extraction principle and therefore do not indicate the *available* levels of nutrients in the soil but rather the total amounts of *soluble* nutrients.

Laboratory analysis

The availability of free laboratory analysis services varies greatly, but it is unlikely that there are any areas in Britain where laboratory analysis is not available on payment of a fee. The range of services carried out also differs according to the body concerned, but the following are the most important issues:

Organic matter Where a *soil*-based media for growing is involved, the percentage of organic matter is a useful figure, especially for border cultivation. Figures of 8–10% (*including moisture*) are average, although some soils may have figures as high as 15–16%, or indeed much higher. The significance of the organic matter content of soilless growing media will be discussed later.

Any gardener with a small crucible and accurate scientific-type scales can note the weight difference in a soil sample before and after combustion over a gas jet, and, by calculation, find out the percentage of organic matter content, which will include the moisture content unless the soil is oven-dried beforehand.

Lime requirement Exchangeable calcium is determined by several means, but usually by a pH meter, when lime requirement is then calculated by reference to a chart prepared by a series of buffering experiments. Most bodies report not only the pH figure, but the amount of calcium carbonate (ground limestone) necessary to achieve the required pH which will vary according to the plant species concerned. Small meters give an immediate reading of pH.

Available nitrogen This is not a test carried out by every laboratory unless specially requested, as it varies so considerably according to temperature, season, whether soil has been heat sterilized, and other related issues. The analyst usually states whether his test indicates high, medium or low availability and either (mg/litre) p.p.m. or index factors, e.g. 51–150 mg/litre (ppm.) = Index 2.

Available phosphorous (P$_2$O$_5$ or P) This is reported as mg/litre (ppm) P, or index factor; also stated as low, medium or high. Index factor P:4–5 is standard for most greenhouse crops; below this, phosphorous is needed; above 4–5 little phosphorous required.

Available potassium: (K$_2$O or K) This is reported in similar fashion to phosphorus mg/litre (ppm) K, or index factor; also stated as low, medium or high.

Index factor K:4–5 is standard for greenhouse crops.

NOTE: *Exact* conversions from P$_2$O$_5$ to P and K$_2$O to K and vice versa are complicated by differing extraction methods.

Magnesium Some bodies now report magnesium, usually as an index factor, levels of around 3–5 being normal.

Soluble salt This is a very important issue in greenhouse culture and is usually stated as low, normal or high. Some laboratories quote the figure as pC while others quote CF, the respective values of which are as follows, the index factor also being stated to give their true significance. Index 3 is the safe level for most greenhouse plants, up to 4 for tomatoes and chrysanthemums, but above this level there is danger of damage. Most analytical bodies now report conductivity figures in μmhos. Index 3–5 = μmhos 2610–3000. These figures are equal to approximately pC 2.8–3.00, or CF 15–10. It cannot be over-emphasized how important these figures are; spot checks should be carried out on a regular basis before and after planting on a large scale. Salt concentration meters are considered a good investment by commercial growers, especially for checking the salt concentration of liquid feeds, and also of growing media to ensure even distribution of the fertilizers. It is vital that all laboratory analysis be interpreted by the analysing body who will generally give advice on the nutrient needs of the particular crop or crops or purpose concerned.

Spectrochemical analysis

This is used for determining the levels of trace elements in both soil and plant tissue. The elements mainly concerned are *zinc,* *manganese, copper and iron.* Spectrochemical analysis is generally used as a further check following normal soil analysis, more so with plant tissue than with soils.

Tissue analysis

In addition to spectrochemical analysis for the trace elements, tissue analysis ensures that the plant is assimilating the correct amount of nutrient. It is generally necessary to carry out a comparison between normal and abnormal tissue. Tissue analysis is becoming very much a part of commercial growing in countries such as the U.S.A. and increasingly in the U.K.

Observation of cultures

Fungal and other cultures are developed under laboratory conditions in specimens of soil. It is claimed that these methods give a much more accurate account of the nutrient levels actually available to the plant, as compared with those determined chemically. Visual assessment of actual plant response still remains a vital part of plant nutrition, and can be learned only by practical experience.

Eelworm determination

Soil or growing media infested with the cysts of the potato cyst eelworm *Globodera (Heterodera) rostochiensis* are unsuitable for the culture of tomatoes, potatoes and other solanaceous plants, which crops it attacks with equal severity. A determination of the number of cysts per gramme (or 100g) of soil or growing media can be made by most advisory bodies, along with a similar statement of the number containing live larvae.

Taking samples of growing media

It is essential that any samples sent for analysis are representative of the main bulk of the growing media. For a greenhouse border, several small samples should be taken with a trowel, auger or other instrument, from a uniform depth of around 13–15cm (5–6in) Bulked together the sample should weigh about 1kg(2lb) Where batches of compost are being made up, the same basic procedure should be followed, selecting small quantities of the media from various parts of the heap and bulking them together. It is sometimes advisable to have the basic ingredients analysed before mixing, especially if there is any doubt about extreme acidity, toxicity or other factors. Samples should be placed in a strong paper or polythene bag and clearly labelled for dispatch to the laboratory. One sample of 1kg (2lb) will generally suffice for some 100m^2 (1,000 sq ft) of border. Always label samples clearly with the exact location and source, and give previous cropping history, if any, and proposed cropping programme, as this will assist the advisory body to give any corrective treatment that may prove to be necessary.

Analysis of solid or liquid fertilizers

Quality control is very strict at the manufacturing stage for all solid or liquid fertilizers, and analysis is seldom necessary, except in the case of doubtful identity. The checking of diluted liquid feeds for salt concentration (pC or CF) is useful, particularly if a doubtful dilutor/dilution method is involved.

Examination of soil for weeds, pests and diseases

It would obviously be folly to use a soil known to contain pests, diseases or weeds, yet it is not always possible to tell visually whether a soil or 'clean' or not, or for that matter to carry out sterilization. The larger pests like wireworms, leatherjackets and other pests can of course be observed when working with the soil in any way, and particularly if putting it through a riddle or screen prior to mixing up a compost. Vegetative underground portions of many perennial weeds such as couch grass, horsetail, coltsfoot and others can also be fairly readily detected by visual examination, even if not specifically. Smaller pests and diseases, however, can seldon be detected visually, most of the disease organisms or spores being microscopic in size. It is not always feasible to examine soil for the presence of disease using the usual pathological techniques of plating and incubation, although an indicator plant could be grown and later sectioned and examined if a pathological service is able and willing to carry out this work. Kits to detect common soilborne diseases are now available. There is now also a laboratory test for detecting club root disease. Usually the previous history of a soil or growing media gives a good indication of what to look for in the way of both pests and diseases, and if in any doubt it is folly to use a doubtful growing medium unless it can be sterilized.

Where a 'new' soil is involved and there is some idea of the cropping pattern carried out in that soil previously, then this also gives guidance. If in any doubt about soil, or to make doubly sure that no trouble does overtake the plants which will be grown in it, the obvious answer, where possible, is to sterilize it either by heat or chemical means. Alternatively, prepared compost can be bought in.

The increasing popularity of soilless mixes owes much to the cleanliness of the basic ingredients (peat, sand or peat alternative) and to the fact that sterilization is seldom, if ever, necessary. Peats, however, can carry rhizoctonia root rots which affect a wide range of plants. Peat can also contain weeds.

CHAPTER 14
Sterilization of Soil

The advantage of using a growing medium free of damaging pests, diseases and weeds cannot be over-emphasized in all spheres of greenhouse culture.

Soil sickness is a term which is difficult if not impossible to define accurately. Organic gardening adherents claim that soil sickness can be avoided by practising organic husbandry principles, so maintaining a soil 'in balance'. While this is an admirable solution, it gives rise to practical problems. Copious and regular supplies of properly made compost must be available, and even then there can often be a 'wait' period before the considerable forces of nature exert their influence, this taking longer than many gardeners have patience for.

Crop rotation principles for border grown crops would obviously do much to prevent the soil becoming sick in the first case, yet without a mobile or easily portable greenhouse, this cannot readily be accomplished. The use of a new soil or growing medium does of course achieve the same object, and provide the plants with an ideal start. This is why, under many circumstances, a strong case can be made out for container-growing of crops such as tomatoes.

The other answer is to pasteurize the soil, endeavouring to rectify the ills, while leaving behind beneficial elements to function to full advantage. The term sterilization is most frequently used in this connection, whereas partial sterilization or pasteurization would be more accurate. *Sterilization implies rendering the growing media completely sterile, which would give rise to many problems with a soil-containing medium. Nevertheless it is a term which will be used for convenience.*

Sterilization of soil or soilless media can take several different forms, all of which have their limitations and drawbacks. The sterilized medium is not rendered immune from future trouble; it may in fact be more prone to invasion because competing organisms will have been killed off in the sterilizing process. But heat sterilization in most of its forms does help to render plant toxins soluble, so that they can be washed but, the same being true of toxic fertilizer residues; organic matter is usually broken down by heat sterilization, rendering it more palatable to micro-organisms as a ready source of food. Perhaps the most significant advantage is in the survival of the thicker-walled spore forming ammonifying bacteria which, in the absence of competition, re-establish themselves completely uninhibited, resulting in a great flood of ammonia.

One vital aspect of sterilization is that there are limits to the degree of penetration achieved over the growing medium. In the case of a greenhouse border, it is only practical to sterilize the top 25—30cm (10—12in) of soil; if the lower depths contain pests and diseases they can act as a potent source of trouble for deep rooted crops. Virus disease of tomatoes, for example, can remain in the lower depths of a greenhouse border, ready to infect a subsequent tomato crop, even when the top 25—30 (10—12in) is sterilized, as the roots soon penetrate into the subsoil. Sterilization can only be considered as 100% efficient in connection with culture in troughs and containers, preferably when the ingredients of compost are being prepared for formulation—and even then contamination from airborne spores or pests cannot be either ensured or ignored.

Sterilization by heat

Most pests, diseases and weeds in both vegetative and seed form have a temperature at which they are organically destroyed, the same being true of micro-organisms. The temperature aimed at during partial sterilization, while taking into account the destruction temperatures of various organisms, also bears some relation to the sheer practicality of applying a certain temperature range. The boiling point of water is 100°C (212°F) and it is neither practical nor desirable greatly to exceed this. It is in this temperature range that most sterilization processes operate, and recourse to a detailed reference book on fungal and virus diseases will show that such a temperature range is highly effective. Indeed many of the weaker parasitic diseases are destroyed at temperatures as low as 54−60°C (130−150°F); but many virus diseases require fully 92°C (200°F) to be completely destroyed, the same being true of the eelworm cysts *Globodera rostochiensis*.

One of the greatest problems when applying a heat process to a soil or growing media is achieving a uniform temperature throughout the bulk. It merely requires the centre of a lump of soil to remain at low temperature for it to act as a potent source of re-infection for the sterilized area of the growing medium. Over-sterilization also raises problems of sterility and formation of toxic substances. Obviously too it is undesirable to incorporate doubtful bulky organics, especially farmyard manure, until they also have been sterilized although it is common practice not to sterilize them.

The moisture content of a growing medium will greatly affect the passage of heat and the degree of penetration achieved in a given time.

Methods of applying steam
Hoddesdon grid method (Fig. 42)
Named after the town of Hoddesdon, Herts, where the system was originally

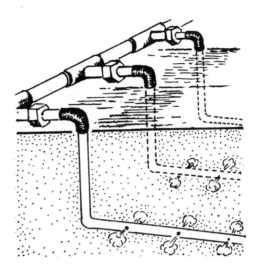

Fig. 42 Hoddesdon Grid. The basic principle of this steaming method is to dispense steam evenly through the soil or medium being sterilized.

developed at the then existing Cheshunt Research Station, this process is used for borders in commercial greenhouses and involves the leading of steam under pressure into perforated steel pipes laid below the soil surface, which has previously been rendered moist and friable by deep cultivation. The many technicalities connected with the grid process can be studied in detail in *Ministry of Agriculture Bulletin No. 22*. The sheer cost of providing steam and the labour for digging in the grids have caused concern in recent years.

Lately mobile steam systems of various designs have been developed for commercial growers and there are gardeners who have improvised, but it should be pointed out that steam can be a very dangerous thing and must be treated with respect.

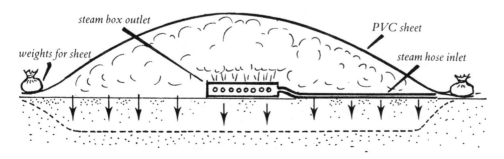

Fig. 43 Sheet steaming. A low-labour method of sterilizing border soil for growing areas.

Sheet steaming (Fig. 43)

This process was developed originally in the Netherlands and involves leading pressurized steam into either a coffin-type box with outlet holes or perforated hosepipe under a heavy grade PVC sheet secured at the edges by long sandbags or other means. With a boiler output of 454kg (1,000lb) steam per hour it is possible to sheet steam an area of approximately 75–93m² (800–1,000sq ft) in one operation.

One of the obvious advantages of sheet steaming over the grid method is the tremendous saving in labour, whereas its main disadvantage lies in the difficulty of achieving adequate penetration of the steam, which may take several hours to reach sufficient depth.

Low pressure steam sterilization

This has much more application for smaller growers, professional and amateur gardeners, although it is doubtful whether the setting up of the apparatus can now be merited in view of ready and reasonably cheap availability of prepared composts. When the John Innes composts were originally formulated and the specifications laid down, the John Innes low pressure sterilizers were built in their thousands all over Britain (see Fig. 44). Here shredded loam was evenly spread in a 25–30cm (10–12in) layer on perforated steel sheeting over a shallow tray of water kept boiling by a coal fire, the steam passing slowly through the soil, being trapped by a tarpaulin or sack covering (now PVC). It took several hours

for the soil at the top of the layer to reach the necessary 82–88°C (180–190°F) and careful checking was necessary to ensure that the whole batch of soil was evenly sterilized. Various models were available, most of which are no longer manufactured; low pressure sterilizers are now usually improvised.

Another form of steam sterilization is to drench shallow layers of soil on a clean surface with boiling water, covering with clean sacks or PVC sheets to retain the heat. On a still smaller scale suspending small sacks of soil in the steam given off by a water boiler can be remarkably successful. The efficiency of all these methods depends much upon the care which is exercised in ensuring even distribution of temperature.

Dry heat sterilization

By the application of dry heat to the soil at a sufficiently high temperature, its moisture content is converted to steam. The crudest form of this method is the use of a fire under a sheet of metal on which is placed a shallow layer of soil. The soil should be wet and care must be taken not to over-sterilize it. It is usual to stir the soil constantly to keep it from 'burning'. The careful use of a flame gun can achieve the same result if the wet soil is spread in a shallow layer on a clean surface.

Rotary drum sterilizers rely on sterilization at 'flash point', the soil being rotated round a metal drum and falling through a fierce flame. The angle of the drum determines the number of times the soil is subjected to 'flash point' heat before being ejected out of the other end of the drum. The efficiency of rotary drum sterilizers depends not only on the correct adjustment of the burner and the angle of the rotating drum, but very much on the moisture content of the soil, which if too wet will 'ball' badly. Conversely if the soil is too dry it tends to 'burn', which destroys its structure. The ejected soil must be carefully checked to ensure that it has reached a temperature of at least 71–76°C (160–170°F) and that this is maintained in the heap for a reasonable period. Where potato cyst eelworm or virus is a problem, higher sterilization temperatures are advisable.

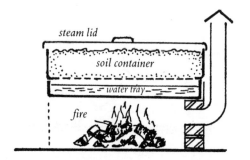

Fig. 44 Low pressure soil sterilizers. John Innes low pressure sterilizers can be built by an enthusiast.

Electric soil sterilizers are available in different sizes, the soil being heated by panel type elements to a uniform 82°C (180°F); although the soil in the vicinity of the panels may be overheated and rendered sterile, it is soon reconstituted by the bulk of soil.

Chemical soil sterilization

Various chemicals are used for this purpose, and *in commercial spheres* these have become extremely popular for economic reasons. They are also useful for the amateur gardener, but great care must be taken to follow the directions implicitly. The fumes, however, can be toxic to young plants, which raises problems in greenhouses where there is mixed cropping.

The chemicals, to be effective, must give off gas which is sufficiently toxic to ensure the destruction of pests, diseases and weeds, yet without harming the beneficial organisms in the soil. The efficiency of chemical sterilization varies greatly, not because of the precise chemicals involved, but because of the condition of the soil, its moisture content and, most important, the prevailing temperature. You should also ensure even distribution in the soil to be sterilized.

Formaldehyde This is reasonably effective on some fungal diseases, but relatively ineffective against many pests. It is used at a strength of 1 part formalin 38–40% to 49 parts water (approximately 0.5 litre in 25 litres or 1 pint to 6 gallons) and the soil is

Sterilization chart *(Note the regulations affecting availability and use of chemicals)*

Material	Root Eelworm Root-Knot Eelworm	Root Rots	Fusarium and verti-cillium wilts	(TMV) and Mosaic Virus	Damping-off diseases	Weeds	Treatment to planting or use in days on average
Chloropicrin	X	C	C	X	C	X	20
Chloropicrin + Methyl Bromide Methyl Bromide	C	C	P	X	C	C	4
D-D Telone by injection	C	X	X	X	X	X	18–20
Cresylic Acid Phenol & Tar oil (Jeyes fluid)	P	X	P	X	C	X	40
Formaldehyde	X	P	P	X	P	X	20–40
Metham Sodium Dazomet Basamid	C/P	C	P	X	C	C	40
Steam, dry heat (correctly applied), water above 180°F/82°C	C	C	C	C	C	C	7–14
Rotary drum sterilizer	As per steam						

C = control   P = partial control   X = no control

Only a few of these chemicals are freely available to amateurs. These include Jeyes fluid, Armillatox and possibly Formaldehyde. Serious gardeners can perhaps use Basamid by co-operation with professional horticulturists under their guidance.

thoroughly drenched—approximately 23 litres (5 gallons) being required per m^2 (square yard) to 23cm (9in) depth. There is a wait period of 20–40 days according to temperature (which must be sufficiently high otherwise the formaldehyde will become polymerized) before the soil can be used.

Phenols, Cresylic Acid etc. Various forms are available such as 'Sterizal' (phenol), Brays Emulsion and Armillatox (cresylic acid), also Jeyes fluid (tar oil plus vegetable oil). They should be used according to directions, noting the 'wait' period and using enough of the mixed material to thoroughly drench the soil or growing media. These materials vary in their effectiveness against pests and diseases and are possibly more effective against pests with some fungal action. (See chart).

Other chemicals used commercially or by approved contractors are Chloropicrin, Chloropicrin + Methyl Bromide, Dazomet, Basamid (granular Dazomet), D-D Fumigant (mainly for eelworm), 1, 3 – Dichloropropane Metham Sodium. Of these, Basamid (Dazomet Granular) is probably the most widely used as it is in a convenient dust-free prill (a coarse powder) in 5kg packs. It is used at the rate of 1kg per 28–30m^2 (1½lb per 20 sq yd). It must be thoroughly mixed with the top 20cm (8in) of damp soil, ideally by rotary cultivator or in heaps of damp soil or growing media spread out on a clean surface in shallow layers. Note the rates of applications can vary. Soil or compost ingredients should be moderately moist and at a temperature of around 9.5°C (49–50°F).

While a form of sealing can be carried out by applying water to the surface, it is better to cover the area or material being sterilized with a clean plastic sheet for several weeks, as this contains the fumes at a toxic level. All these chemicals must be used strictly according to directions, which generally state that the soil should be cultivated, the sterilants applied and, with the powdered or prilled form, rotovated in before 'sealing' with water.

To ensure that these chemicals are effective, the termperature of the soil should ideally be above 9.5°C (49–50°F). The soil should be rotary cultivated or forked to release the fumes after a few weeks. Heaps of potting soil can be treated with chemicals in the same way as border soil. Methyl bromide has found favour in recent years because of its effectiveness on pests and diseases and also its rapid dissipation. *It must be applied by a contractor.* There are recent complaints about water pollution where methyl bromide is used and restrictions on use may be pending.

Checking for chemical sterilants

Cress tests using duplicated wide mouth glass jars are useful techniques for checking whether chemically treated soil is free of sterilizing chemicals. Fill one jam jar with untreated soil and another with treated soil. Scatter cress seed lightly in both jars and seal them, or suspend wet balls of cotton wool dipped in cress seed on wires above the soil. In both cases compare germination.

It is stressed that most of the chemicals mentioned are not intended for use by amateur gardeners. Certain chemicals require a certificate of competence on the part of the user before they can be obtained and used. Refer to a current copy of Pesticides (MAFF) for further information.

The information given in the chart should not be taken too literally, due to the varying conditions of soil, temperature, evenness and depth of incorporation etc.

CHAPTER 15
Greenhouse Growing Composts

The need for good compost

The soil in the garden is usually satisfactory for growing plants there but it is not so suitable for use as a growing medium in pots or boxes, particularly under intensive culture under glass. The reason is that the soil will settle into a compacted state in the pot, especially when watered continually. In the garden the soil is constantly being turned and agitated by the action of worms and insect life within the soil (not to mention larger beings using a spade or hoe!) but these creatures are not generally present in the plant pot, the result being that the soil settles, becomes inadequately aerated and therefore increasingly difficult for water to penetrate; growth will be poor and eventually the plant may die. It is therefore necessary to improve the soil as a growing medium if it is to be used successfully in a pot. This is normally done by the addition of suitable materials to the basic soil and by correct treatment, but more recently composts made without soil have become important.

The John Innes Composts

In 1939 W.J.C. Lawrence and J. Newell of the John Innes Horticultural Institution published the results of their intensive research into the characteristics of compost, and the John Innes Composts, which were to revolutionize the growing of plants in pots and boxes, were born. The gardener for the first time had standard formulae that could be reasonably well reproduced and when properly used would give excellent results. Prior to this, he had had no means of deciding what particular factor a failure might be due to, whether it was a bad loam or diseased leaf-mould and so on. The ingredients of these composts were neither expensive nor difficult to obtain at that time, and the mixing of them was a comparatively simple job which did not require the use of such variable material as stable manure or leaf-mould.

There are two basic JI composts, one for seed sowing and one for potting, differing in their physical and nutrient make up. Two were considered necessary because of the differing conditions required. In the seed sowing composts, the structure had to be free-draining so that the compost was warm and free of excess moisture which can cause rotting. The potting compost was more moisture retentive but still well aerated to ensure good root action.

The basic formulae are given here for the mixes but the specifications of the individual raw materials given later must be studied. These are well and strictly defined so that the composts will be as uniform as possible.

Seed compost

This consists of two parts sterilized loam, one part peat and one part sand, by volume (i.e. using containers of known size). To this is added superphosphate of lime at 1g/litre (1½oz) per bushel and chalk or ground limestone at 0.5g/litre (¾oz) per bushel (36 litres/8 gallons). Metrication has embraced composts more than many other spheres of horticulture and soilless types are now invariably sold in litres. There are 36 litres in one bushel.

During their early life, most of the nutrients required by seedlings are present within the seed itself but phosphates are required for the growth of new cells and good root action. The chalk is added to neutralize the acidity of the peat.

Potting composts

The formula for John Innes potting compost No 1 strength is shown overleaf.
The No 2 strength was made by adding double the amount of John Innes base and chalk, ie 6g/litre (8oz) and 1g/litre (1½oz)

Parts by volume			
7 sterilized loam	J.I. base	3g/litre (4oz)	per bushel of compost
	chalk	0.5g/litre (¾oz)	
3 peat	+	or	
	J.I. base	3.2 kg/m³ (5lb)	per cu yd of compost
2 sand	chalk	800g/m³ (1lb)	

per bushel respectively, and the potting compost No 3 by adding three times the amounts, ie 12oz of John Innes base and 1.5g/litre (2¼oz) of chalk per bushel of compost.

It should be noted that a mix of say 7 bushels of loam, 3 bushels of peat and 2 bushels of sand will not in all probability yield 12 bushels of compost and correspondingly if calculating in litres. The reason is that particles of loam and sand will enter the pore spaces in the peat, thus reducing the volume of compost produced. Therefore, the compost volume, *after* mixing, will have to be measured or estimated, and the John Innes base and chalk added at the rates given above per actual bushel or cu yd of compost produced (see measurement of volume below).

For certain acid-loving plants such as the heathers (*Erica* varieties), etc, a special acid compost may be used. It is known as the John Innes seedling compost (A), the A standing for acid. As the name indicates, it is prepared by making the normal J.I. seed compost—2 parts sterilized loam, one part peat and one part sand, but the lime is omitted and replaced by 1g/litre (¾oz) of flowers of sulphur per bushel of compost. The pH should then be between 5.0 and 6.0.

Measurement of volume
The most common unit of measurement of composts and their raw materials is the bushel. This is a volume, and one bushel is defined as 2,200cu in. For convenience, a standard bushel box may be made or purchased having a standard size 55 × 25 × 25cm (22 × 10 × 10in). One bushel is roughly equivalent to 36 litres (8 gallons) and, therefore, for convenience a bucket containing a 9 litres (2 gallon) mark may be used for measuring smaller quantities of compost ingredients as this represents one quarter of a bushel.

The other standard measurement of compost volume is the m³ or cubic yard. This is a volume of 1m × 1m × 1m (36 × 36 ×36in) and there are 21.7 bushels in a cu yd and 27 bushels (1000 litres) in a cubic metre. This unit is rather large for the amateur and working with litre or bushels is probably adequate for most purposes. *Most compost in Europe is now sold in litres.*

Specifications and preparation of the raw materials – loam

The main ingredient of a John Innes compost is the loam. It gives the compost body, and its chief function is to supply the clay and actively decomposing humus which are so essential for good plant growth.

A loam is defined as a soil in which the porportions of sand, silt and clay are well balanced, typically 7–27% clay, 28–50% silt with less than 52% sand. A medium loam contains just enough clay to be slightly greasy when smeared between the fingers without being sticky. A light loam contains a greater amount of sand, and heavy loam a greater amount of clay. A medium loam should be used for a John Innes Compost; light, heavy and chalky loams should not be used; medium loam will have a good crumb structure and is usually a little acid (pH 5.5–6.3). The loam may be obtained either from arable or pasture land and is therefore known as arable loam and turf or garden loam.

The best loam is turf loam, which is the product obtained when turves cut from a *good* pasture on a loam soil are stacked in a heap until the grass and some of the roots have rotted. The turves should be cut from the top 10–13cm (4–5in) of turf and soil, and measure roughly 30 × 23cm (12 × 9in) for stacking.

Standardization of the loam
The clay content is reasonably well stan-

dardized by choosing a medium or medium-heavy loam, and the humus content by choosing a turf loam as described above.

The pH value of the loam must be standardized to 6.3 (including moisture). If the soil is more acid than 6.3, ie if its pH is below this figure, calcium carbonate must be added in the form of ground limestone or chalk. For medium-heavy loams, the approximate amount of calcium carbonate in g/m^2 (oz per sq yd), for every 23cm (9in) depth of turves is (6.3−pH of loam) × 23. For example, if the pH of the loam is 5.8, the calculation is:

$$(6.3-5.8) = 0.05 \times 760 = 380g/m^2$$
$$(6.3-5.8) \times 23 = 0.5 \times 23 = 11.5oz \text{ per sq yd}$$

Therefore, as the loam is stacked (as detailed below), for every 23cm (9in) depth of turves 380g (11½oz) of calcium carbonate should be evenly applied per m^2/sq yd. For medium loams the formula should be altered to:

$$6.3 - pH \times 594 \text{ g/m}^2$$
$$6.3 - pH \times 18 \text{ oz/yd}^2$$

The standardization of the pH of the loam is essential as excess acidity is a common cause of poor growth in pot plants.

The stacking

It is preferable to cut the turves in late spring or early summer as at these times the grass is thick and lush. The stack, which should not be more than 1.8m (6ft) in height or width, is built up in 12cm (4½in) layers (the approximate thickness of the cut turves). On top of the first layer is added a 5cm (2in) layer of strawy animal manure or half-composted straw, on the next layer the lime is spread evenly−and so on alternately, until the stack is completed. The straw layer assists in the aeration of the stack and serves as an activator by providing a ready supply of bacteria. As moisture is essential to encourage rapid rotting the turves should be thoroughly wetted with a hosepipe as stacking proceeds. Finally, the stack is covered against rain and is left undisturbed for about six months. At the end of this time the grass should have decomposed, the pH should have standardized to 6.3, and the whole thing dried out.

When the stack is being broken down, it should be cut with a spade downwards from the top to bottom so that mixing of the layers occurs to ensure a uniform material. The soil is sieved through a 1cm (⅜in)sieve and it is then ready for sterilization. Care should be taken that the soil is not unnecessarily contaminated.

Sterilization

This is necessary to ensure that the compost is free from harmful pests and diseases. Only the loam requires sterilization, and it has been found that heating to 82°C (180°F) for ten minutes reduces the likelihood of high ammonia levels in the compost. The soil should be brought up to this temperature and cooled as quickly as possible.

Peat

The type of peat recommended for use in JI composts is known as granulated sphagnum moss peat. It should be graded so that most of the particles are of approximately 3cm (⅛in) in size. Normally, this type of peat has a pH of between 3.5 and 4.0. Other peats, including sedge peat, are not recommended, although possibly cheaper. After purchase keep it dry and clean under cover so that it cannot be contaminated by weed seeds floating about in the air. Because it is comparatively sterile, it is not necessary to sterilize the peat before use in the compost.

Sand

As with the other raw materials, the sand should be chosen with care as its structure contributes much to the drainage of the compost and to its aeration. It should be grit/sand, clean, chemically inert, and sharp with little or no clay, silt, lime (such as sea shells) or organic matter. Between 60 and 70% of the particles should be 3−1.5mm (⅛−1/16in), a typical grit/sand being sold as 3mm (⅛in) down. Builder's sand and sea sand are usually too fine. To ease mixing, the sand should be dry. It does not require sterilization.

The food supply−John Innes base

To grow plants well the compost must contain an adequate and well-balanced food supply. John Innes base is made up of three fertilizers in the following proportions:

    2 parts by weight hoof and horn, $\frac{1}{8}$in grist (13% nitrogen)

    2 parts by weight superphosphate (18% phosphoric acid)

    1 part by weight sulphate of potash (48% to 50% potash)

It may be made up by the amateur from the raw materials or it may be purchased ready mixed. The analysis of the complete fertilizer is 5.1% nitrogen, 7.2% phosphate and 9.7% potash. Note that no magnesium or trace elements were added as these were presumed to be adequately supplied by the loam.

Mixing and storing compost

The loam, with its pH standardized, has been sieved and sterilized. The peat from a compressed bale should be broken up by rubbing through a 9mm ($\frac{3}{8}$in) sieve. Because it is usually very dry, the peat should be wetted, using a watering can or hosepipe, otherwise it may cause a temporary check to growth.

After the careful selection and preparation of the compost ingredients it would be senseless to spoil the compost by poor mixing. The correct method for hand-mixing is to spread the sterilized loam a few centimetres (inches) deep evenly over the mixing floor (which should be clean) with the moistened peat on top of the loam and the dry sand last. Part of the sand is kept back and the fertilizers and chalk added to this and thoroughly mixed. This pre-mixes the fertilizer and chalk in some of the sand and makes their distribution through the compost easier and more even. The mixed sand and fertilizer is then spread as evenly as possible over the top of the rest of the sand. The pile of ingredients is cut down and turned over three or four times with a spade. When turning the soil over, it is important to scatter it as widely as possible, not just throw a shovelful from place to place. It cannot be stressed too much that the compost should be mixed as evenly as possible. Alternatively, a mechanical mixer, such as a concrete mixer, may be used.

Enough compost may be mixed for several weeks' use but it is not desirable to store compost for more than one month. *In no case should it be stored for longer than six weeks or harmful ammonia fumes will build up from the breakdown of the hoof and horn meal and cause damage to the plants.* Commercially formulated brands of John Innes compost have in some cases substituted the hoof and horn meal for slow release bases, which means that in theory the compost can be stored for some time. Temperature of storage is still an important factor, however, and every effort should be made to store compost under cool conditions.

The disadvantages of soil-based composts

The John Innes composts had a profound effect on the quality of greenhouse and pot plants and on the success rate of growing them.

However, there are disadvantages with these composts today that were not so apparent in the early years of their use. They are as follows:

1 There is an increasing difficulty in obtaining turf loam. When it is obtainable it is often of indifferent quality and rather variable, producing results that may be disappointing.

2 The cost of loam is increasing because of the labour involved, and therefore not only is the compost becoming more expensive, but undesirable short cuts in production are practised.

3 Because it is based on soil, the compost tends to be heavy to move and its transport is costly.

4 The composts will not store as they become toxic due to the release of ammonia.

5 There is no source of readily available nitrogen (nitrate), magnesium or trace elements. It is presumed that the loam will provide these but this is not always a valid assumption, especially nowadays.

If a good reliable source of loam can be found, the John Innes composts are satisfactory. They have stood the test of time and do have advantages, among them the gradual release of water and nutrients to the plants. However, for many commercial growers and gardeners the disadvantages outweigh the advantages.

The development of soilless composts

The first pioneering work on soilless composts to make a big impact on the horticultural world was that done at the University of California and published in 1957. In fact, soilless composts are frequently referred to as UC composts or mixes (the UC standing for the University of California), even if they are not in fact following any UC formulae. Work was begun in the Department of Plant Pathology at the University of California, L.A., in 1941 to find a better compost for growing plants in containers. Because of the difficulty of finding turf for composting and problems of toxicity after steaming, the John Innes method was not satisfactory and a substitute had to be found.

The UC composts

Eventually five basic compost mixes were evolved, ranging from all peat to all sand, with varying proportions of each in between. To these basic composts could be added one of six fertilizer formulae, three containing readily available nitrogen in the form of potassium nitrate and the others reserve, or longer-availability nitrogen.

When the UC system was first tried in Britain it was not very successful. It must be remembered that these composts were developed for conditions in California where the climate is distinctly Mediterranean. In Britain the lower temperature and light intensity resulted in nitrogen starvation in plants in UC composts as the breakdown rate of organic nitrogen was too slow. The fine structure of the compost, designed to retain moisture in the high transpiration conditions of California, caused waterlogging in the cooler, more humid climate of Great Britain. The result was to make many people deeply suspicious of the whole idea of soilless composts; others however realized that it was just a matter of adjusting the formulations to the British climate, altering the water-holding capacity and the proportions of nitrogen to potash in the fertilizers.

Nitrogen supply in soil-based and soilless composts

The key to success in the nutrition of soilless compost is the supply of nitrogen, which must be provided in both readily available and "slow release" forms. When slow release nitrogen is added to soil or compost, it undergoes a number of changes into other compounds before it is available to the plants. Some of these compounds become toxic to plants in comparatively moderate concentrations and all of them are toxic in excess.

When an organic material such as hoof and horn is applied to the soil, the nitrogen it contains is made up of complicated protein-like compounds which are converted by the soil micro-organisms into inorganic ammonium form which is in turn converted into nitrate form – the form in which it can be taken up by the plants. The first stage is performed by what may be called the ammonifying bacteria and the second stage is performed by what may be called the nitrifying bacteria.

Obviously any condition which affects the population or the activity of these organisms will affect the rate of breakdown of the organic nitrogen into ammonium and nitrate compounds. The soil contains a very large number of micro-organisms including bacteria, fungi, actinomycetes, algae, nematodes and protozoa. All these forms of microscopic life exist in the soil in a state of dynamic equilibrium or ever-changing balance among themselves. Many of these organisms are harmful to plant life, therefore soil to be used in compost is sterilized to try to remove the harmful micro-organisms while leaving the beneficial micro-organisms as unaffected as possible.

In a soilless compost, the situation is rather different. The peat and sand are naturally almost sterile without sterilization and hence the compost when made up will contain few, if any, of the micro-organisms that can convert organic nitrogen into the readily available nitrogen. Because of this it can be seen that readily available nitrogen must be provided in the compost in the form of nitrate until such time as the population of micro-organisms has been built up so that they in turn can provide the nitrates that the plants require. This is an important difference between soil-based and soilless composts and it led to the development of the 'starter' solution for the UC composts. The use of calcium nitrate provided the readily available nitrogen until the hoof and horn began breaking down. The grade of hoof and horn would influence the speed with which nitrogen was released. Finer particles present a larger surface area for the bacteria to work on and hence the nitrogen release would be more rapid than from a coarser grade of hoof and horn.

Two other factors concerning the release of nitrogen must be pointed out. Firstly, the bacteria that convert the organic nitrogen to ammonium nitrogen are able to carry out the conversion even in the absence of oxygen. By contrast, the bacteria that convert the ammonium nitrogen into nitrate nitrogen must have an adequate supply of oxygen so that the ammonia may be converted to nitrate.

Secondly, the rate of nitrification is dependent on the pH of the compost and it occurs in two distinct stages:

$$(1) \qquad (2)$$
$$\text{Ammonium} \rightarrow \text{Nitrite} \rightarrow \text{Nitrate}$$

The conversion of ammonium to nitrate goes through an intermediate stage known as nitrite. The first stage to nitrite will proceed up to a pH of 7.5 but the second stage from nitrite to nitrate will only proceed satisfactorily up to a pH of 7.0. It is obvious that between a pH of 7.0 and 7.5 the ammonium nitrogen will be converted as far as the nitrite but conversion of the nitrite to nitrate will be much slower, leading to a build-up of nitrite in the compost. Excess nitrite is damaging to all plants, but one of the most sensitive is antirrhinum. The first sign of damage is the yellowing of the younger leaves, turning to white in the presence of nitrite. On examination, the roots of the plants will be found to be brown and scorched.

Below a pH of about 5.5, the ammonium to nitrate conversion is slowed down but the breaking down of organic nitrogen to ammonium nitrogen continues. This time, at too acid a pH, ammonia will accumulate which is also damaging to plants.

From the above, it can be seen that the rate and type of nitrogen applied to a compost must be carefully controlled. *Composts containing organic sources such as the John Innes composts and the UC mixes with hoof and horn must not be stored for periods longer than one or two weeks before use, as ammonia will build up from the breakdown but nitrification of it cannot proceed as oxygen will not be able to penetrate the compost.* The pH should be kept in the range of 5.5 to 7.0 because, above this pH, nitrite will accumulate while below this pH range ammonia will build up.

Further differences in the physical properties of soil-based and soilless composts

An important difference between soil-based and soilless composts is in the supply of nutrients. Soil-based composts contain relatively large quantities of nutrients supplied at rather infrequent intervals, but soilless composts contain smaller quantities of nutrients which need to be supplemented more frequently. Incorrectly this is put down to the poor absorption of nutrients by the peat in the soilless compost. It is in fact because of the lower fixing capacity (storage) in peat. This may be best explained by a brief description of clay particles in the soil. These are very fine particles that contain nutrients within themselves which are not exchangeable in the normal soil solution. The exchangeable nutrients are held on to the surface of the clay particles by electrical charges and are removed into the soil solution to be taken up by the plant roots. This leaves a gap on the outside of the clay particle which is replaced from the nutrients within the clay particle. Thus the clay particle acts as a reserve or storage of nutrients. It is this reserve that peat itself lacks. Peat may be compared to a sponge that absorbs water and nutrients and releases them on demand, but once all the nutrients previously given have been removed, there is no reserve supply. The peat itself will gradually decompose but this breakdown is too slow to meet the needs of rapidly growing plants.

This is both an important weakness and strength in a soilless compost. Because of the lack of a reserve a wider range of nutrients must be added and added more frequently. But the grower has a tighter control over the growth of the plants because the plants will respond more readily to changes in nutrition without the reserve of plant foods in the background.

A final difference between the two composts may aptly be mentioned now. Nearly all forms of peat suitable for use in compost have a higher water-holding capacity than loam. Again peat may be likened to a sponge as it contains very large quantities of space for holding water. In a soilless compost, which usually contains peat as the largest proportion of all the ingredients, this may result in over-watering. This is dangerous because the compost will become poorly aerated and this in turn will quickly lead to death of the roots. To overcome this, several precautions are usually taken when using a soilless compost in place of a soil-based compost. The pot should be loosely filled with soilless compost whereas a pot of soil-based compost should be pressed well in. *Pressing down a soilless compost will result in immediate trouble due to the lack of air.* It should be emphasized just how important the air is in a soilless compost. To prevent over-watering, the pot is filled to the top with compost, whereas with a soil based compost approximately 0.6−1.25cm ($\frac{1}{4}$−$\frac{1}{2}$in) is left at the top of the pot to allow for watering.

The compost may be made free draining by adding a very coarse sand or grit to 'open up' the compost structure but it is not advisable to add too much otherwise the compost will require frequent watering and nutrients will be leached away, making high demands on the supplementary feeding. When watering a soil-based compost, the normal procedure is to allow the compost to become dry before watering well. Following this procedure with soilless compost will cause many problems, especially as the peat could be very difficult to re-wet. For soilless compost, the procedure is to water little and often, always keeping the compost more moist than a comparative soil-based compost.

Lastly, to keep the aeration good, the peat used should not be too fine or too decayed. Either would make the compost structure too close and result in a lower proportion of air to water.

Soilless compost: raw materials
Peat

By far the most important raw material is peat, and sphagnum moss peat is ideally structured for soilless compost, with good water retention and aeration characteristics. As it is naturally highly sterile and relatively free from pests, diseases and weed seeds, sterilization is not necessary. Composts consisting of moss-sedge peat mixes or even sedge peat alone (*Carex* spp, not the dark, well-decomposed peat popularly referred to as sedge) have, however, been used successfully. Note that sphagnum peat is acid in nature and sedge peat much less so, which affects quantities of lime to be added when mixing a compost.

Because of environmental pressures, organic materials other than peat are increasingly being used as compost ingredients. These include coir (coconut pith), composted timber and paper waste, brewery waste and other composted materials. As peat is still being widely used, reference to it remains in this book. Readers can be assured that as the properties of coir and other peat alternatives are gradually evaluated by researchers, growers and gardeners, compost formulae will be subject to modifications. Some adjustment in watering and feeding techniques seem presently required when peat alternatives are used.

Composted or pulverized wood bark

There is increasing use of composted or pulverized wood bark in gardening spheres − and this includes its inclusion in composts.

Early problems which arose when using this material related to the varying degrees of composition. If the bark was not sufficiently well decomposed, a shortage of the element nitrogen arises in the plants being grown in it.

Sand or grit

Soilless composts may be made with peat alone but these are not as popular as the composts which have other materials added. Sand or grit is the most widely used additive, making mixing the nutrients easier and the structure of the peat less critical, although still important. Naturally, the compost is heavier with the inclusion of sand but the weight is still only half that of a John Innes compost. The increase in weight is helpful in that it improves the stability of pots.

Rate of addition With different formulations of compost (see later) there are different proportions of peat to sand. The most common ratios are three parts peat to one part sand, 2 parts peat to 1 part sand, 1 part peat to 1 part sand; all these are based on volume not weight, ie 1 bushel of peat to 1 bushel (36 litres) of sand, or 1cu yd of peat to 1m³/cu yd of sand, or even 1 bucket of peat to 1 bucket of sand. Generally speaking, as the amount of sand is increased, the retention of water and nutrients will decrease. It is also reasonably safe to say that the aeration of the compost will be increased as the proportion of sand is increased. This is known as 'opening up' the compost.

Size The particle size of the sand has a great influence on aeration and water retention, permitting variations to suit the type of plant being grown. Three points should be considered in selecting particle size. Firstly, the fine sands as recommended in the original UC compost should be avoided. They were very successful in California but are not generally suitable for the moister and cooler climate in Britain. Secondly, if a coarser sand is being used, the peat should always be moistened before mixing to prevent separation of the peat and sand, which might give variabilities in the compost. Lastly, if the peat is fine, balance this by using a coarser sand; if the peat is coarse a finer sand may be included. However, such variability is not to be recommended as a general practice. It is preferable to standardize soilless compost by using a medium grade sphagnum moss peat (ie neither too fine nor too coarse) and a medium grade grit (say particles as in the John Innes recommendations of 3mm/$\frac{1}{8}$in down). This combination will give a free drainage compost that will retain adequate water but will not be easily waterlogged. In general practice, three parts peat to 1 part sand by volume is the preferred proportion of peat to sand.

Lime content Sand should be lime-free for most subjects, and this is essential for growing the lime-hating plants such as heathers and azaleas. The compost formulations given in this book all contain lime as calcium carbonate and/or dolomitic limestone. This assumes that sand is lime-free, usually with a pH between 6.0 and 6.5. As the pH of the sand rises, so the amount of lime added to the compost should be reduced, until with an alkaline sand having a pH of 8.3–8.5 (not normally recommended), no lime should be added to the mix.

Useful conversions for volumetric measurements

1 bushel	= 8 gallons = 2200 cubic inches = 1.28 cubic feet = 36 litres	
21.7 bushels	= 1 cubic yard = 27 cubic feet = 0.76 cubic metre	
27 bushels	= 1 cubic metre	
6$\frac{1}{4}$ gallons	= 1 cubic foot = 0.028 cubic metre	
1 gallon	= 277$\frac{1}{4}$ cubic inches = 4.5 litres	
1 ounce	= 28gms	

Approximate conversions

oz/bushel →	lb/cu yd → g/cu m³	1b/cu yd → oz/bushel → g/litre
$\frac{1}{4}$oz/bushel =	5$\frac{1}{4}$oz/yd³ = 200g/m³	$\frac{1}{4}$lb/yd³ = $\frac{3}{16}$oz/bushel =125 g/litre
$\frac{1}{2}$oz/bushel =	10$\frac{1}{2}$oz/yd³ = 400g/m³	$\frac{1}{2}$lb/yd³ = $\frac{3}{8}$oz/bushel =0.25g/litre
1oz/bushel = 1lb	5oz/yd³ = 800g/m³	1lb/yd³ = $\frac{3}{4}$oz/bushel = 0.5g/litre
2oz/bushel = 2lb	10oz/yd³ = 1600g/m³	2lb/yd³ = 1$\frac{1}{2}$oz/bushel = 1.0g/litre
3oz/bushel = 3lb	15oz/yd³ = 2400g/m³	3lb/yd³ = 2$\frac{1}{4}$oz/bushel = 1.5g/litre
4oz/bushel = 5lb	4oz/yd³ = 3200g/m³	4lb/yd³ = 3oz/bushel = 2.0g/litre

It may be difficult for the amateur to assess the pH of the sand, unless the supplier is able to state it. The sand may be simply tested by using hydrochloric acid, which may be obtained in small quantities from a local chemist, but because it is a strong acid it should be handled with care. Hydrochloric acid reacts chemically with calcium carbonate (lime, chalk etc) to release carbon dioxide gas and this chemical reaction is used to test the sand for the presence of calcium carbonate. About one dessert—spoonful of sand is placed in a non-corrosive (eg plastic) container and about a teaspoonful of hydrochloric acid is added to it. If no fizzing occurs (ie no carbon-dioxide gas is released), the sand will contain little (less than 0.25%) or no calcium carbonate and it will thus be suitable for use in the compost. If fizzing occurs, then the sand contains over 0.25% lime and an alternative supply should preferably be found.

Occasionally, sands from the seashore are sold for horticultural use. These may contain common salt from the sea water, which is harmful to plants. However, generally speaking, these sands are washed and dried before sale, and provided they are structurally satisfactory they may be used in composts.

Alternative compost materials

Alternatives to sand or grit are usually more expensive and more difficult to obtain. Various advantages for them may be claimed and interest in them varies. These materials may be naturally occurring or they may be synthetic (man-made). Usually they are light, non-toxic, sterile, and slow to break down.

Vermiculite

This is produced from a naturally occurring material called mica which is a glassy type of mineral consisting of flat layers or wafers. It is mined, mainly in South Africa. When it is heated to a temperature of about 1,400°C it expands considerably, thus providing a very large surface area for water retention and rooting. It also has a good capacity for retaining the plant foods added to the compost and itself contains high levels of magnesium, calcium and potassium. Thus it is a useful additive at approximately 10% by volume to composts, but it can be expensive, so its advantages have to be weighed against the extra cost. Because of its light weight it has been widely used as a base for the production of lightweight fertilizers.

Perlite

Although very different from vermiculite this mineral is processed in a similar manner by heat. The basic raw material is a dense, glass-like rock formed by volcanic action in much the same way as pumice stone. The rock is crushed and heated so that it expands like popcorn to twenty or more times its original volume. This gives it water and air-retaining properties and, as in the case of vermiculite, lightens it. Unlike vermiculite, it naturally contains few nutrients and its capacity to absorb water is less. Perlite has been used as a base for lightweight fertilizers but its use in composts is extending considerably because of the excellent air/moisture balance it gives a compost. It is also used for plant culture.

Polystyrene

Factories producing polystyrene products such as ceiling tiles and insulation boards have a waste problem that is an embarrassment to them beause of difficulties of disposal of rejects and off-cuts. A small but increasing use for this waste has been in the addition of the broken-down pieces to composts. Various claims have been made as to the benefits obtained, such as improved aeration and drainage, even to increasing the temperature of the compost by 1−2°C but these are still early days and there is little experimental evidence to substantiate these claims. The material is very light and this causes problems as it tends to "float" to the surface of the compost during the mixing. There are little or no plant foods present and the capacity to retain added plant foods is very low.

Polystyrene may be added to compost at up to 20% by volume but the compost must not be heat sterilized, for example by steam, after incorporation, as the polystyrene will melt.

Compost formulae summary

A bushel is a box measuring 55 × 25 × 25cm (22 × 10 × 10in)
A nine litre (2 gallon) bucket = $\frac{1}{4}$ bushel (9 litres)
One bushel = 36 litres
Peat and compost are now sold in litres in the UK and Europe, less so elsewhere

John Innes soil based composts

Seed sowing
2 parts (by bulk) loam (good soil) ideally sterilized
1 part (by bulk) peat (good quality, well textured)
1 part (by bulk) sharp sand or fine gravel
Allow for 15−20% shrinkage

	per 36 litres (bushel)	*per* cu yd	*per* m^3
Superphosphate	42g (1$\frac{1}{2}$oz)	900g (2lb)	1−2kg
Ground limestone	21g ($\frac{3}{4}$oz)	450g (1lb)	600g

Or use proprietary slow release base such as Vitax Q4, Chempak (no lime needed), Osmocote etc, according to directions. Perlite can be used in place of sand at recommended rates.

Potting

No 1 mix − most vegetables and flowers at early potting stage
7 parts (by bulk) loam
3 parts (by bulk) peat
2 parts (by bulk) sand or gravel (or perlite if
  used)

	per 36 litres (bushel)	*per* cu yd	*per* m^3
John Innes Base, which is	112g (4oz)	2−3kg (5lb 4oz)	3.2kg
2 parts (by weight) hoof & horn meal			
2 parts (by weight) superphosphates			
1 part (by weight) sulphate of potash			
Ground limestone	21g ($\frac{3}{4}$oz)	50g (1lb)	600g

For John Innes No 2 strength — potting stage for many plants

	per 36 litres (bushel)	*per* cu yd	*per* m^3
John Innes Base	224g (8oz)	4.7kg (10lb 8oz)	6.4kg
Ground limestone	42g (1$\frac{1}{2}$oz)	900g (2lb)	1.2kg

For John Innes No 3 strength — For long term culture of plants demanding a lot of plant foods

	per 36 litres (bushel)	per cu yd	per m³
John Innes Base	336g (12oz)	7kg (15¾lb)	9.6kg
Ground limestone	63g (2¼oz)	1.3kg (3lb)	1.8kg

Storage period for composts

This has been referred to, but readers are reminded that *all* compost formulae containing plant foods in any of their various forms do deteriorate or change with storage. The higher the temperature, generally speaking, the quicker fertilizers are rendered into more available form. Generally speaking it is better to mix or buy composts in quantities which allows for their use within a reasonable period, and store the unused composts in a cool place.

Kinsealy Composts (General purpose)

Seed sowing
100% peat

	per 36 litres (bushel)	per cu yd	per m³
‡ Calcium ammonium nitrate	7g (¼oz)	140g (5oz)	200g
★ Urea formaldehyde	7g (¼oz)	140g (5oz)	200g
Superphosphate	14g (½oz)	280g (10oz)	400g
Potassium sulphate	7g (¼oz)	140g (5oz)	200g
Keiserite	14g (½oz)	280g (10oz)	400g
Ground limestone	182g (6½oz)	3.8kg (8lb 5oz)	5.2kg

Kinsealy Composts (General purpose)

Potting (general)
100% peat

	per 36 litres (bushel)	per cu yd	per m³
‡ Calcium ammonium nitrate	28g (1oz)	560g (1¼lb)	800g
★ Urea formaldehyde	28g (1oz)	560g (1¼lb)	800g
Superphosphate	49g (1¾oz)	1kg (2¼lb)	1.4kg
Potassium sulphate	28g (1oz)	560g (1¼lb)	800g
Keiserite	63g (2¼oz)	1.26kg (2lb 13oz)	1.8kg
Ground limestone	182g (6½oz)	3.5kg (8lb 10oz)	5kg
Frit 253 A or WN 255	14g (½oz)	280g (10oz)	400g

Kinsealy Composts (for tomatoes)

Growing on
100% peat

	per 36 litres (bushel)	per cu yd	per m³
‡ Calcium ammonium nitrate	28g (1oz)	560g (1¼lb)	800g
★ Urea formaldehyde	28g (1oz)	560g (1¼lb)	800g
Superphosphates	49g (1¾oz)	1kg (2¼lb)	1.4kg
Potassium sulphate	49g (1¾oz)	1kg (2¼lb)	1.4kg
Dolomitic lime	332g (11½oz)	10.7kg (15lb)	11.2kg
Frit 253 A or WN 255	14g (½oz)	280g (10oz)	400g

Kinsealy Composts

General potting compost (tomatoes)
100% peat

	per 36 litres (bushel)	per cu yd	per m³
‡ Calcium ammonium nitrate	56g (2oz)	1.1kg (2lb 8oz)	1.6kg
Superphosphate	28g (1oz)	560g (1lb 4oz)	800g
Keiserite	63g (2¼oz)	1.26kg (2lb 13oz)	1.8kg
Ground Limestone	182g (6⅓oz)	3.8kg (8lb 10oz)	5.2kg
Frit 253 A or WN 255	14g (½oz)	280g (10oz)	400g

‡ *Calcium ammonium nitrate available as NITRO-CHALK or NITRA-SHELL. Use at rates of approximately 20% greater quantity.*
★ *Watch storage period.*

Modified GCRI Mixes

Seed sowing
50% peat (good fine texture) OR 75% peat
50% sand or fine gravel   25% sand or fine gravel

	per 36 litres (bushel)	per cu yd	per m³
Ground limestone	5–6oz	3–3.6kg (6½–8lbs)	4–4.8kg

Proprietary base – as recommended by manufacturers

For Potting
75% peat
25% sand
Add same quantity of lime as stated for seed sowing but half ground limestone and half dolomitic limestone, plus quantities of prepared base as recommended by manufacturers (Vitax Q4, Osmocote, Chempak or others — see Appendix), noting carefully whether these bases contain lime or not (Chempak *does*).

Soilless composts — 'standard' UK formulae (using straight chemicals which can be replaced with proprietary bases)

Seed sowing (and rooting)
50% Peat
50% Sand   By volume

	per 36 litres (bushel)		per cu yd	per m³
	g	oz		
Superphosphates (18%)	28–56	1–2	560–1120g (1¼–2½lb)	800g–1.6kg
Potassium nitrate	14	½	280g (10oz)	400g
‡ Ground limestone	112–168	4–6	80–120g (5–7½lb)	3.2kg
★ Sulphate of potash	7	¼	140g (5oz)	200g

★ Optional — include for tomatoes
‡ leave out for acid loving plants such as heathers, rhododendrons etc.

Pricking out and potting
75% Peat
25% Sand   By volume

	per 36 litres (bushel)		per cu yd	per m³
	g	oz		
Urea				
★ Formaldehyde − winter	21	¾	448g (1lb)	500g
(Nitroform) − spring	28	1	560g (1¼lb)	900g
− summer	42	1½	900g (2lb)	1000g
Superphosphates (18%)	56	2	1.1kg (2½lb)	1600g
Potassium nitrate	28	1	560g (1¼lb)	800g
Sulphate of potash				
(for tomatoes)	14	½	280g (¾lb)	400g
‡ Dolomitic limestone	84	3oz of each	1.8kg (4lb) of each	2.4kg of each
‡ Ground limestone				
Frit WN 255 or 253A	14	½	280g (10oz)	400g

★ Avoid if to be stored more than 7 days. Include instead:
   Amonium nitrate   14 ½   280g (10oz)   400g
‡ Leave out or reduce for acid loving species

Bedding plants
Standard compost for growing-on (as used at Lee Valley EHS)
75% Irish sphagnum peat, medium grade
25% 3mm non-calcareous grit   By volume

	per 36 litres (bushel)		per cu yd	per m³
	g	oz		
Ammonium nitrate	14	½	280g (10oz)	400g
Potassium nitrate	28	1	560g (1¼lb)	900g
Superphosphates 18%	56	2	1.1kg (2½lb)	1600g
Ground limestone	84	3	1.8kg (4lb)	2.4kg
Magnesium limestone	84	3	1.8kg (4lb)	2.4kg
Fritted trace elements 253A	14	½	280g (10oz)	400g

Average number of pots per 36 litres (bushel) cu yd, m³ of compost

Size of pot in	mm (approx)	Pots filled per bushel (36 litres)	Pots filled per cu yd	per m³
2¼	58	370	7770	9990
2½	65	320	4620	5940
3	75	150	3150	4050
4	100	55	1155	1485
5	125	30	630	810
6	150	18	378	486

Figures vary according to compost type and firmness of potting.

Number of seed trays per bushel (36 litres), cu yd, m³ of compost

Standard seed tray size — 2 × 9 × 14½in (5 × 23 × 36cm) external measurements but they may vary in size and depth. Each tray takes approx 1/10th of a bushel, so — 1 bushel = fills 8−10 trays — 1 cu yd = fills 180−210 trays −1m³ = fills 220−270 trays approximately.

For plant packs, Fyba packs or pots or containers of various sizes, a trial run on a bushel or litre basis will quickly give quantities filled. Multiply by 21 for cu yd and 27 for cubic m. Manufacturers can supply compost volume information. 'Jiffys' (7s and 9s) are bought by quantity, not size. Remember that peat-based composts are not firmed up in the container so much as soil-based composts.

Pulverized fuel ash (PFA)
Large amounts of clinker-type materials must be disposed of by the large furnaces of power stations and one of the uses of this material is as a compost additive. The clinker is broken up (pulverized) and used as a replacement in whole or in part for the sand fraction of the compost. It is lighter than sand although heavier than the alternative materials mentioned above, and the PFA itself has some pore space within the particles. It is used with success by some growers but there have been reservations from certain authorities on its use because of possible excess levels of some trace elements.

Other materials
Synthetic foams have been used in the manufacture of composts as well as on land that is being reclaimed and for conserving water in dry areas. The most useful for horticultural purposes are the urea−formaldehyde foams as these have a cotton-wool-like texture. Shredded polyurethane foam can be obtained as a waste product of the cushion and bedding industry quite

cheaply. Ideally, it should be shredded as finely as possible for addition to compost. Its addition is claimed to improve aeration and heat retention in the compost; roots appear to be attracted to the foam. Polyurethane blocks are also now produced for rooting cuttings. The blocks are available in sheet form, each block being a cube 3−4cm. They are wetted before use and the cuttings inserted into the blocks. Advantages claimed are that the rooting medium is light, sterile and uniform, maintaining the correct balance of air and water, giving even root development. It is likely that this type of medium will find increasing usage in the future. Indeed, the more these synthetic foams are used the more advantages are found for them. Mineral rockwool is also used in block form as a growing substrate.

Comparison of soilless compost mixes (see tables)
Kinsealy composts
These were developed by the Glasshouse Crops Department at the Horticultural Research Centre of the Agricultural In-

stitute, Kinsealy, Dublin, Eire, after the UC composts had been found unsatisfactory. The present formulae for the Kinsealy composts are based on peat alone. Three basic composts are given, two specific tomato composts and a general potting compost. In addition, there is a tomato seedling compost, with a quarter of the plant food of the tomato potting compost. This division between the tomato and general composts would not appear to be too important because the nutrient content of both follow similar lines to composts from other organizations, the main difference lying in the proportion of readily available to slow-release nitrogen. It is interesting to note that the Kinsealy formulae are the only ones to specify the use of kieserite as the source of magnesium. The other formulae used dolomite lime as the magnesium source, which also neutralizes the compost. Hence if kieserite is used, the rate of addition of ground limestone is higher than in a dolomite lime-ground limestone mixture, although the total amount of lime used will be similar.

Tomato seeds are sown in the seedling compost. The seedlings are then pricked out into the propagating compost where they remain until planting out. The tomato growing-on compost has a higher rate of potassium and magnesium addition and the magnesium source has been altered from kieserite to dolomite limestone which is available over a larger period of time. Owing to the high rate of addition of dolomite limestone, no ground limestone or chalk is required.

General potting compost was formulated after a wide range (over 70 species) of plants had been grown in it, including cucumbers. The basic formula is the tomato propagating compost, with half the rate of superphosphate, twice the amount of calcium ammonium nitrate and no source of slow-release nitrogen, so that the compost can be stored after mixing. Although higher rates of superphosphates have been tried, there has been no benefit reported by Kinsealy. It is interesting to note that this compost is similar in nutrient level to the GCRI compost as described. For ready-mixed composts made to the Kinsealy formulae, see

later under the section on ready-made compost.

Difficulty may be experienced with weighing out and evenly mixing the low trace elements in these formulae. The problems may be reduced by the replacement of these individual trace elements by $400g/m^3$ (10oz) of trace element frit 253A per cubic yard of compost.

GCRI mixes

These were first formulated by A. C. Bunt at the Glasshouse Crops Research Institute at Littlehampton in Sussex, England. There were three composts recommended at first, all adaptations of UC formulae: a seed-sowing or propagating compost based on equal volumes of peat and fine sand, and two 75 peat/25 fine sand composts for pricking out or potting on.

In the seed-sowing compost the only source of nitrogen was that readily available from potassium nitrate as seedlings are not in the compost long enough to require slower-release nitrogen. Most growers now use proprietary bases as recommended by manufacturers.

The two potting composts varied in the nitrogen reserve. The compost known as High N Reserve Compost used urea formaldehyde as the source of slow-release nitrogen and must be used fairly soon after mixing as it will not store. The organic nitrogen level is varied according to the season (see table); the readily available nitrogen level is higher than in the comparable UC compost and, to give a balanced growth, the phosphate and potash levels are also higher.

GCRI Low N Reserve Compost was developed as a compost that can be mixed and stored before use. It has a low level of readily available nitrogen and no slow-release nitrogen. Because of this, liquid feeding should commence earlier after potting up in this compost than in the High N Reserve Compost.

The GCRI potting composts use mixtures of dolomite lime and ground limestone for neutralizing the compost to a pH of 5.5, the dolomite lime supplying the necessary magnesium. They also contain fritted trace elements to rectify deficiencies of boron, zinc and manganese in the peat, as well as supplying copper and molybdenum.

Cornell lightweight composts (Peat-lite)
These were developed for the container growing of bedding plants at Cornell University, although subsequently they have been used for potting plants. Standardization was the main theme and this was achieved by including 25–50% vermiculite or perlite with the moss peat. This gave rise to the name of peat-lite for these composts, mix A containing vermiculite and mix B perlite.

The seed mix supplies nitrogen and phosphate as the major elements and boron and iron as trace elements, plus lime of course to neutralize the peat. Mixes A and B for growing on are fertilized with potassium nitrate and superphosphate but the potassium nitrate may be substituted by 1.6–8kg/m^3 (2–12lb per cuyd) of a slow release fertilizer. It must be remembered that the natural levels of potash and magnesium in vermiculite are high to supplement the added fertilizers but calcium content is variable. Because of this, ground limestone is used in preference to dolomite for the neutralizing of the compost to provide calcium. These mixes may be stored.

Peat-lite composts
These have undergone considerable modification in recent years and are now based on varying proportions of peat and vermiculite or perlite, usually 50–75% peat to 50–25% vermiculite or perlite, with slow release base fertilizers added at varying rates according to manufacturers' recommendations, plus lime at 3oz per bushel (4 lb cu yd/2.4kg/m^3), split between ground limestone and magnesium limestone (see note re magnesium levels in vermiculite).

If there are no trace elements in the base fertilizer these are added at 14g ($\frac{1}{2}$oz) per bushel/28g (1oz) per cu yd/ 400g/m^3. (Frit 253A or WM255)

Problems may arise from the good drainage characteristics of the peat-lite composts, the water tending to run through the compost before it is completely wetted. Watering should therefore be done only

lightly initially. Generally the formulae suggested for this compost seem rather vague. (See tables).

Other formulations
Above are given the better known of the compost formulations but there are many more, particularly from the various Experimental Horticultural Stations scattered throughout this and other countries. However, these are all rather similar to the GCRI type compost and it would serve no purpose to list them here.

Mixing composts – ready-made bases

The formulae given above can be rather bewildering for the commercial grower, let alone the amateur. Production of these composts requires the accurate weighing out of comparatively small quantities of fertilizers which have to be evenly mixed with large quantities of compost. This is not easily done and many of the composts used by the commercial growers are made from ready mixed compost fertilizers containing the major plant foods nitrogen, phosphates and potash with in some cases trace elements also. Most also include a balance between readily available and slow-release nitrogen. As a great simplification this reduces the chance of error, with usually a single weighing out of the fertilizer plus a further weighing out of the lime (but see below on reduction of compost volume).

Lime in soilless composts
Lime is essential in a soilless compost and it performs two functions: it neutralizes the acidity of the peat and supplies the nutrient calcium to the compost.

Sphagnum moss peat recommended for soilless compost has a pH of between 3.3 and 4.3 approximately, but commonly in the narrower range of 3.8 to 4.1. For a 3:1 peat-sand compost, the pH recommended is 5.5, ie approximately one pH unit lower than is recommended for a soil-based compost. If only the peat and sand are mixed together, the resultant pH will be about 4.3, assuming the use of an acid sand. To increase the pH to 5.5, 4.5g/litre (6oz) of ground limestone will have to be added per bushel of compost or approximately 4.8kg/m^3 (8lb per cu yd).

Ground limestone is chemically calcium carbonate. Chalk is also calcium carbonate but it is white and softer than limestone. Ground limestone is to be preferred for compost work as it will dissolve more slowly and maintain a reasonably consistent pH over the life of the compost. The grading (or size range) of the ground limestone is important: small particles will raise the pH initially but coarser particles (up to 1.5mm/$\frac{1}{16}$in) are needed to maintain the pH with time, Generally about ten days is required for the pH of the compost to reach 5.5. If the lime contains many fine particles, as in dolomite lime, the pH may reach 5.5 in only three days but the coarser particles must still be provided to maintain this level.

In some of the compost formulae, mixtures of ground limestone and dolomite are used. The reason for this is that dolomite provides magnesium, which may not be present in the other plant foods added to the compost. Dolomite is usually sold as a fine dust rather than as a graded material like ground limestone and it will therefore raise the pH of the compost initially quite quickly. All the formulae give mixtures of dolomite and ground limestone since ground limestone is necessary for the calcium. Both materials have similar neutralizing powers, so that in a formula containing 5.5kg (9lb) ground limestone per m^3 (cu yd) of compost, 3.1kg/m^3 (5lb) ground limestone and 2.4kg/m^3 (4lb) dolomite may be used instead if no other source of magnesium is included in the compost—5.5g/litre (7$\frac{1}{2}$oz) per bushel.

Finally, the adjustment of the pH in an all-peat compost is a simple matter if the pH of the peat is known. It is known that 600g/m^3 (1lb) of limestone will raise the pH of 1cu yd of peat by 0.3 of a pH unit. For example, if the peat has a pH of 3.5 and the compost pH required is 5.0 (the most suitable pH for an all-peat compost), the pH is to be raised by 5.0−3.5 = 1.5. Therefore the amount of ground limestone required per cu yd of peat is $\frac{1.5}{0.3}$ or 3.1kg/m^3 (5lb per cu yd) of peat. If a smaller quantity of peat is being mixed, 3.1kg/m^3 (5lb per cu yd) is equivalent to 3g/litre (4oz) per

bushel (Guideline figures only: peat pH varies greatly as do peat substitutes).

Reduction in compost volume of peat/sand mixtures

When peat and sand are mixed, there is a reduction in the volume of compost produced. For example, if a normal 3 peat/1 sand mix is being made and say 9 litres or bushels of peat and 3 litres or bushels of sand are mixed together, 12 litres or bushels of compost will not be produced since the particles of sand will tend to be absorbed into the spaces in the peat, resulting in an average reduction of one-sixth in volume. In the example quoted above, probably around 10 litres or bushels of compost will be produced and it is this volume that is used to calculate the addition of lime and fertilizer. If 4.5g/litre (6oz) ground limestone and 3g/litre (4oz) compound fertilizer were being added to each bushel of compost, then the mix above would require 10 × 4.5 (45g) 10 × 3 (3oz) 10 × 3 (3oz) of fertilizer. Unless the reduction in volume is allowed for, too much lime and fertilizer will be added, causing damage to the plants.

Therefore for the first mix of compost, the peat and sand should be measured out and then mixed. The volume of the compost thus produced should be measured and the amounts of lime and fertilizer to be added calculated. These same amounts may then be added to further mixes without measurement of the final compost volume as this will be similar for the same volumes of peat and sand initially.

High salt levels in compost
Causes

The higher the fertilizer level in a compost, the higher the salt concentration and the more risk of plant injury. However, different fertilizers have a different effect on the salt level. Obviously slow-release fertilizers will have little effect on it initially, but as they are acted upon by the soil bacteria, the breakdown products which are soluble will contribute to the salt level. However, in the pot, part of this level will be removed as food by the plants and part will be washed away during watering. So that provided the release is not excessive, there is little risk of a dangerously high level accumulating. If such compost is stored in a bag the situation is rather different, because the system is closed and the salt and ammonia levels can build up as the slow release nitrogen becomes available, especially at high temperature.

The more readily available plant foods have the greatest effect on the salt level: ammonium nitrate comes first, closely followed by potassium nitrate and potassium sulphate. Superphosphate has the least effect on the salt level. Soilless composts can be more heavily fertilized than comparable soil-based composts without dangerous build-up, possibly because the peat acts as a sponge, absorbing the dissolved fertilizer which does not then harm the plant roots, possibly because soilless compost is better aerated.

The compost components may contribute to the salt level. Peat and sand have little effect but if soil is used it may contain a high level of salts. This is one reason why, when the John Innes composts were formulated, the soil was obtained from meadowland that had only low plant foods and hence a low salt level; an old greenhouse soil is not suitable because it is likely to contain fertilizer residues which may be harmful.

The last source of salt levels in compost is the water. Sometimes this may contain dissolved salts, particularly in bore-hole water. Tap water is usually safe but rain water is the safest of all.

Effect of high salt levels

The effect of a high salt level in a compost may vary from no apparent damage to rapid plant death. If the salt level is just on the limit of danger, there will probably be only a reduction in the rate of growth. As the salt level increases, the plant will absorb considerable quantities of fertilizer which will tend to accumulate in the leaf margins or tips, causing burning as the water evaporates and leaves the fertilizer behind. Root damage also occurs. If the salt level becomes very high, water will actually be removed from the root into the growing medium, causing the root to brown and dry up. This will aggravate the problem since the plant will be able to take up less water, with the possibility of the leaves wilting and further damage to the leaf margins and tips. A frequent symptom is yellowing of the leaves which may be diagnosed by the inexperienced as a shortage of nitrogen and the plant may be promptly fed with liquid fertilizer, increasing the salt level of the compost still further and making the situation worse. Very often the first sign of root trouble is a yellowing of the foliage and if the plant is knocked out of its pot, the effect of the high salt level is evident by the browning of the roots. *This must not be confused with damage due to over-watering or waterlogging.*

Cure

If the damage is not too severe the compost can be leached out of its excess salt level by generously watering the compost. A free-draining well-aerated compost will help this. Alternatively, the plant should have as much of the damaging compost as possible removed from its roots and be repotted into a fresh, safe compost. Damaged plants should be given plenty of shade and high humidity, thus reducing the rate of transpiration of water through the plant. The damaged roots are under less stress and new roots will be able to form. However, with most things prevention is better than cure and the compost should be made correctly in the first place.

Ready-mixed composts

For the gardener who does not want the bother of mixing his own soilless compost either by the standard formulae or using one of the compost fertilizers given earlier, there are available on the market several ready-made composts. All the gardener has to do is to purchase a bag of compost from the local gardening shop, open it and start using it straight away. The disadvantage is that it is not known exactly what is in the compost, how much fertilizer it contains, how old it is etc. However, it is sold to do a specific job and therefore it is presumed that it will do it well.

There are also many smaller firms who produce soilless compost and sell it through a few local garden shops and garden centres. Often, these producers supply the local commercial growers as well, or it may even be a local nurseryman who packs his own compost. It is obviously not possible to comment specifically on these locally available mixes. Some are excellent, based either on a GCRI type formula or a proprietary compost fertilizer but some may be rather variable in quality.

A general purpose mix is available in ready mixed compost, suitable for seed sowing, rooting cuttings and potting. This type of universal compost must contain only small amounts of plant food so that it will not be damaging to the tender seedlings. When it is used for potting, as it only contains these limited plant foods, the plants must have regular supplementary liquid feeding quite soon after potting if they are not to starve. The advantage in these products is simplicity, having only the one compost for all jobs, but the after-care required is higher.

Other ready-mixed composts are available in two forms, one for seed sowing and rooting cuttings and the other for potting. The seed-sowing compost is similar to the general purpose compost already mentioned above, having low plant foods. The potting compost has higher plant foods that will sustain the plants longer but nevertheless, supplementary feeding is usually necessary in approximately six to eight weeks after potting. Occasionally, three potting strengths will be offered, as with the John Innes potting composts.

Plant propagation

A very important use for compost is in the propagation of plants. This may involve either seed sowing or taking cuttings and rooting them. The basic requirements of these composts are that they are free from pests and diseases, well aerated and well drained. The need for freedom from pest or diseases is obvious since at this stage both seedlings and cuttings are very susceptible to attack. The main danger is from the damping-off fungi or the so−called "water moulds" such as *Phytophthora* and *Pythium* either before or after the seedlings emerge from the soil. The damage caused by these

fungi is usually most severe under conditions when germination of the seed, or rooting of the cutting is slow, for example early in the season or in cold, wet soils. Keeping the compost well-aerated and free draining will keep it warmer and combined with less saturation with water, this will discourage the diseases. There are other means of giving protection such as the use of seed dressings containing fungicides such as captan or thiram and insecticides such as gamma-HCH. A fungicide may be added to the hormone rooting powders used for cuttings. Even these precautions will be less effective or even ineffective if the compost structure is not suitable.

For seed sowing, the soil-based John Innes seed compost is suitable. The soil is sterilized and, provided that has been done effectively, the soil will be free from harmful organisms, the grit is sterile anyway and the peat will be almost or completely sterile—so the compost should be satisfactory. Improved germination and growth have been obtained by using soilless seed sowing composts in place of the soil-based seed compost. There are several formulas that may be made up such as the G.C.R.I. and Kinsealy formulae or equal volumes of sphagnum moss peat and sharp sand may be mixed (50:50 peat:sand) together with a small amount (approximately 0.75g/litre (1oz) per bushel) of a compost fertilizer and ground limestone at 4g/litre (5oz) per bushel of compost for a lime-free (acid) sand.

For rooting cuttings, there is a whole variety of recommendations, ranging from all peat through various combinations of peat and sand to all sand, even using different composts for rooting different cuttings. However, this complication seems rather unnecessary as most subjects can be rooted very successfully in the 50:50 peat-sand compost recommended above for seed sowing using one of the standard formulae or a compost fertilizer. Ready-made soilless composts can be obtained that are suitable for seed sowing and cuttings, or for growbags or bolsters. It is stressed, however, that despite many claims from manufacturers, bought-in composts can vary.

Cropping plants

Recently there has been an increasing interest in growing cropping plants such as tomatoes in compost in place of the more normal greenhouse soil. The main advantage is that the risk of pest or disease attack from the soil is prevented, as the compost is removed each year and replaced. The growing medium is known to be nutritionally good whereas there may be some doubt as to the suitability of the greenhouse soil, such as pH and fertilizer level, as well as the actual soil structure. The three different approaches to this method of growing-containers, modified ring culture and troughs, are dealt with in the chapters on tomato cultivation. In the container system, the compost is placed in pots (plastic), bags or tubes which are then spaced out in the greenhouse. Plants are put individually in pots but bags or tubes may have more than one plant. It is possible to buy the bags or tubes filled with composts from various firms. The main dangers of the bag method, the modified ring culture and the trough method are the drainage of water and the problems of the build-up of the salt concentration in the compost. Watering must be done with care so that the compost does not become waterlogged and feeding, whilst very necessary, must not be overdone in case the compost becomes toxic through excess fertilizer. One method of removing the problem is to slit the side of the growing bag or trough to allow excess water to drain away, but the disadvantage is that if the roots grow through the slits into diseased greenhouse soil, the plants will become infected. An alternative method with the bed for trough system is to place drainage tiles at the bottom of the trough, a system developed at the Kinsealy Institute in Ireland. A tile drain is laid in a central groove running along the bottom of the trough with a 2.5cm (1in) layer of gravel over the drain to prevent the compost entering it. The trough is topped up with not less than 15cm (6in) of soilless compost. At Kinsealy, these troughs have been used successfully for three years without replacement, but the compost is sterilized by steam through the drainage tile at the end of each season to prevent the build-up of pests and diseases.

Compost strengths

Plants vary in their tolerance of the fertilizer level in the compost. In a ready-made compost the level of fertilizer is kept reasonably low so that the least tolerant plants may be grown. But problems arise when the gardener wishes to make up his own compost and has to decide on the stength of fertilizer to be used.

Seed is sown or cuttings rooted in the standard composts detailed earlier. The plants in the first group are pricked out or potted into a compost with a strength of approximately John Innes Potting $\frac{1}{2}$ or the equivalent in soilless. The final potting of these plants is done at John Innes Potting No 1 strength. In the second group the plants are pricked out into John Innes Potting No 1, and potted on into John Innes Potting No 2. All plants may be liquid fed after the roots have filled the pots (gently tap out the root ball to examine). Certain of these plants will tolerate higher levels of plant foods, but for the sake of simplicity the groupings have been kept to two.

Plants that are grown in the early stages in a greenhouse and later planted out in an outside soil, eg bedding plants, chrysanthemums, cucumbers, should be pricked out or potted on into John Innes Potting No 1 or its soilless equivalent. If the plants are to stay in the compost longer than approximately four weeks, some supplementary feeding should be given.

Hydroponics

Various systems of culture involving the growing of plants in nutrient solutions contained in tanks, as shallow films in troughs (Nutrient Film Technique), rockwool, perlite or other aggregates have been widely adopted by commercial growers in the last few years.

All plants take up their nutrients in liquid form under any system of culture, but with hydroponic systems no soil or compost is involved. A specialized approach to such systems is required and details are available from suppliers of equipment (see Appendix).

CHAPTER 16

Propagation by Seed

The word propagation literally means to increase by natural means, and this opens the flood gates for a discussion on what is 'natural' and what is 'artificial'. Setting aside this provocative argument there is, in the whole sphere of greenhouse culture, great scope for examining every facet of propagation under conditions where success is more likely than in the widely varying out-of-door conditions which prevail in most countries.

The living plant

Before propagation can be fully understood it is necessary to consider the basic botanical make-up of the living plant. Flowering plants are divided broadly into two main groups: *dicotyledons* to which most broad-leaved plants belong, and *monocotyledons* which consist of narrow-leaved plants including lilies and most bulbous plants. The basic difference as far as propagation is concerned lies in the existence of a cambium layer in dicotyledons which is lacking in monocotyledons. The cambium cell layer exists between the vital xylem and phloem (see Fig. 45) necessary for conducting water and nutrients in the plant, and its task is to replace worn out cells and act as a source for regenerating the whole plant. Cambium cells are in fact the vital key to some aspects of successful propagation from miscellaneous sections of plant; it is mainly only the cambium cells which are able to bring about physical union between plants in grafting and give rise to the formation of new roots when rooting cutting. It is fairly obvious therefore that one cannot propagate monocotyledons in the same way as they do not possess a cambium layer (see Fig. 46), which imposes definite limitations in propagating methods (with the exception of *Dracaena*).

In addition to monocotyledons and dicotyledons, a further grouping of plants relates to their longevity, there being three well-known groups:

1 Annuals These arise only from seed and die after forming seed, though not necessarily in the one calendar year, eg calendula, annual asters, clarkia, and many more (many annuals are of course half-hardy, living only a part of their lives out of doors).

2 Biennials These live for two seasons or, to be more specific, part of two seasons; in the first they prepare for flowering and in the second they flower, when thereafter they produce seed and die, eg foxgloves.

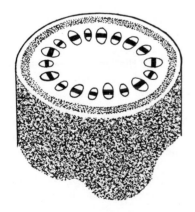

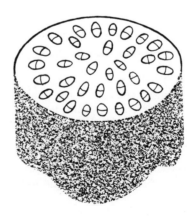

Fig. 45 (*Far left*) A young dicotyledonous stem (cambium layer in black).

Fig. 46 (*Left*) A monocotyledonous stem.

129

3 Perennials Plants in this group carry on flowering and producing seed for a great number of years, storing up their food in roots or stems, which enables them to survive the dormant period, although they may die down out of doors. Woody perennials have a permanent shoot system which usually does not die back to the ground (eg shrubs).

Annuals and biennials are rarely propagated by methods other than from seed, whereas perennials can be propagated either from seed, cuttings, or other parts of them such as roots, stems leaves, and cells.

It must not be imagined that the gardener can choose the method of propagation he prefers, as plants exhibit considerable temperament in respect of how they increase themselves. A cutting from a large soft bush such as an elder may be extremely difficult to propagate, and likewise holly which has a very hard stem. Snips of coleus or tradescantia (wandering Jew or Sailor) root in a few days, whereas many tender ericas (eg *Erica hymealis*) can be very tricky to root. The leaves of many plants can seldom be induced to root, whereas others such as those of *Begonia rex* produce roots with ease (see p. 213).

The eccentricities of seed are well known, where due to cross pollination and other causes the germinated offspring is different in colour or form from the parent plant. But though it may be assumed in the majority of cases that any portion of a plant's anatomy which can be successfully rooted will produce a plant of identical character and pattern of growth to the plant from which it was taken (setting aside 'sporting'), this is not always the case. Cuttings taken from mature plants generally produce plants which flower earlier than those produced from young plant cuttings. Where cuttings are taken from juvenile types of seed-raised conifers, the juvenile form persists. Straggly cuttings taken from older conifers will produce straggly plants, unlike those produced from young short-jointed cuttings from the terminal shoots. There would also appear to be a need to select particular types of chrysanthemum, carnations or other cuttings for stem propagation.

Propagation from seed

While propagation by seed appears to be an extremely cheap and simple method of producing new plants, it is not without drawbacks. Parentage and whether or not a seed is a true offspring of its parent is a critical matter. The grower of early commercial tomatoes purchases a certain variety of seed because of its special qualities in early fruiting, along with fruit size and quality, and the economic consequences of any performance variation are enormous, and this is true of many other plants at all centres of production. The exhibitor of a flower or vegetable, while not involved in economic results, stands to lose much if the seed he sows does not produce plants true to form. Indeed, the ordinary gardener seeking a special colour of flower or shape of turnip would be bitterly disappointed by considerable variation from inherent form. Conversely of course there is always the possibility of finding a form better than the parent. Fortunately there are many plants which produce seed that can, in most cases, be accepted as true to type because of many years of careful re-selection and controlled seed production. The whole secret of a seed house acquiring a good reputation lies in ensuring careful and rigorous selection.

Hybridization

Matters are much more complicated today than in past years, due to the considerable degree of hybridization which has taken place in an effort to produce better form, colour, size, shape, and indeed improve on every characteristic imaginable. The seeds of true species of plants such as common broom *Cytisus scoparius* and many others do however breed true to type from seed with little noticeable variation. In recent years much use has been made of F_1 (and F_2) hybrid seed. In the case of F_1 seed this is the result of controlled fertilization between the two parents *annually* selected from those plants which are either annuals or treated as such. Mendel's Law refers to the true exhibition of the parental characteristics of both male and female parents in the first generation of seed produced, when thereafter segregation occurs in fixed proportions into respective male or female parent characteristics. The important issue with F_1 seed is the true and vigorous exhibition of the parents' qualities in 'blended' form, called hybrid vigour. This has very special significance also as far as the inbred resistance to disease is concerned, such resistances which are bestowed manifesting themselves strongly. The success which has been achieved with flowers and vegetables in F_1 seed form allows the seedsman to predict with certainty that certain qualities will be present in the offspring, whereas with ordinary seed there can be variations, loss of disease resistance, loss of vigour and many other deficiencies, particularly over a period of time unless vigorous re-selection is practised. It follows also that the same re-selection is required to maintain the qualities of the selected male or female parent of an F_1 hybrid. This perhaps serves to explain why seeds can give variable results, and the popularity of F_1 hybrids, but it must be emphasized once more that the careful selection and re-selection of 'ordinary' seed over a great many years will still, in many cases, give results of a high order.

It was said earlier that seed was cheap, and while this is true to a certain extent, the obviously high cost of producing F_1 seed, involving a re-cross annually, has raised the price of many seeds considerably. Examples of this are the F_1 geraniums, whose seeds are sufficiently expensive to cause gardeners some thought as to whether vegetative or seed propagation is cheaper, an issue still further complicated by the rather slower speed at which the F_1 geranium seed produces a flowering plant. F_2 seed is generally cheaper.

Speed of propagation
Where a plant can be propagated either from seed or vegetatively by cuttings or from other parts of the plant's anatomy, vegetative production is the quicker way of producing a *mature* plant. But the F_1 seedling may in turn overtake the vegetatively propagated plant and become bigger, more floriferous and productive.

The advantage of seed is that it is an easily stored embryonic plant. An interesting technique is primed seed, the seed being germinated and then held in suspense pending immediate growth.

Transmission of disease
In the more technical aspects of disease transmission, it is obvious that seed offers a method of plant production much less prone to disease transmission than vegetative propagation. Virus and fungal diseases usually exist in the vegetative tissue of the plant, and it is not thought that the seminal reproductive section of the plant is affected, which means that the seed produced even by virus infected parents should be free from virus. One cannot, however, be too emphatic on this matter, as research is still probing into the facts surrounding the introduction of disease, but for all practical purposes non-transmission of disease by seminal means is a fact, although the importance of inheritance and disease susceptibility cannot be overlooked. It is also possible that the embryo itself may well be free of disease but the tissue surrounding it is not, which in practical terms gives rise to immense problems.

Containers for seed sowing, propagation and growing on
Pots are available in a wide range of sizes and shapes in plastic, clay, bituminized or treated paper, polystyrene or peat, in addition to which there are soil or peat blocks to consider. There has in recent years been many advances in containers and the trend has been towards space sowing in compartment or cell trays to avoid, where practical, the chore of pricking out when larger seeds are involved.

Plastic pots
The swing to these in recent years has been dramatic, occasioned by hygiene, their very low manufacturing costs, transport, and their impermeability. When plastic pots made their debut they were viewed with considerable scepticism by older gardeners who failed to see how plants could grow in a non-sympathetic material incapable of admitting a sufficient supply of air to the roots. Clay with its porous nature seemed to offer all the advantages, yet

practical experience has in the main shown otherwise. In a clay pot drying out occurs not only from the top but from the sides, whereas with a plastic pot the main area of evaporation is through the top surface. Plant physiologists have been at a loss to say whether or not this in itself is a good thing, but less water is certainly lost by plastic pots and this must surely be considered an advantage, though admittedly over-watering can occur by failure to take into account the respective differences in 'transpiration' loss. On the question of hygiene there can be no argument; plastic can be cleaned in warm water without scrubbing, and there is no risk of it absorbing disease as there is with clay. Plastic pots are also highly effective on capillary benches, coming in a wide range of sizes, round or square, light to handle and easy to store. Strips or blocks of small plastic pots are used commercially for a variety of purposes and are particularly useful for growing room activities where space is at a premium. The pot readily detaches by tearing, though some disturbance can occur when young plants require removal.

Paper pots

The role of paper pots is not so clear. While excellent as short-term containers for seeds or growing plants their cellulose content invariably results in a temporary nitrogen shortage until the cellulose decomposing fungi satisfy their own needs for nitrogen. There have been problems also with the saprophytic fungal agencies delaying the germination of seeds and the growth of plants. A major advantage of paper pots is that for seed sowing there is no disturbance on planting out or potting on, as the pot is planted intact, although the implications of temporary nitrogen shortage should not be overlooked. Paper pots are available in round or hexagonal shape, also in concertina-like strips from which pots can be taken as needed. Tubes of paper are very useful for sweet peas.

Red bituminized paper pots are available in large sizes and can be used for growing shrubs, tomatoes, chrysanthemums, and other long-term plants, lasting for about six months with normal handling.

Polythene

Being inert, polythene offers no nutritional problems. While young plants can be lined out with their polythene pots intact, removal on planting is advisable in most cases, and must be effected with care to avoid damage to roots.

Peat pots

Their main advantage is to allow plants to be grown and planted out without check. They are made from a mixture of approximately 75% sterilized peat and 25% wood fibre, the proportions varying with different manufacturers. Small quantities of nitrogen, phosphorus and potash are usually contained in the peat/wood fibre, which is compressed to form a thin wall. Experience is needed to get the best out of peat pots, which retain moisture with tenacity, thus necessitating less frequent watering particularly if the peat pots are housed in boxes or trays on top of a layer of peat. Space should be allowed between the individual pots, otherwise they can deteriorate quickly. They must not be handled any more than is strictly necessary, otherwise after a certain stage they disintegrate easily. Nutritionally peat pots do not present great difficulties, although extra nitrogen may be required at a certain stage of decomposition, as indicated by paler green leaves on the plants.

Peat pots are more suitable for pricking off and growing on than for seed sowing, although for single large seeds or pelleted seed they are excellent, as the roots penetrate the walls and are poised ready for action when the peat pot is potted on or planted out. They are also available in strip form to save space.

Jiffy 7s are compressed peat pots contained in a thin mesh net made from a mixture of polyethylene and polypropylene; they have made a tremendous impact in all spheres of propagation throughout Europe and further afield in recent years. The pots are expanded by saturating with water on a clean surface, or by standing in a tray of water or placing in a tub; the overhead method of expansion is said to be better for seed sowing. Capillary or tub expansion allows more air in the Jiffy 7 and provides better conditions for the rooting of cut-tings. Plants as they develop can be fed with a complete liquid fertilizer high in nitrogen and potash. Seeds can be sown or cuttings rooted individually in each Jiffy 7, which is then potted on or planted out, avoiding all check to growth. Compressed peat blocks without netting (e.g. Jiffy 9s) are now available.

Plastic blocks

Developed in the early 1970s, these consist of foam plastic cut into blocks which serve for seed sowing, rooting cuttings, or prick-ing off. They simply provide a compatible and moist medium for the production of growth, but experience in their use is limited. Rock wool cubes are also now available in different sizes/see Chapter 16.

Soil and peat blocks

Soil blocks have been used for a great many years with changing popularity. Either soil-containing compost or peat can be blocked with suitable machinery, manually or automatically operated, the latter being essential for blocks required by the large scale commercial grower. In the early days of soil blocks they were used as a substitute for pots, largely for pricking off seedlings, but in more recent years they have also been used for the rooting of cuttings and seed sowing. The automatic blockmaker not only makes the block but sows pelleted or split pill seeds automatically and is used mainly by large scale vegetable growers. Soil or peat blocks must be sufficiently compacted otherwise they can disintegrate, and it is essential to hold the blocks in trays or boxes.

Bedding plant pots, trays, seed boxes and propagators (see page 194)

While wooden seed boxes suitably treated against rapid deterioration are still available in standard sizes of 36.8 × 23.2 × 5cm (14 × 9 × 2in), these are tending to be ousted by plastic or trays. Fish boxes have long been the main plant container for com-mercial bedding plant production, but the trend is now towards polystyrene or plastic trays. Drainage occurs in wooden boxes through the spaces left between the bottom

spars, although some gardeners make further holes. Ex-fish boxes tend to be smelly and salt contaminated; they are best kept outside for a weathering period.

Plastic seed trays are usually available in varying sizes with slight variations accord-ing to suppliers.

Polystyrene trays are generally of stand-ard size (14 × 9 × 2in) although they are also available as break-up units (four units each constructed for 10-cell plants) so that customers can buy their bedding plants in small quantities without root disturbance. Commercial growers widely use four or five section polystyrene trays with 10 or 12 plants in each section, but it should be noted that these section trays are not generally available to the public. Gardeners with commercial aspirations can purchase the four or five section trays from whole-sale sundry suppliers, or possibly by ar-rangement with a commercial grower. The trend towards cell trays is pronounced and it is ironical that in the U.K. bedding plants are still produced and sold in communal trays, a practice which can find no fav-our whatsoever in any of the continental countries, U.S.A. or further afield. Plastic packs are also available in the same basic forms.

Apart from the break-up units, the role of all these boxes or trays is similar – seed sowing, rooting of cuttings and pricking off. Their respective merits culturally cause tremendous conflict of opinion; hygiene is a major advantage with plastic trays whereas the risk of disease carry-over in wooden boxes is very real, necessitating washing with a solution of 1:49 formal-dehyde, or cresylic acid at 1:39, some weeks before use. Expanded polystyrene, due to its insulating properties, offers a warm home for the plant, but in some quarters the opinion is that plants do not thrive so readily in polystyrene as in plastic or wood; this is possibly because its poro-sity makes water application more tricky.

Plastic dome covers are designed to cover all sizes of plastic trays, forming very convenient mini-propagating cases, pos-sibly an ideal arrangement for the gardener with limited propagating space in the greenhouse and needing to use a porch or even a light window in the home for additional space. Polythene bags make a very useful cover and conserve moisture effectively. Propagating cases play an increasing role for seed sowing.

Seed sowing

Preparation

Where soil-containing compost is to be used in clay pots follow the filling procedure shown in Fig 51. With plastic pots it is perhaps doubtful whether the layer of roughage is justified (except for very fine slow-germinating seeds) especially if a modern soilless mix is used. For boxes or containers it is doubtful whether any crocks are needed, as the admittance of air and moisture movement are more influenced by evenness of consolidation than anything else, provided the compost has a good texture.

Always use *warm* compost, firming it well with the fingers to the corners and then levelling off with a pot-firmer or the base of another pot or suitably sized box about 1.25cm (½in) below the pot or box level. Compartmentalized trays should be filled in the same general manner, although firming is more readily achieved by 'dumping'. The surface of the compost can be finished off with some light coloured fine sand, especially for very tiny seeds like lobelia or primula, as it not only enables the distribution of seeds to be observed but ensures intimate contact of seed on compost. Once again with special soilless seed composts this procedure may not be thought essential. A level surface on top of the receptacle is, however, necessary for fine seeds in all circumstances.

Prior to sowing, all compost-filled receptacles should be thoroughly watered with a fine rose and allowed to drain, during which interval labels should be prepared, showing plant species, variety and date of sowing. Plastic labels have almost entirely ousted wooden tallies, although there is a lot to be said for the cheapness of the latter on a short-term basis.

Sowing methods

Open the seed packet by tearing off a corner, shake the seed into a piece of paper and use the finger and thumb to distribute it evenly on the prepared compost—this can be difficult if the seed is very dust-like. Alternatively a folded piece of paper can be used as a spill and the seeds encouraged to come out evenly by gentle shaking. At what density to sow seeds depends a lot on circumstances; it is always better to err on the thin side than to sow so thickly that the little seedlings are overcrowded, a state of affairs that leads to the encouragement of damping-off disease.

Fine seeds are not covered, merely being pressed into the top of the compost; most other seeds are covered with a little sifted compost, either scattered on with the fingers or worked through a fine 0.31—0.62cm (⅛—¼in) riddle or sieve, a soup strainer being a useful item of equipment at amateur level. The depth of covering is related directly to the size of the seed. The covering can be gently firmed if thought necesesary. When seeds are sown individually they are simply inserted into the receptacle by hand just below the surface. Pelleted and pilled seeds are best sown *on* the surface.

Germination

Whether to follow the traditional practice and cover seeds first with a sheet of glass and then paper, or to leave the seeds on an open bench, perhaps with mist irrigation, or alternatively to place them in a germinating cabinet, is definitely a matter of personal choice and the facilities available. Germinating temperatures vary greatly, but as a general rule 18—24°C (65—75°F) is desirable day and night, although for more specific recommendations see cultural notes in Part II. In 90% of cases the amateur gardener will use the glass and paper method to ensure humid conditions and avoid drying out, examining the seedlings regularly to observe signs of germination and wiping moisture from the glass, although use of dome covers or polythene bags is increasing and is a valuable technique. Where mist propagation is practised in boxes or receptacles such surveillance is not so necessary, but in a germinating cabinet (which is dark) constant vigilance is required. It is important, as soon as a major percentage of the seedings *germinate*, to bring them into the light, otherwise etiolation occurs, which results in a badly weakened plant very prone to disease attack. At the same time care must be taken *not* to subject the little seedlings to excess sunlight, which can burn them up badly, and this means using temporary shading, blinds or green coloured polythene.

Watering

Whether watering is required before germination occurs depends much on species, coupled with temperature level and humidity of atmosphere. Drying out *must not* occur, and the practice of using capillary benches for germinating purposes has much in its favour in this respect, as applying water overhead can expose the seeds and leave them proud of the compost. Alternatively the receptacle can be immersed in a tray of water or the seeds covered to reduce moisture loss during the critical germination period, or polythene bags used.

One reason why germinating cabinets are favoured in commercial circles is to avoid the watering problem, as the humidity in them is so high that watering is seldom, if ever, needed before germination occurs. Where mist units are used for germinating purposes it matters little whether the seedling is exposed, as it is kept continually moist by the watering, and damage by excessive exposure to the sun is unlikely. The same is true of polythene bags.

Once seedlings are developing freely on the greenhouse bench in a position of good light they should be watered freely according to demands, avoiding over-watering and the provision of too humid an atmosphere which will encourage damping-off. Preventive measures for damping-off are described in the last chapter.

Difficulties

Under most circumstances and with seed of a non-temperamental nature, air, moisture and correct temperature will bring about germination in a specific number of days. Delay in germination may be caused by faulty seed or careless storing, or by the wrong germinating conditions for the species, especially in respect of temperature and light. Compost with poor structure, inhibiting the entry of oxygen, will literally stop the seed breathing, as indeed will saturation of the compost. *Drying out could also be disastrous.*

Some seeds have naturally hard testas or coats (eg sweet peas) and some pre-soaking treatment can speed up germination – by chipping, rubbing with sandpaper, soaking briefly in very hot water, or in warm water for a longer period, or alternatively for a specified period in strong sulphuric acid (this requires precise reference to a botanical list). Sometimes a period of cold followed by warmth will bring about germination; hardy primulas for example can be sown and left outside over the winter, then brought in to germinate in the spring with ease. Such complications are, however, more the exception than the rule.

Seed sowing in frames and borders

What has been said about the sowing of seed in pots, pans or boxes applies generally in the case of sowing seeds in frames, the seed being sown in many cases in the actual ground, although it can be sown in receptacles; follow the same principles of shade for a few days and regular watering thereafter. No special conditions apply other than adequate soil preparation, checking its lime and nutrient content by analysis, a good firm seed bed and the avoidance of drying out. Seed can be sown in drills, or spaced out, or sown broadcast, as with brassicas, which can be merely scattered on the surface before either being covered with some riddled soil or pressed in with the back of a spade.

Weed control may be a **problem** in frames, necessitating sterilization either with chemicals or by heat, although weedkillers such as paraquat can be used on the delayed seed bed technique, i.e. soil is prepared some weeks in advance of sowing and paraquat applied 2–3 days *after* sowing. Alternatively specific weedkillers, such as CIPC (Commercially available only) for lettuce, can be applied.

The same general principles apply when sowing seeds direct in greenhouse borders.

Ancillary propagating equipment

Dibbers can be made with any convenient piece of stick 10–13cm (4–5in) in length and pointed at one end, or plastic dibbers can be purchased. Dibbers are used for space-sowing seed; marking holes for the insertion of cuttings; for pricking off, making the indentation necessary to receive the little plants; and either a dibber or tally can be used for easing young plants out of their pots or boxes.

A series of round or rectangular firmers with handles are invaluable where a lot of seed sowing is involved. Any handyman can make these up. A similar sort of item with nails or wooden pegs inserted is useful for pricking off on a large scale, being pressed into the prepared box to make the little holes to take the young plants (see Fig. 47). A fine-rosed watering can is an essential, as also are some trays for immersing the trays or pots when water is to be given from below. Seed sowers made of plastic are also available, although many gardeners prefer to use their fingers. A professional gardener sowing many boxes of bedding plants every year will find a series of little measures extremely useful to measure the correct amount of seed per box. A series of fine sieves can be made from metal mesh material tacked on to wooden framework, or fine riddles can be purchased. Sheets of glass of various sizes for covering boxes are essential, unless plastic dome covers or bags are available for trays. For removing cuttings from plants use either a *sharp* thin knife or razor blade, preferably one-sided for safety or in a special holder.

Pricking off procedures

It is essential to move seedlings on or prick them off when they are sown broadcast; those which are sown individually are left undisturbed, which apart from the saving in time, is in fact one of the major advantages of this technique. Pricking off involves very careful extraction of individual seedlings or groups of seedlings (in the case of lobelia) using a dibber or tally and avoid-

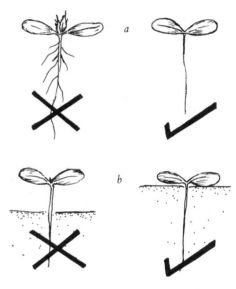

Fig. 48 Pricking off seedlings. (*a*) This should be carried out when first seed leaves have just expanded, *not* when true leaves emerge. (*b*) Prick off seedlings so that leaves are just level with compost surface *not* well above soil level.

Fig. 47 A marker board is a great asset when pricking off bedding plants (available from B. Hopkins, Brick Hill, Hook Norton, Banbury, OX15 5PV).

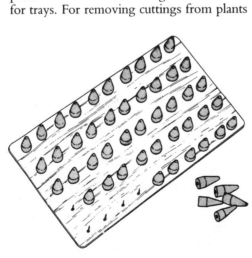

Fig. 49 Pricking off seedlings – number per tray. Space seedlings 5 × 4 (20) per half tray. Mark positions before starting. For a full tray prick off 40 (8 × 5) or 48 (8 × 6).

ing serious damage to roots. The advantages of early pricking off were emphasized by the John Innes Horticultural Institute many years ago (see Fig. 48).

Boxes are generally used for pricking out, using a compost nutritionally acceptable for the time of year. For most bedding plants allow about forty-eight or fifty per standard tray (see Fig. 49). The little seedlings must not be planted too deeply and they should be firmed gently with the base of the dibber. Recent years have seen a variety of propagating techniques being developed. Notable in this respect are the expanded polystyrene propagating system (a compartmentalized container with push out pegs) and the Arcol or similar (see Appendix) trays.

Rather close, humid conditions are given for a few days after pricking off the plants then being given good light and plenty of air, subsequent treatment depending on method of culture dictated by species. A period of hardening off or acclimatization will be necessary for plants being moved to cooler quarters or out of doors, whereas permanently housed greenhouse plants will eventually be potted on, the same being true of plants being maintained in the greenhouse for stock supply purposes.

Propagation of ferns from spores

Spore sowing involves the use of very well-crocked pots and a *very* fine compost, the compost being watered by immersion before the spores are pressed into the surface and covered with glass. Place in a saucer or water to retain moisture. The little plants which appear should be pricked off individually (see also Chapter 29).

Labelling

Always label seed boxes, pots and so on, with either plastic or wooden labels, giving dates, species and variety.

CHAPTER 17
Vegetative Propagation

Many plants propagate themselves vegetatively by means of crowns, runners, suckers, rhizomes, tubers, natural layering, and of course by bulbs and corms. We are concerned in this chapter not with natural but with 'artificial' methods of vegetative propagation, primarily the use of stem cuttings.

Inducing the sections of vegetative tissue taken from a plant to form roots is a technique with many advantages over seed propagation. Speed is one of them, so also is the production of a plant with identical characteristics to the parent (with certain exceptions). Obviously this has great advantages in propagation, as it enables good forms to be readily perpetuated. *Coleus blumei*, for example, is readily raised from seed and the resulting seedlings are generally varied and in many cases of interesting colour form. To sow seed selected from a desirable openly pollinated plant would most likely result in further variance, whereas cuttings taken and rooted will perpetuate the form and colour. These are commonly called 'clones'.

The main disadvantage of vegetative propagation concerns possible disease transmission. Some degree of selection must of course be constantly exercised by a vigorous process of roguing, as is necessary with dahlias propagated from cuttings arising from over-wintered tubers. While the F_1 seedlings of dahlias offer endless possibilities for bedding display, cuttings are the only simple way of ensuring the fixed forms and disease transmission is therefore a major problem in both commercial and amateur circles. This is also true of chrysanthemums. The use of heat therapy to "burn out" virus infection and so enable only clean stock to be vegetatively propagated is referred to in specialist books. The technique is one which amateurs may hesitate to use (see p. 144).

Botanical aspects of vegetative propagation

The ability of a plant to 'think' and pursue a deliberate course of planned action is still a matter of dispute in the botanical world. That a plant is without feelings and merely accepts its fate with stoicism is not accepted by some botanists, the most recent work in this direction being done in Russia. The fact remains, however, that the gardener, not the plant, must generally make the decision when and how to propagate, and at the same time try to interpret the optimum conditions for encouraging the portion of plant selected to become self-supporting as soon as possible. 'Wound shock' invariably arises when it is severed from its parent; it must be encouraged over the shock, and simultaneously persuaded to put out roots.

The first stage of propagation is when the cambium layer which exists between the phloem and the xylem in dicotyledonous plants forms a skin or callus over the wound. This is both to prevent loss of moisture and to protect against fungal and bacterial invasion. This cambium layer then stimulates either dormant buds or root primordia to form, both in the area of severance and further up the stem. It is interesting to note that while buds form stems above ground from external tissue, roots are formed from internal tissue. There must obviously be a subtle differentiation in root origin between different types and portions of plants. If, for example, one takes a cutting from a chrysanthemum stool or dahlia tuber well down near the root ('Irishman's cuttings') when there will no doubt be root initials present, then roots will develop externally. What significance this may have on the ultimate performance of the newly formed plant is a matter for hot debate in specialist exhibition circles, yet for the average gardener the theory of it all matters little, the important issue being the formation of roots. It must also be repeated that the role of the cambium is vital in most aspects of propagation (including grafting and budding) to bring about union betweeen two sections of a plant.

Hygiene is important when removing a portion of plant from its parent, and so is the avoidance of jagged tears, so leaving tissue without a cambium layer to form a skin and protect itself against attack from weak pathogenic organisms. On the other hand, there is an increasing use of the snap-off technique of severing cuttings (avoiding any mechanical means other than those necessary to remove the stipules or leaves), this being practised almost universally in the nurseries of specialist chrysanthemum and pelargonium raisers. This is perhaps mainly a preventive measure against the spreading of disease, though it is also contended that the tissue is more severely wounded by mechanical means, whether it be with a knife or a razor blade, cells actually being dissected, whereas with snapping the cells break off at the cell walls. This raises the further interesting line of thought that the urge to recover from the shock of snapping off might be less than that experienced on mechanical removal.

Hormones or auxins

Hormones or auxins occur naturally in all living plants and are responsible for triggering off cell activity or chemical processes. They are chemical 'messengers' which encourage changes in activity without themselves becoming changed in nature. Their effect on growth behaviour is profound and they are conveyed rapidly around the plant according to the special demands necessitated by changing circumstances, of which the initiation of new roots on plant sections removed from the parent is a typical example. Should there be a shortage of hormones or auxins in the portion of plant removed from the parent, research work has shown that certain chemical substances will produce a response similar to that produced by natural hormones, and indeed may in fact be more effective than natural hormones in certain instances. Such materials are called growth regulators and are used for a wide range of purposes including weed control, growth suppression and, most important in the context of propagation, inducing new roots to form. How these hormones act on plants is complicated in the extreme, but obtaining the right response is largely a matter of using the correct material and the proper dilution at the right time.

While, generally speaking, the use of hormones speeds up the rooting process, this is not always the case, nor is it certain that the hormones will induce roots to form on difficult species. Experience over the years shows that an artificial hormone material is more useful on soft leafy material and at fairly high propagating temperatures in the 18–24°C (65–75°F) range. Solutions of the hormone can be used to immerse the base of the prepared cutting material for 18–24 hours; it is rinsed with water before insertion. The more popular method is to dip the wet base of the prepared cutting in a powder containing the hormone and this is perhaps more hygienic. Directions on the use of hormones are issued with the respective products and should be closely followed.

Types of stem cuttings

It is important that the selected cutting is in good physical condition, free from obvious pests and diseases and with sufficient reserves of food in the form of carbohydrates and proteins to sustain it until it is capable of separate existence and consequent vegetative increase in root, stem and leaf.

It has been stated over the years that soft cuttings are undesirable, this relating to their high ratio of nitrogen to carbohydrates, and while there is undoubtedly some foundation for such a belief, it would not appear to be wholly substantiated by the more modern methods of propagating practised on commercial holdings. Here soft, actively growing cuttings of chrysanthemums and other plants are often preferred to those of a harder nature. There is obviously a difference between active growth in good light and lush softness, however, and the latter should generally be avoided as there are unlikely to be sufficient food reserves to sustain the tissue. Whether, in the light of modern technology, it is desirable to follow older practice and let stock plants intended for provision of cuttings become pot bound and harden their growth in any way by limited nitrogen application and other means is open to debate, it now being thought better to encourage more liberal growth. The age of material selected for cuttings varies, but as a general rule younger tissue contains a higher proportion of meristematic (actively dividing) cells.

There are three main types of stem cuttings – soft, semi-hard and hard, but in greenhouse culture we are more concerned with the soft or semi-hard group (see Figs. 50 and 51).

Soft cuttings

A great variety of greenhouse plants are raised from soft cuttings because the growth of many greenhouse plants is of a soft nature. Soft cuttings are, however, also taken from a vast number of outside plants herbaceous, alpine and shrub. As the name implies, the cuttings are selected from soft new growth which either arises from the base of the plant in the spring, eg basal cuttings from chrysanthemums, cuttings arising from dahlia tubers or from the new growth which frequently develops out of doors after a plant has completed flowering, as with pelargoniums. Plants can often be cut back to induce fresh new growth to develop, this being true of ericas and a great many more.

Removing soft cuttings from the plant involves first of all careful selection of balanced non-etiolated (not drawn or spindly) growth which snaps off cleanly, generally but not always below a node, which is the area from which leaves and buds arise and generally possessed of a wealth of meristematic cells. Many plants can be rooted very simply from internodal cuttings, but gardeners generally prefer to take cuttings below a node as their rooting conditions are not as sophisticated as those of the commercial grower; internodal cuttings could suffer a period of die-back and the risk of disease. Certainly with those plants having a soft or hollow stem, nodal cuttings are more reliable. Heels can be left on some plants to advantage as this exposes a larger cambium area and is very useful for a lot of soft wooded cuttings removed from shrubs such as deutzia, philadelphus and many more. While non-flowering section cuttings are desirable others can be used, although the flowering stem should be removed to avoid using up valuable reserves of food. The base of cuttings should be trimmed, removing stipules or other superfluous tissue which would merely rot if left.

The size of cuttings varies, but 10–15cm (4–6in) is average. Lower leaves should be removed, not only to reduce the transpiration area, but to avoid rotting. Where a shrub has very large leaves (eg hydrangea) it is permissible to reduce the leaf area by half or thereabouts, but a reasonable area of active leaf is essential to the rooting process, as a soft shrub deprived of its leaves to the extreme tends to debilitate rather than produce root. Pipings of carnations are simply pulled out of a node and, after removing the lower leaves, inserted in the rooting medium.

Rooting

Apart from some cacti and succulents, all cuttings should be placed in rooting medium as soon as possible. Where rooting hormones are used, the cuttings should be immersed or dipped in this according to directions. Fungicidal waterings or dustings may be advisable, especially with soft material in very bad weather to avoid ever present disease such as botrytis. The rooting period for soft cuttings can vary from 2–3 days for coleus, up to 3–4 weeks or even longer; the average is 10–21 days. A high success rate is usually possible in mist units, propagating cases or polythene tents. In many cases rooting can be highly successful by putting cuttings in jars of water with a shallow layer of water only and leaving this unchanged, simply adding to it as required.

The provision of a humid atmosphere is a basic essential for the successful rooting of all *soft stem* cuttings. This is achieved by the use of mist propagation units, propagating cases, plastic domes or white polythene tents or bags, the basic objective of these techniques being to reduce transpiration and enable the cutting to conserve its energies for the vital process of producing new roots. It is advisable to group cuttings, the quicker rooting species being kept apart from those that take longer. Quick-rooting dahlias, chrysanthemums and coleus should obviously not be grouped with conifers and heathers. Stating a precise rooting period for each species is difficult owing to varying conditions, but when possible an indication will be given in the cultural notes. Downy leaved species tend to rot in too close an atmosphere such as that under polythene tents because of moisture collecting on the leaves, resulting in botrytis.

An open, free-draining, warm rooting medium is the prime requisite for maintaining cuttings turgid and in good condition for the quick formation of roots. They can readily be housed in boxes or

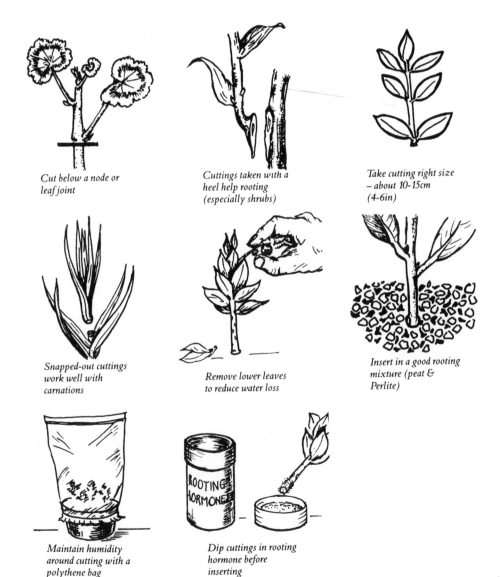

Cut below a node or leaf joint

Cuttings taken with a heel help rooting (especially shrubs)

Take cutting right size – about 10-15cm (4-6in)

Snapped-out cuttings work well with carnations

Remove lower leaves to reduce water loss

Insert in a good rooting mixture (peat & Perlite)

Maintain humidity around cutting with a polythene bag

Dip cuttings in rooting hormone before inserting

Fig. 50 Eight important facts about taking, preparing and rooting cuttings.

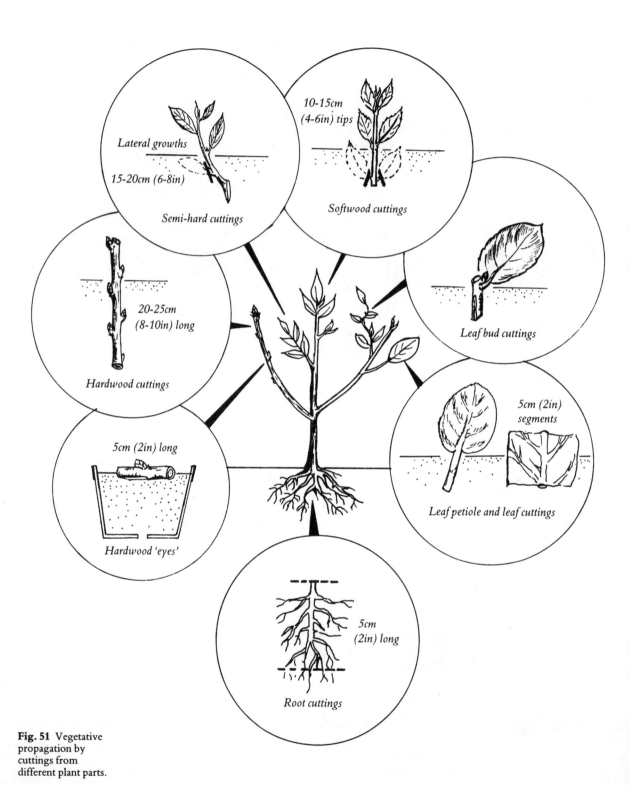

Lateral growths

15-20cm (6-8in)

Semi-hard cuttings

10-15cm (4-6in) tips

Softwood cuttings

20-25cm (8-10in) long

Hardwood cuttings

Leaf bud cuttings

5cm (2in) long

Hardwood 'eyes'

5cm (2in) segments

Leaf petiole and leaf cuttings

5cm (2in) long

Root cuttings

Fig. 51 Vegetative propagation by cuttings from different plant parts.

benches of rooting media with bottom heat provided either by soil warming cables or mini-bore or under-bench heating. Many cuttings can be rooted, perhaps less quickly but with great success, under cooler conditions, either in a greenhouse or frame, heated or cold, or in white polythene tunnels.

The qualities of rooting media are fully discussed elsewhere and the importance of studying this subject in depth cannot be over-emphasized. In the most general terms mixtures of half peat and half sand or perlite are most frequently used for rooting a wide range of species. Preparation of the cuttings and insertion distances vary according to species; again, in general most soft cuttings are inserted 2.5−5cm (1−2in) apart.

Semi-hard cuttings

This term relates to material which has become partly lignified or, in other words, has started to become woody, especially at the base. Propagation by means of semi-hard cuttings relates almost exclusively to the propagation of shrubs from July until September, a wide range of shrubs being propagated during this period with shoots carefully pulled off with a heel, which is trimmed of any surplus thin tissue obviously not containing any cambium cells. Rooting time depends not only on the maturity of the tissue (with many species 2−7 weeks is average), but also on temperature provided.

Hardwood cuttings

As the name implies, this mode of propagation involves the use of mature lignified wood and is a technique which has application both out of doors and under glass. It is usual to select well-matured one-year-old growth of various lengths: up to 90cm−1.2m (3−4ft) long in the case of salix (willow); a more usual length is 20−25cm (8−10in), as for blackcurrants; but cuttings can also be very short, eg 5−8cm (2−3in) in the case of roses. A heel of older wood is not only advantageous in some cases, but thought to be essential with many conifers, although once again with modern propagation methods views are changing in this direction. It is essential that each cutting

has at least one live bud near its tip, and when the unripe tips of the shoots are removed care should be taken to leave the bud at the apex of the tip, otherwise dieback to the bud will occur with consequent risk of disease. The base is trimmed below a node in the majority of cases. Buds may be left at the base of the cutting when a "stool" is required, as for blackcurrants; conversely where a "leg" is required, eg for red currants, the lower buds are removed, leaving only buds at the tip.

The etiolation of hardwood cuttings by earthing is thought to be desirable for many fruit trees, although more recent techniques concerned with storage of the normal cuttings in temperature controlled bins have given highly successful results.

'Eyes' are hardwood cuttings with a section of stem on both sides of the node, as in vines, although they can readily be propagated from soft shoots also.

Hardwood cuttings are usually taken in the autumn when they may be inserted individually out of doors or in a cool greenhouse or, as with fruit cuttings, stored in heated bins until spring. it is interesting to note that while evergreen species of shrubs bear leaves, deciduous species do not, and this would lead one to assume that only the leaf-bearing species would respond to a heated propagating case. Such is not always the case, however, and quite dramatic results have been obtained by inserting nearly dormant hardwood cuttings bereft of leaves into warm propagating benches, where under the influence of moisture and heat they have broken into growth and been rooted with ease (eg roses). Research is proceeding with the rooting of a great many other species of dormant hardwood cuttings under propagating house conditions and under white polythene.

Root cuttings

These are not commonly used for greenhouse plants, although many species of shrubs and border plants may conveniently be rooted in a frame or greenhouse. The method is to lay suitably sized portions of root (in the case of *Phlox paniculata* these are about 3.8−5cm (1½−2in) long in a box of compost, covered by about 1.25−1.9cm

($\frac{1}{2}$—$\frac{3}{4}$in) of the same compost; but here again reference should be made to books relating to the propagation of shrubs, herbaceous plants and fruit trees. In the case of phlox root cuttings are used not only for convenience but to avoid the spread of eelworm. Root cuttings may sometimes not give rise to identical progeny.

Leaf and leaf petiole cuttings
The production of adventitious buds in the fleshy leaves of many plants is well known, the best example being *Begonia rex*, where the fleshy leaves, if cut at the main veins and pegged down with small pebbles or rooting media in a propagating case, will invariably produce little plants at the points of incision. Leaf petioles of streptocarpus and saintpaulia are well known examples of greenhouse plants propagated by detaching the plant with the petioles, which are inserted fairly deeply in a rooting medium in pots or boxes. Streptocarpus leaves are often better reduced to half their size to avoid excess moisture loss. Many shrubs also lend themselves to this technique.

Leaf bud cuttings
This involves the use of a bud stem section with the cambium exposed either by removing a bud, as carried out for rose budding, or with a leaf left in the case of camellias, although both of these can be propagated by leaving the stem intact and making a cut at its base. In both cases the cuttings are inserted around the edge of a pot.

Meristem propagation (now termed tissue or cell culture)
This is a technique used by specialist raisers whereby the tip of the growing plant involving the meristem is selected and grown in agar solution. It is thought that this area is free from fungal and virus infection. In addition, the technique of cell culture has increased where portions of the plant, usually the meristem area, are split into cells which are then encouraged to grow in sterile media. This also has considerable implications in respect of disease elimination and ability to produce large numbers of plants from exclusive plant species.

There are now several commercial firms specializing in the production of a wide range of plants using the tissue culture method and it is possible to buy young tissue cultured plants for growing on, provided the quantity required is sufficiently large. In actual fact, many gardeners buying a wide range of herbaceous plants, shrubs or pot plants can be sure that a high percentage of these are now produced from tissue culture, and results in the majority of cases are excellent.

Layering
This has not a great deal of application in greenhouse culture, although an exception is chlorophytum; the flower tips can be pegged to the ground (Fig. 52). Layering can be applied, however, to a vast range of woody specimens grown in the greenhouse, when it is convenient to layer a stem into a pot of compost. Border carnations grown indoors are also typical of the layering technique, when stems are pegged down into compost after making a short elongated cut through the stem.

Air layering can also be carried out with plants such as ficus which become too tall, although it can also be applied to a number of species by removing a ring around the stem, dusting the wound with a hormone powder before wrapping moist sphagnum moss around the wound and covering this with a ring of polythene secured carefully top and bottom with rubber bands (see Fig. 53). The polythene allows same air to enter but prevents loss of moisture.

The practice of grafting under glass
The process of grafting involves the bringing together of the cambium layers of selected stocks and scions, there being several methods of achieving this, only a limited number of which have application under glass. Grafting is a more likely operation under glass commercially than in amateur spheres, although there is nothing to stop the gardener with specialized interests carrying it out successfully. If there is one vital clue to successful grafting in most of its forms, including budding, it is to appreciate the importance of a union of

Nutrient Film Technique (NFT) is a hydroponic system (of growing plants) with a great future. A shallow film of liquid nutrient is circulated in polythene troughs — as shown here at Renfrew District Central Nursery in Paisley, Scotland.

The early days of any crop are important, especially tomatoes, which are very subject to root rot when young. Here a batch has been pricked off into peat pots.

ix

The key to success
with tomatoes is
producing a lot of
quality fruit.
Spraying with water
regularly greatly
assists the setting of
flowers which
eventually form the
fruit.

All the work of
growing tomatoes is
worth while when
the end result is a
heavy crop of perfect
fruit ready for the
salad bowl.

Like tomatoes, fresh
cucumbers are
always welcome.
Here the variety
'Petita' has been
grown to perfection.

Perhaps not everybody's choice, a few aubergines are something different to grow. This is the variety 'Dusky'.

Capsicums or peppers are becoming more popular all the time and fit in well with tomatoes. The variety 'Gypsy' produces excellent weight and quality of fruits.

Fig. 52 One of the best known examples of layering plants is the house plant *Chlorophytum*.

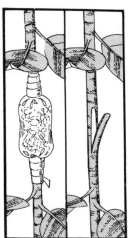

Fig. 53 Air layering is one way of propagating many plants. Here a rubber plant is being air layered, to reduce its height and produce a new plant.

cambium layer, without which failure is inevitable.

Grafting under glass allows work to be carried on over a longer period, and as humid conditions can invariably be created, the normal protection and sealing of the graft area is not so essential.

Saddle grafting of rhododendrons

Perhaps the most usual operation is the saddle grafting of rhododendrons (Fig. 54), when selected variety scions are grafted on to *R. ponticum* stocks. Stock and scion should be approximately of the same diameter, the stock being previously potted up 23–30cm (9–12in high) in a 13–15cm (5–6in) pot and brought into the greenhouse from outside in January, February or March, and after a few days cut back to 3.8–5cm (1½–2in). By making a cut with a sharp knife an inverted V is formed, compensating cuts being made in a 8–10cm (3–4in) four-leaf terminal bud-bearing section of the selected scion. After fitting the scion carefully in the stock, ensuring that at least one and preferably both sides of the respective cambiums correspond, the union is bound up tightly with raffia. They are then placed in a warm propagating case until a union is effected, when fresh vegetative development appears on the scion. Magnolias and fruit trees can be raised by this method also. *Many rhododendrons previously saddle grafted are now rooted from cuttings.*

Splice grafting is also practised under glass, especially with *Cytisus battandieri*, which is a weak grower on its own roots and is frequently grafted on to a stock of common laburnum, potted up in the same way as rhododendrons and brought under glass. A splice graft is the same as a whip and tongue graft without the tongue, and simply involves two slanting cuts, it once again being imperative that one side of both stock and scion corresponds, before binding up with raffia. Roses and clematis (on *C. vitalba* stock) are also propagated in this way, although clematis are now frequently grown on their own roots. The method is to take soft shoots from a greenhouse-grown plant of the desired variety and make two scions from one but cutting the stem down the centre. Roots of

145

Fig. 54 The three stages of saddle grafting rhododendrons.

(*a*) Cut back stock for 3.8 – 5cm (1½ – 2in) with sloping sides.

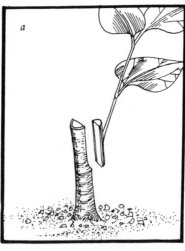
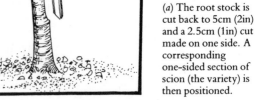

Fig. 55 The three stages of splice grafting are:

(*a*) The root stock is cut back to 5cm (2in) and a 2.5cm (1in) cut made on one side. A corresponding one-sided section of scion (the variety) is then positioned.

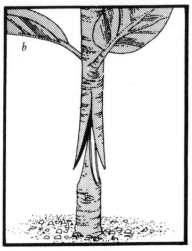

(*b*) Fit previously prepared scion variety over the stock.

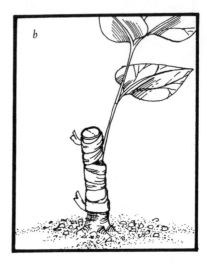

(*b*) The two sections are fitted together and bound with raffia.

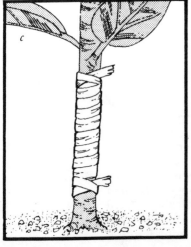

(*c*) Bind tightly with raffia or plastic tape.

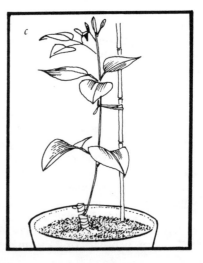

(*c*) The graft is placed in a warm propagating case, taking care to support the scion.

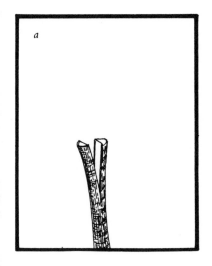
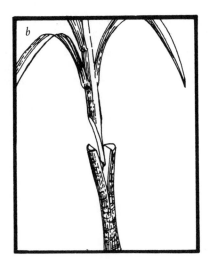

C. vitalba raised from seed sown in the previous March are cut back to 5cm (2in) above ground-level and a compensating 2.5cm (1in) cut is made in the stock, with a lip, allowing the half stem of the variety to be fitted in and bound with raffia before placing in a closed propagating frame (see Fig. 55).

Double forms of *Gypsophila paniculata* are grafted on to seed-raised stocks of the single form, but in this case wedge-shaped stocks of the double form are inserted in split root stocks before being bound up with raffia (see Fig. 56). This is usually carried out during February or March. Here again this practice has tended to fall into disuse as double forms are now raised successfully on their own roots or with tissue culture. Cacti also are grafted in this way.

Inarching or approach grafting is sometimes carried out under glass, when the stock and scions of roughly similar size and growth, and in pots, are bared of a 5cm (2in) slip of bark and brought together by tying with raffia.

Conventional budding can be carried out under glass with roses and other species, although there is no great advantage in this other than perhaps speed for the specialist gardener or plant breeder (see Fig. 57).

Sources of propagating material

These are many and varied. With increased specialization taking place in most spheres of greenhouse culture, there are many central sources of cuttings produced by specialist raisers under strict supervision (virus diseases and fungal disorders are readily distributed by vegetative propagation). Due to poor winter light in Britain, provision is also made for cutting material from the Mediterranean zone, particularly with chrysanthemums and carnations.

The constant stream of new varieties to replace worn out or deteriorating stocks of

Fig. 56 Wedge grafting can be carried out with many plants.
(*a*) The root stock is cut back and the stem split.
(*b*) A wedge shaped section of scion (the variety) is inserted. It must match the cambium at one side.
(*c*) The two are bound with raffia.

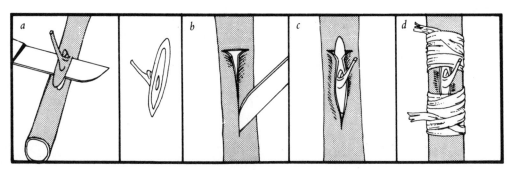

Fig. 57 Budding.
(*a*) A bud from the scion (variety) is carefully removed with a sharp knife.
(*b*) A 'T' shaped cut made in the bark of the root stock.
(*c*) The bud is inserted.
(*d*) Bound with raffia or plastic shield.

plants, more especially chrysanthemums and dahlias, necessitates constant reappraisal of the situation and the purchase of reliable new stock at fairly regular intervals, a lot depending on the intensity of culture. With specialized pot plants such as pelargoniums the same pattern prevails, and specialist producers of young plants retain stock plants under strict supervision; the same is true of specialist fruit tree or soft fruit producers.

Many species of plants which were formerly grown from cuttings are now largely grown from seed. This is because of intensive breeding work (e.g. pelargoniums). The same is true of tissue culture.

PART 2

On the Growing of Plants in Greenhouses

The reader is advised against considering these cultural notes in complete isolation. Reference should be made back to Part I where appropriate, especially to those chapters dealing with soil analysis, nutrition and growing media.

For varieties the reader is urged to make full use of the current issue of the excellent catalogues published by the major seed houses and nursery firms, especially the firms whose names are acknowledged in the preface or Appendix.

The use of peat is frequently recommended in the following chapters. Peat substitutes based on coir, timber products and other materials are increasingly being used. The experience of the author is limited in the use of many peat substitutes.

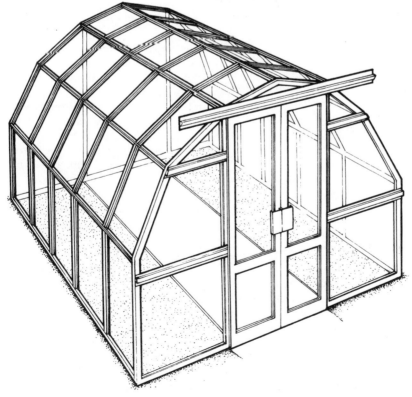

CHAPTER 18

Tomatoes Under Glass

The tomato, originally a small prostrate spreading plant from South America, belongs to the genus *Lycopersicon* and two distinct species, *L. esculentum* and *L. pimpinellifolium*, and several botanical varieties exist. The large-fruited tomato as we know it today still yearns for the high light conditions and warmth inherent in its make-up. Most crops of tomatoes are likely to be earlier and more successful in areas of good light in well-sited, modern, light-admitting greenhouses than they are in dull areas in greenhouses of poor design. For early crops the level of heating should also be sufficiently high and effectively distributed.

Nutritional standards for tomatoes

Tomatoes are greedy plants, especially when grown under glass and coerced into producing their maximum weight of fruit. It is generally accepted that for 125-150 tonne/ha (50—60 tons per acre) which is 4—4.5kg (9—10lb) of fruit per plant, the following nutrients are necessary. Commercial yields are now much in excess of this — as much as double or treble.

Kg *per* ha	lb *per* acre	Amount *per plant*
900—1100	800—1000 potash (K$_2$O)	28g 1oz
450—550	400—500 nitrogen (N)	14g $\frac{1}{2}$oz
80—110	75—100 phosphorus (P$_2$O$_5$)	7g $\frac{1}{8}$oz
120—140	110—130 magnesium (MgO)	7oz $\frac{1}{8}$oz
550—660	500—600 calcium (CaO)	14g $\frac{1}{2}$oz

Allowing for loss through drainage and 'fixing' of phosphorus, especially in soil-based growing media, it is general to provide for about one-third of the plants' needs in the base dressing, this being made up to almost half by the nutrient reserves present in most soils or growing media, the remainder of the nutrients being supplied

by liquid feeding or top dressing applications during the growing season. The calcium is supplied by adjustment of the pH figure. When border soils are intended for tomato culture it is advisable to have the soil analysed, the acceptable standards being as follows:

pH 6—6.5; 5.5—6 for soilless media
Nitrogen Owing to the extreme variability of the nitrogen figure and its presence in different forms and at different temperatures, ie as ammonia, nitrate, etc. this figure is not always available from soil laboratories, but when it is it should be stated as:

100—150 mg/litres (ppm) N Index 2—3
Phosphorous 41—70 mg/litres (ppm) P Index 5
Potash 500—700 mg/litre (ppm) K Index 5
Conductivity Index 3—4.

The nutrient levels of various composts used for tomato culture, ie John Innes Potting No 2/3 and soilless mixtures, are discussed in Chapter 15. A point of some importance which will be repeatedly stressed is the *need to avoid high salt contents*, especially at the propagating stage. *It should also be noted that figures for nutrients vary according to analysis procedures*, but index factors are reasonably standard.

Deciding on cultural methods

The many and varied cultural methods for tomatoes which have been developed over the last decade tend to make a decision on any particular cultural method difficult. The main reason why so many methods have developed is to avoid soil sickness, persistent diseases such as deep-seated virus infection and brown root rot, and pests like the cyst-forming potato root eelworm. In addition, variation of cultural methods avoids most of the physiological disorders arising from monoculture.

Comparison of cultural methods

Conventional border culture   Plants grown in greenhouse borders.

For
Stable water and nutritional regime.
Generally speaking less water loss than
from containers, bales or troughs.
Excellent crops with *new* reliable soils.

Against
Seepage of water from outside may chill
soil. Control of water and nutrients
difficult as searching root system develops.
Soil slow and costly to warm up. Build-up
of pests, diseases, salts and plant acids.
Problems of excess vigour, especially when
soil sterilized by heat.

Grafted plants in borders   Standard varieties of tomatoes grafted on to root stocks with
inherent resistances. Note the need to use 'Signal' rootstock with non TMV resistant
varieties.

For
Similar advantages to border culture in
respect of water regimes. Plants usually
grow well in unsterilized soil. (Certain
varieties are now available with inherent
resistance to wilt or diseases, making
grafting less attactive).

Against
As for border culture. Grafting is tedious
and costly, and requires extra propagating
space. Virus disease can readily be spread
during grafting, apart from which the
vigorous roots penetrate to virus infested
soil. Fruit can be later in developing. A
severe check to growth *can* occur if variety
root is removed on planting.

Ring culture   Plants are grown in 23cm (9cm) bottomless pots or other suitable 'rings',
spaced out on 15–20cm (6–8in) layer of clean inert porous material (grit, ashes or gravel).

For
Only small quantities of clean or sterilized
media are required annually to ensure a
pest- and disease-free start at relatively low
cost. Growing media warms up quickly
and excellent vigour control can be
maintained. Ring culture successfully
overcomes deep-seated pest and disease
problems.

Against
Feeding and watering are constant and
precise tasks; water loss is high, especially
in hot weather and early in the season
before roots are well developed in the
aggregate. The aggregate restricts border
use later for other crops (although
chrysanthemums in pots can be grown on
ring culture systems) Nutritional problems
can arise from the limited amount of
growing media in the ring.

Straw bale or wad culture   Plants are set out on small ridges of soil or soilless media on
'heated' straw bales or wads. Ideal system for organic gardeners.

For
An excellent warm start for plants with no
cold checks. Provides pest- and disease-free
conditions (provided clean compost is
used). A degree of CO_2 enrichment is
provided by the decomposing straw.

Against
Large amounts of water are needed initially
and to keep the plants moist throughout
the season. Bales take up a lot of room
('wads' can be used instead), are costly in
some areas, and there is a risk of weedkiller
contamination.

Plastic bags, peat troughs, polythene trenches, peat mattresses, growbags, bolsters, etc   There are many variations of these methods, all involving limited quantities of growing media, renewed annually or biennially (and sometimes less often).

For
Advantages similar to those for ring culture. Excellent control of growth can be exercised and crops of a high order achieved

Against
Watering and feeding require great care to avoid build-up of salts. This is not the system for the occasional gardener, absent from home for long periods.

Hydroponics including NFT   Tomatoes can be grown successfully by various methods including Rockwool slabs, perlite bags. The advantages and disadvantages are as for the above systems. (See note on new cultural techniques at end of this chapter.)

Hydroponics With hydroponics the tank method as distinct from NFT is most likely to appeal to gardeners.

The advantages and disadvantages are as for the above systems.

Planning for tomato growing

The two basic decisions which must be made concern the growing method and the timing of the crop, all other cultural aspects revolving around them. Given a new site on which a greenhouse is erected, where the soil by physical examination is of good structure and drainage, by laboratory analysis of acceptable nutritional status, and by eelworm determination found to be free of potato eelworm cysts containing live larvae, there is much to be said for using the existing soil. It should be borne in mind, however, that as the border soil becomes progressively more sick, sterilization by either heat or chemicals will invariably be necessary if it is intended to continue border culture without grafting. Here again cost cannot be ignored, nor indeed can the practicability or otherwise of sterilization. Where sterilization or soil renewal is not feasible then the way is open for alternative cultural methods.

Crop schedules

A decision on timing needs careful assessment of all the factors: whether or not there is good natural light in the district concerned, the light-admitting qualities of the greenhouse, the efficiency of the heating system, whether or not one is prepared to

pay the heating bill for early crops (remembering the availability of tomatoes all the year round from countries climatically more favourably placed). Some districts are known to be late maturing because of sun shut-off, exposure, industrial pollution, and so on. Conversely, the early cropping potential of favourable areas is also well known.
(See Chapter 10 for details on lighting and growing rooms)

Early crop, no supplementary lighting
Propagation 12–14 weeks
period
Sowing the   Late autumn
seed
Pricking off   End autumn/early winter
               (8–12 days after sowing)
Spacing out   1st spacing early winter
               15–20cm (6–8in)
               2nd spacing mid-winter
               30cm (12in)
               final spacing mid-winter
               38–40cm (15–16in) if space
               available
Planting out   1st–3rd week late winter
               (according to natural light
               levels)
Harvesting   Early to mid-spring.

NOTE With later crops this time is considerably reduced, and there will be variation according to region and natural light level. As stated earlier, *very early crops should not be attempted unless cultural facilities are excellent and light levels good.*

Early crop, supplementary lighting

Propagation period	9−10 weeks
Sowing the seed	late autumn/early winter
Pricking off	early winter (after 8−12 days); light treatment then given for 17−21 days at 20°C (68°F) 'day' 16°C (60°F) 'night' according to growth rate or until spacing out the plants
Spacing out	As for the unlit crop, generally 2−3 times
Planting out	Variable; generally mid to late winter. Earlier plantings are achieved because of benefits derived from supplementary lighting
Harvesting	Early to late spring, the effects of supplementary lighting depending greatly on area and type of season

Early crop, 'growing−room' propagation

Propagation period	7−8 weeks
Sowing the seed	Early winter
Pricking off	Early winter (after 8−12 days), when light treatment (12−16 hours daily) at 26°C (78°F) 'day' 19°C (66°F) 'night' is given in the growing room for 14−21 days at 1,000 lumens until first truss is initiated. Small pots are required during light treatment, when thereafter the plants are potted up in 11−12cm (4¼in) pots
Spacing out	15 × 15cm (6 × 6 in) in propagation house, when some supplementary lighting is beneficial (12−16 hours daily) for 7−10 days
Planting out	Mid to late winter
Harvesting	Early to mid-spring (depending on natural light level of the area)

Second early crop, natural propagation

Propagation period	10−12 weeks (shorter if lights are used)
Sowing the seed	Early winter
Pricking off	Early to mid-winter (after 10−14 days)
Spacing out	as for early crops
Planting out	late winter/early spring
Harvesting	Mid- to late spring

Mid-season crop

Propagation period	9−10 weeks (variable according to natural light level of the area)
Sowing the seed	Early to mid-winter
Pricking off	(8−12 days mid-winter after)
Spacing out	as before
Planting out	Early to mid-spring
Harvesting	Late spring

Late crop, in moderately heated greenhouse

Propagation period	8−9 weeks (or less)
Sowing the seed	from late winter
Pricking off	late winter
Spacing out	generally twice
Planting out	mid/late spring
Harvesting	Early/mid summer

Later or cold crops, including follow-on crop

Propagating with heat, cold cropping in greenhouse. Mild heat in the greenhouse is, however, always advantageous, especially at night, to avoid high humidity.

Propagation period	6−7 weeks or less (8 in colder greenhouses)
Sowing the seed	early spring/mid-spring (in heat) until mid-spring for very late crops
Pricking off	early to mid-spring (heat for early period) until late spring for very late crops; in the latter case potting can be into large pots
Spacing out	As for late crop
Planting out	late spring/early summer
Harvesting	mid-summer/early autumn

Propagation procedures

Many gardeners prefer to obtain their tomato plants from a nurseryman for a specific planting time, but there are those who prefer to raise their own, particularly when there are other propagating activities in progress. They should note that initiation of the first and second trusses within the plant takes place at a very early stage of development, long before the trusses are visible. The temperature and light intensity at which this initiation occurs is thought by some research workers and experienced growers to have a profound effect on the ability of the flower to produce fertile pollen and set. Temperature levels also have a considerable effect on the number of flowers on the truss. Satisfactory conditions in these respects must be provided to ensure the production of good plants.

While tomatoes can be propagated vegetatively from 10–13cm (4–5in) cuttings rooted in a peat/sand mix at 18°C (65°F), it is not a practice which has enjoyed any great popularity, due to the risk of virus disease transmission, and also because of the expense of maintaining stock plants throughout the winter months. It is, however, a useful procedure for making up any loss later in the season, simply rooting strong side shoots as they are removed, particularly those from ground-level.

Seed sowing

Sowing can be carried out in a receptacle compatible with the scale of operations, a standard seed tray being suitable for 250–300 seeds and a 13–15cm (5–6in) pot for about 50–60 seeds. (10g of seed produces about 1,000 plants). Use John Innes seed compost, Levington, or peat/sand mixes, which are all suitable; or germinate seeds in a peat/sand mix with lime only added, using liquid feed as soon as germination occurs, thus avoiding possible ammonium damage and subsequent possible damping-off. Space sowing in strip pots, blocks, or in boxes is becoming very popular, especially prior to grafting, and is made simpler by the ready availability of pelleted or pilled seed.

The chosen receptacles are filled with suitably warmed compost, struck off level then pressed down to within 0.6cm (¼in) of the top. The seed is broadcast thinly (2–3 per sq in) or in 0.3cm (⅛in) drills made with a piece of cardboard, before being covered lightly and gently firmed to keep, if possible, the seed coat below compost level during germination and so avoid the risk of virus infection which occurs when the seed leaves of one plant catch the outside of the seed coat of another. Pelleted seed is sown on the surface and kept moist by covering with polythene. Space sowing in the actual containers, according to some authorities, avoids the check which inevitably occurs during pricking off, but it is not always convenient. When grafting is to be carried out it is advisable to sow the seed of the root stock about 4–5 days before the variety, owing to the slower germination of the former.

Shade boxes or pots, or cover with paper or black polythene (especially pelleted seed). Germination can also be carried out in a germinating cabinet. A germinating day/night temperature of 18°C (65°F) is now accepted as optimal to avoid the predominance of the short jointed nonproductive rogues or males which may be induced by higher temperatures.

Pricking off or potting

While there are differences of opinion on the need for early pricking off owing to possible coincidence with truss initiation, it is at present generally accepted that pricking off should take place within 8–12 days of sowing, before roots have developed to any extent. To maintain plants in good condition, especially for the early crop and more particularly if they are to be allowed to flower *before* planting, a pot size of 12cm (4¼in) (or equivalent block size) is generally recommended. Pots may be of clay, plastic, peat or polythene. Blocks should be retained in trays or boxes to avoid disintegration, especially when wet. Dark coloured pots absorb solar radiation better (see also Chapter 16 on plastic versus clay pots).

The compost for potting is usually John Innes No 1 or soilless potting media. Soilless media tend to give softer plants than those raised in soil-containing media. Less nitrogen would also seem to be required in poor light areas, especially for early raising. The use of supplementary or replacement light is almost standard practice for commercial growers growing early crops of tomatoes, especially in northern areas where natural light can be of low order early in the year. For further details refer to Chapter 10. Where plants are raised under artificial lights on capillary watering systems, a very rough sand should be used to give good porosity. Whatever compost is selected, the salt content should not be excessively high, otherwise growth restriction can occur.

Handling seedlings

Except where space sown these are removed from the containers with a tally, carefully holding the leaf tip *not* the stem, and inserted into half-filled pots; the remaining compost is then pressed around the seedlings. Alternatively they can be inserted into dibber holes sufficiently deep to take the seedling without root restriction. The compost should be firmed by giving a sharp tap on a bench before the seedlings are lightly watered in. Seedlings can also be pricked off into boxes prior to grafting (12–24 per box) in which case the dibber method is used.

Place plants preferably on a slatted type bench with bottom heat, unless soil-warming benches or propagating cases are being utilized.

Temperature levels from pricking off to cropping

Generally speaking, higher temperatures under conditions of good light invariably increase rate of growth and reduce the number of flowers and therefore potential fruit on the bottom truss, although earlier ripening of the fruit is achieved. Conversely lower daytime temperatures will give larger bottom trusses but later development, and this could have some effect on the viability of the pollen. High night temperatures result in taller plants and low night temperatures in squat plants, often with leaves curled upwards; high daytime temperatures in low light intensity areas will induce leggy plants, simply because

Northern growers (latitude 54–58°N)

Stage		Night		Positive day		Ventilation commences at	
	°C	°F	°C	°F	°C	°F	
1	13	56	20	68	23	74	
2	13	56	20	68	23	74	
3	13	56	20	68	23	74	
4	17	62	18	64	20	68	

Southern growers (latitude 50–54°N)

1	16	60	20	68	23	74	
2	16	60	18	64	23	74	
3	17	62	20	68	23	74	
4	17	62	18	64	20	68	

Stage 1 From pricking out the seedlings to visible appearance of the flower buds in the first truss

Stage 2 From first truss flower buds to anthesis (the opening of the first flower in that truss)

Stage 3 With the first blooms bursting into colour, the plants are planted out into borders or still in pots and the period extends to 4 weeks after picking the first ripe fruit

Stage 4 To end of cropping

the plants cannot manufacture sufficient carbohydrates to sustain balanced growth. The charts on page 155 show the generally accepted temperature patterns in the UK for north and south respectively, positive day temperatures referring to recordings in a screened or at least sun-shaded or digital thermometer.

Propagation periods involve stages 1 and 2, but generally speaking few gardeners would be able to adhere to the stated temperatures with the same precision as the sophisticated commercial grower, which makes the case for purchasing plants stronger. Compromise overall day/night temperatures in the order of 16°C (60°F) plus or minus a few degrees either way are now general in average gardening circles, ventilating at 21–23°C (70–74°F) under all circumstances.

General care of young plants

Reference back to the production programmes will show that spacing is an essential part of tomato propagation to ensure sturdy well-developed plants with the production of the bottom truss of fruit low down.

Watering should be carried out according to the container and the compost. All-peat composts require less water than more porous peat/sand or soil/sand mixes, peat and paper pots less water than clay or plastic pots, while soil blocks can dry out quickly unless kept close together initially. Peat and paper pots should be kept wider apart than plastic or clay pots to avoid their becoming soggy and disintegrating. It is essential that plants' water needs are gauged carefully, as either under- or over-watering can have serious consequences. Many gardeners use water at air temperature in preference to tap water, although research has shown that this makes little difference.

Whether to feed young plants or not depends much on the compost, although in general regular feeding is advisable to keep plants growing strongly, particularly in soilless mixes when regular feeding is most certainly always advisable, taking care to avoid the build-up of soluble salts. Either proprietary or self-formulated feeds may be used. Later propagated plants with their quicker development may not need such

constant feeding, unless in soilless mixes.

Support with split canes may be required for tall plants which are allowed to flower before planting.

Constant attention to detail is essential for young plants, as any disorder can have serious long-term repercussions. The main points to look for are shown on p. 157.

Production of grafted tomato plants

Root stocks resistant to various maladies are used to overcome weaknesses in the desired variety. These are F_1 hybrids and are available as follows:

HIRES "SIGNAL"
T.M.P.V.F_2.N., resistant to tomato mosaic, phytophthora, verticillium, fusarium and nematodes (root knot eelworms).
K.V.F.N., resistant to corky root, verticillium wilt, fusarium and nematodes.

The current range of rootstocks therefore provides resistance to most common disorders of tomatoes. Remember it is advisable to use 'Signal' rootstock when grafting non TMV resistant varieties.

Root stock is generally slower to germinate than the fruiting variety, and should be sown on average 4–5 days earlier. Root stock seed is sown as for the fruiting varieties in trays or in pots and pricked off into boxes at a density of 12–24 per box, the object being to raise sturdy easy-to-graft plants. Grafting is carried out when plants of both the fruiting variety and root stock are about 10–15cm (4–6in) tall and 0.3cm (⅛in) thick, although for inexperienced gardeners the plants may be allowed to become larger.

After removing the seed leaves a downward sloping cut is made in the root stock 1.25–1.8cm (½–¾in) long, and a corresponding upward cut is made in the fruiting variety, the tongues then being fitted together and bound up with lead strips or transparent adhesive tape, this being easier if two people are doing the work. The top leaves of the root stock above the graft are then removed and the two plants potted up in a 10–12cm (3½–4¼in) pot. Union of the grafts will occur readily on an open bench

Care of Young Tomato Plants

Symptoms	Cause	Treatment
Pale green plants	Lack of light. Too high temperatures. Excess nitrogen	Drop day and night temperatures slightly, balance feeding
Very dark green plants Curling leaves. Shrivelled edges	High salt concentration. Too much feed being given	Reduction in feeding. Flush out salts with plain water
Dark blue coloration of leaves. Stocky hard growth	Greenhouse too cold or affected by draughts	Check heating efficiency with maximum/minimum thermometer. Restrict draughts with polythene curtains
Seed leaves dead. Pale or stunted plants	Either of the above	Check growing conditions. Use liquid fertilizer at correct dilution
Spindly leggy growth. Shrivelling and burning of leaf tips	Too much heat caused by lack of ventilation. Dryness and overfeeding also contributory factors	Damp down frequently. Ventilate at 21°C (70°F). If no automatic ventilation, leave vents open during absence
Poor growth and colour with yellowing lower leaves despite regular feeding	Too much water	Give organic stimulant such as dried blood at 13g/litre (2oz/gal). Reduce watering
Wilting, debility or distortion, often associated with dark green coloration	Virus or fungal disease or pest attack	See later chapter for prevention and control of pests and diseases
Leaf mottling	Unbalanced fertilizer or shortage of trace elements	Check feed concentration. Possible weedkiller damage?

if the plants are closely spaced, although they can be draped with a polythene 'tent' to ensure more humid conditions. Plants are given similar temperatures and treatment as previously stated (see Fig. 58).

When planting out it is generally advisable for the root of the fruiting variety to be removed to avoid the transmission of various diseases by the non-resistant variety root, although this can result in a severe check to the plants. In most cases the fruiting variety root seldom develops to any extent. Care should be taken to ensure the utmost hygiene during grafting, and it is advisable to dip the blade frequently in a solution of 2% trisodium phosphate or other disinfectant to avoid the spread of virus. Note the new root stock T.M.P.V.F_2.N. and ask for this.

The time and trouble involved in grafting, or alternatively the high cost of purchasing plants at nearly twice the price of normal plants, must be weighed carefully against alternative cultural systems involving clean media.

Border culture — pre-planting preparations
No chances should be taken with border soil. It is advisable to have some form of analysis carried out, even if it is only a pH and potato cyst eelworm check.

Borders should be cultivated carefully by digging, adding supplies of clean organic

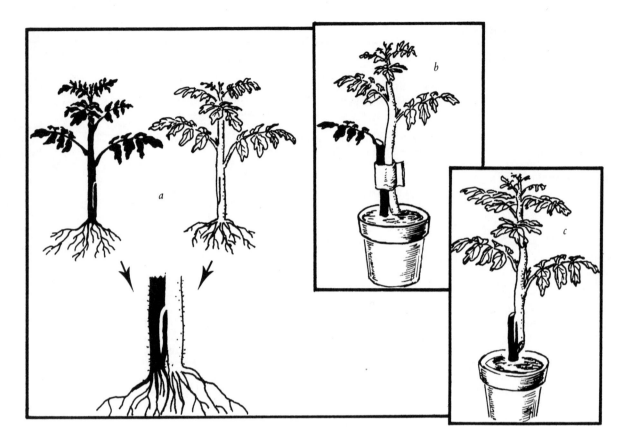

Fig. 58 Tomato Grafting.
(*a*) Grow stocks (black) & scions (white). Prepare a simple tongue graft (*b*) Tape together and pot up (7cm (3in) pot). Remove scion top, leaving one leaf to grow. (*c*) After union has occurred (2–3 weeks) cut off and pull out scion roots.

matter to condition the soil. Many of the troubles which occur when growing tomatoes in borders emanate not from any specific pest or disease or lack of nutrients but simply because of the poor physical condition of the soil. If good well-rotted farmyard manure is available, this should be used at 50kg per 9m² (1cwt per 8–10sq yd), provided that the border has not been heat sterilized—this could cause excess nitrogen problems. Peat is especially reliable at 3–5kg (6–10lb per sq yd). Where sphagnum peat is used in quantity for conditioning tomato borders (or growing borders generally) it is wise to add extra lime, ie in addition to that shown to be necessary by soil analysis, generally 3–6 g/litre (4–6oz) per bushel of peat. Organic composts can be used at rates of up to about one-fifth or one-sixth of the soil bulk, although on a long-term basis they can give rise to heavy metal build-up if used to excess from some sources. (Check analysis).

Organic gardening enthusiasts will obviously wish to use 'properly made compost', and this will invariably result in fruit of excellent quality, although in my experience disease problems can still develop in time, especially if something goes wrong with the compost-making system or rotation programme.

Soluble salt problems
A problem with tomato borders, especially if they are not 'new', is the build-up of soluble salts, and flooding may be necessary to flush these salts out. This process should be carried out to the following levels.

| Border area | | Heavy soil | | Light soil | |
m²	sq yd	litres	gallons	litres	gallons
8	10	363	80	180	40
17	20	160	725	362	80
24	30	1100	240	550	120
33	40	1450	320	725	160
66	80	2900	640	1450	320

Soil analysis will determine the need for flooding or otherwise, it being unnecessary to flood if the salt content falls within the normal level. Flooding should certainly be avoided if possible, as, apart from chilling the border, it can be detrimental to soil structure. In the majority of cases and where previous crops have been grown with adequate water supplies, it will merely be necessary to water the border to ensure that it is sufficiently moist at planting time. Larger quantities of water are best applied in mist form to minimize soil structure damage.

Application of lime
Lime will be necessary to adjust the pH to the 6–6.5 level, and should be lightly forked or watered in after even application. Either ground limestone or magnesian limestone can be used as required by analysis, lacking which information a 270–340g/m^2 (8–10oz per sq yd) application will normally suffice. Direct contact between lime and any farmyard manure applied should be avoided, as ammonia gas may be generated, by digging in the latter before applying lime to the soil.

Application of tomato bases
It is necessary to apply fertilizers as a pre-planting base dressing to provide a 'bank'

or reserve of nutrients. Owing to differing circumstances, including whether the soil is heat-sterilized, chemically sterilized or new, there are several procedures (see table below).

Pre-planting preparations for other cultural systems (Fig. 59)
Grafted plants are set out in prepared borders, sterilization not normally being carried out unless there is a serious weed problem.
Ring culture It is usual to take out the border soil, if any exists in the first case, and replace this with a 15–20 cm (6–8in) layer of inert aggregate which can be weathered ash, perlite, granite chips, coarse sand or gravel. This must be inert and free from chemical residues such as the sulphur which would be found in fresh ashes. The aggregrate should be in an even layer with free drainage. The usual 'ring' is a whale-hide pot (bituminized paper) or 23cm (9in) diameter with or without a bottom. Plants are potted up in a warm greenhouse and grown on to a certain stage before setting out in the aggregate (if pots have bottoms). Rings are generally spaced out 45–60 cm (20–24in) apart and filled to within 5cm (2in) of the top with the chosen compost, usually John Innes No 2. Soilless media can

Crop	Soil	g/m^2	Quantity oz per sq yd	Base-type
Early and main crop tomatoes	Sterilized by heat	204 68–101 68–101	6 2–3 2–3	High potash base Sulphate of potash *Magnesium sulphate
Early and main	Chemically sterilized or unsterilized	204 101	6 3	Medium (standard) potash base *Magnesium sulphate
Late tomatoes (heated or cold grown)	Heat sterilized	204 101	6 3	High potash base *Magnesium sulphate
"	Chemically sterilized or unsterilized	204 101	6 3	Medium potash base *Magnesium sulphate

* Do not apply magnesium sulphate if there is a high soluble salt problem and flooding is not practicable. Vigorous or weak varieties may necessitate modifications to these quantities, as will soil analysis. Following lettuce or other crops a high nitrogen base feed at 204g/m^2 (6oz per sq yd) should be applied unless analysis shows otherwise.

Fig. 59 (*Below*)
Some tomato
growing systems.
(*a*) 'Whalehide' rings
set on ashes
(*b*) Black polythene
bags
(*c*) Home-made
troughs lined with
polythene and filled
with peat. Growing
rings placed on peat.
(*e*) Straw, peat or
fibre blocks, Perlite
and rockwool
systems now being
used on modular
systems to avoid
disease spread
between plants.

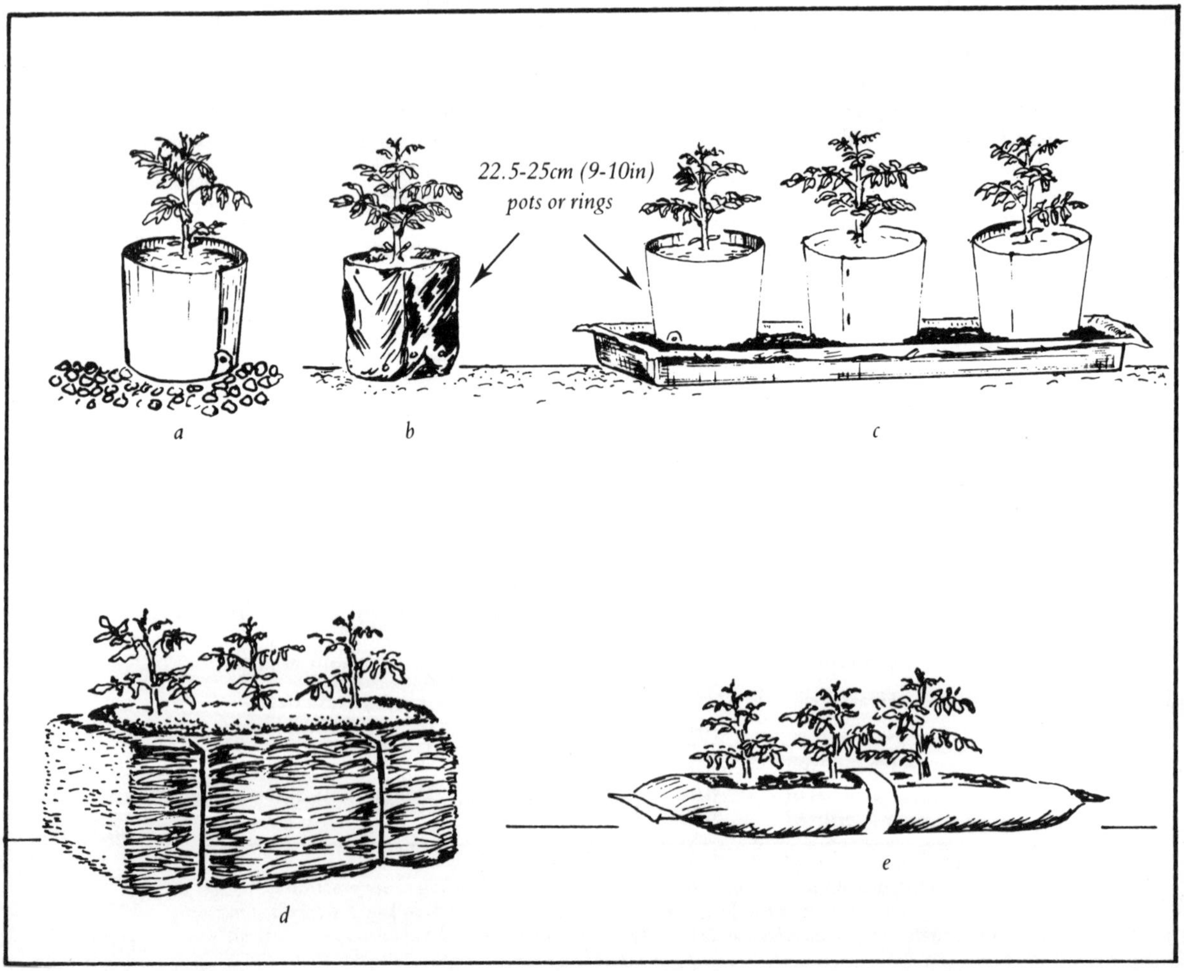

Typical Base Fertilizers

Base fertilizer	Nitrogen % N	Phosphorus % P_2O_2		Potash % K_2O
		Sol.	Insol.	
Standard	9.5	9	0.5	13.2
High potash	6	10	0.5	17.5
High nitrogen (seldom necessary)	12	5.5	0.5	6
John Innes base (use as high potash)	5.2	7	0.5	10

Base fertilizers are applied 7−10 days before planting and the border is then lightly forked and raked to be reasonably level and firm.

22.5-25cm (9-10in) pots or rings

a   *b*   *c*   *d*   *e*

An 'Iceberg' type of crisp lettuce of which there are many excellent varieties available for cropping under glass or plastic.

Vines are a rewarding fruit to grow in a greenhouse provided there is sufficient space to do them justice. Training, support and fruit thinning are key issues.

This superb crop of peaches produced by gardener Ronald MacDonald at Gleddoch House Hotel on the Firth of Clyde must delight many a hotel guest.

Ipomea, variety 'Heavenly Blue', is a vigorous climbing plant of great charm for a corner in the greenhouse. It dislikes excess dampness at the roots.

Stocks, 'Giant Perfection' mixed, make an ideal cut flower crop for the cool greenhouse with their dense columns of highly scented flowers.

(*Near right*) One of the most reliable and colourful greenhouse shrubs, the Abutilon, is relatively easy to grow. There are many beautiful hybrids.

(*Far right*) Begonia semperflorens, variety 'Treasure Trove', is indeed a gem as a pot plant or for outdoor bedding.

(*Near right*) Begonias make ideal hanging basket or pot subjects and come in many different forms.

(*Far right*) Capsicums are superb pot plants requiring care if their fruits are to set and form properly.

also be used, although in this case plants will require feeding much earlier than if grown in a good John Innes compost, of which about 5.5g (12lb) per 22.5cm (9in) whalehide will be required.

Polythene bag culture   Large black polythene bags (medium gauge) with drainage holes, holding approximately a quarter of a bushel of a soilless media, are spaced out on top of the border soil on a layer of polythene, or preferably on a layer of free-draining inert aggregate. Bolsters or growbags can also be used, these simply being bags of growing media which have the top sections removed to allow planting, drainage being provided by making slits in the sides of the bags. Boxes of soil are filled *in situ* at the appropriate distance apart, old wooden apple or orange boxes frequently being used for this purpose on a short-term basis.

Trough and trench culture   Troughs made up with pegs and wire to a 15−20cm (6−8in) depth, or alternatively trenches set in the ground with plastic drainage tiles running through them, were popular for tomato culture in commercial circles, soilless media generally being used. There are many variations on these systems, some of which involve the use of troughs made of concrete or expanded metal; in all cases the necessary criteria are the use of dependable soilless media and outlets for surplus moisture.

Polythene buckets   9−10 litre (2 gallon size) with drainage holes are filled with soilless media, this system being perhaps most successful with lignite or peat/perlite media, or various other aggregates for hydroponic culture.

Peat mattress systems   involve the use of whalehide pots on top of a 5−8cm (2−3in) layer of peat in a shallow polythene trough, and Levington compost has been used with some success for this system in recent years. The method, however, has been employed for many years among smaller commercial growers with pest and disease problems. Many growers merely place whalehide pots on top of the existing border soil, a practice which should be attempted only when border soils are not badly 'diseased'.

Straw bale culture   Deep-seated virus infection or eelworm problems led initially to the development of this system which is based on the old 'hot bed' and uses the beneficial aspects of composted straw and the production of carbon dioxide. Wheat straw is preferable to oat or barley straw, as it is harder textured and does not decompose so quickly. Straw bales do, however, take up a lot of room and alternatively 20−25cm (8−10in) wads may be used, particularly where height is limited. Isolation from border soil can be readily effected by laying the bales or wads on a layer of black polythene. A trench can be taken out before laying down the polythene and this can act as a moisture reservoir very effectively. The straw is first of all saturated with water over a period of several days in a greenhouse temperature of about 10°C (50°F), the heating system being put into operation if the weather is cold. After soaking, the fertilizer (see below) is added to the bales and flushed in with more water.

In recent years it has been found that a shorter period and smaller quantities of fertilizer are required for the fermentation process than were once thought necessary. *Quantities of fertilizer required to induce fermentation vary with the weight of the bales*, but the following average quantities per 50kg (cwt) of straw (2 bales) provide a good guide (*pro rata* for wads). For each 50kg (cwt) straw apply: 336g ($\frac{3}{4}$lb) ammonium nitrate-lime (Nitro-Chalk or similar); 170g (6oz) triple superphosphates; 170g (6oz) magnesium sulphate; 170g (6oz) potassium nitrate; 85g (3oz) ferrous sulphate.

Some gardeners still favour the older practice of a longer decomposition period. This involves ammonium nitrate-lime applied at the rate of 675gm (1$\frac{1}{2}$lb) per 50kg (cwt) straw after the straw is wet, followed by a further 450gm (1lb) per 50kg (cwt) straw in 3−4 days, and followed 3−4 days later by the quantities of fertilizer given above, but reducing the ammonium nitrate-lime to 170g ($\frac{3}{4}$lb) As an alternative 675g (1$\frac{1}{2}$lb) compound fertilizer can be used for the final dressing in addition to the 340g ($\frac{3}{4}$lb) ammonium nitrate-lime. Copious amounts of water are needed which should be applied through spraylines to thoroughly flush in the fertilizers. Organic gardening enthusiasts invariably turn towards organic fertilizers such as Maxi-Crop Tomato Special, which is used on several occasions to ferment the straw. In addition some form of lime should ideally be applied, to prevent tomatoes suffering from calcium deficiency, which will exhibit itself as blossom end rot.

After the full application of the nutrients a shallow ridge of compost (of low nutrient status) is run along the top of the bales. The temperature of the bales in the centre should reach about 43–54°C (10–130°F) and when the temperature drops to about 38°C (100°F) planting can take place, although this is not a vital matter as the plants seem to respond to the heat generated. It is usual to set out three plants per bale, angled and subsequently trained obliquely so that they are not unduly congested, as they will be if planted and trained straight up. It may be found that straw wads do not ferment or heat up as readily as complete bales, and even then fermentation is not always fully achieved.

Planting – for all systems

As the main source of light in the northern hemisphere is southerly (conversely in the southern hemisphere), it is advisable to plant in rows running north–south to avoid restriction of light, or alternatively to plant on the square system. Commercial planting distances allow between 25,000 and 30,000 plants (or more) per hectare (10,000 and 12,000 per acre), but for all practical purposes in smaller greenhouses it is usual to allow about 0.372m² (4 sq ft) of border area or trough per plant for the *total area* of the greenhouse which means about 45 × 45cm (18 × 18in) or 65 × 35cm (26 × 14in) or thereabouts. Spacing is not a vital matter, but close planting is not generally advised, as while it may seem at first sight to guarantee a larger crop, the reverse is often the case, as it restricts air movement and encourages disease. For ring and straw bale culture see relevant notes in respective sections.

Whatever system of culture is involved, the planting of tomatoes *must not take* place until a temperature of 14°C (56–57°F) can be achieved in the growing medium at a 13–15cm (5–6in) depth, as checked by a soil thermometer. With this must go the proviso that light levels must be suitably high, a matter for adjustment in relation to the selected cultural programme. Heating systems must obviously be operating sufficiently in advance of planting time for the necessary temperature level to be achieved. This of course shows the benefit of well-designed systems capable of imparting radiation warmth to the soil in addition to raising the air temperature to the level stated.

Where very early crops are involved, special care must be exercised; it is folly to plant automatically on a certain date every year, when the soil may still be cold. Early crops are planted in good light areas with efficient heating systems from mid winter to late winter onwards, although for the majority of amateur gardeners with a fair level of heat, early spring to mid spring is the most usual time, waiting until mid spring or late spring for crops grown without heat.

Plants should ideally be 30–35cm (12–14in) high at planting, with the first truss of flowers fully developed and showing colour on one or two blooms for the early plantings, so that the developing fruit will act as a brake on rank vegetative development, especially in rich media. For planting in borders generous holes are taken out at the appropriate distance apart with a trowel or planting tool a few days before actually planting, to allow the soil at the sides and base of the hole to be warmed by solar radiation and air currents. Plants are then set out with reasonable firmness, the seed leaves an inch or so above soil-level. Previously watered plants in clay or plastic pots should be carefully removed by tapping them out on a hard surface; paper or peat pots and blocks can be planted intact and can be left on the surface to root gradually but not allow to dry out. Should plants be unduly leggy, perhaps because planting is delayed by another crop such as lettuce, they can be layered by setting the plants on their sides.

With other systems of culture the same general procedure should be followed, but in all cases take care to check planting distances.

Successful establishment

The first task of the young tomato plant is to establish itself successfully, and to achieve this the roots must develop out from the root ball into the growing medium. Where the growing medium is too wet and cold, air will be excluded and the production of new roots inhibited to the extent that they may die back and become infected with weak pathogens. The young plant will often put out new surface adventitious roots in an effort to survive, but a checked plant will inevitably collapse in the end. A dry growing medium will also hinder root development, as will a heavy concentration of soluble salts.

Ideally, therefore, the growing medium should be rendered compatible with the production of new roots in respect of temperature, moisture and soluble salt content. Soil temperature and moisture content are issues which can readily be checked whereas soluble salt concentration cannot (without a salt meter), although troubles in this direction should not arise if preliminary soil analysis is followed by careful base fertilizer application. With formulated growing media it is essential that these be obtained from a reliable source or correctly mixed. If, on the other hand, a plant is able to develop new roots with great rapidity, especially in a heat sterilized soil rich in nitrogen and ammonia, it can rush into non-productive vegetative growth.

Watering Procedure for Young Tomato Plants

Cultural system	First waterings of plants	Moisture state of growing medium	Humidity of atmosphere
Border, including grafted plants	Minimal waterings in area of root ball to prevent wilting	Keep merely moist by damping	Damp frequently with fine rose overhead, especially in mid-morning
Ring	Adequate and frequent watering of root ball	Also give light waterings to whole growing medium to prevent drying out	Dry atmosphere usually prevails, making very frequent damping necessary
Straw bale or wads	Daily or twice daily to keep whole growing medium ridge moist	Use hose or overhead sprays to keep bales or wads wet	The atmosphere is usually sufficiently moist due to straw being kept wet, but damp down also if necessary
Polythene bag, trough, bolster and trench culture	Only minimal watering in area of root ball required	Provided they are sufficiently damp at planting time, peat-based media usually retain moisture content well	Damp down as for border culture
Peat mattress	A compromise of treatment between ring and bag culture. Light ball waterings only	As above, but ensure that the small amount or growing medium in ring does not dry out	A sufficiently high humidity is generally maintained if peat mattress is moist, but damp down on bright days
Container systems	Treat as for border culture where soil-based media is used. For soilless media the same care should be taken as for bags	No further watering will generally be necessary for large bulks of growing medium, apart from damping until plants are established	Frequent damping down, especially for raised box systems
Hydroponics	Intermittent until established	Not applicable (on NFT)	Keep atmosphere moist and ventilate as required

Air temperature should also be at the desirable level, it being especially important that night temperatures do not drop excessively in relation to day temperatures. High humidity encouraged by frequent damping down and avoidance of too early ventilation will also assist with the establishment of plants. In completely cold greenhouses (with no heating), establishment of plants can be very difficult, particularly during periods when cold nights are followed by hot days. But when environmental control equipment is available to regulate temperature and humidity within fine limits, successful establishment is relatively easy.

Support, training and pruning

There are several ways of supporting tomato plants — tying to tall canes, or better still by the use of 3–5 ply fillis, Italian hemp or polypropylene twine (the last mentioned in many ways being preferable to string), tied in a loose knot above the cotyledons but under the lower leaves, and secured to a sufficiently strong horizontal wire 1.8–2.4m (Fig. 60) above ground-level, and firmly secured to the structure (fully laden tomato plants are extremely heavy). The plants are carefully twisted clockwise round the twine as they grow. Netting and plant wires are often used for oblique and layering systems of training. Training methods are extremely varied (Fig. 61), and may be summarized as follows:

Vertical training (A) Plants are stopped on reaching horizontal wires on short-term cultural systems. On long-term crops plants are arched over wires (A2).

V-training (B) Plants are trained out obliquely and alternately in different directions. Useful with straw bales where plants are set closely together.

S-hook system (C) This involves the use of 16 gauge S-hooks set 35cm (14in) apart, plants being supported so many hooks along and dropped a hook as the season progresses, thus being progressively layered obliquely at an angle of 30–35°. Wires or hooks should be used to prevent bottom truss trailing on growing medium. At ends of row plants are turned on to next row (C2).

Layering (D) Initially trained vertically, plants on their strings are detached before reaching the horizontal wire, and dropped to an angle of 30°, usually when lower trusses are picked. Layering in all its forms allows greater stem lengths at a convenient height.

Lateral training (E) The plants are trained obliquely at a 35–40° angle, wide mesh or polypropylene netting being a useful supporting medium. Tie plants on to netting with loops of string or wire/paper clips. Lower plants as season progresses. Interlocking hooks or similar devices can also be used.

Fig 61a shows the use of a simple frame fitted over a growbag. Choice of any particular training system will depend on length of growing season, type and height of greenhouse, consistent with access to plants and whether there is adequate ven-

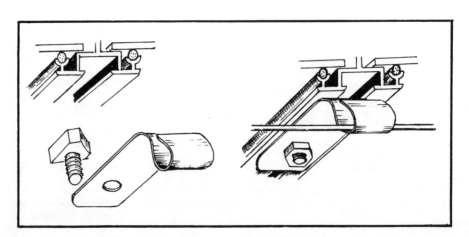

Fig. 60 A simple system for attaching hooks to suspend wires in aluminium glasshouses for tomato training.

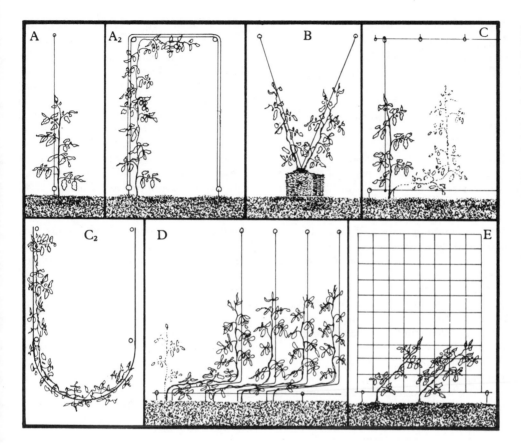

Fig. 61 Some tomato plant training systems. (*A*) Vertical training; (*A₂*) Plants when taller can be trained over in an arch (*B*) 'V' training is ideal for straw bales or where plants are closely planted. (*C*) 'S' system; (*C₂*), plants are turned into the next row at the ends of rows. (*D*) Layering (a modification of (*C*); ideally 'coathangers' (small wire holders) can be used to hold extra twine if required. (*E*) Lateral training from the outset.

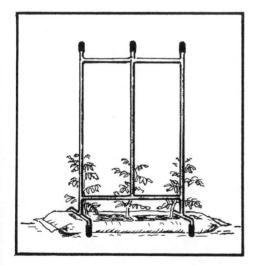

Fig. 61a Tomato training — a simple frame for training tomatoes fits over the growing bolster. This vertical system is likely to suit the majority of gardeners with a short-term crop.

tilation to avoid the problem of disease which frequently occurs in systems other than vertical, due to restriction of air movement.

Training systems for tomatoes depend greatly on the space available and length of growing season.

Pruning Side shoots are removed when small and the lower leaves when they start to yellow, indicating that they have served their purpose. Opinions differ on the severity of de-leafing, but generally speaking defoliation up to the ripening truss is sufficient to allow free circulation of air. Leaves are best removed when the plant is turgid, with a quick up-and-down movement, although a knife can be used, making sure that no snags are left. Plants are generally stopped at a certain height, both to facilitate their handling and to restrict unproductive development of foliage at a time when flowers are unlikely to set and form fruit.

165

Watering and feeding during the season

The amount of water and the method of applying nutrients to the plant vary greatly according to cultural methods and the medium involved. As plants grow larger they obviously make greater demands on both water and nutrients.

Assessment of water requirement

Visual determination is perhaps the most widely practised method. Moisture meters are useful for small scale growers and can either be related to a water requirement table, or state whether the soil is wet, medium or dry. An evaporimeter is a simple piece of apparatus which, by reference to tables, enables the evaporation loss of the plants and the amount of water necessary to compensate for it to be calculated. More sophisticated equipment indicates water requirement in relation to light intensity.

The following figures apply to the quantity of water required over 24 hours by plants with a canopy of leaves and over 90 cm (3ft) tall, no allowance being made for loss by drainage or surface evaporation:

Weather pattern	Water requirement per plant for full 24 hr day in temperate climates	
	litres	pints
Very dull/cloudy and dull most of the day	0.14–0.28	$\frac{1}{4}$– $\frac{1}{2}$
Dull/overcast most of the day	0.28–0.42	$\frac{1}{2}$– $\frac{3}{4}$
Fairly sunny/cloudy with bright periods	0.71–0.85	$1\frac{1}{4}$–$1\frac{1}{2}$
Sunny/only occasional cloud	1.1–1.2	2–$2\frac{1}{4}$
Very sunny/sky clear and sunny all day	1.5–1.8	$2\frac{3}{4}$–$3\frac{1}{4}$

★ For practical purposes 1 pint = $\frac{1}{2}$ litre, 1 gallon = 4.5 litres

Taking an average of about 9 litres (2 gallons) per week from mid spring to early autumn – about 22 weeks – this gives a total of 200 litres (44 gallons) per plant, not counting water lost in drainage and evaporation. For ring culture, polythene bags or straw bales, very considerable amounts extra to the above may be required. To calculate the amount of water delivered by a hosepipe, spray lines or other means when there is no meter, check the amount delivered per minute and then calculate how much water will be applied in a certain time. In a small greenhouse with a hose running at 9 litres (2 gallons) per minute, one merely needs to water for 20 minutes to deliver 180 litres (40 gallons) of water – common practice with about 40 border grown plants in an average greenhouse.

Mulching is a useful technique for preventing surface evaporation of moisture in border growing, using either granulated peat or short straw, taking care to add about 3.5g (4–5oz) of ground limestone per bushel/litre to offset the acidity of sphagnum peat.

Judging whether plants are over- or under-supplied with water can be difficult due to nutritional complications, but over-watered plants will usually tend to go lighter in colour with a yellowing of the bottom leaves due to the exclusion of air from the growing medium and the inability of the plant to extract nutrients from it, particularly nitrogen. Apart from wilting, under-watered plants go dark green and become hard or brittle; there can also be scorching of the foliage and dry set. It is important to note also that if the growing medium becomes dry its salt content rises, making it still more difficult for the plant to obtain water and nutrients.

Feeding

There is a considerable difference of opinion on whether constant or intermittent feeding is more successful, not only for tomatoes but for all crops. Ideally a plant with a constant and easily obtainable supply of nutrients and in a well prepared border soil of good physical structure containing slow-release nutrients may well enjoy excellent growth without the need for constant feeding. Conversely, soilless media have not the ability to store up nutrients in the same way as soil, and plants given only plain water will quickly become starved looking, as indicated by small pale-coloured leaves. Much of the success of tomato growing lies in being able to balance the quantities of nitrogen and potash the plant requires. Excess of nitrogen will result in lush over-vigorous growth, while shortage will give rise to thin hard stems, with yellowing of bottom leaves in severe cases. Excess of potash will produce hard squat plants with very curly leaves, whereas shortage usually allows the nitrogen content of the soil to predominate, with symptoms of excess nitrogen developing. Constant application of liquid feeds, which can be either self-formulated or proprietary, is essential, applying the feeds in nitrogen/potash ratio according to the needs of the plant, the same practice being followed with solid fertilizers.

It is usual to give high potash (3/1) early in the season, more balanced feeds later (2/1), finishing in many cases with high nitrogen feeds.

Composition of feeds						Nutrient (% weight/vol)	
K²O to N ratio	Potassium nitrate		Urea or		Ammonium nitrate		K²O N
	g/l	oz/g	g/l	oz/g	g/l	oz/g	
3:1 (high potash)	150	24	–	–	–	–	6.7–2.1
2:1 (standard)	150	24	31	5	37	6	6.7–3.4
1:1 (high nitrogen)	150	24	100	16	130	21	6.7–6.7

NOTE: This is the stock solution prepared by careful mixing in warm water. It is often diluted to 1:200, generally with a calibrated dilutor. When using a watering can the solution is 6ml *of the stock solution* in 1 litre (1 fluid ounce in 1¼ gallons) of water.

It is impossible to predict with any degree of certainty the amount of nutrients required by plants, owing to variable drainage loss, vigour of plants, temperature levels and many other factors.

Care must always be taken *not* to apply either concentrated liquid or solid feeds to dry plants, as this will not only result in a rapid rise in salt concentration, but may physically damage the roots or necks of the plants due to the caustic nature of many fertilizers. When applying fertilizer in solid form, care should be taken to avoid 'swirling' by the use of a hosepipe, which can give rise to high concentrations in localized areas.

Foliar feeding is an extremely useful method of feeding plants, and tomatoes are no exception, but it is important to avoid the application of these feeds in hot sun, and to adhere strictly to recommended dilution rates.

Cultural systems other than border culture may require some modification to ball watering and feeding methods, especially where limited quantities of soilless media are involved. In containers constant liquid feeding can frequently result in a build-up of salt concentration and give rise to 'black bottoms' due to low water availability or temporary deficiency in calcium caused by high salt concentration. It is necessary to flush out with plain water on one or two occasions.

Straw bale culture may give rise to problems, a shortage of nitrogen frequently occurring early in the season due to its 'locking up' by the straw decomposition process. Later on there may be excess supply, necessitating extra potash at a time of year when the reverse is more usual.

Fruit picking

This should be carried out with care, removing the fruit by snapping the stem, leaving the calyx on the tomato. Fruit should not be left under a hot sun, as it quickly goes soft and deteriorates. *When wholesale marketing of fruit is intended, it is usually picked fairly green and must be graded according to accepted standards.*

Amounts of fruit per plant vary from 3–8kg (6–15lb) (or more). A good average is around 4.5 kg (10 lb). A material called 'Ethrel-C' can be used to ripen green fruit on the plant at the end of the season.

Removal of plants
At the close of the season the top of the plant is cut off 23–30 cm (9–12in) from ground-level and the rest removed with as much of the root as possible, necessitating

in some cases the watering of the growing medium. Both foliage and roots should be deposited as far away from the greenhouse as possible. It is also sound practice to examine roots and estimate the degree of pest and disease attack, after which the greenhouse is then thoroughly cleaned by carefully burning sulphur at $45g/28m^3$ (1lb per 1,000cu ft), or by other means (see Chapter 31 on tomato pests and diseases).

New cultural techniques for tomatoes

Since the early 1970s much interest has centred around hydroponic systems, in aggregate or pure nutrient solution, either in plastic mouldings or latterly in troughs, nutrient film technique (NFT), perlite and rockwool. Rock wool systems are developing very quickly in commercial spheres, as are perlite bag systems. Compressed peat, straw and wood pulp systems are also being developed.

It may take some time for these systems to be introduced into amateur growing circles, but perlite systems seem likely to be introduced before too long. Production-line methods are beginning to develop, including two or three crops per year on a concentrated basis from a succession of plants taken only to the first or second truss stages.

Single and double truss cropping

A square area of cropping in a greenhouse is able to produce a certain number of kg/lbs per year on conventional cropping. If taking the plant to ten or more trusses gives a yield of, say, 1—3kg (3lb per sq ft), it should be possible to improve this by setting the plants closely together and obtaining 226—450g ($\frac{3}{4}$—1lb) from each. Allowing a succession of crops per year there is scope for enormous yields.

Gardeners wishing to experiment with this technique in borders should set out the plants at 25—35m (10—14in) apart each way, supporting them with canes or netting and allowing two trusses to form. Under this method, however, there could be problems with soil sterilization, and poor light may limit the number of crops per year to two instead of three.

Carbon dixoide (CO_2) enrichment

There has been in recent years much publicity about accelerating the growth of plants under glass by supplementing the natural complement of carbon dixoide gas in the atmosphere. In the case of tomatoes three-fold enrichment is carried out from half an hour after sunrise until one hour before sunset. Specific equipment is obtainable for the purpose, the amount of CO_2 supplied for a given period being measured by weight, not volume. Burning paraffin, propane, dry ice or liquid CO_2 are the various methods used, the requirement for tomatoes being 45—60kg (100—130lb) for propagation and 300—360 kg (700—800lb) for the growing period per $28m^3$ (1,000 sq ft)

Varieties of tomatoes

Most varieties grown by amateur gardeners and commercial growers conform to a fairly standard type but there is great variation in stem colour and hairiness, leaf shape and colour, plant habit and vigour, flower and fruit, size and colour. New varieties are being constantly introduced, most of these being F_1 hybrids of specific habit, some with some inbred disease resistance. The fruit colour types have a particular attraction, pale lemon, pink, yellow, tangerine, chartreuse, red with golden stripes, or brown with green stripes adding a superb rainbow effect to any salad and much appreciated by floral art enthusiasts. Most important, they are delicious to eat. Information and seeds can be obtained from Practical Plant Genetics, 18 Harsfold Road, Rustington, Littlehampton, Sussex, England.

See Chapter 31 for tomato disorders, diseases and pests, and current catalogues for varieties. It is essential to choose a variety suited to the growing conditions, whether cold or warm, and whether a compact or a vigorous variety is required. In general practice under amateur growing conditions compact varieties are more useful. One should always seek information from up to date seed catalogues (see Appendix).

CHAPTER 19
Cucumbers, Melons & Peppers

The cucumber

Cucumis sativus is frequently grown commercially, like the tomato, in a single cordon, but is unlikely to be so treated by the majority of gardeners. The following method of culture will be found satisfactory on either a large or small scale.

Early crops should only be attempted in areas of good natural light and in a well-constructed greenhouse of good design. Cucumbers are lovers of warmth, demanding a minimum of 19°C (66°F) for optimum production, although they will produce worthwhile crops on a smaller scale at lower temperatures. Cucumbers are frequently grown on an amateur scale as a "follow-on" short-season crop subsequent to general propagating activities when the outside temperature levels are sufficiently high to avoid the high cost of heating necessary for early crops.

Programme of production

Earliest crop

propagation period	About 8 weeks
Sow seed	From mid autumn in very good light areas until early winter in poor light areas
Potting on	7–10 days after germination (or sooner)
Planting	from early winter until late winter
Cropping	late winter/early spring until early autumn

Mid-season crop

Propagation period	6–7 weeks
Sow seed	throughout mid winter
Potting on	7–8 days after germination (sooner if necessary)
Planting	throughout early spring
Cropping	Early summer onwards

Late crop

Propagation period	4–5 weeks
Sow seed	Late winter – early spring
Potting on	2–5 days later
Planting	Mid spring (until late spring for frames)
Cropping	Mid summer – mid autumn

Seed sowing and germination

It is essential to observe almost clinical hygiene throughout the propagation stage of cucumbers, since they are extremely susceptible to infection by weak parasitic diseases. Good light is highly desirable for cucumber propagation, which means very clean glass to admit maximum light.

The compost for seed sowing should be absolutely clean, porous and free-draining, necessitating the use of coarse grit to give good aeration. All materials including pots should be sterilized by washing in disinfectant.

It is now general practice to sow the seeds, usually sold by number, individually in paper tubes or peat pots and plant up in 11–13cm (4½–5in) pots when large enough, thus avoiding root disturbance and damage. On a larger scale seeds can be sown in seed trays, 40–48 per box, for potting direct into 11–13cm (4½–5in) peat or paper pots thereafter.

Use plump seeds only (flat ones being discarded) and cover with 1cm (½in) layer of compost. It matters little whether the seeds are placed flat, on their sides, or with the pointed end downwards; a convenient method for the amateur is to push them into the compost with the finger and thumb.

A temperature of 27°C (80°F) to ensure quick and even germination is desirable, although lower temperatures, down to 21°C (70°F), will give fair although more erratic results. Lower temperatures than this tend to give patchy germination, a lot depending on variety. Once sown, the seeds are covered with black polythene or paper and glass. Germination usually occurs with viable seed in about two days at higher temperatures and in up to four days at lower temperatures. Germinating cabinets can be used. Immediately the cotyledon appears the little plants should be given maximum light. A practice still followed by some gardeners is to germinate seeds in between thick blotting paper kept thoroughly soaked in a shallow tray, at a temperature of 27°C (80°F), the seedlings being potted up with tweezers immediately.

NOTE: Root stock *Cucurbita ficifolia* is available for grafting varieties on to, and imparts resistance to wilt disease. Grafting procedure is similar to that described for tomatoes. Sow root stock seed earlier than the variety.

Treatment of young plants

The potting sequence varies, but the following is a summary of the accepted procedure.

Box sown plants	Potted in 8cm (3in) pots 7–10 days after germination in winter, or 2–5 days in spring. After 10–14 days the plants are potted on in (4½–5in) pots
Small pot sown	After 10–14 days potted in 11–13cm (4½–5in) pots
Large pot sown	This method is used for late sowing and avoids all re-potting

Some gardeners sow the seed direct into 15–18cm (6–7in) pots to enable the plants to be housed for a longer period in propagating temperatures. The temperature during the propagating stage (excluding germination) should be 21°C (70°F) day, 18°C (66°F) night, ventilating at 26°C (80°F).

Composts for potting
John Innes No 1 in winter and up to John Innes No 2 in spring is usual, although peat or peat/sand mixes can be equally satisfactory. Plants must be handled with extreme care, the compost being firmed up only loosely. Plants are put closely together to begin with, and finally spaced out to 30 × 30cm (12 × 12in). They are ready for setting out when the roots are sufficiently developed to avoid disintegration of the root ball. Open benches have been shown to be more successful than solid benches for cucumber propagation.

Feeding
Plants may require feeding in John Innes compost, particularly towards the end of the propagating period; with soilless mixes feeding is essential, using either proprietary feeds or home-made feeds at a dilution rate of 1:400 (not 1:200 as for tomatoes) – .

Artificial illumination

The need to use supplementary lighting depends on time of year and natural light levels. When conditions are poor, cucumbers with their very large leaves will respond reasonably well to artificial light, which may shorten the propagation period considerably.

Specification of supplementary lighting
HLRG mercury fluorescent reflector lamps 75cm (2.5ft) above bench, 1.2m (4ft) apart. Alternatively MBFR/U lamps suspended 90cm (3ft) above bench at 1.2m (4ft) apart can be used. All types of lamp can either be permanently fixed or on a sliding rail to allow batch treatment. Either type will cover 200 seedlings. Fluorescent tubes can also be used and in fact are the main source of lighting by commercial growers Sungro-Lites have a very useful application here. Lighting period should not be in excess of 17 hours in each 24, the plants having 7 hours of darkness daily over a period of 14–20 days. (In experimental work plants treated for longer have responded well.) A 12 hour lighting cycle, the lights being changed at 10.00 hours and 22.00 hours, gives two batches their share of supplementary light. The plants are placed under the lights when the seed leaves or cotyledons are fully open (see Appendix).

Enrichment with carbon dioxide
There is insufficient evidence to show that CO_2 enrichment is of great assistance during the propagation period, although it can certainly be experimented with, particularly in areas of good light.

Preparation of beds
Cucumbers are most successfully grown in beds raised above the ground soil level, as this ensures good drainage and soil areation.

For commercial growing soil sterilization by one or other of the methods discussed in Chapter 14 will be necessary, while on a smaller scale special beds or straw bales will be used and the need for sterilization diminishes. Whatever soil is used must be sterilized or clean, there being much to be said for a good loam derived from stacked turf put through a 0.6cm ($\frac{1}{4}$in) riddle.

Beds must be made up on an area of perfect drainage, which may involve the incorporation of very coarse sand or gravel through the border soil below the selected bed area. The farmyard manure selected should preferably be from a farm where the animals are straw bedded, avoiding if possible manure containing wood shavings or peat, particularly the former. The first layer of manure is spread on the ground 15cm (6in) deep and about 50–60m (20–24in) wide, followed by 10cm (4in) of soil; further layers of manure and soil are added. The beds should be about 50cm (20in) high with straight sides and a flat top. The beds are prepared about 2 weeks ahead of planting and watered for 7–10 days before planting, to induce fermentation and rapid release of ammonia. The temperature of the beds will rise quickly and planting can commence when it has fallen to about 27–32°C (80–90°F).

Straw bales and wads
The procedure for straw bale fermentation is very similar to that described for tomatoes. Many gardeners thoroughly soak the bales over a period of around 3 weeks or so before the intended planting date, applying 680g (1$\frac{1}{2}$lb) of ammonium nitrate lime after the straw is wet, followed by another 454g

(1lb) in 3 days and a further 680g (1$\frac{1}{2}$lb) of a complete slow-release trace-element-containing fertilizer, the above being quantities per 50kg (cwt) of dry straw. Cucumbers appear more susceptible to salt damage than tomatoes, necessitating caution when ammonium nitrate lime is applied, although owing to the varying nature of the straw, plants can suffer from nitrogen deficiency when insufficient nitrogen has been applied during the fermentation process. At all events, the fertilizer applications are watered in thoroughly. A check should be kept on the temperature of the bales, planting commencing when the temperature of the inside of the bales has dropped to about 27–32°C (80–90°F).

Straw wads 20–25cm (8–10in) wide can be used, applying the fertilizer *pro rata* to the total quantity of straw used. As with tomatoes, organic gardening enthusiasts should use organic based liquid fertilizers such as Maxicrop Tomato Special for the fermentation process.

Isolated beds
Several systems are involved here, the main criteria being to isolate the beds from pests and diseases contained in the greenhouse border by using large clay pots, 23cm (9in) whale-hide pots, bolsters (growbags) or conveniently designed boxes, rockwool, peat, wood pulp or straw blocks. But good aeration and drainage are necessary or fungal diseases may attack. Rockwool, NFT, Perlite and other specialist systems require advice.

Planting
Cucumber plants are ready for planting when 30–38cm (12–15in) high with eight to ten leaves formed, although smaller plants are often set out with great success, especially for later planting. The actual planting procedure is to set about 45–60 cm (18–24in) apart directly into soil-manure beds, with a trowel, making sure each is firmly set with no air pockets. If the root ball is a little 'proud' of the bed, this often helps to avoid fungal disorders at the plant's neck. No plant which shows the least evidence of disease should be planted under any circumstances. Always water the

plants well before knocking them out of their pots, unless they are in peat or paper pots when the whole pot is planted. Where straw bales are being used, run a ridge of clean soil and peat 13—15cm (5—6in) deep on top of the bales, or better still peat plus lime at 114—170g (5—6oz) ground limestone per bushel, 4.5g/litre as this avoids the possibility of disease introduction when using unsterilized soil.

After planting the plants are initially watered in and the greenhouse kept humid for a few days. When it is seen that the roots have started to run, general watering can commence.

Greenhouse temperatures should *ideally* be 21°C (70°F) day and 19°C (66°F) night, ventilating at 27°C (80°F) for the first 8—9 weeks of cropping. Thereafter temperatures are reduced to 19°C (66°F) day and 17°C (62°F) night, ventilating at 24°C (75°F) to ensure good quality and colour. Few gardeners can maintain such high temperatures or will want to for economic reasons. Try to average 15—16°C (60°F). *It is important to avoid cold draughts.*

Training systems

Some planning is obviously necessary before planting to ensure that means of adequately supporting the plants exists. Indeed the actual placement of the beds or bales will depend almost entirely on the training system adopted. Broadly speaking there are three basic ways of training: (1) arch training, (2) oblique cordons and (3) vertical cordons. The method chosen must relate not only to the size of greenhouse but to the numbr of plants being grown. In many amateur-sized greenhouses one row of arch-trained or single cordons will invariably suffice, vertical cordon systems being more suitable where other crops such as tomatoes are being grown in the greenhouse. Where arch training is adopted it will be necessary to erect a framework of wood and wire on which the plants are arched (see Fig. 62).

Vertical and oblique systems are more likely to interest the smaller scale grower. Basically all that is involved is having a strong wire horizontally above or at an oblique angle to the plants in a similar manner to that employed when growing tomatoes. The plants are bent over to give 'slack' before securing fillis or polypropylene twine around the neck of the plants in a non-slip loop. They are then twisted around the string as for tomatoes, removing all the laterals which first appear, then allowing short laterals to form, followed by longer laterals higher up the plant. This is to avoid spoilage of fruit from trailing on the beds. Male flowers are removed to avoid pollination, allowing a reasonable quantity of female cucumbers to develop. Failure to remove the male flowers may result in fertilized and malformed fruits. The use of all-female cucumbers has helped to alleviate this chore.

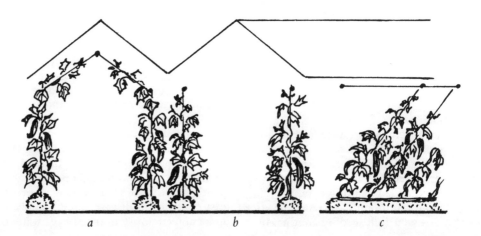

Fig. 62 Systems for training cucumbers. (a) Archway training. (b) Cordon training. (c) Oblique cordon (along the row).

a   b   c

Seasonal feeding and general culture

Cucumbers require regular watering, a regular supply of nutrients and good environmental control if they are to be a highly successful or economically viable crop. Constant visual assessment of the nutrient situation is necessary. For short-season crops grown in properly made up beds supplementary feeding may not be needed. Guidance on this matter can be forthcoming from having an analysis made of the soil used for the soil/manure bed. A pH of 6.5 is the aim, with phosphate and potash figures at index 3/4 (see soil analysis, Chapter 13). The use of nitrogen as Nitram or Nitro-Chalk (or other form of ammonium nitrate lime) at approximately 34g/m (1oz per sq yd) run of bed about 6 weeks after planting is fairly standard practice for long-season crops. Alternatively 6.5g/litre (18oz) of ammonium nitrate may be dissolved in 1 gallon of water and applied at a dilution of 1 in 200. Potash can be applied by giving sulphate of potash at 34/m² (1 oz per sq yd) at intervals of 4 weeks, commencing 8 weeks after planting. Alternatively use a complete proprietary liquid feed at 1–2 week intervals or, if self-formulating the feeds, concentrate on high nitrogen feeds early in the season, changing to higher potash feeds later. The plants themselves should give a good indication of their requirements. If thin and hard, nitrogen is required; if gross and overvigorous, potash is required. A nicely balanced growth should be kept as such by a good balanced nutrient approach.

CO_2 enrichment later in the season

This has been shown to be beneficial in specialized situations, particularly later in the season, but it should be noted that considerable natural enrichment takes place from the decomposing beds or straw bales and for all normal purposes it is doubtful whether the use of artificial enrichment would be economically justified, the exception being a late planted crop to yield into the winter.

Necking up

This practice is useful for promoting the development of surface adventitious roots, later in the season using soil or peat (peat plus 170g (5–6oz) ground limestone) per m²/yd² in a mulch 15–23cm (6–8in) deep. *Shading* will not normally be necessary with a healthy crop.

Mulching (not practical with bolsters)

This involves the application of composted, well rotted farmyard manure, when the white roots are seen on the surface of the beds. *It is a practice not without risk, however, as ammonia gas can cause irrevocable damage if released from too fresh manure.* It is better, therefore, to store the manure out of doors for a few days before bringing it into the greenhouse to be spread on the beds and well damped down. The manure should be kept away from the main stem to avoid stem rot. The number of mulches given depends on the length of season, but usually two or three will suffice. The use of only one, or at the most two mulches of straw is a useful and often more acceptable alternative. The value of mulching, apart from providing a source of nutrient in the case of FYM, is to prevent 'capping' of the beds when they lose porosity and fail to absorb water freely. Note that some lime should be used along with peat.

Watering

Fairly large quantities of water will be required initially, keeping the beds moist after planting by twice or thrice weekly dampings. Then after 3 or 4 weeks a heavy watering is given once a week in combination with damping of the beds two or three times a week in hot weather. Methods of watering can involve spraylines, drip irrigation, or hosepipes, and the amounts of water to apply, in very broad terms, are about one and a half to two times the quantity of water required by tomatoes in borders and up to twice as much more than tomatoes grown on straw bales. The amount of water given to the beds is usually sufficient to maintain a humid enough atmosphere without resorting to the frequent damping down once thought to be essential with cucumbers, since disease is associated with constant high humidity. It will be noted that cucumbers can readily be fitted in with a crop of tomatoes, with largely similar temperature and humidity requirements.

Picking the crop

Carefully pick cucumbers by cutting the supporting stalk. It is usual to harvest every 4–5 days. Fruit should be kept reasonably cool after detaching from the plant. Compulsory grading standards apply for cucumbers if they are offered for sale in *wholesale* markets and details of the gradings can be obtained from any marketing officer or horticultural adviser. Cucumbers are usually packed in cardboard flats in 10s, 12s, 14s, 16s or more, well covered with paper.

Frame culture

Cucumbers make a useful frame crop, usually being planted following lettuce during mid to late spring, according to district, when all risk of frost is past (see frame varieties in catalogues). While it is possible to make up hot beds this is seldom practicable; soil warming cables are frequently used to give sufficient warmth to allow early planting or quicker development.

It is frequent practice merely to take out holes 30cm (12in) wide and 23cm (9in) deep, replacing the soil with equal parts of well-rotted stable manure and good garden soil. Alternatively use well-dug soil dressed with 101–135g/m² (3–4oz) per sq yd of fertilizer. Either one or two plants 20–25cm (8–10in) high can be set out per frame sash, the single plant in the centre or the two plants at diagonally opposite corners.

A coat of whitewash or shading material should be put on the glass over the planting station to assist establishment, especially if weather is hot, and the tops should be pinched out when the little plants start to grow quickly. The resulting side shoots are turned out either to the four corners or to the sides, no further pruning being carried out until fruits are well formed. Unless they are all-female flowering varieties, male flowers should be carefully removed and the plants carefully watered and ventilated. Straw may be laid on the ground to keep fruit from rotting on the soil. Considerable yields can be achieved with comparatively little attention.

For later crops, seeds can be sown direct into the frame, using two seeds at each station and selecting the stronger plant. Cucumbers may also be grown under cloches, being planted out 60–90cm (2–3ft) apart in late spring or early summer. There are many excellent varieties ideal for frame culture.

See Chapter 31 for pests, diseases and physiological troubles.

The melon

Cucumis melo is closely related to the cucumber, requiring for its cultivation a hot arid atmosphere with at least 16°C (60°F), and it is happier at temperates well above this. It is not therefore a commercially profitable crop in temperate climates when imported melons from warm countries are available at reasonable prices all the year round. However, on a smaller scale, melons are grown following general propagating activities on benches and also make an excellent frame crop. There are many varieties in the catalogues outside the usual range, eg among the canteloupes, which can be produced as delicacies.

Cultural programme in greenhouses

Seed sown	Early to mid-spring
Planted	Mid to late spring
Harvested	Mid summer to early autumn

In frames

Seed sown	Early to mid spring in greenhouses
Planted in frame	Mid to late spring
Harvested	Late summer to Early autumn.

Seed sowing

Sow seeds either on their side or end in 8–10cm (3¼–4in) pots of clay, plastic or peat, using JI potting compost No 1 or soilless compost of high nutrient level. Germination occurs best at 18–21°C (65–70°F) in a propagating case, it being advisable, as with cucumbers, to ensure a brisk germination in astringent conditions because the young plants are extremely disease prone.

Preparations for planting

The older method of cultivation for the early crop was to make up a "hot bed" with farmyard manure, preferably in the greenhouse border or bench (underbench heating generally being unnecessary) and leave it over a period of days to allow dispersal of ammonia, not always very practical in a mixed culture greenhouse. More usually these days, and in particular with a warm greenhouse, good riddled loam is used with a small proportion (one-fifth to one-sixth part) of well-rotted farmyard manure. Alternatively leaf-mould, or peat can be used. Where a "hot bed" is used the soil mixture is placed on top of the bed after it has cooled down a little and the ammonia dispersed. John Innes No 2 compost can be used instead of the soil/manure mix with reasonable success. The placement of the bed must be in relation to a trellis or other means of support and depends on the length of the season and level of management. While a continuous bed 30−45cm (12−18in) high takes a lot of soil, it is more retentive of moisture than the mounds 25−30cm (10−12in) high, frequently recommended, which dry out all too quickly during absence on business.

The young melon plants grow strongly in good light, being supported if necessary with a short cane and planted out (like cucumbers) slightly proud of the soil at 75cm (2½ft) apart when the soil mix is sufficiently warm, preferably 18−20°C (65−68°F). The plants are well watered in. If possible the greenhouse should be kept warm and made more humid by limited ventilation for a few days, though melons can cope with some departure from the rules.

Constant watering is necessary, especially when rapid growth is seen. The leading shoot should be trained up the supporting trellis with soft twine before pinching out the growing tip, which encourages the development of the side shoots which bear the flowers. Some restriction in side-shoot growth will be necessary to avoid a clutter of leaves, bearing in mind that it will only be necessary to leave a small number of female flowers, pinching side shoots out a leaf or so beyond the selected female flower. The unisexual nature of melons necessitates manual pollination by removing the male flowers and placing them into the open centre of the female flowers, which can be readily recognized by the swelling behind the petals. It is important to do this when the sun is shining and to pollinate five to six flowers on each plant simultaneously, otherwise there will be varying development and size, although this to a degree may be desirable on smaller scale culture.

Top dressing with soil, plus the use of liquid fertilizers, are the main cultural requirements. Avoid saturation of the soil, which appears to predispose the plants to disease, especially at the neck of the plant. To prevent stem collapse some gardeners use broken pots as a shield against moisture. A moist growing atmosphere is frequently advised but is not now in favour as it provides ideal conditions for many diseases to flourish.

Support for the plant

Fruit must be individually tied in to the trellis or supported by small nets. There will be on average 5−6 melons per plant, it being unwise to allow any more to develop.

When the fruit begins to change colour this is a sign that it is ripening, at which time water quantities are reduced and, if possible, freer ventilation given, the fruit being carefully detached with scissors when ripe.

Culture in frames

The cultivation of melons in frames is basically similar to their cultivation in greenhouses, it being better to remove the soil at the planting station and replace it with a suitable compost of soil/manure mix. Normally only one plant per Dutch light frame is allowed, being conveniently planted in the middle of the sash, generally at a time of year when lettuces have been harvested, preferably in late spring or early summer. After setting out young plants, whitewash the glass to give shade to prevent the plants wilting particularly in hot weather. The top of each plant is pinched out when the young plants are 15cm (6in) high to encourage early side shoot development. This results in bushy plants which produce sufficient flowers, generally 5–6, to pollinate as before, observing the same general procedure.

Watering and feeding requirements are the same as for greenhouse culture, ensuring adequate supplies of moisture and reasonably free ventilation during hot weather. As for cucumbers, a layer of straw on the soil helps to prevent deterioration of fruit.

Vegetable marrows and courgettes
(Cucurbita pepo ovifera)

Members of the cucumber family, the vegetable marrows are becoming much more popular as a greenhouse crop, some listed varieties having been specially bred for forcing either in frames, cloches or greenhouses, the small, immature fruits produced being known as *courgettes*. They are raised in a similar manner to cucumbers by sowing the seed singly in pots from mid-winter onwards, depending on whether heat is to be used for their culture, late-winter sowing in heat being advisable for culture under relatively cool conditions.

The plants are grown to planting stage in 10–13cm (4–5in) pots in JIP2 or similar, being fed if necessary to encourage vigorous growth. They are planted 60–90m (2–3ft) apart in either heaps of soil plus well-rotted farmyard manure, or holes in the ground filled with this mixture. If too vigorous growth is noted, the pollination of blooms may not be achieved despite assistance by hand pollination (as for melons). The leading shoots should be pinched out to encourage side growth, which in time is also pinched out and side growth restricted to reasonable levels. Can be trained on nets or allowed to 'sprawl'.

Vegetable marrows need cool, slow, but frost-free growth, and do not lend themselves to short-season culture. For the amateur gardener with limited growing space it may be better to raise the plants initially under glass and then grow in frames or cloches. Sow seed in late winter for planting in frames during mid-late spring; for outdoor growing sow seed in early spring for planting outside in late or early summer when all risk of frost is past.

Peppers *(Capsicum annuum var. grossum)*

Peppers, like tomatoes, belong to the family solanaceae and their culture is in many ways similar. Indeed a number of nurserymen previously specializing in tomatoes have become interested in the commercial production of peppers. Many varieties are offered, most of them prolific and several resistant to tomato mosaic virus (see Chapter 31).

Cultural details

Seed is sown, as for tomatoes, in John Innes seed compost or soilless equivalents from mid-winter onwards, being germinated at 18.3°C (65°F) and covered by paper or glass. Seedlings are pricked off into 11–12cm (4¼in) pots in John Innes potting No 1 or soilless equivalents and given good light and temperatures of a similar regime to that given to tomatoes. They are frequently planted up singly in 20–23m (8–9in) pots using John Innes No 2 or soilless compost, although in the latter case liquid feeding must be commenced earlier. Alternatively they can be grown like tomatoes after similar soil preparation or the use of growbags. Support is usually with a combination of canes and string, the plants achieving a height of about 1–1.5m (3–5ft) with a 3–4 stem plant. Strings are run around the stems to stop the plant sprawling.

Aubergines *(Solanum melongena)*

These 'egg plants' also belong to the Solanaceae. Sow seed in late winter/early spring, following the instructions for peppers above. They do, however, require cooler growing conditions than either tomatoes or peppers, otherwise they do not set too well

CHAPTER 20
Other Vegetables Under Glass

Lettuce in greenhouses and frames

The lettuce *Lactuca sativa* is increasing in importance as a greenhouse crop since the breeding of short-day varieties has made year-round production possible. The quality of greenhouse lettuce, furthermore, is better than that of lettuce grown out of doors and it needs only relatively cool conditions for cultivation.

Lettuce thrives in a fairly rich soil, pH 6–6.5, of fairly high nutritional status—potash and phosphate index 4 and medium nitrogen levels. It is particularly susceptible to high salt concentration and grows best in a moist regime. Lettuce culture in a greenhouse is almost entirely confined to growing in borders, although on an amateur scale pots may be used. The culture of lettuce on capillary matting (NFT) has recently been developed. It requires *relatively* high light intensity, and light levels during the winter months in many areas are too low for entirely successful year-round growing.

Production programme

The provisional programme outlined below is subject to considerable variation according to region and natural light levels:

Seed sowing procedure

For many years it was the practice to sow lettuce in standard seed trays at the rate of 300–500 per tray in either John Innes or a soilless seed compost (low nutrient for winter, high nutrient for spring/summer), but there is now much interest in individual sowing of pelleted or split pill seed in soil or peat blocks, the block making and sowing being carried out mechanically on a large scale. Small peat pots can also be used to good advantage for space sowing. Alternatively seed can be sown direct in greenhouse borders or frames. There are approx 500–600 lettuce seeds per gm and the germination percentage is usually fairly high; 10/64–12/64 grading pelleted seed contains approximately 13,200 per kg (6,000 per lb.) Pellets and split pills are now generally sold by number not weight.

Seed sowing in greenhouses or frames	Planting under glass	Cutting	Comments
Late summer	Early autumn	Late autumn–Early winter	Can be very difficult in poor light areas
Early autumn	Mid autumn	Early–mid-winter	
Early–mid-autumn	Mid–late autumn	Late winter–early spring	Growing room propagation can considerably reduce propagation period
Late autumn–early winter	Early–mid-winter	Early–mid-spring	
Mid-winter	Late winter★ Early spring★	Mid-late spring Late spring	An "easy" crop to produce
Late winter			

Late winter★ Can be planted outside Early-mid-spring in soil blocks or grown in greenhouse†

Early spring to mid-summer	Mid-spring–late summer	Late spring to mid-autumn	

★ Do not require heat apart from propagation period. † According to district.

When sowing seed fill boxes (or pots), strike off level, then firm up with a board. Scatter seed on thinly and cover lightly before firming in. Water with a fine rose and place seed either in a germinating cabinet or cover with black polythene. Pelleted or pilled seed should be sown individually in the selected container, watered in, and covered with polythene. These germinate more evenly in high humidity with plenty of air and moisture, germination frequently being delayed by covering the seed too deeply. There is increased interest in space sowing pelleted seed directly into borders, singly or doubly at 23 × 23cm (8 × 8in) intervals, or at 10 × 10cm (4 × 4in), thinning out. Firm and thorough preparation is essential.

Germination occurs under a wide range of temperatures, although 13–16°C (55–60°F) is the optimum *and too high temperatures will depress germination.* Polystyrene sheets are useful. Good light levels must be given to seedlings as soon as they germinate, otherwise they become etiolated and drawn.

To avoid damage to roots prick off before too large, either directly into prepared borders or into small peat pots or peat blocks when direct sowing into these is not practised in the first case. The soil for peat or paper pots should be of John Innes Potting No 1 nutrient level, and the same is true of peat or soil block composts.

The use of growing rooms

The use of growing rooms in the raising of plants considerably shortens the propagating period, and is increasingly practised. Seed is sown normally and germinated either in a germinating cabinet or a warm greenhouse in stacked boxes. As soon as the seedlings have germinated they are placed under lights at and given *continuous* 24 hour light at a temperature of 20°C (68°F) for 3 days, before being pricked off into blocks and given continuous 24 hour light for 8 days 6000 lux. They are watered and fed regularly when in the growing room and develop very rapidly, being ready for planting 3 weeks after sowing. Alternatively 15,000 lux/lumens can be given on a double batch system (12 hour lighting in each 24 hours) for 8–10 days more or less according to development.

Space sowing techniques are also readily adaptable to growing room conditions. it is difficult to quote exact techniques for growing rooms as they tend to be the subject of frequent modification, but the basic principle is quite clear; to raise plants on a programmed basis (and a planned cropping scheme) irrespective of weather conditions, utilizing 'waste heat' from the lights to warm the growing room or whatever other erection is being used. Carbon dioxide enrichment is beneficial in growing rooms at 2–3 fold rate (600–900 or 1,000 ppm).

Preparation of borders

Greenhouse borders should be analysed to check the nutrient level with particular reference to the pH figure, the greenhouse thoroughly washed down and consideration given to whether sterilization in any of its forms is necessary. Lettuce, while prone to certain fungal maladies, does not make a soil "sick", particularly if grown as a single crop and then followed by tomatoes. For successive cropping, however, some sterilization would inevitably be needed, there being much use made of the sheet steaming technique in commercial circles. Chemical sterilization in one or other of its forms will also be effective since, apart from the incidence of fungal disease, weeds can be very troublesome with this closely grown crop, chickweed being a particular menace, although chlorpropham mixtures have been used with some success in this instance under glass (commercially only!).

Lettuces are frequently grown before a tomato crop and therefore the soil treatment is complementary to both crops. If *clean* FYM is available this should be dug in at 50kg/8m² (1cwt per 8–9sq yd), care being taken that the FYM does not introduce weeds (alternatively sterilize the soil thereafter, flooding after heat sterilization to reduce the salt content to around pC index 2). Base feeds in the order of 34–68g/m² (1–2oz per sq yd) of hoof and horn meal and 130–170g/m² (4–5oz per sq yd) of a medium potash fertilizer are general, although when soil is found on analysis to be well supplied with phosphate and potash (index 4), apply only the hoof and horn meal, particularly if FYM has also been applied.

Borders should be well forked, firmed, and raked to a reasonable tilth, being of a moisture content where the surface only dries out after a few days but plenty of moisture is available at lower depths. If this is not the case, borders will require a light watering or alternatively the plants should be well watered in after planting.

As a preventative against root rot, quintozene* dust is applied evenly a day or two before planting, being raked well into the surface.

Planting
The soil should be warmed to 10–11°C (50–52°F), which may mean turning the heating on a week or so before planting in the winter months. Spacing is important for hearting and health; 20 × 20cm (8 × 8in) square or staggered is general, give or take a little for size and growing habit of varieties. Use a dibber when planting from a seed box, checking for brown discoloration indicative of disease. Plants in peat pots or blocks should be planted with a trowel, or on a larger scale by a mechanical planter which indents the soil. Water the plants in lightly with a fine rose on a hosepipe, or spray-lines.

Temperature patterns
Lettuces respond to low night (7–9°C/ 45–48°F, or lower) and slightly higher day temperatures of 13–16°C (55–60°F), especially when carbon dioxide enrichment is being carried out – approximately 63–68 kg (140–150lb) CO_2 per 93m² (1,000sq ft) being required for the winter crop from half an hour after sunrise to one and a half hours before sunset for approximately 4–5 weeks. Continuous daytime carbon dioxide enrichment is only feasible during the lower temperature winter months when no ventilation is necessary, and day temperatures tend to reach 18°C (65°F).

Some of the hardier varieties will tolerate reasonably low temperatures. The rule should be to select a variety suitable for the likely environment, or else to adhere to the

temperature recommendations for a particular variety.

Light intensity is also an important factor to bear in mind: the net effect of too high a temperature under poor light being non-hearting, apart from physiological troubles such as tip burn of the leaves and botrytis.

Watering and ventilation
Better lettuce is produced in high moisture regimes. Where soil is of a retentive nature and water tables high, it may be unnecessary to water lettuce at all, but in general watering commences when the lettuces have a leaf spread of 5–8cm (2–3in), an average application overall being about 27 litres per m² (5 gallons per square yard). Too heavy dampings or overhead sprayings should be avoided as this encourages fungal diseases. Two dustings of Benomyl (Benlate) or other fungicide are generally given during the season, especially in dull, wet areas with a high risk of botrytis during the winter months.

Ventilation is important in preventing excessively high day temperatures, particularly following upon a relatively cold night. Rapid fluctuation of temperature causes tip burn. Ventilation should be given at the 18°C (65°F) level. (See also NFT culture.)

Harvesting
Lettuces are cut when they have achieved a reasonable size. This varies from 13 weeks down to 6 weeks for the later spring crop. Using growing rooms shortens the period. Begin cutting early to prevent wastage.

Varieties
Basically there are two main types, the tight hearted and the bigger, crisp type. Red leaved lettuce are very popular now. Select varieties suitable to environment and time of year, ie short day lettuces for the dull winter months, and note resistances offered in the catalogues with reference to local conditions (see Chapter 31 on diseases and pests).

Mustard and cress
Both outside mustard (*Brassica alba*) and greenhouse cress (*Lepidium sativum*) are annuals belonging to the Cruciferae, grown

* Commercially available only.

as a salad crop for the young leaves. Success lies in a brief growing period under conditions of good light. Either sow thickly on well-prepared soil and cover with damp sacks until germination, or sow in boxes or punnets of compost, soak, and cover with black polythene. The seedlings are ready for cutting in 10–14 days or less, according to heat level and time of year. Weeds are the main problem. Soil should be sterilized, pH of about 6.5, and the compost selected should be of reasonable nutritional standard, index 3 for phosphate and potash levels and high level of nitrogen. Soilless compost can be used especially if growing in punnets.

French beans

The French bean (*Phaseolus vulgaris*) is a mouth-watering delicacy which can be grown to tender perfection in a greenhouse, whereas out of doors cropping can be severely restricted in a poor summer.

Dwarf French beans may be grown in large pots, either plastic, clay or whalehide. The pots are half filled with John Innes No 2 potting (or similar nutrient level) compost; 4–5 seeds are put in each 20cm (8in) pot and 5–6 seeds in each 23–25cm (9–10in) pot, and top dressed with more soil when they have made 6–8in of growth. Support is achieved by using beech twigs.

Climbing French beans are best grown in well-prepared greenhouse borders 30–45cm (12–18in) apart in rows 1.5–1.6m (5–6ft) apart, or alternatively given 45–50m (18–20in) apart each way in a square system. Seeds may be sown directly into the border, but are better germinated in small peat pots in peat for planting cold during mid-spring. Support is by cane or twine, the growth being 'twisted' in, in much the same way as for tomatoes, although the tips may have to be tied in. If frequently sprayed with water, kept warm and given free ventilation on sunny days, they generally grow vigorously and produce remarkably heavy crops of very tender pods. The plants should be kept rigorously pruned by removal of basal growth. This is a crop which can give a surprisingly high return for a modest area.

See Chapter 31 for notes on diseases.

Forced vegetables

In addition to the vegetables so far discussed, there are others which are "forced" in greenhouses:

Seakale *(Crambe maritima)*

This plant, which is found wild in maritime districts of Europe, is grown for the blanched shoots which are produced in heat and darkness during winter and spring. A batch of plants is raised initially by sowing seed out of doors in mid-spring in deeply dug soil enriched with manure. Seed is sown thinly in drills 2.5cm (1in) deep and 30m (12in) apart and seedlings thinned to 15m (6in) apart. Plants are kept well hoed and free from weeds and left undisturbed until the following late winter or early spring, when they are lifted and planted about 75cm (2½ft) apart each way in a well-prepared site. The plants are prevented from forming a flowering stem by cutting off the crown of each plant when planting just below soil level. The plants are restricted to one stem and the foliage allowed to die down before lifting for forcing in the autumn.

When lifting plants for forcing, trim all but the central root and pack closely, either in soil under the staging or in boxes of good soil. If given a temperature of 7–10°C (45–50°F), plenty of water and complete darkness, succulent blanched shoots will be produced.

The side shoots or root cuttings are stored in batches for planting the following late winter or early spring, it being important to make a straight cut at the top and a slanting cut at the base. They are set out vertically in well prepared soil in dibber holes 38–45 cm (15–18in) apart in rows 60cm (2ft) apart with the *top* (straight cut) of the cutting just below the soil surface, again limiting each plant to one strong shoot. These plants will provide a supply of forcing roots, the same rotation as previously described being carried out in the autumn.

The blanched shoots are ready for use when 15cm (6in) or so long. Once the roots have been forced they are destroyed after removing any suitably sized sections of root to reserve as a further source of cuttings.

Rhubarb *(Rheum rhaponticum)*

Early forced rhubarb is a commercial crop of some significance. It is forced in dark heated sheds at 10—13°C (50—55°F), usually fan ventilated to avoid the risk of fungal and bacterial diseases (see Chapter 31). On an amateur or professional scale it is first of all necessary to build up a stock of two-to three-year-old rhubarb crowns.

Propagation

Commercial practice is to divide established crowns, this being quicker and more dependable than propagation from seed. Each section must bear one or more terminal buds, these being planted in well-cultivated soil with a pH of 5.5—6.0, phosphate and potash index 2, on a 90cm—1.2m (3—4ft) square-planting system. Large areas are treated with a simazine based weedkiller at 2.2kg/ha (2lb active ingredient per acre). Vigorous growth is encouraged by dressing with nitrogen at 251—376kg/ha (2—3cwt per acre) 34—40g/m² (1—1½oz per sq yd).

Preparation for forcing

Forcing crowns are those which have been established for at least two years. They are ploughed, dug or forked out of the ground and allowed to become frosted. A points system is used to determine the optimum time for housing the various varieties. To install the necessary soil thermometer make a vertical hole 10cm (4 in) deep with a cane the same diameter as the bulb. Insert the thermometer so that the bulb is in direct contact with the soil, with the graduated part of the stem lying horizontally along the surface. Fill the hole gently with sifted soil, disturbing the soil as little as possible. Leave the thermometer in position *undisturbed* until the end of the season and do not cover with a box for protection. The temperature should be read every day at 9 am (10 am before British Summer Time ends). Any readings above 9°C (49°F) are ignored. All readings below are subtracted from this base of 9°C (49°F) and the daily differences added up: these are the 'cold units'. By 1972 three varieties had been tested at H.R.I. Stockbridge House, Yorkshire, and the optimum stage for lifting from the field was

found to be as shown in the table below.

	Celsius	Fahrenheit
Timperley Early	111	200
Prince Albert	166	300
Victoria	288	520

1 cold unit = 1°C or 1°F

Forcing

The lifted crowns are placed in forcing sheds or in boxes under the greenhouse staging, packed tightly together with soil or peat to fill up the spaces and cover the crowns. If given warmth and moisture and *complete* darkness, blanched shoots will be formed according to the temperature level. After forcing the crowns are discarded. Planting in large whalehide pots and lifting into a warm, dark place for forcing is now practised.

Asparagus

There is not a great deal of interest commercially in forcing *Asparagus officinalis*, a member of the Lilaceae. But it is worth while lifting a few plants to produce succulent early shoots. Make up a hot bed out of manure and old leaves in a corner of the greenhouse; rapid fermentation should take place. When the temperature has dropped, put a thin layer of soil or peat over the manure and pack in the asparagus plants tightly before covering with a further layer of soil or peat.

Alternatively they may be planted up in the greenhouse border, or in boxes of soil, in early mid-winter, and early shoots will be produced according to the temperature level provided. After harvesting the plants are generally destroyed.

Chicory

Known botanically as *Cichorium intybus*, this vegetable is grown for its leafy blanched shoots in the winter months. Seed is sown out of doors in late spring in well-prepared soil 1.25cm (½in) deep in rows 38cm (15in) apart; thin out to 20—23 cm (8—9in) apart.

The plants are kept clean by hosing and are lifted in the autumn, the tops cut off and stored between layers of fine sand in lines in a dry place or at the foot of a dry wall. The roots are lifted in as required and packed tightly together in boxes with some soil between them. If kept moist, dark and at a temperature of 12.8°C (55°F) shoots will be ready for cutting in 3–4 weeks, or longer at lower temperatures.

A useful place is beneath suitable draped greenhouse staging, providing a succession of blanched shoots which can be forced every fortnight.

Mint and parsley

Plants can be lifted into the greenhouse to continue growth during the winter. Parsley should be in 15–20cm (6–8in) pots; mint should be planted closely in deep boxes of good loamy soil, when with warmth and moisture new shoots will form. Parsley pots are also popular.

Other vegetables

A number of outdoor vegetables can also be grown in cold or heated greenhouses/ plastic structures, where they will be ready for harvesting a great deal earlier, e.g. beetroot, chinese cabbage, carrots (special forcing varieties), onions, peas, radish, spinach, turnip. Give adequate watering and free ventilation during the spring months. All require fertile soil, pH 6–6.5 and potash and phosphate index 2–4. Beetroot and turnip do not stand frost.

Many vegetables can be started off under glass for eventual growing outside, e.g. early brussels sprouts, early cabbage, early cauliflower, sweet corn, leeks and parsley, in addition to those already mentioned. Seed is best sown in peat pots, Jiffy 7s or peat blocks and germinated at 13–15.6°C (55–60°F) before hardening off for planting out at the appropriate time for the district concerned.

The growing of herbs – in pots, or borders in greenhouses or plastic structures – to give a continuity of 'crop', is becoming very popular.

CHAPTER 21
Greenhouse Fruits

The grape vine *(Vitis vinifera)*

Ideally vines should be planted in a specially prepared border either inside or just outside the greenhouse, the stem being led in just above ground level and the roots able to spread freely and derive benefit from rainfall. Culture in large pots or tubs 30cm (12in) or more in diameter may be an excellent arrangement for the smaller greenhouse.

Preparation of vine borders

A vigorous vine will demand a section of greenhouse border at least 90cm—1.2m (3—4ft) wide and 1.8—2.4m (6—8ft) long with a prepared soil depth of 60cm (2ft) or more. It would be folly to try to grow a vine in a diminutive structure.

The preparation of a vine border in traditional pattern is exacting in the extreme, demanding (1) complete removal of the soil to a full depth of 75cm (2ft 6in), (2) a 15cm (6in) layer of rubble or broken brick with drainage (it is sometimes advisable to dig much deeper and arrange for an *in situ* sump of rubble), (3) a layer of inverted turves, (4) a mixture of 5 parts good sifted loam, 1 part mortar rubble (if not procurable broken brick will suffice), 1 part decayed manure, and any wood ash which may be available, (5) 68—136g/m² (2—4oz per sq yd) of bone meal and, if mortar rubble was not used, 270—400g/m² ground limestone ($\frac{1}{2}$—$\frac{3}{4}$lb per sq yd). This compost was used over generations; it may not be practicable now. Good soil plus a little manure can be used instead, so long as good drainage is provided. JIP3 compost is used when planting in large pots or other containers.

When placing the roots out of doors the same procedure should ideally be followed for the make-up of the bed, but the same compromise may have to be made, with attention again to drainage. The idea that the carcass of a dead animal forms a good foundation for a vine may be true, although it is a practice seldom acceptable.

Propagation and planting

Vines are frequently bought as young roots, although they can readily be propagated from 5cm (2in) 'eyes' taken in late winter and put in a pot with the 'eye' at soil level. Also layers, 3 bud stems, or young growths. Given heat, young plants are ready for setting out in early or mid-summer of the following year.

Dormant vines are usually planted between mid-autumn and late winter anything from 1.5—3m (5—10ft) apart according to the system of training employed. For a single cordon 1.5m (5ft) apart will suffice, but one vine is usually sufficient for the amateur greenhouse. If the greenhouse is oriented with the ridge running north-south it would be advisable to plant the vine in the centre or to one side of the north end. This will allow the vine to travel along the one sloping roof and, provided it is ruthlessly restricted, still allow the culture of other crops. A better arrangement can be made if the greenhouse is oriented east-west, when the vine could then be trained along the north side and largely confined to this to avoid the restriction of light from the southerly aspect (ie if in the northern hemisphere). Where the whole greenhouse can be devoted to the culture of the vine, then the centre at the end away from the door is as convenient a location as any. In lean-to structures it is usual to train vines on the glass side.

Support is usually provided by a series of wires run horizontally 20—25cm (8—10in) apart through wire eyes screwed into the astragals (glazing bars). Alternatively, mesh materials can be used. With an alloy house it will be necessary to make a wooden framework or use sucker supports.

Planting

The vine, self-raised or bought, is taken out of its pot and the roots opened up or disentangled, it not being advisable to leave them in a compact ball. It is then planted into container or border by spreading out the roots well, setting not too deeply, watering in and, after a good firming, mulching the surface of the soil with peat or well-rotted farmyard manure. When the root is planted out of doors it will be necessary to remove a brick or two, or a section of glass or wood, keeping the opening to a minimum and covering one root and wrapping the stem with sacking and filling any air space with straw and sacking.

Pruning and training

Dormant vines *must* be cut back to 1.2 or 1.5m (4 or 5ft) after planting; a young growing vine planted in summer is cut back to two buds after planting. Strong growth should invariably result, encouraged by plentiful watering and spraying the young leaves and stems. In the small greenhouse there is much to be said for allowing only one main rod, but vine rods are very

accommodating and at any stage the decision can be altered and another 'main' growth allowed to develop.

In the winter subsequent to planting *new growth* on the main rod or rods is cut back to 90−1.2m (3 or 4ft) and any lateral shoots to two plump base buds which can readily be found if searched for, although not obvious.

Annual pruning follows the same general pattern of cutting back a proportion of new growth, although there will come a time when this cannot be achieved and the vine has to be restricted according to space available.

The number of laterals must be determined at a fairly early stage, it generally being convenient to have a lateral running off about every 60cm (2ft) of rod. It is also important to decide in which direction the shoots are to be allowed to form; if the main rod is run along under the ridge of the greenhouse the laterals can be tied down one side to the gutter, or the other way round (see Fig. 63).

It is general practice to allow the vine to become established over two or three years before any fruit is allowed to form, but in the restricted conditions of amateur greenhouses it would seem futile to carry out this practice, it being more desirable to restrict the vigour by early cropping or any other means, always provided of course that the vine has at least enough root system to sustain growth. After cutting back the laterals to two plump buds, two shoots are allowed to form each spring; the stronger and preferably the one bearing a bunch of embryo fruit is selected, the other being removed completely. This procedure is followed (spread out over a period to avoid shock) at each lateral growth point until in the end the single, double or treble rod is left with a number of single laterals growing out in one or both directions.

The laterals are gradually pulled in to the supporting wire or mesh material and tied, progressively shortening the string used. The tip of each lateral should be nipped off at the second leaf past the bunch of grapes, or if no grapes, as with a young vine, the lateral is stopped at about the seventh leaf. Sub-laterals formed after stopping are re-

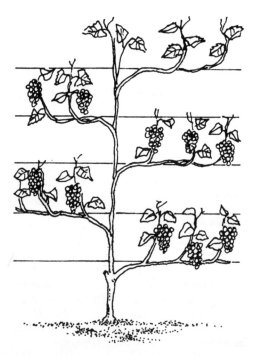

Fig. 63 The normal way of training a vine if space allows it.

stricted to one leaf or so, although this is not critical. *No system of pruning is rigid; it must be adapted to circumstances and space.*

Cultural treatment

Early vines will start into growth by mid- or late winter in the greenhouse if there is sufficient heat. With unheated greenhouses growth will start later. Water is applied to the roots, and the vents are shut a little to encourage a humid atmosphere, while the rods may be syringed well with plain water. In order to get an even break of buds it may be necessary to arch the leading shoots over by untying the rod from its support, but with younger vines this is seldom necessary. When the flowers appear the greenhouse should, if possible, be kept drier, ceasing syringeing and avoiding damping down. Pollination and fertilization generally occur readily, but it may be necessary to tap the rod or dust the flowers with a little cotton wool on the end of a cane.

Vines should never be allowed to dry out. Borders should be watered with a fine rose, keeping the surface moderately moist, and a good thick mulch of peat will assist in this direction. Vines growing in pots or boxes must be watered regularly, indeed this is one of the main disadvantages of growing them in this manner.

About 12.8°C (55°F) is satisfactory for flowering, and for rapid swelling of the berries the ideal is 18.3°C (65°F) day and about 15.6°C (60°F) at night. Feed with weak liquid manure at this stage. During ripening plenty of air should be given to avoid botrytis. Vines will resent sudden temperature changes just as much as any other crop, and can react very positively by 'shanking', when the stems of the berries shrivel or the berries 'scald'. Ideally a little air should be left on at night always, particularly when the berries are ripening.

Thinning and harvesting

The thinning of grapes is most important. A start should be made when the berries are about the size of peas, using special vine scissors and leaving the berries about half an inch apart. Success at shows depends much on the shape of a bunch of grapes and a little practical experience goes further than pages of description. A few weeks after thinning the rapidly swelling berries appear to stop growing, this being because they are stoning, and ideally the temperature should be dropped a little during this period. It is important not to allow too many bunches of grapes to remain on a vine, about 2.5kg per m (1lb per foot) or rod being usual. The bunches will ripen according to variety, temperature and season, and should be harvested when ready; in a cold greenhouse in a northerly latitude there can be difficulty in fully ripening the grapes of some varieties such as 'Black Hamburg'.

Winter pruning follows the sequence described previously and should be carried out annually when the vine is dormant. After pruning lift all dead leaves and rubbish and then rub all loose bark from the main rod of the vine and paint with a strong solution of malathion, or other general insecticide, avoiding the buds which can otherwise be damaged. This procedure is to kill off over-wintering pests.

The border should be given a good top dressing of well-rotted farmyard manure annually, and in addition a dressing of $101-136g/m^2$ (3–4oz per sq yd) of a good balanced general fertilizer as growth commences.

Varieties

For heated greenhouses: Alicante (black), Black Muscat, Gros Colmar (black), Lady Downes (black), Madresfield Court (black), Muscat of Alexandria (white), White Frontignan.

For cold or cool greenhouses: Black Hamburg, Buckland Sweetwater (white), Fosters Seedling (white), Forbes Seedling (white), Gros Maroc (black), Reine Olga (reddish).

Note new varieties are appearing.

For pests, diseases and physiological disorders see Chapter 31.

The cultivation of peaches and nectarines

Peaches and nectarines are types of *Prunus persica*, the difference between them lying in the felt-like skin of the former and the smooth skin of the latter. Like the vine, the peach and the nectarine post problems for cultivation in small greenhouses. It is asking too much to expect a vigorous bush to perform well under severe restriction, and gardeners would be well advised to consider these problems before embarking too enthusiastically on their cultivation. An alternative may well be to grow them in pots.

Traditionally peaches are grown on the wall of a south-facing lean-to, a practice which fits in well with vines being grown against the glass. Alternatively the peaches can be grown against the glass 30—38cm (12—15in) from it and a vine run along the ridge from the end. To do real justice to a peach, a wall height of 3—3.5m (10—11ft) will be necessary, with commensurate height for the glass portion. They can be excellently grown in a spanroofed structure on an alternate staggered arrangement where more than one bush is grown, and a greenhouse with a width of 3—3.5m (10—12ft) and 2.5—2.75m (8—9ft) high will give reasonable room for development.

Greenhouses may be cold or heated. Adequate roof and side ventilation is important. Supporting wires should be run 23—25cm (9—10in) apart in vine eyes 8—10m (3—4in) from the wall or 23—25cm (9—10in) from the glass, or some other support provided.

Production programme
Heat given early/mid-winter—fruit harvested early summer
No heat—fruit harvested mid—late summer/early autumn according to variety

Preparation for planting
The long-term nature of a peach or nectarine demands a thorough approach to border preparation. When the soil is initially of good quality and drainage is in no way impeded, it will suffice to work through a reasonable quantity of broken rubble and well-rotted manure or compost to an area of 2×1m (6×3ft) per tree. Peat is now frequently used in quantity for soil improvement and in this case lime should be applied at 120—150g (4—5oz) per bushel of peat to offset its acidity and in addition at

approximately 1lb or more per sq yd of border, according to analysis, to bring the pH up to about 6.5, with a phosphate and potash index of between 2 and 3. Where the soil is completely unsuitable excavate to a depth of 60—75cm (2—2½ft) for the area of 2×1m (6×3ft) referred to above. Fill up with a good layer of rubble through which is mixed any *clean* garden rubbish available, along with a liberal application of bonemeal and basic slag. Once again a good John Innes type compost (JIP2) will suffice, but the magnitude of the task shows the need to think in terms of improvement rather than substitution if at all possible. The roots of peaches and nectarines in modern greenhouses will invariably gain access to the outside soil and therefore it may be necessary to improve the outside area concerned.

A heavy mulch of well rotted farmyard manure should be spread over the surface sufficiently long before planting to allow a degree of drying out yet keep the mixture moist.

Planting
On delivery from the nursery the tree should have its roots spread out in a wide shallow hole, after removing any roots damaged in transit. Deep planting is not advisable, 5—8cm (2—3in) of soil over the top roots being all that is required. Leave a space of 10—13cm (4—5in) against the wall or the side of the greenhouse. Water in thoroughly. Tie branches loosely to support wires or trellis framework; these are finally spaced out and secured after pruning and before growth starts in the spring. If trees are bought with a well-developed fan shape, the main branches should in the first pruning be cut back to about half their length to encourage the development of new side shoots, as peaches and nectarines *fruit on the previous year's new wood* and a constant supply of this is necessary to keep the tree productive. The training of a young plant requires more detailed information than can be given here.

It is important that from the time growth commences there should be a plentiful supply of moisture, otherwise a newly planted tree will draw on reserves of sap and possibly collapse and die back completely.

Flowering, pollination and setting fruit

Blooms will be produced very early in the season, being formed while there is very little leaf growth. Pollination must be assisted by tapping the branches and dusting the open blooms with a rabbit's tail or cotton wool on a cane, keeping the air dry and the house relatively cool at 7.2–10°C (45–50°F) – if this is not made impossible by other activities. If it is, then the peach or nectarine must take 'pot luck' and there may be very erratic setting and fruit production.

Much can be done to encourage growth and good setting by syringeing or hosing with a *fine* rose early in the morning of a day which promises to be bright, this being a practice which should be persevered with until fruit is well formed. Dryness of atmosphere will also induce red spider attack.

After it is seen that tiny fruits have set, the temperature may be gradually increased to 18.3–21.1°C (65–70°F) by day and 12.8–15.6°C (55–60°F) by night, emulating the conditions experienced in out-of-doors culture later in the season. Vents should be shut down early at night to conserve heat as much as possible.

Thinning of fruit

Thinning to avoid over-cropping is generally done first to a limited extent after the tiny fruits are set, then later to about one fruit per 30cm² (square foot), or roughly one fruit per shoot, this taking place over a period when the fruits are the size of small walnuts 1.25–2cm (½–¾in). Remove with scissors to avoid tearing the bark. During this second thinning period high or erratic temperatures must be avoided, or a large fall of fruit may be induced.

Summer pruning

Surplus growth must be rubbed out (gradually, to avoid shock) throughout the season when 2.5 centimetres or an inch or so long, except during the flowering period, the object being to rub out *all* buds growing outward, leaving only two or three well placed to replace the shoots presently bearing fruit. Failure to remove surplus shoots and loosely tie in the remaining young growth will result in a forest of growth and a completely unmanageable tree.

Harvesting

As the fruit ripens it should be allowed the full benefit of the sun by tying aside any growths that shade it. When picking the fruit handle it very carefully, especially peaches which bruise very easily.

After the fruit is gathered, frequent hosing of the foliage should be carried out and full ventilation given, along with plenty of water at the roots to coincide with the mild autumn rains they would receive out of doors. The application of very diluted liquid manure is also advisable to strengthen the shoots and buds for next year.

Winter pruning

When leaf fall is complete the tree should be carefully pruned, cutting out suitable old shoots which have borne fruit and tying in well-placed new shoots. There must obviously be compromise here, e.g. a fair proportion of old shoots must be left because of new shoots coming from them. As the tree grows pruning becomes more exacting, and gardeners are again reminded that they should not enter into the growing of peaches or nectarines unless they are prepared to give the detailed attention necessary.

Root pruning

Where trees are over-vigorous and non-productive it may be necessary to carry out root pruning by completely lifting trees up to 5 or 6 years old, cutting off strong tap and coarse lateral roots and replanting. This is carried out in the dormant period.

Nutrition

Each mid to late winter give a top dressing per tree of 200–226g (7–8oz) of a good compound trace-element-containing fertilizer, scattered evenly over the ground for a reasonable area out from the tree. Each autumn after the fruit is gathered apply 270–400g/m² of hydrated or 540g/m² (1lb per sq yd) of ground limestone. Over-vigorous trees should not be too liberally fed. Weak trees can be fed more generously to the extent of applying stimulants during the growing season or giving additional nitrogen as in sulphate of ammonia in late winter at 34–65g/m² (1–2oz per sq yd).

Varieties
White fleshed and yellow fleshed peaches and nectarines are available, fruiting according to level of heat and variety from early summer to the end of early autumn.

For pests, diseases and physiological disorders see Chapter 31.

Figs
The fruit of the fig *Ficus carica* does not ripen fully outside in northerly latitudes except in favoured sheltered situations, but under glass two (or even three) crops of fruit can be achieved per year.

Planting
Avoid any greenhouse area likely to be in shade. The sunny wall of a lean-to structure is ideal. They can be grown in pots.

It is best if borders are excavated to a depth of about 90cm (3 ft) and some concrete or corrugated iron put down, followed by a 15cm (6in) layer of broken brick, on top of which is placed good leafy loam with some mortar rubble worked through. The purpose of sealing off the bottom is to prevent downward growing roots which can result in rank unproductive growth. Really deep digging will generally suffice, broken concrete slabs being laid down in the process. Allow plenty of room, 3.6m (12ft) or more for each fig (unless of course they are grown in pots).

Fan-trained trees 3–4 years old are generally purchased, and planted either in autumn or late winter according to the level of heat; late winter is suitable for colder growing conditions. Trees are trained out in fan form on suitable wires or trellis, the bottom 30cm (12in) from ground level being kept clear of all growth. Congested branches should be thinned out before planting and dense growth avoided during the growing season as this encourages disease. One does not need to be too fastidious about pruning methods, trying to keep 'open' bushes is the important issue.

Seasonal culture
Figs respond to regular watering, a steadily rising temperature from early winter onwards, starting at 12.8°C (55°F) and reaching 18.3°C (65°F). Humidity should be maintained by regular spraying with clean water. The figs will grow at a rate commensurate with prevailing temperatures, and cooler growing is the more usual procedure in these days of high fuel costs. When fruit is seen to be well formed and ripening, freer ventilation should be given where possible. A second crop can be achieved in a reasonably cool greenhouse by cutting away older shoots to allow development of new shoots to bear the next crop. This practice is repeated after the second crop has been picked, leaving a fair balance of well-spaced shoots – and this is the whole essence of pruning procedure. In addition some shoots should be rubbed out in spring and summer and lateral shoots stopped at the fifth or sixth leaf from the base. Once again the aim should be to avoid overcrowding.

Regular watering coupled with the application of weak liquid manure should keep the figs growing healthily, as they are greedy plants.

Over-cropping is the main cause of failure, especially on young trees, and some restriction of fruiting should always be aimed at.

Culture in pots
The culture of figs in pots follows the same general pattern as all pot-grown fruit, the essence of success being to stop young lateral shoots at 4 or 5 leaves in summer, then cut out over-crowded wood in winter and, most important, avoid over-cropping.

Propagation
Figs are propagated by seed, layering, budding or grafting, layering being a ready way of getting a new young bush by pegging down a suitably placed shoot into the top of a pot and by mulching it to induce roots to form. Budding and grafting are also useful techniques. It is important to produce a bush with some formal shape, ideally fan trained, and to produce well shaped trees takes time and a lot of patience.

Varieties
Consult specialist catalogues. For pests, diseases and physiological disorders see Chapter 31.

Strawberries

Strawberries are native to Europe in small-fruited forms, *Fragaria vesca* and several others. The cultivation of large-fruited strawberries is attributed to the introduction of *F. virginiana* from North America in the 17th century, the first British raised large-fruited variety being Keen's 'Imperial' by Marshall Keen in 1806.

General culture
Much research has gone into the techniques of growing strawberries successfully under glass, as they are a high value crop. It is highly important in the first place that runners be selected only from plants of the highest quality and as free as possible from all strawberry ailments, virus and eelworm in particular. Every effort must be made to get young runners established in their forcing grounds as soon as possible. Mobile structures are frequently used in Holland and Belgium for early strawberry culture and the young newly rooted runners are planted out in their respective plots directly they are severed from the parent plant and irrigated until they are growing strongly.

For mobile greenhouse culture the plants are planted at 25 × 25cm (10 × 10in) or 30–30cm (12 × 12in) or thereabouts in 1.35m (4ft 6in) beds, the greenhouse being pushed over the plots in December or January. The Belgians plant at the same density in beds 75–90cm (2ft 6in–3ft) and 60–90cm (2–3ft) apart in a static greenhouse in autumn. Black polythene mulch with lay-flat irrigation underneath the polythene is invariably used, and irrigation is once more relied upon to prevent any set back.

A more modern system of culture is the waiting bed technique when multi-crown plants are grown on outdoor beds, de-blossomed and planted under protection in sequence, generally three or six plants per Growbag, watered by trickle systems. On a still smaller scale the young rooted runners are potted into 13–15cm (5–6in) pots after severing from the parent plant, using John Innes No 2 compost or similar. Growbags can be used to excellent effect.

A vernalization period is thought beneficial for strawberries in order to initiate flower buds, and is brought about by periods of lower temperatures. In small scale growing the pots are left outside until mid to late winter, being protected from severe frost by straw or other means. The necessary vernalization period is completed by the time they are lifted into the greenhouse or covered. The plants are kept cool for 3–4 weeks and then heat is applied to coax them gradually into growth. Flowers will form according to the temperature level given, generally in late winter or early spring, during which time the flowers should be dusted with a rabbit's tail or cotton wool to assist pollination. Strawberries are, in the main, self-fertile, but at that time of year and in the environment of a greenhouse there will be few, if any, pollinating insects, though high temperatures will encourage bees if a hive is placed in or near the greenhouse. If kept well watered and given weak liquid feeding the plants can be encouraged to produce fruit by mid to late spring, considerably earlier than out of doors. At lower heat levels they will still crop much earlier than out of doors. Commercially they are only grown for one year in greenhouses, new 'maidens' being planted annually, although two-year-old plants can be lifted when dormant and can perform extremely well.

Strawberries ideal under NFT systems in "A" frames.

Cold frame culture
Strawberries can also be grown most successfully in cold frames, the runners being established in 25 × 25 cm (10 × 10in), the sashes being put on during late winter. Drying out or lack of pollination is the risk in frames, resulting in small malformed fruits. When possible the sashes should be left off during the day in the flowering period to allow entry of insects for pollination, or this can be done artificially by dusting the flowers, a practice essential with early flowering in heated frames. The plants can be left in frames for two or three years,

but kept well cleaned of runners. When strawberries are grown under cloches, polythene tunnel or floating mulches the same general procedure is followed. It is important to avoid the soil becoming 'sick' due to repetitive growing on the same site.

Environmental control

Environmental control is particularly important with strawberries grown in greenhouses, frames, cloches or tunnels, and it may be necessary to take preventive measures in wet humid areas by spraying with fungicides. Support for the fruit by wires or other means will help by preventing fruit/soil contact. Strawberries in greenhouses respond to low intensity artificial lighting at 9–10W per m²/sq yd given during the night for 2–3 hours, this encouraging earlier flowering.

Cold storage for runners

The putting of runners into cold storage will allow planting in early and mid-summer for autumn cropping under glass, or alternatively the early establishment of plants in pots in late spring, deblossoming by removing flowers and bringing well-established plants into the greenhouse in mid-winter. If when runners are lifted they are tied in bundles of 25 or 50 and stored long-term in 38mu gauge polythene bags at −2 to −1°C (28–30°F), this allows planting out over a period and provides for successional cropping. This is complementary to waiting beds.

Varieties

Note that Gorella and other similar types are especially good for early forcing and is one of the main varieties grown in continental Europe for this purpose. Royal Sovereign tends to be susceptible to botrytis under glass. Redgauntlet (early) and Talisman (late) can both be double cropped in a good year. For other varieties see specialist suppliers catalogues.

For pests, diseases and physiological disorders see Chapter 31

Fruit growing in pots

The growing of fruit in pots is a very old practice which has tended to fall out of favour in recent years. The full range of fruits may be grown including apricots, apples, pears, cherries, plums, peaches, vines, figs, nectarines, citrus fruits, strawberries and so on. No great demand on space is made and greenhouses are available for other activities at various times of the year. The growing of fruit in pots allows the production of limited quantities of superlative quality fruit in areas which may be so bleak and exposed that outdoor culture is impossible. It is also useful for the production of fruit for the show bench.

Only greenhouses of good design and well situated to receive full sunlight should be considered: a greenhouse partially shaded by a vigorous peach or vine is not really suitable, although if it is a lean-to structure and a peach is grown on the rear wall, pots may certainly be grown in the front portion. Fruit in pots is an interesting and tempting subject for the conservatory that is also used for recreation. It is not generally necessary to think in terms of artificial heat, except perhaps the very minimum in the coldest areas. The pots are placed on the greenhouse floor–soil, ashes or concrete– and frequently on bricks to prevent supplementary rooting.

Type of bush

A restricted growing habit is essential, which involves the use or training of specially shaped trees grown on dwarfing rootstocks obtained from a reliable nurseryman. The skilled gardener can start with a 'maiden' (one year grafted) on a dwarf root stock and shape the tree, but it is generally better to buy specially shaped trees from a nurseryman, and better still if the bushes are already established in pots, three years old, and well furnished with buds so that fruiting can start immediately. With maidens it takes time to build up the framework before fruiting commences.

Cultural procedure

Delivery of trees is best taken in the autumn at dormancy or leaf fall, when they are potted up into 23cm (9in) pots. It is unwise to put a small bush into a large pot of 25–30cm (10–12in) diameter, as the secret of success with pot-grown trees is root restriction, though as the trees get older they may eventually graduate to 25–30 cm (10–12in) or even larger pots. The pots used should be very sturdy and have drainage holes in the sides as well as in the base. Only the heaviest gauge plastic pots should be used, it being necessary in some cases to put one inside the other to impart sufficient strength, boring holes in the sides with an electric drill. If new clay pots are used they must be soaked well before use, and all pots must be scrupulously cleaned by washing. All pots are given a deep layer of drainage in the form of broken pots of pebbles over which is put a layer of coarse peat or coarsely shredded peat.

Much is made of the need for a good turf-based compost derived from stacked turf and it is unlikely that this can be bettered by any of the modern composts. Through the loam for apples and pears should be mixed one-third part of very well rotted farmyard manure or well-made, reliable garden compost. For apricots, peaches, nectarines and figs avoid the farmyard manure but add bonemeal and lime at 114g (4oz) and 56g (2oz) per 36 litres/bushel respectively. The compost should be well mixed and under cover for a few weeks before use, finally adding some coarse bonemeal plus a liberal scattering of ground limestone. The compost should be sufficiently moist, rendering it so by watering if necessary.

Shorten all vigorous lateral and downward growing roots before potting up with great care, packing the compost in with a potting stick in layers until it is 2.5cm (1in) below the rim of the pot.

After potting the trees must be well watered and placed in a sheltered situation at the foot of a sunny wall, the pots of 'hardy' trees being plunged to their rims in good soil or ashes or alternatively protected with straw or peat to avoid damage by freezing, care being taken that they are not waterlogged. Hardy trees – apples, pears, plums and cherries – can remain out of doors until the buds begin to swell; apricots, peaches, nectarines, vines, figs and citrus fruits are better brought into the greenhouse immediately after potting, being given plenty of room and ventilation.

Seasonal treatment
While the culture of fruit in pots demands considerable care and attention to detail, it is remarkable what can be achieved by regular watering and feeding; indeed, *because of the limited root area the importance of this cannot be over-stressed.* It is also essential that free ventilation should be given in the morning and excessively high temperatures avoided, particularly during the initial period of stoning in the case of peaches and nectarines. Assistance with pollination of all trees is desirable, using a rabbit's tail or cotton wool.

Regular spraying is essential to encourage healthy growth of leaves and to discourage attacks of red spider, which can have a disastrous effect. Feeding with liquid manure should be practised after the fruits are set, once fortnightly at first, increasing the applications to once weekly later. As soon as the trees are in full growth a top dressing of equal parts of well rotted farmyard manure and soil should be given and moulded up round the edge of the pots, raising their height several inches to allow watering. Alternatively rings of linoleum or other suitable material can be used to contain the top-dressing material effectively.

Pruning and fruit thinning
In spring and summer there should be reduction of new growth. With apples and pears lateral growths should be pinched back to about 10–13cm (4–5in) or less, leaving only a proportion of them in the case of apples, otherwise the tree will become a tangled mat of growth. Peaches and nectarines, which fruit on new wood, should have well-placed shoots selected and allowed to make reasonable growth before having the tips pinched out. Some thinning of fruit will be necessary, leaving only one fruit per cluster on apples and pears and thinning plums out singly every 5–8cm (2–3in) or more, while peaches and nectarines should only be allowed to form one fruit per reasonable area of tree to avoid overcrowding. Figs should only have their shoots thinned. Apples and pears can be taken out of doors when the fruit is ripening and the pot plunged in soil for safety and conservation of moisture. Wind

damage can be avoided by securing each fruit with raffia to a convenient branch.

After fruiting, all types of trees are ripened off by placing out of doors, carrying out any re-potting in mid autumn along similar lines to those already described. Annual re-potting is advisable in many cases, moving vigorous trees to a slightly larger pot. Again, the hardy trees can remain out of doors in a sheltered spot but the rest should be brought into the greenhouse.

Pruning is carried out by reducing the laterals in apples, pears and plums to within two or three buds of the base, and on trees such as peaches, which fruit on new wood, leaving only a proportion of well-placed sturdy shoots to bear the following year's crop.

Specific pest and disease control is best (see Chapter 31); there is generally not the same need for the routine practices necessary with bushes out of doors.

CHAPTER 22
Summer Bedding Plant Production

Many types of plants are grown as 'summer bedders' for planting in the period mid-spring—early summer. Greenhouse production considerably shortens the propagation period, especially where germination is under mist or in cabinets, followed by the use of either growing rooms or supplementary lighting. (see Chapter 10).

The majority of bedders are seed raised; others are propagated by cuttings or division. Containers for bedding plants are shown in Fig. 64.

Cuttings are taken in late summer—mid-autumn before and during plant lifting at the end of the summer bedding season, or in spring from over-wintered plants, or from over-wintered tubers in the case of dahlias. Autumn rooting can take place in either cool greenhouses or cold frames; lush growth is not desirable as plants tend to become too large before the spring—keep very much on the dry side. Early spring rooting can be carried out at higher temperatures and the plants kept growing strongly. Plenty of light and as free ventilation as possible within the limits of the weather should be the rule for all over-wintered plants. Dahlias, begonias and other tender plants are of course over-wintered in heated or frost free greenhouses or, in the case of tubers, in a mulch of peat in frost-free cellars.

There is much to be said for using Jiffy 7s for the rooting of all cuttings as they sustain the plants for a considerable period before potting on is necessary.

Seed sowing procedures for bedding plants are on traditional lines (see Chapter 16). Damping off disease is frequently encoun- tered with bedding plants especially when sterilized soil forms part of the compost with the resultant release of ammonia. Antirrhinums and lobelia are particularly prone to damping off.

Pricking off is required at an early stage in the development of seed sown bedding plants to avoid tangled roots and etiolation. Break-up cell containers or peat blocks are useful as root distrubance is avoided at planting. This is especially so when linked to direct sowing of seeds, which with larger seeds is relatively simple. With smaller seeds, mixing the seed with a gel, such as wallpaper paste, and 'sowing' it with a cake icer or other suitable dispenser emulates to a certain extent the commercial practice of "fluid sowing" using special apparatus or pelleted seed. While some thinning down or gapping up may be necessary, direct sowing is becoming very popular with the high cost of seed and because it avoids the check received by plants on pricking out, plus the saving in time. Note primed seed is now available, also seedlings and "plugs". Nutrition is important with the use of soil-less media; many bedding plants will suffer acutely from starvation if diluted liquid feeds are not given regularly.

Acclimatization through a period of progressively cooler temperatures is necessary. Normally plants are placed out in frames in spring, depending on the region; less water is given and ventilation gradually increased. Feeding with diluted liquid fertilizer may be necessary to sustain growth, but not to the extent of inducing lushness. For pests, diseases and physiological disorders see Chapter 31.

Fig. 64 Containers for bedding plants.

POLYSTYRENE TRAYS

Segmented trays

12 or 15 cell trays

40 cell trays

Double half trays

MOULDED THIN PLASTIC

Segmented trays

12 cell trays

15 cell trays

Half trays

THICK PLASTIC TRAYS

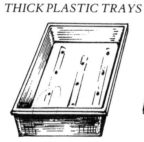
Full seed tray

Half tray

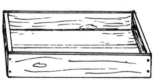
Wooden seed tray

POTS AND BLOCKS

Plastic

'Whalehide'

Peat pots

Peat blocks

Summer Bedding Plants (Note Average germination temperatures are 18−21°C (65−70°F)

Name and approx. seed count per gram	Propagation method and approx. full germination time (variable)	Colour and average height
Acrolinium. Annual. 200	Seed in Feb/March. Lightly covered. 2−3 weeks	Wide variety of shades. Everlasting, ideal for cutting. 38−45cm (15−18in)
Ageratum houstonianum (*A. mexicanum*). Annual. F$_1$ hybrid and 'straight'. 7000	Seed in Feb/March. Sown on surface. 3 weeks	Blue shades. 10−23cm (4−9in)
Amaranthus (Love lies bleeding). Annual	Seed in Feb/March. 2−3 weeks	Red plumes. 45cm (18in)
Anchusa capensis. Annual variety. 30	Seed in Feb. 2−3 weeks	Blue. 20cm (8in)
Antirrhinum majus. Perennial treated as half-hardy annual. Many F$_1$ hybrids available. 7500	Seed in Feb. 10−21 days	Various shades, pinks, whites, reds 30−60cm (12−24in)
Aster *Callistephus chinensis*. Tender annual. 450	Seed in March. 2−3 weeks	Various. 30−60cm (12−24in)
Balsam. Annual. See also *Impatiens*. Note – Balsam needs warmth.	Seed in March. 2−3 weeks	White, pink, salmon, scarlet. 20−45cm (8−18in)
Begonia, fibrous, *B. semperflorens*. Half-hardy perennial treated as annual. 70,000	Seed Dec−March for smaller plants. Sow thinly on surface. Apply liquid feeding after germination. 2−3 weeks	Wide range of colours. Some with dark leaves. 15−30cm (6−12in)
*Begonia, tuberous, *B.* × *tuber-hybrida*. Half-hardy perennial. 60,000	Seed in Nov/Dec. By division of tubers after starting them into growth. By planting tubers dormant. Short-day plants and may need supplementary light and day length control.	Extremely large range of colours and flower form. 23−30cm (9−12in)
Cabbage. Ornamental mixed types. 250	Sow March/April under glass in gentle heat.	Unusual. Cream, green, pink and rose in decorative marking. 30−40cm (12−16in)
*Calceolaria *C. integrifolia*, *C. rugosa* and others. Half-hardy perennials treated as annuals. F$_1$ hybrids available. 25,000	Herbaceous types from cuttings in autumn or spring. Seed Nov−Jan 2−3 weeks	Red, yellow, orange, scarlet and crimson. 25−30cm (10−18in)
C. gracilis. Annual	Sow March/April. 2−3 weeks	Yellow 23−25cm (18in)
Calendula. Annual. 150	Usually sown direct, where it is to flower March-May. But can be sown under gentle heat for pricking off to plant outdoors when large enough	Wide range of shades. 30−45cm (12−18in)
Campanula isophylla. See Pot Plants p. 203		
Carnation *Dianthus caryophyllus* Annuals, including 'Chabaud'. 500	Annuals sown Jan/Feb. 2−3 weeks	Various. 25−35cm (10−14in)
*Perennial carnations	Cuttings or layering in summer. Seed in spring. Do not flower well until following year	Various. 30−45cm (12−18in)

Name and approx. seed count per gram	Propagation method and approx. seed germination time	Colour and average height
Castor-oil plant *Ricinus*	Useful as pot plants. (See Pot Plants p. 215)	
Celosia flamosa. Annual. 1200	Sow Feb−April in moderate warmth. 2−3 weeks	Wide range of shades. 20−38cm (8−15in)
Centaurea. Perennial. 650	Seed in Feb. 2−3 weeks	Silver foliage. Dwarf. 20cm (8in)
Chrysanthemum *C. carinatum*. Annual. 600	Seed in Feb/March. 2−3 weeks	Various. Singles and doubles. 40−60cm (18−24in)
★C. leucanthemum. Perennial. (See also Chapter 25). 1200	Seed in Feb/March. 2−4 weeks	Various. Singles and doubles. 30cm (12in)
Chrysanthemum parthenium. Perennial 'Golden Feather'. 6000	Seed in Feb. Cuttings in spring. 2−3 weeks	Yellow and white. 10−30cm (4−12in)
Cineraria maritima. Annual. See also Senecio.	Seed Feb. 2−3 weeks	Silver foliage.
Cleome spinosa (C. pungens). Tender annual. 500	Seed in Feb/March. Resents root disturbance. 2 weeks	Pink. 90cm (36in)
Coleus (see Pot Plants p. 213) New dwarf forms ideal for window boxes, hanging baskets and other small containers		
Coreopsis. Annual 400	Seed Feb/March 2−3 weeks	Golden yellow, maroon and crimson. 30cm (12in)
Cosmos. Tender annual *Cosmea bipinnata* 200	Seed in Feb/March. 1−2 weeks	Various. 90cm (36in)
Dahlia variabilis. Tender perennial. Hybrids 120	Seed in Feb/March. Cuttings Feb/March or plant tubers direct either dormant or started into growth. Will stand no frost. 2−3 weeks	Wide range of colour and flower form. Singles and doubles. Dwarf seedlings 30−45cm (12−18in). Other varieties 60cm−1.8m (24−72in)
★Dianthus. Annual. F_1 hybrids 900	Sow Sept for the types requiring long season of growth (eg 'Queen of Hearts'). Other types sow March 1−2 weeks	Scarlet and mixed. 15−30cm (6−12in)
D. chinensis (D. sinensis). Perennial. 1000	Sow in Sept or earlier out of doors. Can also be sown in Feb 1−2 weeks	Carmine, pink, salmon, white. 15cm (4−6in)
Dimorphotheca aurantiaca. Annual (half-hardy) 500	Seed in Feb/March. 2−3 weeks	Various. 10−15cm (12in)
Dorotheanthus bellidiformis (Mesembryanthemum criniflorum) (Livingstone daisy). Half-hardy annual. 4000	Seed in Feb/March. 2−3 weeks. Grow cool	Various. Creeping
Echium. Annual. 250	Seed Feb/March in gentle heat	Shades of blue, white, pink, rose and carmine. 30cm (12in)

Name and approx. seed count per gram	Propagation method and approx. seed germination time	Colour and average height
Fuchsia. Half-hardy perennial. 2,500	Seed Feb. Cuttings anytime but ideally ideally early in year.	Superb range of colours. 30−45cm (12−18in)
Gazania splendens. (Half-hardy) Perennial. Hybrids. 220	Seed in Jan/Feb. 1−2 weeks	Various. Daisy-like flowers. 15−23cm (9in)
Geranium. See Pelargonium		
Gerbera. Perennial.	Seed Feb. 2−3 weeks	Many shades. 30−40cm (12−16in)
Gladiolus species and hybrids. Perennials. Corms bought by count	Corms planted direct or started in heat prior to planting outside in May	Wide range of colours. 45cm−1.25cm (18−48in)
Godetia grandiflora. Annual. 1,600	Invariably treated as a hardy annual and sown direct, this is an excellent bedder, lending itself to raising under protection, especially in the north. Seed Feb/March, preferably directly sown to avoid pricking off 2−3 weeks	Wide range of colours
★*Heliotropium aborescens (H. peruvianum).* Tender perennial. 1,500	Seed in Feb/March or cuttings in spring. 2−3 weeks	Blue and mauve. 38−45cm (15−18in)
Helichrysum. Annual. 1,300	Seed Feb/March. 2−3 weeks	Scarlets, golds, etc 30cm (12in)
★*Impatiens wallerana (I. holstii, petersiana,* *sultani).* Tender annuals and perennials. F₁ hybrids (Balsam) (Busy Lizzie). 2000	Sow from early March. Cuttings at any time, but for bedding out April/May. 2−3 weeks. High humidity essential (fungicidal dust also advised). Sow direct	Pink, orange, white, red shades. 30−45cm (12−18in)
Kale or Borecole. Ornamental types. 250	Seed in Feb/March. 2−3 weeks. Mild heat only	Ornamental leaves. 30−45cm (12−18in)
Kochia scoparia (burning bush), cv. 'childsii' (compact), var. 'trichophylla'. Tender annuals 1,200	Seed Feb/March. 1−2 weeks	Lovely foliage in autumn. 30−60cm (12−24in)
Lavatera. Annual. (*Lavandula vera*) 125	Sow seed Jan/Feb. 2−3 weeks	White, rose etc. 60cm (2ft)
Lobelia erinus. Annual 25000	Mid March. Thinly on surface using 'dressed seed'. Prick out in clumps 1−2 weeks	Blue, red, white. Compact and bushy forms. 10−23cm (4−9in)
L. cardinalis and *L. fulgens.* Perennial.	Cuttings in autumn or spring. Seed in spring.	Blue-grey foliage. 60−90cm (24−36in)
Lobularia maritima (Alyssum maritimum) and var. *Benthamii.* Annual. 3000	Seed in Feb/March 2 weeks	White and pink. 10−15cm (4−6in)
★Marigold (American) *Tagetes erecta.* Tender annual. F₁ hybrid (name changed from African marigold 1970, but still called such).	Sow March. 1−2 weeks	Gold, orange, yellow. 30−60cm (12−24in)
Marigold (French) *Tagetes patula.* Tender annual. 300	Seed in Feb/March 1−2 weeks	Orange, red, yellow shades. 15−30cm (6−12in)
★*Matricaria capensis.* Perennial, grown as annual. 6,000	Seed Feb/April 2 weeks	White and yellow 20cm (8in)

Summary Bedding Plants—*continued*

Name and approx. seed count per gram	Propagation method and approx. seed germination time	Colour and average height
Mesembryanthemum. See Dorotheanthus p 196		
Mimulus tigrinus. Perennial. 23,000	Seed in Feb. 2–3 weeks	Reds, pinks, yellows 30–38cm (12–15in)
Nemesia strumosa. Tender annual. 5,000	Seed Feb/March. Avoid check to growth by pricking off early. 2–3 weeks	Various bright shades. 23–30cm (9–12in)
Nicotiana alata (N. affinis var. grandiflora.) Tender annual 9,000	Seed in March 1–2 weeks	Pink, white, yellow 25–60cm (10–24in)
Pansy *Viola tricolor.* Hybrids and F₁ hybrids. Perennial 800	Seed in Dec/Jan until March 2–3 weeks	Various colours. Selfs or mixed shades 15–20cm (6–8in)
Pelargonium × hortorum ('Geranium'). F₁ and F₂ hybrids; *P. zonale* is one of the parents. Tender perennial. Seed size variable; sold by count	Cuttings in autumn and spring. Seed in Jan/Feb. Use dwarfing agent to keep dwarf. 2–3 weeks	Many exciting new hybrids, many with compact habit. 23–45cm (9–18in)
Penstemon × gloxinioides. Half-hardy perennial. Hybrids 4,000	Seed in Dec/Jan. Cuttings autumn/spring 2–3 weeks	Scarlet and carmine shades. 75cm (30in)
Petunia × hybrida. Tender annual. F₁ or F₂ hybrids. 9,000	Seed in Feb/March. Not covered. Germinate cool. 1–2 weeks (or longer)	Brilliant stabs of red, scarlet, pink and white 25–30cm (10–12in)
Phlox drummondii. Tender annual. 500	Seed Feb–April 2–3 weeks	Pink, yellow, scarlet 15–30cm (6–12in)
Polyanthus. Perennials. *Primula veris elatior.* 1,000	Seed Jan–March in gentle heat or in cold frame April/May. Germination variable.	Wide range of shades. 25–30cm (10–12in)
Polygonum capitatum. Tender perennial 1,200	Seed Feb–April 2 weeks	Pink Trailing
Poppy, Iceland, *Papaver nudicaule.* Perennial 7,500	Seed in Jan/Feb. 2 weeks	Bright shades 45cm (18in)
Portulaca (sun rose). Tender annual. 10,000	Seed Feb/March. 2–3 weeks	Various 15cm (6in)
*Primrose. Perennial. *Primula acaulis.* 900–2,000	Seed Apr/July. 2–3 weeks	Many forms and colours, variable heights.
Pyrethrum aureum. Perennial. 13,500	Seed Feb/March.	Golden and silver foliage.
Rudbeckia hirta and *fulgida.* Grown as annuals. 2,000	Seed Feb/April 2–3 weeks	Wide range of colours
*Salpiglossis. Tender annual. F₁ and F₂ hybrids 4,500	Seed in Feb/March 2 weeks	Blue, brown, lavender, scarlet 60cm (24in)
Salvia splendens. Tender annual. 300	Seed Feb–April. 2–3 weeks	Scarlet. 15–30cm (6–12in)

Summer Bedding Plants—*continued*

Name and approx. seed count per gram	Propagation method and approx. seed germination time	Colour and average height
S. Patens. Perennial	Cuttings or seed in Feb.	Blue
Scabiosa atropurpurea (scabious). Treat as annual. 180	Seed Feb/March 2–3 weeks	45–60cm (18–24in) Wide range of colours 50cm–1.2m (24–48in)
Steirodiscus. Annual 3,500	Seed Feb/March 2–3 weeks	Yellow 10cm (4in) A 'new' bedding subject.
Stocks:		
Mathiola incana (Ten-week). Annual. 600	Seed in Feb/March. 2 weeks	White, red, blue, rose. 25–30cm (10–12in)
Brompton (Biennial)	Sow April/May in gentle heat. 2–3 weeks	White, red, blue, rose. 38–45cm (15–18in)
Sweet Peas. Annual.	Seed Feb/March. 2–3 weeks	Wide range of colours and heights.
Tagetes tenuifolia pumila. Tender annual. 1,200	Seed Feb/March. 1–2 weeks	Yellow, golden orange. 20cm (8in)
Torenia foumieri. Annual. 1,300	Seed Feb/March. 2 weeks	White, pink and blue shades. 20–25cm (8–10in)
★*Verbena × hybrida*. Perennials. Treat as annual. 400	Seed in Feb/March. 3–4 weeks	Scarlet shades. 25–30cm (10–12in)
Viola cornuta cultivars. 750	Seed Dec–March. 2–3 weeks	Blue, yellow, purple. 10–20cm (4–8in)
Vinca. Annual. 650	Seed Feb/March. 3–4 weeks	Pink, lavender 15cm (6in)
★*Zinnia elegans* and other species. Annuals. 100	Sow seed direct in small pots or containers. 1–2 weeks. March	Wide range of colours. 30–60cm (12–24in)

★These plants are useful as pot plants.
Note: The above table gives a list of 'conventional bedding plants', including types for hanging baskets, containers, tubs etc. There are a great many plants which might be called 'marginal bedding plants' which can be used for bedding displays. They include a vast range of 'hardy' annuals, pot plants, biennials and perennials, and dwarf shrubs. Some plants have been excluded on account of their aggressive growing and seeding habits.

CHAPTER 23
Pot Plants & Shrubs

Nothing can equal the light-admitting greenhouse for the culture of top-quality pot plants, especially the flowering kinds. Greenhouses should be drip-free or rendered so by sealing strip or other means, benched (preferably in tiers), and with full facilities for watering, shading, ventilating, potting and storing.

Propagation methods are specific to the plant being grown and brief details are given in the cultural notes. Examine all plant material for pest and disease and take any necessary measures before placing in the greenhouse. General hygiene must be of a high order.

Liquid feeding

For seed sowing, vegetative propagation, pricking off and potting, the respective composts are listed in Chapter 15. Actively growing plants generally need additional nutrients, depending on size of pot, leaching due to water requirements, and whether or not the plant is a gross feeder.

In Chapter 15 some formulae are given for liquid feeds, but the self-mixed formula is repeated here for convenience.

This is the stock solution prepared by careful mixing in warm water, it is diluted to 1 in 200 generally with a calibrated dilutor (for pot plants this can be 1 in 300 or 400 where desired). When using a watering-can the dilution (1 in 200) is 5 ml per litre (1 fluid ounce of the *stock solution in* $1\frac{1}{4}$ gallons) of water. The object is to vary the nitrogen/potash ratio to achieve the balance of growth required: high nitrogen for leaf growth, high potash for soft plants when more flowers and less leaf is the aim, and standard potash/nitrogen when balanced growth is exhibited and it is decided to sustain this. Time of year and region can confuse the issue as far as nutrient balance is concerned, plants grown in northerly latitudes generally requiring lower nitrogen feeds, especially during the duller months. There are many excellent proprietary feeds available.

Self-Formulated Liquid Feeds for Feeding Plants and Shrubs

Dilution rate	K_2O to N ratio	Potassium nitrate	Urea or ammonium nitrate		N	PPM K_2O
1−200	3−1 high potash	24oz/gal 150g/l			105	335
1−200	2−1 standard	24oz/gal 150 g/l	5oz/gal 31 g/l	6oz/gal or 37 g/l	170	335
1−300	1−1 high nitrogen	24oz/gal 150 g/l	16oz/gal 100 g/l	21oz/gal or 130 g/l	225	225
1−200	1−1½ medium/high nitrogen	24oz/gal 150 g/l		11oz/gal 68 g/l	225	335

Composition of feeds is in oz/gal and g/litre, or use proprietary feeds as advised. *Dilute as stated.*

Artificial illumination

Supplementary lighting adds to the quality or intensity of natural light and is useful in the duller months for those light–demanding plants which tend to become debilitated. Day length manipulation is used mainly to induce earlier flowering (or to delay it). These matters are discussed in Chapter 10, and interested gardeners should consult advisers on the appropriate electricity boards who will give details of the latest lighting techniques and their application to pot plant culture.

Half-hardy annuals as pot plants

In addition to the plants listed in the following tables, a number of half-hardy annuals and perennials are highly suitable as pot plants and are becoming popular. These are indicated by an asterisk in the previous bedding plant table, and the best varieties for pot growing are listed in seedsmen's catalogues, a wealth of new varieties being produced annually for this purpose. All are sown in the early part of the year and pricked off (except balsam) into Jiffy 7s or peat pots for flowering in 9–10cm (3½–4in) pots or larger. Most require pinching out to induce bushy growth, but their culture is simple.

For pests, diseases and physiological disorders see Chapter 31; for compost details see Chapter 15.

Flowering Pot Plants (for composts see Chapter 15. See also Foliage Plants, Shrubs, Cacti and Ferns)

Type and main varieties/cultivars	Approx height and flowering period	Propagation method and culture
Abutilon × hybridum	30–45cm (12–18in) Summer	Cuttings in spring. Also seed in spring. 18–24°C (65–75°F). Grow cool, 12.8°C (55°F) night
Achimenes grandiflora	15–20cm (6–9in) Summer	Rhizomes (tubers) in March/April. 5–6 per 13cm (5in) pot. Also seed in spring 18–24°C (65–75°F). 12.8°C (55°F) night. Support with twigs

Aechmea
  faciata (pink)
  fulgens (scarlet and black)
  lindenii (scarlet and purple)
  mariae-reginae (violet and crimson)
  veitchii (red)
	30cm (12in) Summer	Suckers removed at base of plant and potted. Minimum of 10–12.8°C (50–55°F). Plenty of moisture. Water little in winter. Avoid draughts

Aechynanthus marmoratus radicans	Summer, trailing	Cuttings in warm spring.

Agapanthus praecox
  subsp. orientalis (blue)
  and orientalis 'Alba' (white)
	60–90cm (2–3ft) Summer	Division in March. Seed in spring. Germinate at 18–24°C (65–75°F). Free drainage necessary. Water liberally in summer

Aloe
  humilis (grey leaved) and vars
  striata (leaves striped)
  variegata (partridge-breasted aloe)
	25–30cm (10–12in) Summer	Seed in April (may not be true due to hybridization), or cuttings taken as suckers from base of plant in summer. Free drainage is essential. Keep dry in winter or plants will rot. Water sparingly in summer. Give plenty of sun. Minimum of 12.8°C (55°F)

Anthurium Andreanum	45cm (18in) Long period	Seed in summer. Germinate at 21–24°C (70–75°F), 150 per seed tray pressed into surface, or division of old plants early in year.

Flowering Pot Plants—*continued*

Type and main varieties/cultivars	Approx height and flowering period	Propagation method and culture
scherzerianum *crystallinum*		Grown at mimium night temperature of 18°C (65°F). Water sparingly in dull cold weather and shade. For flowering raise temperature to 21−24°C (70−75°F)
Aphelandra squarrosa var *louisae* (zebra plant) 'Brockfield' 'Silver Beauty'	30cm (12in) May−Nov	Cuttings 10−15cm (4−6in) in bottom heat (14−21 days) at 24°C (75°F) in peat plus sand. Leaf bud cuttings also. Give heat at 18°C (65°F). Liberal watering and high nitrogen feeding
Arum lily (see *Zantedeschia aethiopica*)		
Asclepias curassavica (blood flower)	45−90cm (1½−3ft) Summer	Seed in spring for planting outdoors or division in Sept−Oct for indoor planting. For forcing, give initial period of 28 days or longer at 6°C (42°F). 6 days at 29.4°C (85°F) then force from end Oct at 16−29°C (60−85°F). May be grown colder, but later
Azalea indica (Japanese azalea), correctly *Rhododendron indicum*. Many vars *A. obtusa*, corrrectly *R. obtusum*	30−45cm (12−18in) Dec−April	Cuttings from strong shoots in June−July. Rooted in peat/sand. Pot at 10°C (50°F) and raise gradually to 18.3°C (65°F). After flowering remove spent blooms. Re-pot and encourage growth, shortening long branches. Plunge out of doors in shady position in July and keep feeding
Begonia × *cheimantha* 'Gloire de Lorraine' *B*. × *hiemalis* 'Optima'	15−30cm (6−12in) Autumn−winter	Leaf and stem cuttings Jan−May at 21°C (70°F) from stock plants. Give lighting to encourage vegetative growth. Leaf cuttings from Oct to Dec rooted at 18°C (65°F) Grow at 15°C (60°F). Give shade in spring and summer and feed regularly. Reduce temperature to 12.6°C (55°F) when in flower. Do not grow too hot or they become vegetative
Begonia *coccinea*, 'President Carnot' *fuschsioides* *manicata* *metallica* *nitida* (*B. minor*) *haageana*	Various Large part of year	Root readily from cuttings 13−15cm (5−6in) long in peat/sand during spring and summer. Very tolerant of a wide range of conditions but prefer some shade from really hot sun, otherwise leaves may 'burn'
Begonia semperflorens (fibrous begonia) New vars constantly produced incl F₁ hybrids	15−30cm (6−12in) Summer−autumn	Seed on top of compost. very small seeds Germinate at 21°C (70°F). Can be pricked off in groups initially for individual potting from Oct−Feb. Minimum 15.6°C (60°F) night temperature. Supplementary lighting helps development
Begonia × *tuberhybrida* (tuberous).	30−38cm (12−15in) Summer−autumn	Seed in February at 18−21°C (65−70°F) for normal varieties. Start tubers growing Feb−Mar. Divide into sections in March, leaving a strong shoot, and pot. Grow at 15.6°C (60°F). Give shade in spring and summer and feed regularly while flowering in cool atmosphere

Flowering Pot Plants—*continued*

Type and main varieties/cultivars	*Approx height and flowering period*	*Propagation method and culture*
Beloperone guttata (shrimp plant).	23–30cm (9–12in) or taller Large part of year. Best in summer/autumn	Cuttings from young shoots in summer rooted in peat/sand at 18°C (65°F), cutting back plant if necessary to provide these. Resents over-watering (yellows leaves) and grows best in well-heated environment
Billbergia *bakeri* *iridifolia* *nutans* *speciosa*	45cm (18in) Late winter but always attractive	By suckers which develop from base Keep cool at 10°C (50°F) in winter
Bouvardia × hybrida (many excellent vars in scarlet, salmon and pink).	30–38cm (12–15in) Winter	Cuttings of young shoots 10cm (4in) long in late spring in propagating case Cut back hard after flowering and pinch new shoots until August. Minimum temperature of 10–12.8°C (50–55°F)
Browallia speciosa 'Major'	45cm (18in) According to sowing date	Sow seed in March for summer flowering, July for winter and spring. Light shade in summer. Grow fairly cool. Do not over-feed or over-water. Requires support with twigs
Brunfelsia calycina and other spp.	60–90cm (2–3ft) Summer	Cuttings of the half-ripe shoots in June or July in propagating case. Re-pot after flowering. Keep on dry side Oct-Feb. Water and feed freely March onwards. Pinch out young branches to keep bushy. Minimum of 10°C (50°F)
Cacti (see Chapter 27)		
Calceolaria × herbeo-hybrida Multiflora Nana' and many excellent cultivars incl F$_1$ hybrids.	30–45cm (12–18in) Spring–Sept	Sow seed pressed into surface or covered with sand to facilitate sowing in July/August for next March/April, or Oct for May. Germinate at 18–24°C (65–75°F). Must be grown cool for good hard maturing and bushy plants. Can be left in cold frame until autumn, at about 13°C (55°F). Reduce water in winter, but keep well fed after growth starts in February
Camellia japonica	45–60cm (18–24in) Feb-Mar	By leaf bud cuttings in March Keep cool and do not over-water
Campanula isophylla 'Alba' and 'Mayi'	13–15cm (5–6in) May–Oct	By cuttings taken in August or Feb/March from cut-back plants inserted around the edge of 13cm (5in) pots. Also seed in early spring Very adaptable plants which can be grown with ease. Require regular watering
Campanula pyramidalis	1.5m (5ft) Summer	Seed in June, transferred to open ground for potting up in October. Will readily grow in cool greenhouses with little trouble

Flowering Pot Plants—*continued*

Type and main varieties/cultivars	Approx height and flowering period	Propagation method and culture
Canna indica and hybrids (Indian Shot)	30–45cm (12–18in) June–Aug	Jan-June, nick seed to induce germination. Put in small pots for planting outdoors in summer. Division of existing roots in spring. Easily grown plants requiring the minimum of attention. They go dormant in winter and can be stored dry
Capsicum annuum	25–30cm (10–12in) Fruit in autumn–winter	Seed in February sown thinly and potted up when very small. Grow at 16–18°C (60–65°F). Pinch hard for bushy growth. Shade to prevent scorch. Spray overhead to encourage setting and feed when fruit forms
Carnations (see Chapter 24)		
Celosia argentea var. *cristata* (cocks-comb) var. *plumosa*	30–38cm (12–15in) May–Sept	Seed in Feb/March. Must be kep growing constantly, with no checks, at not less than 12.8°C (55°F) at night. Keep cooler and drier when flowers are formed. Over-watering can rot stems
Ceropegia woodii	Trailing Summer	Cuttings in April/May. Grow at not less than 12.8°C (55°F)
Chorizema ilicifolium	38–45cm (15–18in) Summer	By seed in pots or cuttings with a heel in August when they root readily in fairly cool conditions. Plant in loamy soil. Minimum of 7°C (45°F). Prune by shortening shoots after flowering by one-third. Plunge out of doors after flowering. Re-pot every second or third year
Chrysanthemums in pots (see Chapter 25)		
Cineraria cruenta. correctly *Senecio cruentus* 'Grandiflora', 'Multi-flora', 'Multiflora Nana'	38–45cm (15–18in) Mar–June	Seed May–September in JI seed compost at 16°C (60°F). Grow cool giving adequate ventilation, especially during dull weather. Give dilute liquid feed adding some Epsom Salts occasionally
Citrus spp (oranges, lemons, grapefruit and tangerines)	Will grow tall if space allows Spring	Seed in spring or at various times. Grow cool and give plenty of air; never allow drying out. Small fruits may be formed
Clivia miniata Many excellent hybrids	30–45cm (12–18in) Spring	Seed in propagating case, but usually division of existing plants. Responds well to slow-acting fertilizer such as bonemeal. Re-pot every 4–5 years or sooner if required
Columnea gloriosa	Trailing or supported. Summer	By cuttings in spring–early summer, taking tips of shoots; rooted in propagating case in peat/sand. Keep moderately cool in summer and water very sparingly in winter
Crassula coccinea (see *Rochea*)		
Cuphea ignea (cigar flower)	15–25cm (6–10in) Summer	Seed in March. Pinch out to form bushy plant. Keep cool

Flowering Pot Plants—*continued*

Type and main varieties/cultivars	Approx height and flowering period	Propagation method and culture
Cyclamen persicum	23—30cm (9—12in) Winter	Soak seed in water 24 hours. Sow thinly in JI seed compost, 16—18°C (60—65°F). Sow July/Aug to flower following autumn; Oct/Nov for smaller plants (in 5—6in pots) the following autumn; Jan/Feb to flower in 10—11cm (4—4½in) pots in Dec. Feb/Mar in 9—10cm (3½—4in) pots to flower December. Corms can be potted up in August or earlier if available. After pricking out, give 18°C (65°F) for a few days, then a steady 15.6°C (60°F) until established. Shade in summer if necessary. Ventilate freely. Feed regularly and try to keep temperatures at 10—13°C (50—55°F) to induce more flowers to form. Remove bloom which forms prematurely. Water carefully, *avoiding the corms*, and water less in winter. New, quick-maturing types now available
Cytisus canariensis ('Genista' of florists) c. racemosis	30—45cm (12—18in) Spring	Firm cuttings in summer after flowering, in peat/sand Requires little more than regular watering and some shading. A succession of young plants necessary to maintain attractive appearance
Daphne odora 'Aureomarginata'	30—45cm (12—18in) March	Cuttings in propagating case in spring or layer for other types. Grafting may also be carried out. Keep outside for most of the year, bring in during the winter. Re-potting may be necessary after cutting back

Dipladenia bolivensis D. × hybrida 'Rosacea'
    sanderi
    splendens
	Climbing or trailing
	Summer
		Cuttings 2.5—5cm (1—2in) long with two leaves in propagating case in November.
		Grow at a minimum of 12.8°C (55°F). As house plant requires trellis for training. Water and feed freely in summer. Keep dry in winter

Echeveria
    derenbergii
    harmsii
    Worfield Wonder
	23—45cm (9—18in)
	Spring—ummer
		Seeds in spring or summer. Cuttings of side shoots in April—August. Offsets.
		Minimum of 7°C (45°F). Water sparingly in winter, but less so in spring. Do not water crowns of plants.

Epacris
    impressa (red and white)
    longiflora (white-tipped crimson flowers)
	1—1.5m (3—5ft)
	Winter
		Cuttings 1—1½in in July—August in propagating case.
		Minimum of 7—10°C (45—50°F). Pinch out growing points to form bushy plant. Cut back hard in spring then repot. Plunge out of doors in summer and bring in during September

Erica (heath)
    canaliculata (white)
    gracilis (pink)
    gracilis 'Alba' (white)
    hyemalis (pink) × willmorei
	30—45cm (12—18in)
	Winter
		Cuttings Nov—Jan in acid peat (3 parts peat/1 part sand), at 60—65°F (16—18°C). Root in 4—6 weeks. No rooting powder advisable.
		After the propagation period keep cool [12.8°C (55°F)], shading all summer, giving liquid feeding, sulphate of ammonia at ⅛oz per gallon until July. Take into greenhouses in September and give gentle heat

Flowering Pot Plants—*continued*

Type and main varieties/cultivars	Approx height and flowering period	Propagation method and culture
Eucharis grandiflora	30—40cm (12—16in) Spring	Plant bulbs in autumn and early spring. A simple plant to grow. Likes shade. Min. temp. 7°C (50°F)
Eucomis punctata (E. comosa)	60cm (2ft) Summer	Plant bulbs or offsets in March Will grow well as long as it is kept frost free
Euphorbia pulcherrima (Poinsettia) (many excellent vars with red or white bracts)	30cm—1.2m (1—4ft) Winter or other period by day-length manipulation	Cuttings from 'rested' plants in July—August under mist or in propagating case. Singly in peat pots or Jiffy 7s. Grow at minimum or 15.6°C (60°F). Size of plant produced will be related to time of taking cuttings. Never allow to dry out. Liquid feeding every 7—10 days. Pinch out leading shoot. High temperature will assist with colouring of bracts. Dwarfing compound can be used

Exacum
    affine
    macranthum
	23—30cm (9—12in) or more
	Summer
		Seed in Feb/March
		Given plenty of water and some shade. Support needed. A simple little plant to grow

Felicia amelloides (blue marguerite)	30—45cm (12—18in) or higher Summer	Seed in March/April at 10°C (50°F) May not bloom until second year. Keep frost free
Francoa ramosa (Bridal wreath)	30—38cm (12—15in) Spring summer	Seed in March and thereafter divide plants each March/April. Also cuttings, March Keep almost dry in winter but frost free. Water freely in summer and give liquid feeding
Fuchsia (lady's eardrop) A vast range of species, varieties and hybrids	23—45cm (9—18in) or higher Summer autumn winter	Cuttings from Feb onwards from stock plants which have been rested and started into growth in Dec/Jan at 15.6°C (60°F). Small cuttings only in peat/sand in close atmosphere. Insert cuttings around edge of pot, with polythene bag covering. Grow on at a steady 15.6°C (60°F). Keep potting light (compost *not* rammed). Water sparingly to begin with then more generously. Give liquid feeding when roots fill pot. Pinch out tips of shoots to encourage side shoots. Shade when necessary. Seed of F1 Chimes now available.
'Geranium' (botanically, *Pelargonium*). Zonal pelargoniums, regal pelargoniums, ivy-leaved, scented. Many excellent hybrids have been produced in recent years, which develop quickly from seed	Various, around 30—45cm (12—18in) Zonals at all times. Regals in summer	Cuttings from stock plants from August to April, or at any time for zonals. Cuttings 6—9cm (2½—3in) in length, preferably *nodal*. Root well at 18.3°C (65°F) with bottom heat. Seed sown in Jan/Feb or in autumn and wintered cool Easy to grow but does not like to be over-watered, especially in winter. Grow fairly cool throughout. Liquid feeding desirable using balanced ratio 1:1:1. If nitrogen shortage evident extra nitrogen may be given. Use dwarfing compound, especially for 'Carefree' and 'Sprinter'

Flowering Pot Plants—*continued*

Type and main varieties/cultivars	Approx height and flowering period	Propagation method and culture
Gesneria, (smithiantha)	15—25cm (6—10in) Summer	Sow seed in January, pressed into surface and covered with polythene. Cuttings from young shoots in spring or tubers in February, singly in small pots or in groups in larger pots. Minimum winter temperature of 12.8°C (55°F). Tubers dried off in winter for potting in February
Gloriosa (glory lily) *rothschildiana superba*	Climber Spring—summer	Grown from tubers planted in March singly in 15—18cm (6—7in) pots. They can be increased by offshoots in spring and by sowing seed in March. Climbs by means of tendrils and must have a winter temperature of not less than 12.8°C (55°F). Dig out tubers for winter
Gloxinia speciosa, correctly *Sinningia speciosa*	23—30cm (9—12in) Summer	Seed in February at 21°C (70°F) on surface. Start tubers in March—April. Leaf cuttings in summer. Cuttings in spring. Minimum of 10°C (50°F). Shading essential. Water with care, only syringeing during hot weather. Feed as buds open. Dry off after flowering for re-potting in March/April
Guzmania, several varieties, foliage and flowering	30—45cm (12—18in) Summer	Offsets any time in warmth.
Haemanthus albiflos (white), *coccineus, katharinae* (red), *multiflorus*	30—90cm (1—3ft) Summer	Pot in March/April or leave undisturbed for several years. Detach off-sets at planting time. Simple plants to grow. Rest after flowering
Hedychium gardnerianum (ginger lily)	60cm—1.8m (2—6ft) Summer	By division of rhizomes in spring. Almost hardy plants which will grow in good garden soil in tubs or borders. Water and feed regularly in summer. Dry out in winter. Re-pot in March if necessary after cutting back
Heliotropium arborescens (*H. peruvianum*) (Heliotrope)	30—90cm (1—3ft) or more Summer	Seeds in Feb/March at 18.3—23.9°C (65—75°F). Cuttings in spring. Old plants can be retained for re-potting every few years
Hippeastrum (popularly but wrongly called amaryllis)	60—90cm (2—3ft) Summer	Pot up bulbs in Nov—Feb. Easy plants to grow in variable conditions. Re-pot every 3 years
Hydrangea macrophylla (*H. hortensis*) in a wide range of cultivars	30—60cm (1—2ft) or more Spring—summer	*Internodal* stem cuttings between February and May (non-flowering shoots) in peat/sand. Requires 'stopping' to produce bushy plant, then careful watering. Grows well at 12.8—15.6°C (55—60°F). Stand outside in shade for summer. Support with canes July and bring into greenhouses in Sept/Oct for gradual forcing from Dec onwards. Keep nitrogen and phosphate levels low during feeding. Use chelated iron if foliage turns white (due to too alkaline a soil). For blue vars use blueing compound, 25g (1oz) aluminium sulphate in 1 litre (2 gal) water at fortnightly intervals. Shading is generally needed

Flowering Pot Plants—*continued*

Type and main varieties/cultivars	Approx height and flowering period	Propagation method and culture
Hymenocallis *narcissiflora (H. calathina)* *speciosa*	45—60cm (18—24in) Spring	Pot up bulbs or offsets in autumn or early in the year when growth is seen to be starting. Cheerful plants for the frost-free greenhouse. Some other types of hymenocallis require more heat but usually very adaptable and require re-potting only every 3 or 4 years. Rest after flowering
Impatiens walleriana *(I. holstii, sultani, petersiana)* (busy Lizzie) F$_1$ hybrids New Guinea types	23—45cm (9—18in) or higher Summer/autumn over a long period	Sow seed to give succession plants. On surface of compost. Cover with polythene. If given 21.1—23.9°C (70—75°F) it will germinate quickly. Remove polythene on germination. Cuttings root easily in pots of peat/sand compost. Keep well watered. Pinch to ensure bushy plants. Give some shade from hot sun
Ixia (corn lily) Usually obtainable as mixed hybrids *I. viridiflora*	38—45cm (15—18in) May/June	Bulbs in 13cm (5in) pots in September. Simple to grow. Keep out of doors like other bulbs until Christmas when they can then be forced gently. Support may be needed
Ixora *chinensis* (red to yellow) *coccinea* (red) *griffithiana (I. congesta)* (red and yellow) many hybrids and cultivars	90cm—1.2m (3—4ft) Summer	Cuttings of firm shoots in spring and summer. Needs warmth to grow well. Prune into shape in February. Keep dry in winter
Jacobinia *carnea* (pink) *coccinea* (red) and others	60—90cm (2—3ft) Late summer—winter	Cuttings in July every second year to keep a supply of young plants raised in peat/sand in propagating case. Prune back after flowering. Keep at not less than 12.8—15.6°C (55—60°F). Water and feed well in summer. Water sparingly in winter or spring after flowering
Kalanchoe blossfeldiana	20—25cm (8—10in) Winter	Seed sown in March at 18.3—21.1°C (65—70°F). Cuttings in March. A plant sensitive to day length. Grow at 15.6—18.3°C (60—65°F). Shade to give short days (see Chrysanthemums, Chapter 25) in July or early Aug from 16.30 to 08.00 hrs for 24 days
Kohleria eriantha *(I. soloma erianthum)*	45—60cm (18—24in) or more Summer—autumn	Grows well in warm humid atmosphere. Not difficult to cultivate in moist greenhouse
Lachenalia aloides (Cap cowslip) 'Burnham Gold' 'Nelsonii' (yellow) Many modern varieties	30—45cm (12—18in) Spring	Pot up 4 or 5 bulbs in 13cm (5in) pot in August. Seed in March. Bulbs dried off after flowering for re-potting. Cool atmosphere. Need plenty of light in winter when growing or they become too vegetative
Lilium *longiflorum* *tigrinum* and others	45cm (18in) Spring	Bulbs are stored at low temperatures 0.6—1.7°C (33—35°F) to enable them to flower early Flowers according to temperature level; 15.6—21°C (60—70°F) is average. Prone to leaf scorching. Use calcium nitrate to offset this

Flowering Pot Plants—*continued*

Type and main varieties/cultivars	Approx height and flowering period	Propagation method and culture
Limonium *suworowii* *profusum*	30–38cm (12–15in) Summer	Seed in Feb–Mar at 18.3°C (65°F). *L. profusum* from cuttings in summer. Grow at minimum of 7.2°C (45°F). A relatively straight-forward plant
Marguerite *Chrysanthemum* *frutescens* (white) *coronarium* (yellow)	45–50cm (18–20in) Summer	Cuttings Aug/Jan. Seed in February. Simple to grow; requires merely the protection of a greenhouse to flower profusely. Over-feeding makes plants too tall
Medinilla magnifica	90cm–1.2m (3–4ft) Summer	Half-ripe shoots with heel in November. Bottom heat essential Minimum of 12.8–15.6°C (55–60°F). Re-pot in February. Water well. Shading necessary to start off. Water and feed frequently in summer; keep dry in winter
'Mesembryanthemum' *Lampranthus* *aureus* (yellow) *blandus roseus* (pink) *coccineus* (scarlet) *haworthii (Erepsia haworthii)* (magenta)	30–35cm (12–14in) Summer	Cuttings after flowering. Keep frost-free for winter. Never over-water, especially in winter
Mimulus glutinosus *(aurantiacus)* (monkey flower)	45–60cm (18–24in) Spring–Summer	Cuttings in summer. To keep dwarf cut back each February and pinch shoots in summer
Myrtus comunis (myrtle)	As pruned Spring–Summer	Cuttings late spring and summer. Must be grown cool in greenhouse
Nerine *bowdenii*, several varieties *samiensis* and hybrids	45cm (18in) Sept–Oct	By offsets and bulbs potted up in July, 3 bulbs in a 15cm (6in) pot and 1 bulb in a 8cm (3in) pot. Re-pot only every few years as they do well if pot-bound. They like resting in the spring and early summer. Water and feed well during growing period and top dress pot with fresh compost
Nerium oleander (oleander)	Up to 1.8m (6ft) Spring–summer	Firm ripe cuttings 8–15cm (3–6in) long in summer. Prune shoots back one-third after flowering. Rub out shoots at base of flower buds. Can be put outside in summer but keep well watered (stand pots in water). Water sparingly in winter
Ornithogalum (chincherinchee) *arabicum* *lacteum* *thyrsoides*	45–60 cm (18–24in) Spring–early summer	Seed in spring–summer. Give 15.6°C (60°F). Division in October. Must be in well crocked pots. Re-pot each spring as new leaves expand
Oxalis *bowiei* (purple) *deppei* (red)	15–23cm (6–9in) Spring	Pot up 4 or 5 tubers in 13cm (5in) pot in autumn. Put in pots for forcing about February then bring into greenhouse. Dry off and re-pot in autumn

Flowering Pot Plants—*continued*

Type and main varieties/cultivars	Approx height and flowering period	Propagation method and culture
Polianthes tuberosa (tuberose)	45cm (18in) Summer	Pot up bulbs in succession in Jan – Feb, singly or in threes. Usual to buy bulbs annually. Keep cool to encourage rooting then force into flower at brisk temperatures
Polyanthus *Primula veris elatior* *Primula acaulis* A wonderful range of vars	23–25cm (9–10in) Dec – Feb	Seed in March – June, pressed into the surface. Cover with clear polythene and give 15.6–21.1°C (60–70°F). Respond well to *cool* growing and regular watering. Give shade from direct sunlight in cool greenhouse. Or keep in pots outside in cold frames for lifting in during December. Use 2:2:1 liquid feeding
Primula kewensis malacoides obconica sinensis	30cm (12in) Spring – summer	Seed thinly in May – June. Germinates at 18.3–21.1°C (65–70°F). Grow cool and keep well watered, potting only lightly. Reduce watering during winter. Apply iron sequestrine if leaves go white
Rehmannia angulata elata	90cm–1.2m (3–4ft) June	Seed in June/July at 15.6°C (60°F) or by cuttings from basal shoots after flowering. Root cuttings can also be taken. Frost-free conditions only. Treat as biennial. Raise cool and light in greenhouse in winter. Feed and water well when flowers form
Richardia (arum lily – see *Zantedeschia*)		
Rochea coccinea (*Crassula coccinea*)	23–30cm (9–12in) Summer	Cuttings in spring and summer. Select from terminal shoots if rooting in peat/sand, at 15.6–18.3°C (60–65°F) round edge pot. Cool greenhouse conditions. Keep dry in winter. Must be well dressed
Roses (see also Chapter 25) Dwarf and miniature types	40–45cm (16–18in) Spring – summer	Buy in plants and pot up dwarf growing varieties. Keep as cool as possible. Pay strict attention to pest and disease control. Root from cuttings
Saintpaulia ionantha (African violet)	20–25cm (8–10in) Various	Seed in Aug/Sept at 21.1–23.9°C (70–75°F) in JIS plus extra peat (can be sown any time to flower 6 months later). Leaf petiole cuttings with petioles inserted in sandy compost at 70°F (21.1°C); lift plants and pot separately. Grow at 18.3°C (65°F). Water from below to avoid leaf marking. Give shade. Feed when plant becomes pot bound each year
Salpiglossis sinuata	30–35cm (12–14in) (dwarf type) up to 90cm (3ft) Summer, autumn – spring	Sow seed in July – Sept in JIP1. Can be difficult to prevent damping off. Overwinter in small pots and pot up to 15cm (6in) in February, giving a minimum of 10°C (50°F). Pinch out leading stem to give bushy plant. Do not overwater in winter

Flowering Pot Plants—*continued*

Type and main varieties/cultivars	Approx height and flowering period	Propagation method and culture
Salvia	23–30cm (9–12in) Summer–autumn	Sow seed from mid-February to May or later. Seed must be germinated at 21.1–23.9°C (70–75°F) Give a growing temperature of 12.8–15.6°C (55–60°F). Too low temperatures and excess watering will yellow the leaves
Saxifraga stolonifera (mother of thousands)	30–40cm (12–16in) Spring–summer	Increase by runners any time. Keep cool and in well-watered pots. Can be grown out of doors in mild areas
Schizanthus (butterfly flower or poor man's orchid)	45–60cm (18–24in) Spring	Sow August until January in 18.3°C (65°F). Grow 3 in a pot for best effect. Likes cool steady growth, plenty of light, pinching to make bushy and support with split canes. Water sparingly in winter, generously in spring
Schlumbergera truncata (*Zygocactus truncatus*) (Christmas cactus)	Pendulous Winter	Propagates with ease from stems rooted any time. Water sparingly in summer. Give light feeding from Oct onwards
Solanum *capsicastrum* *pseudocapsicum*	30–35cm (12–14in) Winter	Like tomatoes. Seed in January and February thinly at 150 per tray at 18.3°C (65°F). Also from cuttings, in propagating cases Needs plenty of light for sturdy growth. Pinch to keep bushy. Stand in frame in summer. Syringe frequently during flowering in July–Sept to induce good setting. Avoid over-watering. Feed with 1:1:1 after berries are set
Spathiphyllum Spathiphyllum	30–60cm (18–24in)	White spathes. Cultivation similar to Zantedeschia (arum)
Strelitzia reginae (Bird of paradise flower)	90cm–1.2m (3–4ft) Spring summer	Division in spring. Plenty of sun and adequate water in spring and summer. Never below 10°C (50°F)
Streptocarpus Many complex hybrids	90cm–1.2m (3–4ft) but dwarf types 38cm (15in) Summer	Seed in Feb–Mar at 18.3°C (65°F) and again in July. Leaf cuttings in August will also root. Grow cool, not less than 7.2°C (45°F). Begin watering in March and feed from April. Encourage to flower again following year by removing old flower stems
Tillandsia lindeniana	38cm (15in) Summer	By suckers which develop at the base of plant. Minimum of 12.8°C (55°F). Requires warmth and humidity to thrive
Torenia fournieri	30cm (12in) Summer–autumn	Seed in March/April. Pot up 3 plants per 15cm (6in) pot. Requires some shade like begonias. Support necessary with twigs
Trachelium caeruleum	45cm (18in) Summer	Seed in July in frames out of doors. Best treated as a biennial. Keep frost-free through the winter, then water and feed liberally

Flowering Pot Plants—*continued*

Type and main varieties/cultivars	Approx height and flowering period	Propagation method and culture
Tulbaghia pulchella	30—45cm (12—18in) Summer	Pot up in March/April. Propagation by detaching offsets. A simple plant to grow. Rest in winter
Vallota speciosa (Scarborough lily)	45—60cm (18—24in) Summer	Pot up deeply in early summer, one per pot. Can be propagated from offsets which form at base. Hates disturbance; leave 3 years in same pot. Feed when growth starts. Very little heat required. Some shade beneficial in May/June
Veltheimia bracteata *(V. viridifolia)*	30—45cm (12—18in) Early spring	Pot up in September. Small bulbs appearing at base form a means of propagation. Frost-free conditions. Do not need potting every year
Zantedeschia *aethiopica* (arum lily) *angustiloba* *elliottiana* and dwarfer varieties	60—90cm (2—3ft) Spring	Divide up in July/August after flowering. A great favourite with the floral art enthusiast, but not popular with gardeners because it introduces green fly. Dry off after flowering

Foliage Pot Plants

Type/variety	Height	Propagation/culture
Acalypha wilkesiana	45—60cm (18—24in)	Half-ripened shoots taken in the summer. Heat is necessary in the propagator. JIP$_2$ with extra peat. Syringe with tepid water in summer
Acorus gramineus 'Variegatus'	20—25cm (8—10in)	By division of the tufts in spring. Cool conditions. Also thrives out of doors. Loves wet conditions as these are aquatic plants
Aglaonema commutatum	30—45cm (12—18in)	By division of the roots in March into small pots. 3 parts loam, 1 part peat, 1 part sharp sand.
Ampelopsis veitchii	Climbing	Cuttings of soft shoots in summer. Ordinary soil. Seed in spring
Araucaria excelsa (Norfolk Island pine)	30—60cm (12—24in)	By seed or cuttings in propagating case. Ordinary soil; is nearly hardy
Aspidistra elatior often mistakenly referred to as *A. lurida*	45—60cm (18—24in)	By division when re-potting. Likes shade. Stand out of doors in summer.
Aucuba japonica variegata	30cm (12in)	By seed or cuttings. Ordinary compost
Begonia masoniana	30—60cm (12—24in)	Leaf or stem cuttings any time in propagating case. Also by leaf or a portion of it with the underside veins cut at 2.5cm (1in) intervals, placed flat on a sandy compost. Slow-growing and requires more heat than other begonias. Needs some shade

Foliage Pot Plants—*continued*

Type/variety	Height	Propagation/culture
Begonia rex hybrids and other foliage types	30–60cm (12–24in)	as above. Water sparingly in winter. Shade from strong sun
Caladium × *hortulanum* (hybrids of *C. bicolor* *C. humboldtii*	30cm (12in)	Leaves die down in winter. Tubers should be stored in the pots at temperatures not below 2.8°C (55°F). Report tubers in March at 18.3°C (65°F) minimum in coarse peaty mixture
Calathea rotundifolia zebrina	25–30cm (10–12in)	Divisions of roots in spring
Chlorophytum comosum 'Variegatum' (spider plant)	30–45cm (12–18in)	Layer from small plantlets which form on flower heads. Useful and easy to grow. Rich soil and much water.
Cissus antarctica (natal vine)	Climbing	By cuttings of hard new growth place in water. This plant will tolerate most conditions but not excessive sunshine
Coleus blumei	30–45cm (12–18in)	By seed. Also by cuttings rooted in propagating case in spring. Shade from strong sun. Keep well watered. Feed regularly.
Collinia elegans (*Chamaedorea elegans*) (stove plant)	2.5–3m (8–10ft)	By seeds in March 2.5cm (1in) deep in pots after soaking for a day or two. Requires high temperatures to germinate 29.4°C (85°F) Do not expose to sun. Minimum of 18.3°C (65°F).
Cordyline terminalis various cultivars	45cm (18in)	Seed in March at 29.4°C (85°F). Main stems cut to 2.5cm (1in) lengths inserted horizontally in sandy soil. March/Apr temperature 23.9–26.7°C (75–80°F) Needs a rich soil containing much peat. Water well in growing season.
Croton, correctly *Codiaeum variegatum* and cultivars	30–60cm (12–24in)	Cuttings with at least 6–7 leaves, also leaf bud cuttings. Both in propagating case. Give full light and keep cool. Shade only in full sun. Tricky but worth while. Minimum of 12.8°C (55°F) in winter
Cyperus alternifolius (umbrella grass)	45–60cm (18–24in)	Division in March or April, or use tips of shoots. Give shade
Dieffenbachia maculata (dumbcane)	30–60cm (12–24in)	Terminal and stem cuttings, the latter with two buds horizontally. Both in propagating case. A fairly easy plant to grow.
Dizygotheca elegantissima (*Aralia elegantissima*)	60–90cm (24–36in)	Root cuttings in March. Seeds sown in March. 18.3–21.1°C (65–70°F). Plenty of water
Dracaena Dracaena various	45cm (18in)	Stem and leaf bud cuttings in propagating case. Shade from bright sunlight. High humidity necessary.
Elettaria cardamomum	30cm (12in)	By division any time. Do not expose to full sun. Give plenty of warmth and moisture.

Foliage Pot Plants—*continued*

Type/variety	Height	Propagation/culture
Euonymus radicans variegata, a form of *E. fortunei*	15cm−20cm (6−8in)	By stem or leaf cuttings or by pegging down runners. Also by division. Good soil, leafy and light.
× *Fatshedera lizei* (fat-headed Lizzie), hybrid *Fatsia* × *Hedera*	45−60cm (18−24in)	Terminal and leaf bud cuttings in propagating case. Half peat/half sand. Must be supported and shaded from bright sun.
Fatsia japonica (rice-paper plant)	45−60cm (18−24in)	From seed or cuttings taken in the spring. Copious watering and regular feeding
Ficus *benjamina* *elastica* (India-rubber plant) *pumila*	60cm (24in) 30−60cm (12−24in)	Leaf bud and terminal cuttings or seed in propagating case. Requires more water than the rubber plant. Not the easiest of plants to grow. Water regularly but sparingly.
Fittonia *verschaffeltii* var *argyroneura*	15−30cm (6−12in)	From cuttings of firm young shoots taken in spring, rooted with bottom heat. Good soil and a warm, moist atmosphere.
Grevillea robusta (silk oak)	30−60cm (12−24in)	From seed sown in early spring, also cuttings with heels of old wood attached. Prune off points of shoots occasionally to induce bushy growth.
Gynura aurantiaca	60−90cm (24−36in)	By cuttings taken in the spring. Give plenty of light, but not direct sun.
Hedera (ivy) *canariensis helix* many cultivars	Climbing 5−10cm	By cuttings taken in spring. A tip cutting 5−10cm (2−4in) long will root in water or sandy soil. Resents over-watering in winter and care should be taken not to over-pot
Helxine soleirolii (mind your own business)	Trailing	By division in spring. Any soil. Can be a nuisance if allowed to develop
Hoffmannia *refulgens* *roezlii*	30cm (12in)	By cuttings of young growth in sandy soil in propagating case with brisk bottom heat. A coarse soil mixture of peat, sand and loam should be satisfactory at all stages of growth
Maranta (prayer plant) *leuconeura*	15−20cm (6−8in)	By division of tubers in February or March, also by leaf cuttings in moist heat. Rich soil and feed during summer. Re-pot each year. Water abundantly March−September.
Microcoelum weddelianum (*Cocos weddaliana*)	30cm−60cm (12−24in)	Seed 2.5cm (1in) deep in light, soil, temperature 29.4°C (85°F). At any time. Minimum temperature 10°C (50°F). Must not stand in draught.
Monstera deliciosa	Climbing	Seed or cuttings and requires a high temperature − a task for the professional. Water freely March − October. Syringe twice daily.

Foliage Pot Plants—*continued*

Type/variety	Height	Propagation/culture
Neoregelia carolinae	23—30cm (9—12in)	From seed or offsets. A temperature of 21.1°C (70°F) is needed. Use potting compost, peat, leaf-mould, or sphagnum moss. Best if they are not over-potted
Nepenthes species (pitcher plant)	Climbing	8—15cm (3—6in) one-year-old shoots in spring and summer. Orchid-type compost
Nephthytis 'Emerald Gem'	Climbing	Stem cuttings, any time. Can be trained to a cane, but better still to a cork bark or wire cylinder filled with moss kept damp for the aerial roots. A rich compost and plenty of feeding in the summer are required
Oplismenus hirtellus 'Variegatus'	20cm (8in)	From stem cuttings. (Needs good winter light, warmth and good soil).
'Palms', including: *Chamaedorea, Chamaeops, Euterpe, Washingtonia, Phoenix* etc.	Various heights	By stratified seeds in spring.
Pandanus veitchii (screw-pine)	30—45cm (12—18in)	By suckers with some heat. Good winter warmth, plenty of water in summer and acid leafy soil
Pellionia repens (*P. daveauana*)		Propagation is easy from cuttings Considerable care in winter with regard to temperature and watering
Peperomia argyreia (*P. sandersii*)	8—15cm (3—6in)	Cut a leaf in half and insert the cut surface about 1.2cm ($\frac{1}{2}$in) deep in a rooting medium with bottom heat. Requires careful watering. Temperature in winter must remain above 10°C (50°F)
Peperomia griseo-argentea (*P. hederifolia*) (pepper elder)	8—15cm (3—6in)	By leaf cuttings in the spring. Leaf complete with stalk is inserted vertically 2.5cm (1in) deep in rooting medium. Requires careful watering. Temperature should remain above 10°C (50°F)
Philodendron erubescens 'Burgundy' (sweetheart plant) and others	Climber	Terminal cuttings, leaf bud cuttings rooted in a temp. of 21.1°C (70°F). Rich leaf soil need. Min. temp. 12.8—15.6°C (55—60°F)
Pilea cadierei (aluminium plant)	30—45cm (12—18in)	Propagation is easy from cuttings. Shade from bright sun. Rich soil and plenty of water in summer
Rhiphidophora aurea (*Scindapsus aureus*) (ivy arum)	30—45cm (12—18in)	By root division in Feb/March in peat, sphagnum moss, sand or a little charcoal. Water with care and keep temperature above 10°C (50°F) in a light situation. Must be stopped occasionally.

Foliage Pot Plants—*continued*

Type/variety	Height	Propagation/culture
Ricinus communis (castor oil plant) 'Gibsonii' *Sanguineus* and others	30−45cm (12−18in)	Seed in February. Plenty of light required for good plants
Sansevieria trifasciata (mother-in-law's tongue) 'Laurentii'	90cm−1.2m (3−4ft)	'Laurentii' has to be increased from suckers to retain the variegated leaves. Others can be propagated by leaf cuttings in May−August. Rich soil with plenty of grit and very sparing watering. Needs winter warmth
Saxifraga stolonifera (*S. sannentosa*) (mother of thousands)	30cm (12in)	By detaching runners, anytime. Grow cool
Schefflera actinophylla	30−45cm (12−18in)	Cuttings in spring. Feed regularly in growing season. Benefits by yearly potting on until in a fairly large pot.
Sedum sieboldii	20cm (8in)	Propagate by short cuttings which root easily. Dies down in winter so must be kept dry. Restarts in February
Selaginella species	10−15cm (4−6in)	Cuttings 3in long in peat at a temperature of 26.7°C (80°F). Equal parts peat and sphagnum moss. Shade from sun
Sparmannia africana	45−60cm (18−24in)	Roots readily from cuttings. It may be cut back severely. Does best in warm conditions and in smallish pot
Tetrastigma voinierianum	Climbing	Leaf bud or terminal cuttings. Feed during the growing season but do not over-water at any time
Tradescantia species (Wandering Jew/Sailor etc)	Trailing	Old plants should be replaced regularly by rooting cuttings in 8cm (3in) pots An ideal plant for the edge of the greenhouse staging
Tillandsia	Various colours of leaf 30cm (12in)	By offsets
Vriesia splendens	30cm−45m (12−18in)	By offsets inserted in small pots of sandy peat. Temperature 23.9−29.4°C (75−85°F) Require warm conditions but not full sun during summer

Plant Identification

Identifying the huge range of pot plants now grown in greenhouses can be a problem, especially when, as often happens, you lose a label or a friend gives you a cutting or a young plant. Browsing round a well stocked garden centre or nursery, where all plants these days are meticulously labelled, is one way of identifying what you have. Alternatively, it is a question of referring to books or wall charts, or taking your plant along to a botanical or society garden where they are almost certain to be able to identify your plant for you.

Greenhouse shrubs

Many of the greenhouse shrubs can also be grown in large pots or tubs and quite a few of the smaller or restricted shrubs have already been described as flowering pot plants. In nearly all cases the necessary space for development is more important than adherence to a strict regime.

The soil for growing greenhouse shrubs need not be of a very high nutritional standard, but it should be in good physical condition. To this end deep cultivation and sometimes excavation of the existing soil may be necessary, especially where shrubs are being grown in borders against walls or on the floor of a conservatory or other largely glass erection. Saturation of the growing media by seepage of water from outside is a very frequent cause of failure, lack of moisture being less of a problem than might be imagined, as many shrubs send down roots to a fair depth, often well outside the greenhouse or conservatory.

Support and pruning

Support for climbing or clinging shrubs is provided either by longitudinal wires or plastic or wooden trellis. Shrubs grown in relatively cramped conditions will certainly require pruning. Broadly speaking shrubs either form flowers on new wood of the current or previous year's growth, or on spurs emanating from older portions of wood. It is important therefore to ascertain the flowering mechanism and prune accordingly. In many cases, however, such a specific approach is not necessary and pruning merely to keep the shrub within limits and well shaped is all that is required.

Temperature levels

Few gardeners maintain a greenhouse exclusively for the well-being of shrubs and it is therefore a case of first of all selecting a suitable shrub for the intended temperature level for the main greenhouse activity (see table which follows).

Shrubs for the Greenhouse or Conservatory (see Chapter 15 for composts)

Name	Minimum winter temperature	Propagation and culture
Abutilon (flowering maple) *megapotamicum striatum* 'Thompsonii' 'Savitzii' *vitifolium* and many others	10°C (50°F)	Cuttings at almost any time of year. Side shoots with heel are best inserted in propagation case. Prune back to two or three branches from the base, merely shortening shoots of pot-grown species by half. Train against a wall or support
Acacia *armata* *dealbata* (mimosa wattle) *drummondii* *longifolia* *riceana* and others	7.2°C (45°F)	Seeds in spring and summer, specially 'chipped'. Cuttings in July of semi-woody heeled side shoots. Cut young plants back one-third and side shoots similarly. Prune annually by thinning out weaker shoots and cutting back side branches. Keep well watered and feed when actively growing
Allamanda cathartica var *hendersonii* and many more	10°C (50°F)	8cm (3in) cuttings in March rooted in frames or inside a mist unit. Plant up in 13cm (5in) pots, put them into benches or borders of good soil. Prune back previous summer's growth to 2–3 buds in February. Water freely in summer, sparingly in winter

Shrubs for the Greenhouse or Conservatory—*continued*

Name	Minimum winter temperature	Propagation and culture
Anemopaegma (formerly *Tecoma* or *Bignonia*) (trumpet flower)	7.2°C (45°F)	By seed if available but generally by three-jointed cuttings in summer, planted up into 13cm (5in) pots when rooted for eventual planting out in well-prepared borders. Cut back side branches after flowering to 30−90cm (1−3ft) of all wood on main branches. Trim back to 25−30cm (10−12in) apart. Remove all weak or superfluous growth in spring. Requires regular feeding
Araucaria excelsa (monkey puzzle, Norfolk Island pine)	Cool culture, being quite hardy	Propagates easily by cuttings in Aug or Sept in warm propagating case. Does best in a loamy compost (JIP2 plus peat). Grow in 13−15cm (5−6in) pots. Must be kept frost free. Re-pot if necessary in Feb. Feed regularly in summer
Aristolochia elegans and other species (calico flower, Dutchman's pipe)	12.8−15.6°C (55−60°F)	Root from cuttings taken in June or July in propagating case. Grow in tubs or borders in good garden soil. Seed can be sown in March. Cut back in Feb if too vigorous. Keep frost free
Bougainvillea *glabra* (rose) *spectabilis* (lilac rose) 'Lindleyana' 'Mrs Butt' (rose) 'Mrs Louis Wathen' (reddish orange)	10°C (50°F)	10cm (4in) half-ripe cuttings in Aug in propagating case. Pot up in 8cm (3in) then 13cm (5in) pots, preparatory to planting out. Prepare 60 × 60cm (2 × 2ft) planting area of good soil plus peat with perfect drainage for planting in autumn. Prune back previous summer's growth to within two buds of base in Feb. Can also be grown in pots.
Bouvardia × *hybrida* Many excellent varieties in scarlet, salmon and pink	10−12.8°C (50−55°F)	Cuttings of young shoots 10cm (4in) long in late spring in propagating case. Pot up in 13−15cm (5 or 6in) pots Cut back hard after flowering and pinch new shoots until Aug
Brunfelsia *B. calycina* and others	10°C (50°F)	Cuttings of half-ripe shoots in June or July in propagating case. Pot on when rooted in 13−15cm (5−6in) pots Re-pot after flowering. Keep on dry side from October till Feb. Water and feed freely from March onwards. Pinch out young branches to keep bushy. Can also be grown as pot plant.
Callistemon citrinus 'Splendens' (bottle brush tree)	4.4−7.2°C (40−45°F)	Seed in April. Cuttings in Aug in propagating case. Fairly hardy. Can be pot grown but at their best in well-prepared greenhouse border with good garden soil. Cut back strong shoots by half and weak shoots by two-thirds after flowering. Water sparingly in winter

Shrubs for the Greenhouse or Conservatory—*continued*

Name	Minimum winter temperature	Propagation and culture
Camellia japonica varieties, and hybrids, especially *C. × Williamsii Donation (C. japonica × C. saluenensis)*	4.4−7.2°C (40−45°F)	Seeds at any time for distinct species. Grafting of several varieties on to *C. Japonica* in spring or cuttings from young shoots in July − Aug in propagating case. Fairly hardy, they thrive in frost-free conditions. Prune into shape after flowering and avoid either excess moisture or dryness (resulting in botrytis or bud drop). Grow as cool and airy as other greenhouse activities allow
Cassia corymbosa	4.4−7.2°C (40−45°F)	Cuttings of young shoots in propagating case in early summer. Grow in frost-free conditions for best results. Prune by cutting back previous year's growth in Feb
Cestrum aurantiacum and other excellent species	4.4°C (40°F)	Cuttings of young wood in Aug in propagating case. Can be grown in large pots but happier in good soil in a wall border. Trim young plants lightly and older plants harder by cutting side shoots to a few buds in late winter. To keep bushy pinch shoots
Chorizema ilicifolium (red)	7.2°C (45°F)	By seed in pots or cuttings with heel in Aug, when they root readily in fairly cool conditions. Plant in loamy soil. Shorten shoots by one-third after flowering, then plunge out of doors. Re-pot every second or third year. Can also be grown in greenhouse border
Clerodendrum (glory bower) *splendens* (scarlet) *Thomsoniae* (crimson and white) *speciosissimum* (syn. *C. fallax*) (scarlet)	15.6°C (60°F)	Seed in March at 18.3°C (65°F) and gradually move up pot size. Cuttings in spring and Aug rooted in propagating case. Also by root cuttings and suckers in some cases. Trim back branches in spring. Plants need plenty of light and resent over-watering
Clianthus *formosus (C. dampieri, C. specious)* (glory pea) *puniceus* (parrot's bill)	4.4−7.2°C (40−45°F)	Seed in spring or summer. For *C. formosus* by grafting on to seedlings of *Colutea arborescens*: insert wedge-shaped section of clianthus in a slit in colutea, bind with soft wool and insert in propagation case. *C. puniceus* can be raised from cuttings on its own roots. Gives little trouble if grown cool and frost-free either in pots or in tubs
Cobea scandens (cup and saucer vine)	10−12.8°C (50−55°F)	Seed in February − March. Pot on, using good garden soil. Simple to grow. Merely requires branches cut back to 2 buds (like a vine) in Feb or March, and occasional restriction when it gets out of hand. A succession of new plants from seed is often less trouble
Crossandra infundibuli-formis (C. undulaefolia)	12.8°C (55°F)	Seed or cuttings in March. Pot into 8cm (3in) then 13cm (5in) pots. Best to raise new plants from seed or cuttings annually. Shorten main shoots to keep bushy

Shrubs for the Greenhouse or Conservatory—*continued*

Name	Minimum winter temperature	Propagation and culture
Datura *cornigera* (angel's trumpet) (white) *sanguinea* (orange—red)	7.2°C (45°F)	Cuttings in spring in pots or open beds or propagating case. Can be a large and vigorous shrub requiring pruning back. Pot up young plants frequently. Water little in winter, but water and feed copiously in summer
Doxantha capreolta (glory flower), previously known as Bignonia	4.4—7.2°C (40—45°F)	Cuttings of short shoots in bottom heat in peat/sand. Potted on into good garden soil. A bushy shrub relatively easy to grow in large tubs or greenhouse borders. Do not over-water in winter
Gardenia *jasminoides* (Cape jasmine) and double form 'Florida' *nitida* *thunbergia*	12.8—15.6°C (55—60°F)	Cuttings of young shoots 8cm (3in) in length in peat/sand in March with bottom heat. Must be 'coddled' by bench warming until established. A succession of young plants should be raised as bush goes straggly. Pinch shoots of young growth to induce side-shoot formation
Hibiscus species (rose mallow)	12.8—15.6°C (55—60°F) in moist atmosphere	Shoots 8cm (3in) long on bottom heat in March, but may be slow Given warmth, a fairly simple shrub to grow, shoots being cut back by about half in Jan or Feb. Pinch out to give a bushy plant
Hoya (wax plant) *bella* *carnosa*	12.8—15.6°C (55—60°F) *H. carnosa* the hardier	By layering of shoots in pots or by cuttings in spring and summer. At its best rambling from good soil in a greenhouse border but could be grown in large pots or tubs, being re-potted every 3/4 years
Humea elegans (incense plant)	7.2—10°C (45—50°F)	Sow seed in summer and pot on. Do not over-water in winter. Support needed, along with regular feeding and watering in spring and summer
Iochroma *coccineum* (scarlet) *fuchsioides* (orange scalet) *grandiflorum* (purple)	4.4—7.2°C (40—50°F)	Cuttings in summer. Must be kept frost-free. Water very little in winter. Support needed
Ipomoea (pharbitis, morning glory) *learii* (perennial) *tricolor* (annual)	12.8—15.6°C (55—60°F)	Seed in March for annual species. Seed in March or cuttings in summer for perennials. Best planted in greenhouse border in good soil. Perennial type, must be kept frost-free but dry. Requires adequate support with string or trellis
Jasminum (jasmine) *angulare* (white) *mesnyi (J. primulinum)* (yellow) *polyanthum* (white, pink in bud) and other species	7.2°C (45°F)	Cuttings in summer, potted on when rooted and then planted either in large pots or in borders. Simple shrub to grow. Cut back after flowering. Merely requires to be frost-free. If in pots stand out for summer
Lagerstroemia indica (crape-myrtle) and cultivars	7.2°C (45°F)	Cuttings of young shoots in March—April. Grow on good soil. Prune back hard in Feb. If in pot stand out for summer period. Keep dry in winter.

Shrubs for the Greenhouse or Conservatory—*continued*

Name	Minimum winter temperature	Propagation and culture
Lantana camara and cultivars	7.2°C (45°F)	Cuttings in spring, or seed in Feb — March in propagating case. Cool greenhouse subjects. Pinch out shoots to keep dwarf if necessary. Prune in winter by cutting back shoots hard
Lapageria rosea (Chilean bellflower)	7.2 — 10°C (45 — 50°F)	Layering in spring and summer is best method of propagation. Do best in specially made-up beds as they like a free root run. Top dress each spring with new soil

Manettia
  bicolor (red and yellow)
  inflata (same with less yellow)
	12.8 — 15.6°C (55 — 60°F)	Cuttings in May — June. Pot up 2 or 3 plants together.
		Must have good warmth and need a fair bit of room. Trim into shape after flowering

Metrosideros (closely related to *Callistemon*)
  diffusa (crimson)
  excelsa (crimson)
  robusta (scarlet)
	7.2°C (45°F)	Seed in April. Cuttings in Aug.
		Frost-free greenhouse. In borders or large pots in good garden soil. Trim into shape after flowering

Passiflora (passion flower) *P. caerulea* and others requiring more heat of which *P. antioquiensis* (red) is popular	7.2°C (45°F)	Cuttings with heel in bottom heat in spring and summer, although node cuttings will also grow. Seed in spring. Cool growing conditions for *P. caerulea*. *P. antioquiensis* needs more heat. Keep dry in winter and cut back fairly hard after flowering
Pelargonium spp (Geranium)	7.2°C (45°F)	Cuttings rooted any time. Plant up in tubs, or borders. Seed of some types available. Will not stand frost. Trim to shape occasionally. Useful as a source of cuttings
Petrea volubilis (purple wreath) (lilac blue) arborea (violet)	7.2°C (45°F)	Cuttings 5cm (2in) long in spring/summer. Seed in spring Grow in borders of good soil only where there is sufficient room for development. Cut back weak branches in Feb

Plumbago (climbing leadwort)
 	
  capensis (blue)
  rosea (red)
	7.2°C (45°F)	Cuttings in spring or early summer.
		Can be grown either in tubs or borders. Prune back when desired in Feb, cutting back shoots by a third to a half once established (before this merely shorten slightly in Feb)

Rhodochiton atrosanguineum	7.2°C (45°F)	Can be treated as annual, raising from seed sown each spring. Pot up 15 — 18cm (6 or 7in) pot or border Uncomplicated plant to grow for the summer period
Sparmannia ofricana (African hemp)	4.4°C (40°F)	Cuttings in spring and summer with bottom heat. Cut back previous year's shoot to within 2.5 — 5cm (1 — 2in) of base
Stephanotis floribunda (Madagascar jasmine)	10°C (50°F) but cool airy conditions	Cuttings in spring. Pot up in large pots or plant in border. Cut out weak shoots and shorten main shoots in Feb. Discard plants if they get too straggly

Shrubs for the Greenhouse or Conservatory—*continued*

Name	Minimum winter temperature	Propagation and culture
Streptosolen jamesonii	7.2–10°C (45–50°F)	Cuttings in summer in bottom heat. Cut back plants in Feb after resting
Trachelospermum jasminoides (Chinese jasmine)	4.4°C (40°F)	Cuttings in propagating case in summer or layering any time. Pot up or plant in borders. Almost hardy but give heat in frost-free greenhouse in cooler areas. Prune back in winter and stake shrubs in summer

CHAPTER 24
Roses & Carnations

The rose as a flower crop

While commercial rose growing is on the decline in Britain it is becoming increasingly popular in amateur and exhibition circles, including floral art. Suitable varieties for forcing can be obtained from specialist rose firms. They tend now to be treated as a short-term crop, the bushes being forced to produce up to five flushes per year, and replaced after two or three years according to their performance.

The amateur gardener, however, may merely concern himself with a few bushes in 23–25cm (9–10in) pots to provide blooms in advance of those grown outside, and for a longer period into the autumn (the Royal National Rose Society has a recommended list).

Ideally roses thrive best in light airy conditions in a well-ventilated greenhouse with a minimum temperature of 10–12.8°C (50–55°F). The soil, of good texture and porosity, should have a pH of 6.5 (too far above this can lead to deficiency problems) and a phosphate/potash index of 3–4. Much use is now made of complete trace-element-containing fertilizers such as Vitax Q4 at 204g/m^2 (6oz per sq yd) in addition to farmyard manure at 50kg/8m^2 (1cwt per 6/10 sq yd). Good drainage is essential, which means thorough cultivation if borders are to be used, and the free use of crocks in pots.

Roses are grown commercially 'on the flat' in borders (4–5ft) wide, planting distances being 25–30cm (10–12in) each way. The situation regarding stocks for roses is a changing one and best taken up with specialist suppliers. The best time for planting is early spring or autumn. Planting should be firm, and the same is true with potting.

Growth should be commenced slowly in January/February with 7.2°C (45°F), rising gradually over 14–21 days to 12.8°C (55°F). Higher temperatures will obviously prevail during the summer months, but excessively high temperatures should be avoided by free use of ventilators. Regular watering, preferably by low level irrigation systems, or on a small scale by hose (with a fine rose) is essential, avoiding either saturation or excessive dryness.

Budded roses when planted should be pruned back to 10–13cm (4–5in) from ground level and main shoots pinched when they develop to encourage lower growth when approximately at the 5-fivers stage (5 leaflets). There should ideally be some selection and thinning of shoots and a degree of disbudding is necessary with hybrid teas.

Following each flush of growth a straight form of nitrogen should be given – Nitro-Chalk, Nitram or urea fromaldehyde, at normal application rates and watered in. Pest and disease control is particularly important, using sulphur if necessary for mildew on a continuous basis (see Chapter 31).

Potted roses can be rested by plunging in ashes out of doors in mid-autumn, being pruned and brought into the greenhouse in late winter/early spring for the production of early blooms. Liquid feeding should be given. Roses should be pruned lightly between flushes.

The culture of carnations

The carnation, like any other crop, reacts unfavourably to monocultural practices, diseases becoming established in border soils which are virtually impossible to eradicate. Border culture should only be considered, therefore, where the soil is 'new'; subsequently isolated beds of one form or another are necessary, and in amateur spheres this includes pot culture.

Raised beds can be constructed of precast concrete, sheet or corrugated plastic; ground or surface beds are best prepared on a concrete base with wood sides and ends; and for small-scale culture sunken beds can be consturcted cheaply by using polythene sides and base, providing outleats for surplus moisture by drainage tiles or slits in the base. Some form of sterilization will be necessary for all beds. Growbags can be used on a short term basis.

Carnations on a long-term basis require support, this being best provided by the use of strong metal supports at the ends of the bed, using wires, cross battens and coars string or alternatively neeting. For pot culture, support is provided by canes and string.

Growing media and nutrition

Carnations make large demands on nutrients and soils should be adjusted following soil analysis as follows:

pH   6.5 at planting time (lower for peat composts—see Chapter 13;
Nitrogen   High (50—150 ppm mg/litre nitrate), a difficult figure to adjust
Phosphorus and potash   Index 3—5
Magnesium   Index 4
Soluble salt   Index 2—3

Such nutrient levels are met by using John Innes No 2 potting compost or equivalent soilless mixes. When the existing soil is being used, and subsequent to adjustment of the pH following analysis, a normal base application is 33—136g/m² (1—4oz sq yd) super-phosphates 68—204g/m² (2—4oz sq yd) magnesium sulphate, and between 18—136g/m² (2—4oz sq yd) hoof and horn according to the time of year and soil analysis. The higher nitrogen dressing is given at times of the year when water requirement is low in winter or early spring and liquid feeding is therefore not practical. Compound base fertilizers can be used at rates of up to 271—305g/m² (8—9oz per sq yd) there being virtue in selecting one with a trace element content. Applications should be reduced if analysis merits it. Hydroponic systems have much application in carnation culture especially aggregate culture.

Propagation

The commercial practice in the UK and Europe generally is to buy in high-quality tested cuttings from specialist raisers. There are some excellent sources of supply open to the amateur grower, and arrangements can sometimes be made to obtain small quantities of cuttings from specialist nurserymen. Gardeners or growers anxious for detailed information on stock build-up are referred to the *Ministry of Agriculture Bulletin No 151* in which the subject is discussed in some detail. This bulletin also deals with the effective storage of cuttings at 0°C ± ½°C (32°F ± ½°F), a technique which assists the rooting process. Research has shown that cuttings taken from flowering plants seldom show the same vigour as cuttings taken from stock plants used solely for the purpose.

Dip cuttings in hormone rooting powder or soak overnight in a diluted solution (alpha napthalene acetic acid formulations give best results). Insert in porous rooting medium (pH 7 being desirable; see also Chapter 17) at a density of 60—84m² (50—70 per sq ft), which is fully 2.5cm (1in) apart each way. Give good light and bottom heat, either by soil warming cables, under-bench or mini-bore pipes, in the region of 21.2—22.2°C (70—72°F) for ten days after cutting insertion, when thereafter temperatures are reduced to 16.7—18.3°C (62—65°F) as a weaning measure. Rooting should take place in 18—21 days. Smaller scale propagation can readily be carried out in seed boxes with plastic domes, and mist benches, if available, are also helpful, especially from early spring to early autumn. No more watering should be carried out than is needed to prevent wilting, since too much watering encourages fungal diseases. There is no advantage in leaving the cuttings after rooting, as this merely results in a greater check when planted or potted.

Programme of production

Carnations can be planted at any time of the year and will start flowering according to the light intensity, heat level and other factors. The following are the advantages of planting in different months:
Mid-winter planting Cuttings rooted in

good light areas will, if left unstopped, produce the first flush of flowers by mid-/ late spring, and the first lateral flowers in early summer. Stopping the plants by nipping out the centre stem will delay flowering by 2–3 weeks.

Mid/late spring Cuttings planted in mid/ late spring and stopped once will flower in late summer/early autumn. A second stop will enable the plant to give greater continuity of flowers into late autumn.

Early summer Most gardeners will find that summer plantings suit them best, stopping the plants to take the first flowers in winter, after which there tends to be a shortage of flowers until about mid- to late summer the second year.

Autumn planting The worst time, as the young plants will have difficulty in developing in the diminishing light and may fall prey to fungal disorders if environmental control is not of a very high order. The first blooms will not appear until the following spring.

Growers and professional gardeners will obviously need to study planting times from an economic angle.

Plant spacing

Average planting distances are 20 × 20cm (8 × 8in) in a square planting system. Closer planting up to 13 × 10cm (5 × 4in) gives an earlier yield but generally increases disease potential. For pot growing, three plants per 23cm (9in) pot is average.

Water requirements

Plants are set out in relatively damp soil or media and should merely be watered in and thereafter watered according to their needs, which will vary enormously according to whether plants are in raised, sunken, or ground beds, or in pots. In commercial spheres water requirements are related to the readings taken from evaporimeters and determined in the UK by Ministry of Agriculture centres. These, and tensiometers, can be used on a small scale with some success.

Stopping and disbudding

Stopping refers to the removal of the terminal growth to encourage lateral bud development; it also delays flowering. The *single stop* is the removal of the first small pair of leaves, the plant being bent over until it snaps off cleanly. Raising the night temperature to 15.6°C (60°F) for 2–3 weeks after stopping, and more frequent damping, encourages lateral growth development. In general, from a single stop about five buds will be produced.

A *stop and a half* relates to a supplementary stopping of some of the subsequent laterals. Commercially this is done to delay flower production over a poor price period. It can also be done for flower show timing. Where no stopping is carried out the plant is allowed to form its terminal buds and flower early, a practice which may well suit the amateur. It is used as a means of avoiding glut periods. Spray blooms are now popular.

Disbudding of stems down to the one terminal bud (except sprays) is necessary weekly in summer and every two to three weeks in winter.

Seasonal feeding

Supplementary feeding is usually necessary soon after planting carnations, this either being applied dry and flushed into the soil or growing media, or applied in liquid form through an irrigation system or a rose on the end of a hosepipe. The dry feed generally used is 3 parts by weight of dried blood (or 2 parts sulphate of ammonia) and 1 part sulphate of potash applied at 68g/m^2 (2oz per sq yd) at 12–14 day intervals. Very considerable research has been carried out in the whole sphere of carnation nutrition at the H.R.I. (Horticultural Research International), Littlehampton in Sussex and elsewhere, and generally speaking equal parts of nitrogen and potash (K_2O) throughout give the best results. Reference back to Chapter 12 shows a range of nutrients in this category, it being important to avoid too high concentrations which can quickly result in salt build-up.

Gardeners using pots may also find it inadvisable to feed too lavishly and there is much to be said for erring on the side of safety, since feeding can always be increased but it is not so easy to remove excess nutrients to repair damage caused.

Temperatures

Accepted regimes now appear to be a night temperature of 10°C (50°F) raised to 12.2°C (54°F) from early spring to mid-autumn and a positive day temperature of 15.6°C (60°F) with ventilation coming into operation at not more than 21.1°C (70°F), although it is doubtful if such precision is possible or necessary in small greenhouses.

Lighting

Research findings indicate that periods of long days or continuous lighting hasten the inducement of flower buds. Lighting is applied from dusk to dawn using tungsten filament lamps, with 150 watt bulbs at (3.6–4.5m) (12–15ft) centres, 1.5m (5ft) higher than the growing point of the plant, for 14 days in summer up to 45 days in winter.

Young shoots remain vegetative until they have formed 5–7 pairs of expanding leaves, after which in forming another 5–6 pairs of leaves a flower bud develops. This means that from mid-spring onwards in the U.K. and countries of similar latitude, plants have 12–14 pairs of leaves to the flower bud, but if the shoot reaches 5–7 pairs of leaves when days are short (ie from early autumn onwards) it will grow up to 22 pairs of leaves before flowering in the spring. Dusk to dawn lighting wil induce all the plants in the 5–7 pairs of leaves category to produce flower buds despite the short days. The whole technique of lighting carnations is still the subject of considerable research, but the general implications are quite clear.

Carbon dioxide enrichment

This is still not a precise technique, but research workers claim that an improvement in the quality of cut flowers is achieved by two-or three-fold carbon dioxide enrichment, especially during the winter period.

Varieties

There is a countless number of varieties demanding constant reappraisal, but in re-

Foliage and flower crops for seed sowing (U.K. timetable)

Type	Seed sowing	Planting distance	Flowering period
Antirrhinum F₁ greenhouse hybrids	October	30 × 30cm (12 × 12in) in well-prepared soil of greenhouse border	March–May
Asparagus plumosus, correctly A. setaceus A. sprengeri correctly *A. densiflorus*	Sow March–April for outdoor planting the following spring. Soak seed for 48 hours	Can be planted out in greenhouse 30cm (12in) apart	For foliage
Gerbera	Sow seed in Feb/March. Prick off the small plants into Jiffy 7s	Plant out in well-prepared land 30 × 30cm (12 × 12in)	Continuous, more productive in winter
Matthiola incana	Sow mid-Oct-Dec. Prick out Jan–Feb in cool greenhouse	Plant 6 × 8in well-prepared bed, pH 6.5. Wider apart for 'Giant Excelsior' strain	April–May
Zinnia elegans and cultivars, double flowered	Sow dressed seed (captan) in March–April in individual small pots. Alternatively prick out 4–5 days after germination	25–30cm (10–12in) apart in well-prepared border preferably dressed with fungicide as a preventive measure against soil-borne diseases	Summer

cent years many new varieties have been developed and to keep up to date, consult specialist suppliers. Spray varieties and Pinks (grown as sprays) are now becoming popular as a greenhouse crop and are generally easier to manage and more productive.

Foliage and flower crops from seed under glass

A number of perennials and annuals are grown in greenhouses for cut flower production, decorative purposes and floral art. Culture is usually straightforward and involves sowing seed and pricking off as described under Bedding Plant Production (see Chapter 22).

Culture of many foliage and flowering plants from seed is becoming more popular in plastic structures or greenhouses, especially with flower arrangement enthusiasts, to provide material on a regular basis, free of weather damage. It is essential to provide free and full ventilation to avoid soft, floppy growth, coupled with regular pest and disease control.

Popular subjects are *Alstroemeria* from seed or division, annual chrysanthemums, *Clarkia*, dahlia from seed or tubers, *Dianthus* from seed, everlasting flowers and foliage such as *Acrolinium, Ammobium, Craspedia, Helichrysum, Rhodanthe, Statice, Xeranthemum* – all from seed sown in early spring – *Gerbera* from seed, *Gypsophila* from seed or root cuttings (perennial type), stocks, sweet peas, sweet William (all from seeds) and *Pyrethrum* (seeds or division). See also bulbs and ferns.

CHAPTER 25
Chrysanthemums

Terms used in chrysanthemum culture

Bud sport One shoot produces flowers of a different colour or shape from those on the rest of the plant. It is a vegetative mutation due to spontaneous genetic change and the sport can usually be perpetuated by cuttings taken from the shoot.

Break bud A chrysanthemum plant growing naturally develops a single stem in the first instance and then produces a flower bud at its tip at varying heights according to variety. This is called the break bud because leafy shoots break into growth immediately below to form a branched plant. While the break bud is usually imperfect, it is satisfactory in the case of late rooted cuttings grown on single stems and many large-flowered exhibition varieties.

Natural break The formation of the bud restricts the extension of the main shoot and further growth of shoots takes place when the buds in the axils of the leaves below the break bud develop. This process and the shoots that form are collectively called the natural break.

Crown buds These shoots, if left to grow, will in time produce a crown flower bud at their tips, below which further leafy shoots will be produced which will again in time form a second crown bud. First crown buds, if left, will produce flowers, or if removed by 'stopping' will allow the second crown buds to develop. First crown buds invariably give fuller flowers than second crown buds though very full flowering varieties are often better on second crowns.

Terminal buds When a shoot which arises from a leaf axil ends in a cluster of flower buds (not a bud with a cluster of leafy shoots) the central bud is known as the terminal bud.

Stopping The removal of the growing point to induce a shoot or a number of shoots to develop lower down on the plant than would be the case if it were left to grow naturally. Varieties differ in the forming of breaks, some producing natural breaks too freely. The number can be reduced by pinching out the top of the plant before the breaks appear. If on the other hand there are not sufficient breaks, it may be necessary to stop subsequent tips to the branches to form more.

Disbudding This is the careful removal of flower buds which form around the terminal bud, this bud being said to be 'taken'. If the buds are all allowed to form this is called a spray, whereas the single flower per stem is called a standard.

The main forms of chrysanthemum culture

1. *Earlies out of doors* Propagation in greenhouses or frames in the early part of the year for planting and flowering out of doors in borders (early flowering types).

2. *Protected flowering* Propagation in greenhouses or frames in the early part of the year for planting out of doors in borders to flower in autumn under the protection of sashes, mobile greenhouses or plastic structures.

3 *Pot culture* Propagation in greenhouses in the early part of the year for planting in pots which can be lifted indoors for flowering, or left outdoors in the case of earlies. Not to be confused with intensive culture of pot chrysanthemums which is dealt with in a separate section at the end of this chapter.

4 *Lifters* Propagation in greenhouses in the early part of the year for growing in borders out of doors, for lifting into greenhouses for flowering.

5 *Semi-direct planting* Late propagation in greenhouses, or purchase of late-struck cuttings, for growing in frames or protected areas (preferably in peat pots to avoid

checks). These are then lifted into greenhouse for continued vegetative growth and flowering.

6 *Direct planting* Planting direct in greenhouses or plastic structures to flower in natural season, this including (a) earlies under glass and (b) late-struck cuttings during mid and late summer. Cuttings can be self-propagated in the case of earlies but are more usually bought in for direct planting in mid or late summer.

7 *Spot cropping* The same as (6) but, by day length manipulation, grown for a specific period out of natural season.

8 *Year-round culture* This, using bought in cuttings, involves day length manipulation with artificial lighting or shortening by shading. Readers are reminded that cultural details on cropping plants are now available from specialist suppliers.

Types of chrysanthemum

Flower form

1 Incurved—where the majority of the petals turn inwards to form a ball-shaped flower

2 Incurving—the same, but flowers are of a looser habit

3 Reflexing—where petals turn outwards or have a dropping habit

4 Singles—which have a ring of petals; up to five rings for exhibition

5 Large exhibition chrysanthemums— which have enormous flowers of incurving, incurved or reflexing habit

6 Other types, including Spiders, Rayonnante, Anemone, in the early, mid- and late-flowering groups

7 Sprays—for cut flower production or in pots (frequently called American sprays)

Further groupings

For indoor culture, natural season, spot cropping or year-round culture, varieties are categorized as tall, medium or short. Still further grouping relates to temperature requirements during bud initiation periods, requiring reference to specialist catalogues. For direct planting and year-round culture chrysanthemums are categorized in response groups, according to the number of weeks from bud initiation to flowering under inside conditions.

The photoperiodic nature of chrysanthemums

Most chrystanthemums (apart from non-photoperiodic earlies and some 'mids' which successfully initiate their flower buds in long days) will only initiate their flower buds when the day length is less than about 12—14 hours. Equal day and night length occurs at equinox. It follows therefore that for natural season cropping it is necessary to plant sufficiently in advance of bud initiation to ensure sufficient vegetative development beforehand, a matter which will be referred to in more detail later. Because of this photoperiodicity, chrysanthemums react very positively to the artificial stimulus of shading to make artificially short days, or lengthening with low intensity light to give artificially long days. Response groups indicate when the chrysanthemum will flower from bud initiation, and cropping can be organized accordingly.

Lighting equipment

This involves the use of 100W tungsten clear filament lamps. For beds 1.2m (4ft) wide tungsten rubber sheathed or polychloroprene cables are suspended 1.2— 1.5m (4—5ft) above the centre of the bed. The 100W lamps are spaced 1.8m (6ft) apart (or 60W 1.2m/4ft apart) in special lampholders made of neoprene with waterproof connection to the cable. *The importance of this cannot be over-emphasized.* Very careful wiring is required; preferably the system should be professionally installed. It may be necessary to increase the amount of light in winter in very poor light areas.

The period of light necessary will be 2 hours in mid- to late spring, late summer and early autumn, 3—4 hours in mid- to late autumn, late winter and early spring, and 5 hours in early and mid-winter. It is usual (and also cheapest) to give light in the middle of the night to ensure that the dark periods do not exceed 7 hours. Cyclic lighting (3 minutes on, 9 minutes off) has been found effective, although it is not a technique which appears to have been widely developed. It is obvious that a time clock is an advantage for the operation of the lights. From early spring to early

Chrysanthemums: cultural programmes (relating to latitudes 50–58°N)

Definition of crop	Propagating time	Planting or potting in frames	Planting or spacing out of doors or in greenhouse	Stopping (may be once or twice)	Flowering time	Temperature
1 Outdoor crop – earlies	Feb – Mar	Mar – April	Late April – May	May – June	July – Sept	Prop at 15.6–18.3°C (60–65°F) and grow cool
2 Flowering with protection	Feb – Mar	Mar – April	Late April – mid-May	May – June	June – Oct or late	as above
3 Pot-grown for flowering out of doors with protection or lifting into greenhouse	Feb – Mar	April – May	Late April – mid-May	May – June	Aug – Oct or later	as above
*Pot-grown** large exhibition types	Dec – Jan	Feb – April	April – May	March – May	Oct – Jan	as above
4 Lifters	Feb – March	Feb – April	April – May	May – June	Sept – Nov or later	as above
5 Natural season (semi-direct)	Cuttings bought in or rooted	End June 15 × 15cm (6 × 6in) or 11–12cm (4½in) peat pots	Planted in greenhouse 22.5 × 22.5cm (9 × 9in) at end of August	3rd week July	Oct – Dec	Minimum of 12.8°C (55°F) (especially during bud initiation)
6 Natural season – direct planting, single stem	Plants normally purchased		10–15 Aug at 13 × 13cm (5 × 5in)	Not topped	December	13.3°C (56°F) for 6 weeks then 10°C (50°F)
as above, two stem	Plants normally purchased		Last week July, at 7 × 8in	10–14 days after planting	December	as above
as above, three stem	Plants normally purchased		2nd week July at 23 × 23cm (9 × 9in)	4th week July	December	as above
7 Direct planted – early flowering crop	December or purchased		Late Jan – Feb 25 × 30cm (10 × 12in)	Mid-end Feb reducing stem to 4 per plant when growing strongly	According to variety but around June	Minimum night temp 7.2°C (45°F)

8 Spot cropping** Date planted	Spacing	Lighting	Shading	Flowering	Temperature
6 January	13 × 13cm (5 × 5in)	6 Jan – 14 Feb	20 March – bud colour	Early May	15.6°C (60°F)
20 May	13 × 13cm (5 × 5in)	Nil	8 June – bud colour	Mid-December	as above
28 August	13 × 13cm 5 × 5in	28 Aug – 27 Sept	Nil	Mid – April	as above

* Although not normally practised, later planting can be carried out for two crops.
** These dates are merely approximate and can be varied considerably.

autumn shading with dense black poly-thene sheeting or other dense material is necessary to simulate short days, usually from 18.00 hours until 07.00 hours. This is achieved by putting the polythene over metal hoops or by block arrangement. Support both in beds out of doors and in greenhouse borders is by means of strained nylon netting.

Year-round cropping

This requires exact programming on a week-by-week basis by specialist cutting suppliers, following the necessary shading and lighting pattern and basically the same cultural, spot cropping or direct planting procedures. Difficulty can be experienced in poorer light areas if considering year-round cropping, especially during the dull-est months of the year.

IMPORTANT NOTE A technique which is finding favour is to root cuttings in 6−7cm (2½in) peat pots or small pots and take them to the 12 leaf stage under glass, giving supplementary lighting if necessary during poor light periods and 'short days' im-mediately on planting out in the green-house border. This technique obviously has application not only in year-round cropping and direct planting.

Cultural procedures

Where propagation material is being re-tained, it is important that this be selected carefully. Hot water treatment of the stock may be desirable for eelworm control be-fore the stools are boxed up with good clean compost, when cuttings will freely form with warmth and moisture. It is im-portant not to induce growth too early, particularly in the case of earlies which often produce better from a shorter period of growth. Initial growths from stools are in any case of poor habit and should be removed and discarded.

Rooting and planting of cuttings

Whether cuttings are prepared below a joint or node or merely snapped off is a matter for individual choice, although cut-tings below a node are more desirable for amateurs who will often have a lower level of heating with consequent slower rooting.

Cuttings are taken 5−7cm (2−2½in) long, trimming off the lower leaves and dipping the base of the cuttings in rooting hormone if this is thought necessary before inserting them 1.25−2cm (½−¾in) deep and 2.5−4cm (1−1½in) apart in seed trays or, on a smaller scale, in pots, in a mixture of equal parts peat and sand or for later propagation in John Innes No 1. Jiffy 7s may also be used with success. Cuttings are well watered-in and given bench heat to 12.8−18.3°C (55−65°F) level. Rooting will take place within 7−21 days. Various techniques are practised to induce quicker rooting: mist propagation, polythene bags over pots or boxes, plastic dome covers. Too high hu-midity can lead to damping off problems.

When rooted, as confirmed by a freshen-ing of the top growth, or visible evidence of root formation (in Jiffy 7s), cuttings can either be potted into 8cm (3in) clay, plastic or peat pots, using John Innes No 1 or a soilless equivalent or, where applicable, planted out 13 × 13cm (5 × 5in) apart in well-prepared soil in frames. Plants should be potted or planted firmly. Early flower-ing varieties which are rooted in mid- to late winter may have to be boxed up in boxes containing compost and kept in the greenhouse until the danger of frost is past and they can be put into frames. Alterna-tively, frames can be protected from frost by the installation of electrical tubular hea-ters (preferably controlled by a thermostat) which will maintain the air temperature above freezing point.

Stopping

Stopping is usually carried out when 15−23cm, (6−9in) growth has been made (up to 38cm/15in with some varieties) and the bottom buds are seen to be breaking naturally (ie anticipating the natural break). It is achieved by the removal of the whole top of the main stem, without removing the first fully developed leaf. With pro-grammed crops under glass it is unnecess-ary to be so exact, the tips of the main shoots being stopped in a routine manner 10−14 days after planting. Stopping should not coincide with planting or potting. Af-ter stopping it is usual to thin down the number of remaining shoots (generally

3–5) according to purpose and of course variety, although one or two extra shoots should be allowed to compensate for breakages.

Time of stopping can be critical, especially when showing is involved and it should be noted that varieties which produce the best flowers on second crown buds (having fewer petals or being ball shaped) will require a second stop, which means, in general terms, stopping varieties to be flowered on their first crown buds (and therefore stopped only once) 14–21 days *later* than those to be flowered on second crown buds, which will be stopped for a second time after an interval of 4–6 weeks, whether in borders or pots. The first stop will, in many cases, be while the plants are in frames or small pots.

Sometimes the break bud develops before the plant has produced sufficient laterals for flowering requirements, and to offset this the top two or three laterals should be stopped by carefully removing their terminal buds before they reach an appreciable size, allowing them to produce second crown flowers which will generally flower about the same time as lower placed laterals or first crown flowers.

Some large exhibition varieties may require stopping 14–20 days earlier than the appearance of the natural break warrants in order to ensure time for the development of a full flower. Conversely, varieties which produce over-full flowers are improved by stopping on the natural break and allowing free development of the upper laterals, removing the lower ones. There can be no general rules, and top exhibitors generally achieve results because they have learned by experience what to do and what not to do.

Outdoor planting

This will apply to earlies, lifters and to chrysanthemums being grown under protected cultivation. Ground must be well prepared with a pH of 6.5, phosphate and potash index 4 or slightly higher, magnesium index 2, and salt concentration index 4. A base feed of 136–204g/m² (4–6oz per sq yd) using one of balanced proportions is usually applied before planting out of doors, but some guidance from analysis is always useful. Planting distances are usually 30 × 30cm (12 × 12in) or 30–36cm (12 × 14in) in beds 1.2m (4ft) wide, although for lifters more space is generally given between the rows to allow easier lifting. Support will be necessary by canes or stout nets, although for lifters nets are obviously not suitable.

Pot-grown chrysanthemums

Plants in 7.5cm (3in) pots are moved to 13cm (5in) pots once the roots are well through the ball, this being ascertained by holding the pot upside down and allowing the root ball to drop into the hand. John Innes No 2 potting compost is invariably used, with plenty of roughage in the bottom of the pot, the plants being well firmed-up. Final potting into 20 or 23cm (8 or 9in) pots is carried out when once again the roots are well through the 13cm (5in) pots, this time using John Innes No 3 or special compost, roughage and a potting stick to ram the soil in firmly, as uneven potting affects water retention and nutrient release.

One of the main requirements of the growing of chrysanthemums in pots is to have a compost with a high fibrous content which assists the retention of moisture and provides improved feeding for the roots. Most exhibitors try to maintain a stack of loam for this purpose (see Chapter 15 for method).

After final potting, three strong canes 10–13cm (4–5in) apart are inserted around the edge of the pot and the plants initially supported by strong twine around the canes, later tying the number of shoots left individually to each cane. Pots are placed close-up against each other for a few days to give them some protection, then placed in a line 15cm (6in) apart, usually on gravel or ash paths not recently weedkiller-treated, especially if the usual weedkiller used is with sodium chlorate which can last up to 2 years in the surface of the soil. The paths must be absolutely level, a spirit level being used to check this if necessary. At least one cane per plant must be tied to a strong wire or fence.

Plants must be fed and watered regularly

Liquid feeds

Crop description	Stock solution g per litre (oz /gal)				Dilution of stock solution 1−400 = 2.5ml in 1litre (1fl oz in 2½ gallons 1−300 = 3ml in 1litre (1fl oz in 15 pints)
	Potassium nitrate g/litre	oz/gal	Ammonium nitrate g/litre	oz/gal[†]	
Direct planted − summer Pots − summer up to bud	156	(24)	136	(21)	★ High nitrogen ★★ 1 in 400
Direct planted − winter Pots − summer after budded	156	(24)	42	(6)	Medium nitrogen 1 in 400
Pots − winter	156	(24)	42	(6)	Medium nitrogen 1 in 300

† 1 oz/gallon = 6.5g/litre (approx)
★ or proprietary feeds at same nitrogen/potash ratios, or as recommended by suppliers
★★ Feed strength may be varied according to circumstances

and the pots given an occasional turn to prevent rooting into base, although it has now been established that a considerable amount of moisture is pulled up from the base.

(Chrysanthemums can of course be grown on the ring culture system in much the same way as tomatoes; see Chapter 18.)

Disbudding and lateral removing
Any generalization on disbudding procedure is impossible owing to the differing cultural methods involved. It is usual, however, where single stem or standards are being grown as opposed to sprays (year-round or spot cropping) to reduce to all but the central or terminal bud in the absence of individual preference to the contrary. With spray varieties being grown either direct or semi-direct it is usual to remove the terminal bud to give a better shape of spray, and in addition some stopping of the lower side shoots may be carried out. Lower laterals must also be removed.

Watering and feeding
Regular watering and feeding with liquid or solid fertilizer is essential on a regular basis for all chrysanthemums, whether growing out of doors or in pots. Trickle irrigation systems are extremely useful for the watering of large pots. Medium nitrogen liquid feeding should be practised unless growth is too hard, when high nitrogen is necessary, or too soft, when less nitrogen is necessary. The above table is a summary largely for greenhouse grown chrysanthemums, but it is broadly applicable also to conventional pot culture.

Lifting in
Plants in pots are better safely housed in early to mid-autumn before any frost occurs, this being particularly important with plants with good bud development. Before housing, the plants and pots should be laid carefully on their sides and given a thorough drenching with a suitable insecticide and a mildew specific. They should then be allowed to dry off before being taken into the greenhouse *pot* first to avoid damage to the breaks. Space about 56cm (18in) apart each way.

Keep the greenhouse fully ventilated for

a few weeks to let the plants sweat; heat is then given to the 7.2−10°C (45−50°F) level. Watering and feeding must be continued with, it being usual in the latter case to concentrate more on potash to limit growth and encourage better flower colour although there can be no hard and fast rules in this case. Mildew can quickly establish itself under conditions which are too humid, so also can botrytis which causes spotting on the blooms, particularly of white varieties. Pest control should also be given regular consideration.

Lifters

Before lifting in plants, greenhouse borders which have previously grown tomatoes are given a good forking and, while fertilizers are usually unnecessary, some ground limestone at 136−204g/m² (4−6oz per sq yd) is advisable to adjust the pH to the 6.5 level. Plants are lifted with a sharp spade, it frequently being advisable to cut around the root area a week or two beforehand. Whether plants can be lifted with a good root ball depends on soil type, this being difficult with light soils, especially if dry. Growing in plastic or wire baskets is sometimes practised to avoid disintegration of the root ball, while at the same time achieving a measure of root restriction. Plants being lifted must be handled very carefully otherwise side shoots can be broken off, particularly with brittle varieties, eg 'Loveliness'. Planting in the greenhouse is usually close; 15−23cm (6−9in) apart in rows 30−45cm (12−18in) apart, and thoroughly soaked-in. The greenhouse is kept cool by ventilation and, while some wilting is unavoidable, the plants usually recover fairly quickly and start growing again when heat is given to the 7.2−10°C (45−50°F) level, the same precautions being carried out against mildew and botrytis as described for pot-grown plants. Feeding is stopped when the buds are showing colour.

The canes invariably used as supports for lifters are of course lifted in along with the plants.

Direct planting techniques (for late-struck cuttings, early planting, spot cropping and year-round planting)

Direct planting is often thought to be a very complicated procedure, whereas in fact it can be a lot simpler and less demanding in care and attention than conventional culture. The only difficulty is in obtaining the necessary cuttings in the small quantities desired, as few specialist suppliers are willing to supply less than 50 of each variety.

It is possible to take and root cuttings at the normal period of the year in late winter or early spring and plant them out in greenhouse borders or frames at 23 × 23cm (9 × 9in). These, if stopped once or twice again, will serve as a source of late cuttings which if necessary can be rooted again and the same procedure followed.

Mid-season varieties

This involves planting from early summer until as per the programme already outlined, selecting the single, double or triple stem crops. Beds in the greenhouse approximately 1.2m (4ft) wide must be put in good physical condition by the liberal addition of peat and adjustment of the pH to 6.5, phosphate index 5, potash index 4, and magnesium index 3−4. This can usually be achieved by the application of a standard base dressing at 136g/m² (4oz per sq yd) or 2 parts hoof and horn, 2 parts superphosphates, and 1 part sulphate of potash and 1 part magnesium sulphate, leaving out the hoof and horn if liquid feeding is to be practised from the outset. Spacings are according to the table previously given. It is important not only to space the plants exactly, but grade out the cuttings so that the smaller ones are placed on the outside of the beds. They are planted firmly and evenly and watered in.

The same procedure is followed for spot or year-round culture.

Seasonal culture for direct planting

It is usual to keep plants more humid for a few days after planting to help them to re-establish temselves. Support by means of stretched 15cm (6in) mesh nylon netting is essential at an early stage of development, raised gradually on posts as the plants grow. Regular, even watering, coupled with temperature control to the level stated in the programme should be the aim, with the object of achieving 12.8–15.6°C (55–60°F), especially during early to mid-autumn when buds are being formed. Feeding programmes are similar to those discussed earlier.

The flowering period will be as outlined in the programme, either summer for early flowering or mid-autumn to early winter for autumn natural season cropping, with flowering at other times according to the programme followed. It cannot be emphasized too strongly that while the culture of natural season direct planters is relatively straightforward, specialist and year-round cropping requires tremendous precision, particularly where quality is important, and a highly specialized approach to cropping and strict planning is necessary.

Semi-direct
The timing for this is stated in chrysanthemum-growing programme 5. Nutrition from an early stage is important to encourage sufficient vegetative growth during the outdoor period, and liquid feeding from the outset may be necessary.

Where plants are put into peat pots, these should be 12–13cm (4¼in) and John Innes No 2 or its soilless equivalent used, the plants being placed in rows 15 × 15cm (6 × 6in) apart on a layer of peat and mulched well with peat in order to reduce watering needs. Alternatively the plants can be planted up 15 × 15cm (6 × 6in) apart in good soil with a pH of 6.5 and the standard stated for outdoor planting.

Growth must not be too soft otherwise breakage readily occurs through wind and when planting: wind protection in one form or another must be provided, and considerable care must be exercised when handling the plants. Very careful watering is necessary to avoid checks.

The plants should be lifted into a more comfortable environment before the third week of September at the latest, unless the weather is very mild or temporary cover can be laid on. It is not desirable that budding should coincide with lifting and planting, but when the plants are indoors too soon they tend to make insufficient vegetative growth and to flower on stems that are far too short.

Stopping is carried out as per the respective programmes, unless for single stem or standard crops which are grown on the break bud.

Pest and disease prevention measures and control should be given constant attention.

Sterilization of borders
Where spot or year-round cropping is practised then soil sterilization, usually by the sheet method (Chapter 14), is imperative. For natural season cropping following tomatoes, experience shows that where the soil is of an acceptable standard nutritionally (generally speaking, if it is acceptable for tomatoes it will be suitable for chrysanthemums) the soil sterilization carried out for the tomatoes will suffice for the following crop of chrysanthemums in that year. There can, however, be no generalization.

More recently raised beds or sunken polythene-lined beds filled with soilless media have been used successfully for chrysanthemum culture, also growbags on a limited scale.

Showing chrysanthemums
Most people who take the growing of chrysanthemums seriously will sooner or later gravitate towards exhibiting them, either at their local shows or at national level. Any properly run show in Britain will conduct its chrysanthemum business in accordance with the rules of the National Chrysanthemum Society and the Society's publications *Code of Rules for Judging Chrysanthemums* and *Exhibiting and Judging* should be read by all intending exhibitors.

Ash Base system for earlies
This method has become popular with exhibitors for the housing of rooted cuttings before planting out. It reduces the attention required and may also give better plants in the end. A frame is prepared with a base of 10–15cm (4–6in) of coarse ashes firmed well. On top of this ash base an 8cm (3in) layer of JI No 3 compost is laid, into which the rooted cuttings are planted about 13 × 13cm (5 × 5in) each way. The compost must not be too dry and an initial watering may be given to settle the plants in. Thereafter water is withheld for 10–14 days (a

light overhead spray being given if the plants wilt excessively) so that the plants send out roots in search of moisture and a good root system is built up. When they are well established and growing strongly, water may be applied liberally and the good drainage conditions ensure that no waterlogging occurs. The plants revel in the cool root conditions and growth is rapid. Supplementary liquid feeding may be given as the plants reach the end of their time in the frame, and normal spraying precautions against pests should be taken. In most cases the plants will be stopped in the frame. Air should be admitted progressively and, weather conditions permitting, the frame lights should be removed altogether in the later stages so that the plants are hardened off before planting out. The plants can be lifted with a small hand fork and if the system has been operated correctly it will be found that the massive root systems have used up practically all the compost in the frame.

B-Nine (and other dwarfing agents)
Some chrysanthemum cultivars have a natural habit of growth which makes them rather taller than is desirable, especially when they have to be housed in greenhouses. Other varieties tend to have a rather long unsightly neck below the bloom, a condition aggravated when grown under frames or covers which draw them up to the light. A chemical known as B-Nine, is of considerable assistance to the exhibiting chrysanthemum grower in alleviating these conditions. It works not by checking the growth of the plant, but by inducing lateral rather than longitudinal expansion of the cells. The result is a stockier, dwarfer plant, with stronger stems and shorter internodes. Normal dilution is 1:40 (1 tablespoon to 0.56 litre/1 pint water) and is applied as a fine spray from a plastic (not metal) sprayer on to the top 15cm (6in) of foliage to run-off point. Two or three applications may be given at any stage considered desirable but it is advisable to make the final application not later than 14 days before the bud is taken. In addition to restricting the height of certain cultivars it is also useful to control the height of plants at certain stages where they are tending to become drawn, eg in poor light conditions or in frames prior to planting out.

Pot chrysanthemums ('Pot mums')
The intensive culture of pot chrysanthemums is practised commercially on a large scale in Britain and Europe generally. It must not be confused with the culture of conventional chrysanthemums in pots since the varieties grown for year-round pot work have been specially bred for this purpose. The categories 'tall', 'medium' and 'short' are further divided into response groups of 9, 10 and 11 weeks, this referring to the time from bud initiation to flowering under a minimum temperature of 15.6°C (60°F). Under the less precise conditions which frequently exist in small-er greenhouses, temperatures frequently fall below this level, resulting in delays to flowering. Conversely, should the weather be abnormally mild in the autumn or spring, flowering may be advanced. In order to maintain production on a year-round basis, day length manipulation by shading and lighting is necessary. The poor winter light in many northerly areas makes successful winter culture difficult and results in plants of etiolated growth and in flowers of low petal number. In general, few professional or amateur gardeners are much concerned with year-round culture, tending to confine their activities to natural season flowering.

Controlled flowering
Short-day varieties of pot chrysanthemums initiate their flower buds in day lengths of 12 hours, which means that *short-day varieties will not require artificial short days by shading between 21 September and 21 March*. Conversely, long days allow vegetative development before the short day period, and this is provided by lighting when the natural day length is less than 12 hours.

As with cut flower chrysanthemums, it is important to remember that for each week the plant is exposed to long days, a week must be added to the time taken to produce the plant in flower, eg an 11 week response plant given 2 weeks of 'long' days will not flower for 11 + 2 = 13 weeks.

The selection of varieties for pot culture is particularly important, as techniques require modification accordingly.

Tall varieties These grow too tall for pots if allowed to develop naturally and require treatment with dwarfing chemicals. As stem length is unduly increased by long day treatment, they are therefore given short day treatment immediately after potting.

Medium varieties Normally speaking, one week of long day treatment is given to these varieties after potting, although in good conditions this week of long days is generally unnecessary in spring and autumn.

Short varieties Three weeks of long days in winter, two weeks in autumn and spring and one week in summer is the normal treatment, with the exception of vigorous varieties which do not need any long day treatment in summer and can be given short days immediately after potting. When these varieties are grown at a time of year when day length is longer than 12 hours they are usually allowed to grow naturally for one or two weeks before being given short days but, on the other hand, if the day length is less than 12 hours artificial light can be used to give artificial long days.

Cultural details

Cuttings from specialist raisers are again desirable, having a special advantage in their uniformity of size for pot work. Amateur gardeners will once again find it difficult to obtain small quantities of cuttings and will need to contact a commercial grower or an amateur chrysanthemum specialist. On a limited scale, plants can be kept as a source of cuttings provided they are kept vegetative by long days.

Pot size and compost

Pot chrysanthemums are commercially grown five or six rooted cuttings to a 14cm (5½in) deep pan. Alternatively three cuttings can be put in an 11–12cm (4½in) deep pan, and one cutting in a 8–10cm (3½in) pot. Plastic pans or pots are invariably used.

Either a compost of JIP2 standard or a soilless equivalent can be used. Standard composts often give rise to trouble as their nitrogen level may be too high for the poor light conditions in northerly latitiudes during the autumn and winter months, giving rise to lanky, unproductive growth. Many growers and gardeners could achieve much greater success by selecting a compost of lower nutrient level and liquid feeding from the outset, modifying the feed according to the growth exhibited. In general terms, higher nitrogen feeds are given in the summer than in the winter, irrespective of region, reducing the nitrogen level in winter commensurate with light levels.

Planting

Pots are loosely filled to within 0.6–1.2cm (¼–½in) of the rim and firmed by dumping on a hard surface. Plants are then set into dibber holes at equal depth and equal spacing around the edge of the pots, with the base of the plant just below the surface of the compost. Cuttings with larger roots may require larger planting holes to allow entry of the root without damage. Cuttings should be watered in and the pots kept close together for a week or two, spacing the pots at 30 × 30cm (12 × 12in) thereafter to allow sufficient room for uninhibited growth.

Pinching

The soft tip of the growing plant is generally removed two weeks after planting, except pinching (7–10 days) is advisable to encourage a lower break. Single stem plants of certain varieties can be grown, being later disbudded so that only the terminal bud remains on each stem, extra plants being required in the centre of each pot in this case.

Disbudding

While many varieties will make good plants with no disbudding, there are exceptions. Plants grown single in 8–10cm (3½in) pots are not disbudded at all, it obviously being an advantage to have as large a number of flowers as possible. It is essential to take specialist advice on this matter.

Dwarfing treatments

Phosfon is a dwarfing agent which is mixed in powder form with the compost for all tall varieties, generally speaking about 21–42g ($\frac{3}{4}$–1$\frac{1}{2}$oz) per bushel according to variety, although makers' recommendations must be closely followed in respect of quantities for different varieties. Delays to flowering have been induced following the use of Phosphon. B-Nine, a liquid form of growth retardant, can be sprayed on the plants 2–4 weeks after pinching when the resultant break shoots are 1.25cm ($\frac{1}{2}$in) or so in length and it is used at the rate of 50ml/litre (8fl oz) per gallon of water, the same distribution rate for all varieties. B-Nine may not be sufficiently dwarfing for some very tall varieties.

Natural season culture

Many gardeners will be interested mainly in natural season culture, in which case either medium or short varieties are potted in the first week of September to allow two weeks or so of long days before 21 September when bud initiation is naturally induced. Assuming bud initiation in late September/early October, varieties will flower during early winter, although much will depend on temperature and other factors such as the application of Phosfon, etc.

For pests, diseases and physiological disorders see Chapter 31.

If you are really keen to learn more about chrysanthemum growing, and meet others of similar enthusiasm, it is a good idea to join the National Chrysanthemum Society.

CHAPTER 26
Greenhouse Bulbs*

Anemones

Although mainly grown as an outdoor crop, anemones lend themselves to protected cropping in cool greenhouses, frames or polythene structures. Single anemones of the De Caen type are usually in demand, and many excellent colour selections have been made available, eg Hollandia (scarlet, very large flowers), His Excellency (scarlet), Sylphide (magenta), Mr Fokker (blue violet), The Bride (white). Bulbs of the double St. Brigid type are available but produce fewer flowers than the singles, especially in winter, and the best varieties are: The Governor (scarlet), Lord Lieutenant (blue), The Admiral (magenta). French doubles are also available, although they are rarely grown for the production of cut flowers.

Anemone corms (tuberous rhizomes) are bought either as pointed pittens or the flatter buttons and are available in various sizes from 1–2cm up to 5–6cm. The 2–3cm size is usually grown commercially, flowering on average 12–13 weeks after planting. Larger sized corms may flower earlier but tend to fade out soon, and conversely smaller corms take longer to flower.

Anemones may also be propagated from seed; new hybrid seed is now available.

Cultural details

Anemone corms must have frost protection. They will thrive in most well cultivated soils with a fairly high lime content. (pH 6.5–7). The phosphate and potash index should be 2–3, and the soil conditioned with farmyard manure at 50kg per 7m² (1cwt per 6–8 sq yd).

Plant 10cm (4in) apart in rows 30–38cm (12–15in) apart, and cover with 5–7.5cm (2–3in) of soil. If corms are planted in mid-summer under glass or plastic, flowering will begin towards the beginning of

mid-autumn, be at its peak in early winter and may well continue into early spring according to region. Planting mid–late summer will give later flowering.

The soil should ideally be in a moist condition early in the development of growth. Reduce watering very considerably during the winter or it will certainly encourage disease. There is no need for high temperatures which will in fact merely spoil the flowers by 'blowing' them.

Freesias

The freesia belongs to the Iris family and is a native of South Africa. The main species is *F. refracta* 'Alba' (white), and in recent years this, together with *F. armstrongii* (red), *F. aurea* and *F. leitchlinii*, has been used for considerable hybridization to produce better coloured and more prolific strains, especially the tetraploid and triploid strains (the usual freesia being a diploid).

The culture of freesias from seed

Sow mid-spring to early summer for flowering early autumn to spring. Freesia seed can be erratic to germinate and a variety of methods are used for 'chitting': soak for 2–4 days in water at 21.1°C (70°F); mixing with damp peat or vermiculite for a similar period at the same temperature, until the seed shows signs of growth; or in the case of slow germinating tetraploid seed, rubbing it between sandpaper before soaking for 24 hours. Darkness is necessary for germination in all cases, the seed being planted 1.25cm ($\frac{1}{2}$in) deep as soon as germination occurs. Later sowings can be made 0.3–0.6cm ($\frac{1}{8}$–$\frac{1}{4}$in) deep, directly into containers out of doors, covering with 1.25–2.5cm ($\frac{1}{2}$–1in) layer of peat; 23cm (9in) whalehide pots, 2.5 × 2.5m (1 × 1in) spacing, and JIP1 are suitable.

After germination plants will require 12.8–15.6°C (55–60°F) but cool moist

(* excluding those already dealt with in plant lists)

growing conditions after the seeds have developed are essential to keep growth sturdy. Containers should be placed on a sheet of polythene or hard slabbing and may be stacked fairly closely together as convenient. Some shelter from wind should be provided. Regular watering should be the rule, plus balanced liquid feeding every 10–14 days to keep growth vigorous, without producing excess soft foliage which flops about. Excessive watering should be avoided, not only to offset fungal disorders, but to avoid leaching out nutrients.

The crop should be brought into the greenhouse in early autumn. The night temperature should not exceed 12.8°C (55°F) in early/mid-autumn and early/mid-spring; drop to 10°C (50°F) from late autumn to late winter. Excessive temperatures will result in unproductive growth. Support will be necessary either by netting or twigs.

Production from corms
Basically similar to production from seed, but spacing up to 7.5 × 7.5cm (3 × 3in) and planting to 5cm (2in) depth in JIP1. Normally corms are planted in spring to flower in the autumn, but see *Ministry of Agriculture Bulletin No 197* for details of storing for year-round production.

After flowering, growth should be encouraged for two months to allow development of the corms, which should then be lifted, dried and stored for two weeks at a temperature of 21.1°C (70°F), though flowering is improved if they can be stored at 30°C (86°F) for ten weeks in an electrically controlled heat treatment chamber. The corms from seed-raised plants can of course also be stored.

Hyacinths
Bulbs are imported from the Netherlands where their culture is a specialized task, especially when required for forcing. It is of interest to note that the two main methods of hyacinth propagation are cross-cutting and scooping. Cross-cutting involves three cuts over the base of the bulb deep enough to inactivate the main bud, bearing in mind that the hyacinth bulb, in common with all true bulbs, is a flower in embryo surrounded by leaves. Scooping is carried out with a special knife, the object once again being to destroy the main bud, yet cut the base of the scale leaves. After either process, the bulbs are placed in a room where the environment can be controlled to fine limit in respect of both temperature and humidity until young bulbs are formed in the cut section at the base of the bulb. Parent bulbs, complete with these young bulbs, are planted in the autumn, generally in late autumn, when they will eventually develop to the selected size after a process of lifting and replanting.

Bulb preparation
Hyacinth bulbs bought for early flowering have been 'prepared', this being a physiological process which affects the development of the flower bud. Bulbs intended for early flowering are lifted in early summer and stored at 30°C (86°F), gradually reduced to 25.6°C (78°F) during a period of 4–5 weeks, and thereafter to between 22.8–20°C (73–68°F) according to variety until the flower is completely developed inside the bulb when the temperature is lowered to 17.2°C (63°F). This treatment varies according to the intended time of flowering. Occasionally there are bad batches of bulbs which fail to flower well.

Bulbs are purchased according to size, from 18–19cm down to 14–15cm, and the price is usually commensurate with size, although in many cases smaller bulbs will flower better than large ones simply because the large flower of top sized bulbs is difficult to support and tricky to handle.

When bulbs come from the supplier they should be unpacked immediately and kept at between 12.8–15.6°C (55–60°F) or preferably cooler, as this will accelerate growth by assisting with the rooting process.

Planting
Hyacinths require little in the way of nutrition, as all the strength necessary is already contained in the flowers and scale leaves. Physical condition of the planting medium is, however, important. Sand and peat or peat alone are the usual choices, it being important in both cases to ensure that sufficient lime is added to bring the pH up to

above 6. When bowls without drainage are used, peat and lime (shell) plus some charcoal (bulb fibre) is frequently used, a medium which tends to keep sweeter than soil-containing media. Whatever the chosen medium, it should be reasonably moist and should not have been used for bulbs before.

All containers, whether boxes, pots or bowls, should be at least 10–12cm (4–5in) deep. Place the bulbs in with the nose showing when they are to be grown to the flowering stage on benches or pots; leave them half-covered for easier lifting if they are to be potted up in bowls after forcing. Spacing of the bulbs will vary according to whether they are being grown to maturity in pots or boxes or for forcing. Space out if growing to maturity, while for forcing they can be packed fairly tight. They should be firmed in moderately. Some gardeners prefer to plant hyacinths in a double layer so that they will have a solid mass of flowers.

Note that for Christmas flowering, bulbs are planted in September; for January flowering in October; up to November for February flowering. When unprepared bulbs are grown for still later flowering planting in October is normal.

Root development
The prime requisites for bulbs after planting are coolness and moisture, during which period they develop sufficient roots to sustain them for flowering. The commercial grower frequently lays out his boxes on a flat surface out of doors and covers them with a thick 5–30cm (10–12in) layer of straw which is kept moist, the bulbs being kept cool by the principle of loss of heat on evaporation. On a small scale a good layer of peat, sand or even well-weathered ashes will suffice. Dark cupboards, sheds or cellars may also be used, it being remembered that a cool moist atmosphere of 9–10°C (48–50°F) is the ideal. Occasional watering may be necessary to achieve this.

Forcing
Bulbs are brought into warmer temperatures when the shoots are about 3.75–5cm (1½–2in) long with the flower bud well through the neck of the bulb. Long shoots result in weak flowers. For the first 10–12 days semi-darkness is desirable, which in a greenhouse will necessitate shading with paper or other material. Shading will induce the flower bud to extend without extensive leaf development. Temperatures of 18.3°C (65°F) initially, raised to 22.8°C (73°F) are ideal; on a small scale much can be done in a heated propagating case to save costs. Excess bottom heat should be avoided and, when benches have heating pipes underneath, a thick layer of peat should be put on the bench to prevent rapid drying out. Bulbs are kept well watered and not exposed to excessive sunlight, but care must be taken not to pour too much water on to the neck of the bulb as this will encourage the development of botrytis. Light spraying helps to keep a humid atmosphere and reduces watering needs. Temperatures should be lowered gradually as flowers begin to open.

For 'natural' growing the bulbs are taken out of the 'plunge' or dark area and merely given normal greenhouse temperatures, or taken into the home. The same philosophy of shade for a period should, however, be adopted for best results.

Commercially bulbs are lifted when in flower and planted up in decorative bowls.

Forcing in daylight-excluded structures
When bulbs are forced in light-excluded structures they are given temperatures of 23.9°C (75°F) until the flowers begin to open, dropping to 21.1°C (70°F) until colour is showing and finally to 18.3°C (65°F) to complete the process. The level of lighting necessary is 100W/m²/sq yd operated for 12 hours in each 24.

Iris
In the last few years the growing of irises under glass has become a major greenhouse crop, particularly as with preparation they can be induced to flower for a major part of the year. Of the numerous species, the main varieties for greenhouse growing have been selected from the Xiphium and Xiphiodes groups which are natives of the Mediterranean zone.

The embryo bud contained in the iris bulb is incompletely developed when the bulbs are lifted, and the development of the bud continues under cool storage at 8.9°C (48°F) or planted in cool soil.

Bulbs for forcing should usually be from 10cm upwards, uniform in size and should not have produced flowers the previous season. Out of season flowering of suitable varieties can be achieved by a combination of heating and cooling, this procedure being generally carried out by the supplier.

Main timings

'Wedgwood' varieties and sports Planting: mid autumn to late winter. Flowering: mid winter to spring (treated bulbs flower earlier) All other varieties   Planting: late autumn – mid-winter. Flowering: mid-winter to early/mid-spring
Retarded bulbs   Plant outdoors in beds or greenhouse borders early spring – late summer. Flowering: mid-summer to mid-autumn or later under cover

Iris danfordiae (yellow) and I. reticulata (blue) are grown in pots, planting early in the year to flower in spring, 3–4 bulbs per 15cm (6in) pot.

Cultural procedures

Irises can be grown either in boxes, pots or borders, in all cases with sufficient depth of soil 10–12.5cm (4–5in) to accommodate the root system. Any good garden soil with good texture and a pH of 6, and reasonably well supplied with nutrients, will suffice. The addition of peat is frequently necessary to improve soil texture. For forcing, plant very shallowly about 7.5cm (3in) apart; for slower growing plant deeper 5–7.5cm (2–3in). For planting between late spring and late summer mulch the ground with damp peat to keep soil temperatures cool.

It is usually recommended that for 'Wedgwood' and its sports 13.3–15°C (56–59°F) should be given for the first two weeks, maintaining or slightly raising the temperature at night to 17.8°C (64°F) to advance flowering. For other varieties give 11.1–12.2°C (52–54°F) for first two weeks, up to 13.3°C (56°F) for smaller bulbs (7–8 and 8–9cm). Coolness and ventilation is the general rule to avoid gross production of foliage and possible 'blindness' (when

the flowers do not form). Support may be needed with nets or canes.

Lily of the valley *(Convallaria majalis)*

These are produced from imported 'pips', generally from Germany. Of the three grades available, only three-year or two-year top grade pips should be used. For very early flowering it is necessary to retard the pips from 10–12 weeks at −4°C to −2°C (28–25°F) treating them as bulbs, thawing them out in a warm bowl of water at 26.7°C (80°F) for 12–15 hours. The retarding will generally have been carried out before purchase.

Forcing procedure

The pips should have their roots trimmed down to 8cm (3in) before planting in 13cm (5in) deep boxes or in a bed of similar depth, using a mixture of peat and sand. They are spaced 2.5–5cm (1–2in) apart, being covered finally by a layer of damp peat. Complete darkness is necessary for the initial forcing process for 10–12 days, which will necessitate the use of a shaded greenhouse bench (using black polythene covers) or a shed. Bottom heat to the 21.1°C (70°F) level is necessary, and this can readily be provided by soil warming cables, with an air temperature of 15.6°C (60°F) for the first three days, 21.1°C (70°F) for the following three days and 26.7°C (80°F) for the remainder of the forcing period. The pips are thoroughly watered-in on planting and watered again in 10–12 days. When shoots appear in 10–12 days the shading is removed. When they are 30cm (12in) long artificial light is given, to provide 16 hours of light and 8 hours of complete darkness until the flowers are ready for cutting. The lighting can be achieved by 100W tungsten filament lamps at 1 per m²/sq yd, 60cm (2ft) above the beds. Too strong a light or light given too soon will restrict stem height. Temperatures are reduced when cutting commences.

Muscari

Muscari armeniacum or grape hyacinths are useful flowers for greenhouse culture, both in bowls and for cut bloom. Specially prepared bulbs for early flowering can be obtained, although in gardening circles the late flowering of unprepared bulbs is usually more acceptable.

For forcing the bulbs are planted in 7.5– 10cm (3–4in) deep boxes in early to mid-autumn, plunged out of doors for a period, and then brought into the greenhouse to flower. More usually, however, they are planted 2.5cm (1in) apart in pots or boxes and kept cool 4.4–7.2°C (40–45°F) for eight weeks or longer, when they are brought into flower in a moderately warm greenhouse.

Narcissus

For early flowering, pre-cooled bulbs (double nosed I, II and III are generally used for forcing) are purchased, these having been given four days of heat at 33°C (93°F), followed by 17.2°C (63°F) for one or two weeks, then cool stored at 7.2°C (45°F) until planting. Bulbs for later flowering are given 17.2°C (63°F) till the flower is complete in the bulb, then stored at 8.9°C (48°F). Variations in temperature treatment are also used to influence flower size.

Planting in borders
Bulbs can be grown either directly in borders, or planted in boxes, bowls or pots. Any good soil with a pH of about 6 and a reasonable nutrient content will suffice. Planting direct into greenhouse borders is done in mid-autumn, in rows 15cm (6in) apart, the bulbs spaced 5–7.5cm (2–3in) apart in the rows. Water in well and cover with straw. Keep as cool as possible by ventilating for 6–7 weeks, then raise temperatures in steps of 2.6–5.5°C (5–10°F) to around 18.3°C (65°F). Keep bulbs well watered, about 75litre/m² (15 gallons per sq yd) being necessary.

Planting in boxes
Push the bulbs into deep 12.5–15cm (5– 6in) boxes of clean soil which has not grown bulbs before, pH adjusted to 6.25, leaving the bulbs with their noses clear. Cover with a layer of sand or other material to act as a barrier between the soil or peat which will be used to cover them in a plunge out of doors to minimum depth of 15cm (6in). This is generally achieved in the first week of mid-autumn and adequate watering

should be given to induce lower temperatures (by evaporation) down to about 7.2°C (45°F).

Boxes are brought into the greenhouse from the late autumn until late winter according to variety, when flowers are clear of the neck of the bulb and there is good root development, and not before (suppliers' catalogues should always be consulted for housing dates). Minimum heat is given for 7–10 days, the temperature gradually being raised to 18.3°C (65°F). Water the boxes as necessary and make sure that they get all the light they need, otherwise the leaves will become gross. Support may be provided with netting or broken canes and string.

Bowls or pots of bulbs should be treated in the same way, strict attention being paid to watering and the amount of light given. Bulbs for later flowering should be left longer in the plunge and given lower temperatures in the greenhouse or home.

Forcing under artificial light
This is carried out in the same way as described for tulips (below) although in general it is better to have higher light levels and lower temperatures 15.6°C (60°F), taking 4–6 weeks on average for the bulbs to flower.
Pests, diseases and *troubles* Narcissi are not difficult to grow, but they can suffer from a number of troubles (see Chapter 31).

Ranunculus

There are three main groups: French, Persian and Turban, and Turkey or paeony-flowering, of which the last mentioned are increasingly grown as outdoor crops in mild districts. They also lend themselves to protected cropping, as this ensures better flower quality.

Planting times can vary from early and mid-summer for autumn flowering with cloche or mobile greenhouse protection, until early autumn for late winter to late spring flowering in the greenhouse. Ranunculus can also be planted in well prepared soil in early/mid-spring with the cover of a mobile greenhouse, to flower out of doors in the summer. The roots are planted with their claws downwards, 15cm (6in) apart and 2.5–5cm (1–2in) deep, and after flowering the tuberous roots are lifted and dried for furture planting. They can also be grown in deep boxes or pots, but care must be taken that they do not dry out.

Schizostylis (Kaffir lily)

Schizostylis coccinea, a native of South Africa, and its two main varieties, 'Miss Hegarty' (early) and 'Viscountess Byng' (late), are tender bulbs grown on a limited scale in the greenhouse. They are propagated by division in spring when 3–4 shooted clumps should be put in 22.5–25cm (9–10in) pots with JIP1 or 2. Given plenty of water they will flower in the winter months.

Sparaxis

These South African plants, *S. grandiflora* and *S. tricola*, are planted in late autumn in greenhouse borders, 10cm (4in) apart and 10cm (4in) deep, in good soil, where they will flower in the spring.

Tulips

A wide range of tulips is grown both for bowl culture and for cut flower production in boxes or greenhouse borders. The flowering times of a tulip and the ability to force it to flower early depends on a range of temperature treatments best left to the suppliers, as wrong treatment will result in the production of deformed flowers. In recent years specially prepared bulbs called 5° tulips have been used to a large extent for cut flower production in greenhouses.

5° tulips

Initially for two weeks the soil or growing medium must be kept cool, in the region of 10–12.8°C (50–55°F). 5° bulbs of a 12cm size are generally planted direct into greenhouse borders with a pH of 6.5 to 7 during the first week of late autumn in rows 15cm (6in) apart, the bulbs being 5cm (2in) apart, with the top of the bulb 1cm ($\frac{3}{8}$in) below soil level. It is usual to grow in beds for easier management. After planting, the beds are thoroughly watered, not only to settle the soil but also to reduce temperature, but water-logging should be avoided. Heat is given after 2 weeks, up to 17.8°C

(64°F) air temperature, and at this temperature flowering occurs. For later flowering a lower soil temperature, 10.6–11.1°C (51–52°F), is necessary for two weeks, then raise air temperature to about 15°C (50°F), a procedure which will keep flower quality high. Ventilation should, however, be given to avoid excess humidity and possible spread of botrytis.

Pre-cooled tulips

These are usually grown in boxes, the bulbs being planted in early October according to their size (generally 11–12cm or larger) from 6 × 11 (66) up to 13 × 7 (91). Boxes should be 7.5–10cm (3–4in) deep, clean and provided with adequate drainage. Soil should be of good texture with a pH of 6.5–7 and should not have been used for bulbs beforehand. Fill to within 2.5cm (1in) of the top and press the bulbs into the surface, adding more soil to leave the nose of the bulbs exposed. A layer of sand or ash is then put on top of the boxes to form a barrier between bulbs and plunge soil.

Boxes are then stacked in rows out of doors and covered with a layer of 15cm (6in) sand or peat, and straw on top of this. The watering of the straw subsequently induces the cool conditions necessary by evaporation. Fungal dusts (quintozene) are useful *before* the bulbs are covered by the soil.

After being in the plunge for a minimum period of 6 weeks, bulbs are brought into the greenhouse when the flower bud is clear of the neck of the bulb (as can be determined by examination) and there is good root growth, the temperature then being raised gradually to 21.1°C (70°F). They should be given shading by newspapers or other means to draw the flower up, or alternatively by putting them under benches. Temperatures are dropped as buds show colour.

Bulbs can be brought into the greenhouse in succession to flower over a period, flowering commencing in early winter. It is important, however to pay attention to the programming provided by the supplier. Uncooled bulbs are given the same general treatment for flowering from mid-winter to early spring.

Celosia is one of the simplest and most attractive greenhouse plants to grow provided it is not over-watered as this will cause the stems to rot. This is 'Century' mixed.

What could be called a traditional plant, the cineraria is now coming back into popularity as a greenhouse plant.

Always interesting with their multi-coloured leaves, coleus are not difficult to grow from seed or from cuttings. Pictured here is 'Wizard' mixed.

Very much in vogue these days are cyclamens, produced from seed.

(*Far left*) Geraniums from seed are now simple to grow with the introduction of F17 hybrids. They can be grown either as pot plants or for mass display out of doors. The variety here is 'Hollywood Star'.

(*Near left*) A mixed batch of *Primula malocoides* make a delightful display in the cool greenhouse. Compost for growing them must not contain too much lime, or leaf chlorosis will result.

Geraniums or pelargoniums grow well under relatively cool conditions on an open slatted bench. To give of their best they require regular feeding and very careful watering.

Almost certain to give a prolonged period of flowering in a cool greenhouse or conservatory is *Primula obconica*. Like its sister *malocoides*, it does not like a limey compost. Its leaves can cause a rash on sensitive gardeners.

Streptocarpus is one of the most delightful flowering plants available for greenhouse or conservatory.

A delightful display of pot plants including streptocarpus, begonias and geraniums in a light, airy greenhouse.

Chrysanthemums tend to be grown more and more only by specialist gardeners yet are relatively simple to grow. Here the variety 'Rynoon' is grown to perfection.

(*Near right*) It is not appreciated how successful gladioli can be under cool protection when they flower earlier and often more prolifically than they do out of doors. They usually require some support with canes or netting.

(*Far right*) Many cacti have highly unusual flowers such as this *Mammillaria*. Cacti in general require gritty, well-drained compost and relatively dry conditions if they are to give of their best.

Ferns require full, shady, moist growing conditions if they are to give of their best. Greenhouses used expressly for their culture should be located in a shady situation.

(*Far right, opposite*) Living surrounded by foliage plants is much in vogue these days. Here is a typical selection of plants including *Fittonia argyroneura*, *Ficus benjamina*, dizygotheca, peperomias, *Rhoeo discolor minima* and *Pseuderanthemem reticulatum*.

Gardeners tend to shun orchids as a highly specialist plant, yet many such as this *Cattleya* are relatively easy to grow.

An Alpine house can open up new horizons for the gardener who dislikes spending a lot of money on heating. This is the Alpine house at RHS Wisley Gardens in Surrey.

Pot culture

Bulbs being grown for pot display are generally of dwarfer varieties of early singles and doubles. They are planted up closely and fairly firmly in pots or bowls of various sizes, either in bulb fibre or clean soil in mid-autumn with the nose of the bulb exposed. The bulbs may be plunged into a deep layer of soil or peat and put into a dark cupboard and after the necesary 6 week period brought into the greenhouse or a warm room where once again *shade is essential* to begin with. At all times where bulbs are being grown in boxes or pots, adequate water supplies should be maintained, but never to the extent of spotting the blooms by careless over-application. Gardeners frequently find that gross foliage and weak flowers result, this being due in the first case to an insufficiently cool rooting period, and latterly to excess temperatures applied too quickly.

There are many variations of tulip culture, including the use of mobile greenhouses, when the bulbs planted out of doors can be brought forward to flower earlier than the outdoor crop by covering in early spring.

Forcing under artificial light

A very successful technique is the use of artificial light at 100W per sq yd and 30–36cm (12–14in) above the top of the bulbs for 12 hours in each 24 at 18.3°C (65°F) to start with, dropping to 15.6°C (60°F) when buds show colour.

Varieties

A classified list of names of all varieties of tulips in cultivation, is available from the Royal General Dutch Bulbgrowers Society and from the Royal Horticultural Society, Vincent Square, London.

Catalogues provided by specialist bulb suppliers list all bulbs available for flowering at various times and for different purposes.

For pests, diseases and physiological disorders see Chapter 31.

Other bulbs

There are several other bulbs which can be grown superbly under protection, some of which have already been mentioned under Pot Plants. These are as follows:

Alstroemeria This is the well-known herbaceous plant which has recently been grown under protection to produce earlier and more continuous blooms. The rhizomes are best established in pots before being planted out 30 × 30cm (12 × 12in) spacing or thereabouts in reasonable soil. They are an aggressive plant once established and can eventually take up a lot of room.

Arum Lillies (See p. 212 Pot Plants) For cut bloom these are usually grown in large pots, being propagated from offsets and repotted every second year, being top dressed with well rotted manure in the intervening year. They can also be spaced out in borders at 30 × 30cm (12 × 12in). They are a very 'dirty' plant, invariably attacked with aphids and red spider which then spread to other crops.

Amaryllis (Bella Donna lily) These have become very popular in recent years as house plants. They can be grown from seed which is slow to develop, or from offsets taken from the parent bulbs. They are best potted or planted in borders in the Spring. For cut blooms.

Chincherinchees (See Pot Plants p. 209) Grown from seed sown in late summer to produce bulbs for planting the following early autumn in beds or pots to flower the following Spring, or alternatively imported bulbs can be planted in early spring to flower in the Autumn. They are useful and attractive cut flowers.

Clivia (See Pot Plants p. 204).

Canna (See Pot Plants p. 203).

Eucharis (See Pot Plants p. 206).

Gladiolus These have enjoyed mixed fortunes under protection due to the prevalence of disease. They are best planted in borders in reasonably good soil early in the year at 10 × 10cm (4 × 4in) spacing, selecting special varieties for indoor flowering.

Ixias These are grown in a similar manner to freesias (see p. 239).

Liliums (See Pot Plants, p. 208) These are grown from seed or from bulbs taken from cold store in succession. They make very attractive indoor flowers.

CHAPTER 27
Cacti

Over the past few years cacti and other succulent plants have become increasingly popular. In the centrally heated conservatory and home they make ideal subjects and revel in the dry air. Their stylized shapes are remarkably in keeping with modern architecture. And all the old wives' tales about flowering only once in seven years have been exploded.

There are certainly many species of cacti that do not flower until they reach a considerable size, but equally so there are many that flower profusely as very small plants. Once plants do reach flowering size they should flower regularly every year providing they are well looked after.

In the wild, cacti are found growing in a wide variety of conditions and climates. Those growing high up in the Andes of South America are covered by snow in winter. Some are epiphytic and grow in humus trapped in the crooks of trees – these are known as orchid cacti and are very popular as house plants because of their exceptionally large and colourful flowers. The majority of cacti, however, are found in naturally arid conditions such as exist in many parts of South America, Mexico and California.

A great many succulent plants are wrongly called cacti, simply because they have spines or thorns. A true cactus can always be identified by the way in which the spines grow, with clusters of several spines arising from central points along the ribs or on tubercles. These central points are known as areoles, and any plant that does not have them is not strictly speaking a cactus, although amongst these succulent plants there are many interesting and bizarre forms. There is one plant that grows like a string of beads, and another that has hairy flowers smelling of decayed meat to attract the horseflies that pollinate it. There are also the 'living stones', plants that grow in the very hot dry deserts of South Africa and have taken on the semblance of small pebbles to prevent themselves from being eaten by animals.

Cacti and succulents will thrive in any dry atmosphere – on a greenhouse bench, conservatory bench, or indoor gardens of various designs, the pattern being set by the cactus houses of many botanical gardens, that in Kew Gardens near London being an outstanding example.

Cultivation
Potting
Purchased cacti will probably be in a tiny pot that does not allow sufficient development room for new roots. Ideally repotting should be done in late autumn or early spring when the plants are semi-dormant, though they do not seem to suffer from being moved carefully during the summer.

The potting compost should allow free drainage of water, otherwise the plants will quickly rot. A mixture of equal parts of good loam and gritty sand is suitable for desert cacti. Succulents need to be kept slightly damper than cacti so one part of peat should be added to this mix for them. Epiphytic cacti need a compost rich in humus, and 2 parts peat, 2 of leafmould and 1 of loam is ideal. Purchased John Innes composts are acceptable provided extra sand is added. Re-potting long-spined cacti may seem a formidable task, but if a piece of twisted paper is wrapped round the middle of the plant leaving a 'handle', the job is made much easier. Once in a reasonable sized pot, eg 9cm (3½in) for globular varieties, further re-potting should be in the same size, being simply a replacement of exhausted compost. Flowering ability is adversely affected by too large a pot. Bowls or indoor gardens should be planted with the tallest plants at the back, low growing plants in the centre, and trailing plants hanging over the front and sides, finished off perhaps with a layer of flint chippings or small pebbles between the plants.

Watering

As with most other types of plants, watering should be done when needed rather than on a regular weekly or fortnightly basis. The amount of water required varies from nothing during the winter to a maximum at the height of summer of a good soaking when the compost is dry. After the winter rest watering should begin very gradually in warm weather around early or mid-spring. When the plants have started growing strongly the amount of water is increased until midsummer, after which it is gradually reduced until by early autumn they are getting very little. By mid-autumn no more water is given until the following spring unless conditions are exceptionally hot.

Feeding

It is not really necessary to feed cacti as long as they are re-potted occasionally to provide new soil for them. After flowering, however, a couple of waterings with very diluted liquid fertilizer does help to get the plants back into peak condition.

Ventilation

Despite the fact that they live in hot climates, cacti need plenty of fresh air. In a greenhouse give ventilation even on sunny days in winter and do leave both ventilators and door wide open at the height of summer, provided the range of other plants being grown allows this.

Heating

Though many varieties of cactus in the wild are covered by snow in the winter, they do not in damp temperate climates dry out before the cold weather as they do in their native lands. So, if exposed to frost, the water inside the plant will freeze, resulting in the death of the plant, and for this reason cacti should be kept at a minimum temperature of 4.4−7.2°C (40−45°F) throughout the winter. Some of the more exotic succulent plants, and the epiphytic cacti, need to be kept at 12.8−15.6°C

(55−60°F). This means that unless expense is no object warmth-loving cacti are better lifted into the dwelling house over the winter.

Propagation

Basically there are four methods of propagating cacti: by dividing up old plants, taking cuttings, raising from seed or by grafting.

Division

This is the easiest way of propagating, as the offshoot has its own roots before it is detached from the parent plant. Unfortunately not very many types of cacti produce offshoots, and those that do are not perhaps the most interesting. The best time for detaching offshoots is in the early spring, as the young plant has the longest possible time to establish itself before the winter resting period.

Cuttings

Most cacti and succulents can be propagated quickly and easily by cuttings, but there are some difficult varieties which tend to rot before they produce roots. Before taking cuttings from a favourite plant one should consider whether this will leave ugly calloused stumps. Cuttings should ideally be taken in late spring, though they may be taken until quite late in the year providing bottom heat is available. It is best to take cuttings at a joint in the case of *Opuntia* species (prickly pear) but with tall upright types which do not make joints, a 7.5−10cm (3 or 4in) cut from the top of the stem will make a good cutting. Let them dry on a shelf for a day or two before attempting to root them in seed trays, pots of pure sand, or half peat and half sand.

Seed

Cacti can also be grown from seed. Mixed packets are available from most garden shops, but several firms deal in packets of single named varieties. The easiest way of building up a large collection quickly and inexpensively is indeed from seed. Some varieties will flower within two or three years of being raised from seed, but the majority take a great deal longer. Cactus seeds are very easy to germinate, the main problem being to keep them alive after they have germinated. Scatter the seeds over the surface of a pan or box or peaty compost, stand it in a few inches of water, and put a sheet of glass over the top. With efficient heat germination generally occurs within a month. Both before and after germination watering must be controlled so that the soil is never dry, or conversely waterlogged. The glass is then removed and the young cactus plants, which are very slow growing, can remain in the pan for a year before pricking out.

Grafting
Grafting is a rather specialized technique. It is used to speed the growth rate of slow-growing varieties by grafting them on to a vigorous root system of another species or culture. Grafting is often done by specialist cactus nurseries to enable them to produce saleable sized plants more quickly. Plants which are forced in this way often bear little resemblance to the same variety grown on its own roots. Spines especially do not seem so strong on grafted plants. One advantage of grafting is that plants flower earlier than they otherwise would. The stock which provides the root part of the graft is generally one of the faster growing *Cereus* group, chosen with a stem the same diameter as the scion. The top is cut off the stock leaving about an inch above soil level; the top of the scion is removed and the two surfaces joined as quickly as possible to prevent drying out. The two parts are held together either by a cactus or spine pin or an elastic band running under the base of the pot and over the top of the scion. The graft should be kept in a warm dry place until the two parts have united, taking care that no drips enter the cut when watering, which invariably starts rotting. Grafts usually take 4—6 weeks to unite and can be made at any time of year when both stock and scion are growing vigorously.

Varieties
Prickly pear types Many of these have short bristly spines that come away easily in the fingers. Whilst not poisonous, they

are difficult to remove and cause severe irritation. Very few of these plants flower at the sort of size suitable for the home and are grown mainly for their attractive pads. *Opuntia ficus-indica* is the plant cultivated in parts of the world for its edible fruit, and is the true 'prickly pear'. The pads are large, up to 45cm (18in) long, and have short spines.
Opuntia microdasys albispina has small dark green pads with pure white bristles at the areoles, giving the plant a spotted appearance.
Opuntia salmiana is a relatively dwarf-growing type which flowers freely even as a small plant. The flowers are pale yellow and measure about half an inch across.

Cacti grown for spines and hair
Echinocactus grusonii makes a large plant, covered in long golden spines.
Espostoa lanata is covered with long white hair which completely overhangs the spines.
Ferocactus wislizeni has long hooked spines, is very slow growing and will not flower until it is very old indeed.
Myrtillocactus geometricans is a very fast-growing variety with very short black spines and a pale blue/green stem covered with a powdery 'bloom' that comes off if the plant is handled too much.
Oreocereus trollii is another hairy variety but it also has very long bright red spines growing out through the hair.

Free-flowering cacti
Aporocactus flagelliformis is commonly known as rat's-tail cactus because of its long thin stems that trail over the edge of the pot. In early spring the whole plant is covered with large red flowers, and for these to be seen at best advantage the plant can be grown in a hanging basket.
Echinopsis eyresii produces masses of off-set, so is very easy to propagate. If a large clump is allowed to build up the mother plant will flower regularly.
Rebutia miniscula is a very small plant, no more than 7.5cm (3in) across even when fully grown. In time it will produce a great many offshoots and so build up a large clump. It is one of the most free-flowering

cacti and will flower within two years of being grown from seed.

Stenocactus multicostatus is unusual in that it has wavy ribs. This plant too will flower when quite young.

Epiphytes, the orchid cacti

These plants are quite unlike the desert cacti in appearance, having flattened leaves like stems with no spines. When not in flower they are relatively uninteresting, but are well worth growing for the flowers alone, which are several inches in diameter and come in shades of red and orange, also white. Some are scented. There are not many natural varieties of epiphyllums, but a great many hybrids have been raised, especially as florists' plants.

Succulent plants

Echeveria derenbergii makes a rosette of pale blue leaves with pink edges. The small yellow flowers appear at the tip of a long stem from the middle of the rosette.

Lithops bella is just one of hundreds of types of stone plants. Individual plants measure about half an inch across and in time build up large clumps. In this particular variety the leaves are brownish-yellow with brown indented markings and white daisy-like flowers.

Sanseveria trifasciata laurentii is the popular mother-in-law's tongue plant. The long narrow leaves are dark green, mottled with light green and edged with yellow.

Senecio herreianus, known as the string of beads plant, is a creeping plant with globular leaves resembling miniature gooseberries.

Stapelia grandiflora consists of short thin angular stems. The flowers are very spectacular, measure 15cm (6in) across, are covered in hairs and smell of decaying meat.

Any of the plants in this list are also quite suitable for growing in the home and present no problems in cultivation. As one becomes more interested in cactus growing one comes across varieties that are rather more exacting in their requirements and need special greenhouse conditions. Such varieties are not usually available from florists but have to be obtained from cactus nurseries.

CHAPTER 28
Ferns

Accommodation requirements

There are something in the region of 9,000 fern species, growing throughout the world. The pleasure from growing them is immense, for though they do not produce exotic flowers they more than compensate for this by their grace, soothing colours and diversity of form. They can be divided roughly into five groups for the purpose of their cultural and accommodation requirements: the tropical group, the temperate group, the filmy ferns, the epiphytic group and the hardy group.

The tropical group

Many of these are fascinating subjects that will grow fairly easily under greenhouse conditions. The temperature range must be maintained around the 21°C (70°F) level, dropping during the winter months to 20°C (67–68°F) to eliminate the risk of etiolation through the effects of poor light and excessive temperature.

The glasshouse used must be equipped with some means by which it can be shaded during the summer from direct sunlight. Heating is best achieved by hot water, through small-bore piping. *Hot air heating is not suitable for fern culture, as this dries the atmosphere considerably, and the all-important relative humidity level drops too low.* Humidity is one of the most important factors to consider when cultivating ferns. The use of the capillary bench system raises the atmospheric humidity level quite considerably, while also allowing the plants to take up water themselves, thus saving both time and effort. Not all ferns respond favourably to this method of culture, many requiring a very free-draining compost or growing medium. However, a simple system of benching with a shingle, gravel or ash layer 5–7.5cm (2–3in) thick, on which the containers and plants are stood, is still a very satisfactory way of housing the plants.

The floor and benching, if of the last type, should be kept moist by damping with a can or hose two or three times per day, more damping being necessary in the summer than winter months.

Ventilation will hardly be required, and should be applied with extreme caution if at all. A little air if and when the temperature reaches 29–32°C (85–90°F) could be given, but the humidity level must be watched and the young growth not allowed to flag badly.

If space and conditions allow, one can landscape an area of the greenhouse and plant out selected ferns to give a more natural appearance. Some of the larger species, eg tree ferns, which include the Cyatheas, lend themselves to landscape work, and can be underplanted with other species, eg *Blechnum, Tectaria* or *Nephrolepis*, to give a pleasing effect. This is a way of saving labour, as such a planted area will hold plenty of moisture and watering need not be carried out so frequently.

Suggested subjects *Nephrolepis* spp and cultivars, eg *N. cordifolia, N. exaltata, N. davallodes; Pityrogramma* spp (the gold and silver ferns); *Adiantum tenerum, A. raddianum*.

The temperate group

This next largest group contains many very pleasing plants, and indeed some from high-altitude tropical regions also. The cool-temperate fern house requires the same general refinements as does the tropical. Blinds must be provided and an efficient heating system is necessary, although the temperature here is kept at about 10–13°C (50–55°F) during the night and up to 18°C (65°F) during the day, above which ventilation must be applied. Being a cooler house, the humidity level is not so critical and is easier to maintain. Plants may be grown in containers on benching, or in a landscaped area. It is possible to incorporate the two methods in one house, using the specimens from the staging as they become larger to replace old plants, or fill gaps in the landscaped section.

Many of the Pteris are good specimens for such a house. *P. cretica* and its cultivars, *P. longifolia* and *P. vittata* are all fast-growing plants. *P. altissima* and *P. tremula* provide larger specimens attaining 60cm−1.2m (2−4ft) in height. These can all be raised from spores. Also suggested: *Cyrtomium falcatum, C. fortunei, C. caryotideum;* the spleenworts *Asplenium bulbiferum, A. mayii.*

The filmy ferns

This is possibly the most interesting of the fern groups. The plants are usually quite small and, as the name suggests, very delicate, much of the fronds being only one cell layer thick, giving the appearance of a thin film of tissue. They are exciting to grow, and some could be accommodated in the cool temperate house if grown in a closed case or frame (there are one or two designs on the market which would prove very suitable). One may, however, experience difficulty in obtaining material of these plants, due to their scarcity. A number are natives of New Zealand and they are all members of the family Hymenophyllaceae.

Humidity is particularly important for the filmy ferns. They require to be grown in a moisture-laden atmosphere, although not liking their feet in waterlogged conditions. They will not take full sunlight either, so must be partially shaded on all but the dullest days. A house devoted entirely to the culture of these plants need only be fitted with enough pipe heating to exclude frost. It must have good ventilation to enable it to be kept cool, but not to lower the atmospheric moisture-level. The proven method is to have a double opaque glass roof, with the ventilation applied between the glass layers.

There are some filmy ferns which originate from tropical environments, and these would require much higher temperatures.

Suggested subjects *Hymenophyllum demissum, H. wilsonii; Trichomanes venosum.*

The hardy fern group

This last group comprises the hardy and slightly tender species. They are natives of the colder parts of the globe, including Britain, and have to tolerate frost during part of the year, but need protection during the winter as much from excessive dampness as from cold. They may be housed in a cold greenhouse or cold frame, with some method of protection against the worst frosts.

These plants must have a dormant period in which to build up reserves, and most form a resting crown of young fronds tightly packed around the centre growing part of the plant. Water should be withheld during the winter, or applied only if the compost becomes quite dry. In this way slight frost will not damage the resting crowns.

Suggested subjects *Phyllitis scolopendrium; Adiantum venustum; Polystichum aristatum.*

The epiphytic group

The cultural needs of this group are discussed fully below.

General Fern Culture

A basic general compost for most terrestrial ferns consists of: 3 parts by volume moss peat, 1 part by volume loam, 1 part by volume coarse sand. The peat need only be put through a 1.8cm (¾in)sieve to eliminate the very large lumps. The loam should be passed through a 1.6m (¼in)riddle and sterilized, preferably by steam. No fertilizers need be added to this mixture, as when the plants have fully permeated their allotted compost with roots, a liquid feed can be used to give added nutrient. To this compost, 'pea' gravel or granite chippings can be added for the temperate group of ferns. This gives sharper drainage, so necessary during wet or cold spells. Special composts can be bought.

The epiphytic group requires a free-draining compost that will retain sufficient moisture without becoming waterlogged and sour. A large number of these epiphytic plants are in the family Polypodiaceae. They respond well to the following compost: 3 parts by volume moss peat, 2 parts by volume fibrous bracken peat, 2 parts by volume sphagnum moss, 1 part by volume charcoal, 1 part by volume leaf-mould or bark chippings.

The majority of ferns object to being over-potted, ie given a large quantity of soil to root in, so it is usual to pot on in small stages, giving only one increase in pot size eg 1.25cm (½in)at a time. There are exceptions to this, however, and a strong-growing plant during the spring and summer months will take a larger move without setback. When repotting, care should be taken not to damage the root ball, as this may cause the fronds to wilt and desiccate as a result. Some types produce a short rootstock and, when repotting, this ought to be partly covered by the new compost. Examples of this type of growth are to be found in *Pteris* species, eg *P. altissima, P. pacifica, P. tripartita*. Others produce a creeping rhizome or rootstock which must not be buried deeply, but kept at soil level and given adequate room to spread over the soil surface.

When potting, one must be guided for drainage not only by the system used but by the plants themselves. With capillary benching no crocking is the general rule: one is aiming at a good contact between bench and compost. However, certain fern species appear to become over-wet with this method, and it is preferable to revert to the old system of crocking and placing rough peat over this, before adding the prepared compost and potting.

Propagation

The quickest way of increasing one's stock is by vegetative propagation. Not all ferns lend themselves to this, however, but many may be so treated.

Bulbils

Quite a number of the ferns produce bulbils on their mature fronds. In many cases, the frond or part of it with the bulbils attached can be removed, pegged down on to a peat/sand growing medium, and placed in a propagating case for rooting to begin. When the plantlets have become established, they can be removed from the frame, separated and potted into general compost, thereby taking about 18 months to become mature plants. Examples of

species that can be propagated in this way are: *Asplenium bulbiferum, A. viviparum, Diplazium proliferum, Tectaria incisa* (viviparous var.).

Rhizomes

The great majority of epiphytic ferns colonize new area by means of rhizomes. These can be separated from the parent plant, preferably with a quantity of root intact, and attached by wire pegs to the medium on which they are to be grown, or tied to cork bark or other material if being grown in a truly epiphytic manner. It is not necessary to place it in a propagating case, unless the piece is small or weak, or a shy plant to establish, eg *Oleandra* spp, *Pyrrosia* spp, *Microgramma* spp. Rhizome propagation works very well for *Phlebodium aureum, Drynaria sparsisora*, species of *Davallia* in general, and some members of the genus *Polypodium*.

Root buds

The best known group which exhibits this feature are the platyceriums, or stag's-horn ferns. Not all the platyceriums produce root buds, but a number including *P. stemmaria, P. bifurcatum* and *P. alcicorne* do so quite readily. When the young plantlets resulting from these adventitious buds have produced their sterile 'nest' frond, they may be removed and potted into a 7cm (2½in) pot, or placed immediately on to a piece of cork bark, on which has been placed a small cushion of sphagnum moss and osmunda fibre to accommodate their roots. Eventually they may be transferred to a larger pot or board, or even planted on a rock area to grow to maturity.

Diplazium esculentum produces a mass of young plantlets around the parent, and, if grown in a container, these can be cut out with some root and soil, potted singly, and will quickly make mature specimens.

Division

This method of propagation can be applied to many species and groups, usually rhizomatous. All that is needed is to slice up the plants. In this way a pan of, say, *Dennstaedtia* or *Drynaria* can be divided into halves or quarters, provided sufficient young growth is left in each section. The sections can now be potted or panned into a container of appropriate size and allowed to settle down and colonize their new home. No initial establishment treatment is necessary.

Spores

Anyone who has become interested in fern growing will sooner or later want to try to raise plants from spores. These are tiny dust-like bodies, which can be compared loosely to the seed of higher plants. The spores germinate to form prothalli, small and usually scale-like. The prothallus is the sexual stage in the life-cycle of ferns, where fertilization takes place. The frond- and spore-bea ing fern-plant grows up from the prothallus.

Raising from spores

The best time of year for sowing is roughly from early spring to early summer inclusive. It may be carried out later than this if need be, as the life of some spores is very short and it is possibly better to sow than to store for a long period. There are a number of different methods for raising plants from spores. The following gives good results, provided one pays attention to hygiene.

1 Sterilize sufficient pots for the number of items to be sown. Clay pots are preferable.
2 Fill to within 1.25cm ($\frac{1}{2}$in)of the lip with compost which should contain the following parts by bulk (each part should be sterilized to 180°F, preferably by steam) screened through a 0.3cm ($\frac{1}{8}$in) sieve: 3 parts moss peat, 1 part loam, 1 part sand. Put one crock (piece of clay pot) over the drainage hole, to stop the compost falling through. After filling, firm slightly with a firming tool (cut a circle of plywood to the required diameter and affix a handle to it).
3 Write labels for subjects to be sown. Plastic T-shaped labels are best, as they allow the covers to sit neatly on the pot rims.
4 After the pots have been prepared, water thoroughly with boiling water, which can be applied through a metal can with fine rose attachment.
5 Immediately (4) has been completed

cover the pots with glass covers (convex watch-galsses are best, but plastic or glass petri dishes can be used; failing this, squares of ordinary glass will suffice).
6 The spore-bearing material, which has been previously collected and dried to allow the spore-cases to dehisce or break open in the packet, may now be sown. One pot is sown at a time, and the glass or plastic cover replaced as soon as sowing is complete. Only a thin dusting of spores is necessary to give the best results. Heavy sowing will cause overcrowding of the prothalli, often resulting in male gametes only being produced. Thus fertilization cannot be achieved as early as is desirable and fungal infection is more likely to occur.
7 The sown pots are now placed in plastic watertight trays. A solution of potassium permanganate is poured into the trays to a depth of 125−2cm ($\frac{1}{2}$−$\frac{3}{4}$in), to suppress any algal and fungal growth. To make up this solution, enough permanganate crystals are added to a gallon of water to produce a deep mauve colour. The plastic trays should be kept topped up with the solution as needed. The depth of solution in the trays should not exceed 2.5cm (1in); more would cause water-logging of the compost in the pots.

The trays can now be put in the greenhouse, and kept under the staging in partially subdued light, and if possible raised above the ground by some method. This reduces water splashes and prevents water from the dampening process from entering the trays and contaminating the permanganate solution. A green flush of growth will be noticed in some pots after 4−5 weeks. Speed of germination depends on the temperature in which the pots are placed: 18−21°C (65−70°F) for the tropical subjects and around 15°C (60°F) for the temperate ones is adequate. This is the stage when fertilization takes place, and as a result the sporophytes (young plants) will start to appear. The plants must now receive more light, and so can be moved on to the benches, but still kept in the trays, to absorb water from beneath. As the sporophytes develop, the covers on the pots may be gradually removed, and eventually the young plants 'patched off' into shallow trays, pans or small pots, depending on the quantity of plants needed. It is better to include three or so plantlets in each group or patch, placing nine or so patches per 10cm (4in) pan. With the tree ferns, eg *Dicksonia* spp, *Cibotium* spp. *Cyathea* spp, a single plant should be selected, as a strong single-stemmed specimen is required. When the patches have filled their allotted space they may be potted on. Each group can now be placed in a 5cm (2in) pot, containing the general compost mixture, except for epiphytic plants, which require a more open growing medium (see above under General Fern Culture). As the plants develop, potting on can continue in stages until a pot about 13cm (5in) diameter has been reached. By this time the majority of ferns will be producing spore-bearing fronds, thus completing their life cycle.

Fern ailments

Due to the delicate nature of most ferns, one has to be most careful in selecting chemicals or other methods of control for pests and diseases. A good growing environment, producing strong plants, will do much to reduce the incidence of fungal or insect attack.

Scale insects   These can be a considerable nuisance and spoil the appearance of the plants, particularly by the sooty mould which grows on the excreta left by them on the fronds. The best time to deal with these is when the young scale-insects emerge from the parent scale case and search for a suitable feeding spot. Derris liquid (Rotenone) can be used without harm, but a more beneficial preparation is diazinon, member of the organophosphorous group of chemicals, which gives a much better degree of success. During the winter months one or two applications of malathion mixed with diazinon in equal proportions will control scale insect.

Mealy bug   Can be controlled by spraying with diazinon and malathion.

Aphids   Mainly appear on *Adiantum*. Providing no young growth in the pink unfolding stage is present, nicotine shreds may be used as a fumigant, but care must be taken in its use, and rare specimens should not be exposed to the fumes, unless previously known to tolerate the treatment without damage. Diazinon and malathion must not be used on *Adiantum*.

Slugs and snails   These can be very destructive. A liquid slug-killer applied to benches and staging will give some protection, and slug pellets can be broken and placed in each pot or container.

Cockroaches   These are particularly fond of the fern-ally *Lycopodium*, and eat the centres of the growing spikes, causing them to become blind. Baits can be tried, but general cleanliness is very important.

Glasshouse red spider mite   Although not a prevalent pest of ferns, this does occur and usually can be controlled with diazinon.

Botrytis   This is the main fungal attacker. It causes a lot of harm, and again the *Adiantum* group suffers most from its ravages if conditions are overcrowded or the atmosphere stagnant. Good plant husbandry should keep the effects of this to a minimum, but if persistent a spray of Benlate may be used.

The frond eelworm   Turns the fronds black. *Adiantum* again susceptible. These should never be watered from overhead, as this will cause the eelworm to spread rapidly. Badly infected fronds should be cut off and burnt.

CHAPTER 29
Orchids

The first orchid plants to arrive in Europe came from the West Indies in the mid-eighteenth century. These were of the species *Bletia verecunda (purpurea), Epidendrum rigidum,* various *Vanilla* species and *Epidendrum fragrans.* Later in the century came the first Asiatic orchids *Cymbidium ensifolium* and *Phaius tancervilleae.* Not until the beginning of the nineteenth century did orchids arrive from South America. Few orchids survived the long journey to Europe, but this only made them the more desirable. At first the cultural systems adopted contributed to the casualties. Irrespective of source, all orchids were kept in excessively hot, damp, humid conditions and poor light. It was a long time before it was realized that few orchids came from steaming jungles and that fresh air and cooler temperatures might bring more success.

Nowadays orchids are still imported but on nothing like the scale of the last century. This is due in part to nature conservancy and the restriction of exports, but even more to the production of hybrids. The first orchid hybrid, × *Calanthe dominyi,* between *Calanthe masuca* and *Calanthe furcata,* was made in the mid-nineteenth century by John Dominy of the firm of Veitch, and in 1859 he exhibited at a meeting of the Royal Horticultural Society in London five seedlings which were hybrids of *Cattleya guttata* and *Cattleya loddigesii (× Cattleya hybrida).* Gradually further hybrids involving other genera were made, frequently in a haphazard manner. In 1904 a breakthrough occurred. This was × *Odontioda vuylstekeae,* the result of crossing *Cochlioda noetzliana* with *Odontoglossum pescatorei,* the first bigeneric hybrid.

The production of hybrid orchids in quantity was limited by the symbiotic method of seed germination, which was the sowing of the seed on the surface of the compost of a healthy adult plant. Losses were heavy under this system. In 1922 Dr Lewis Knudson of Cornell University introduced an artificial medium, providing nutrition for the orchid seed chemically in a base of agar jelly (asymbiotic process), the seed sowing being done under laboratory conditions. This process revolutionized the raising of hybrid orchids, not only by enabling them to be produced in quantity, but because planned breeding programmes could be carried out. Knudson's formula has been superseded by many variations of the original, particularly in the USA, Hawaii, S. Asia and Australia, where due to kinder climates most of the world's orchid raising is now done.

Meristem propagation (tissue culture)

When an orchid hybrid is registered, all the seedlings of the cross receive the same name, even though they may vary tremendously in many respects. Selected plants of the cross may then be given varietal names. Until the introduction of the meristem method of propagation, such plants could only be multiplied by division of the original plant, a slow business which kept prices high. Now, however, the tissue culture process enables practically any number of identical plants to be brought to the flowering stage in 3—5 years, the time taken to produce a flowering seedling. Briefly this technique is as follows: a microscopic section of the growth tip of a young orchid shoot can be raised as if it were an orchid seed. If, however, the seed-raising medium is a liquid, ie without agar, and the medium constantly disturbed—the flasks containing the medium are placed on a rotating wheel—the original growth tip will proliferate. The proliferations are then sectioned and each section treated as the original growth tip. The process can be continued until the desired number of propagations is reached, the rotation is stopped and the sectioned proliferations will then develop into plantlets. These are then treated as orchid seedlings. This method of propagation brings young plants identical to the world's most illustrious orchids within the reach of everyone. Seed raising is of course still necessary, since only by this method can new and better orchids be raised. Tissue culture has not as yet been applied to all genera. It has, however, enabled commercial *Cymbidium* growers to upgrade their stock and amateurs to possess orchids which a few years ago would have been quite beyond their means.

Meristem or tissue propagation for amateurs is probably too difficult to carry out due to the equipment required, but in fact kits are available in America for this purpose though the original propagation is supplied ready for use. Seed raising is by no means beyond the careful amateur, since all the requirements for seed sowing are available in kit form both in Britain and in America and the simple equipment needed can readily be obtained. Raising the seedlings is more difficult than producing them, but temperature and light-controlled Wardian-type cases can be made or purchased.

Starting a collection of orchids

Until fairly recently prospective orchid growers experienced some difficulty in obtaining information of any kind on this subject. Nowadays more orchid nurserymen are advertising in the general garden press, most public libraries contain at least one or two orchid books, and the recently formed British Orchid Council means that it is only necessary to write to the secretary of that body to receive a list of orchid nurserymen and of the orchid societies in Great Britain, with one of whom an early contact should be made for advice. A further and most useful source of advice is one's local botanical garden where at least some orchids will be grown.

Greenhouses for orchids

Specially designed orchid houses are ob-tainable, but orchids may be grown in any kind of greenhouse if certain points are borne in mind. Glazed to the ground structures, due to their high heat loss, are only really suitable for growing *Cymbidium* in beds of compost at ground level. Any greenhouse, however, may be double glazed to help with the control of heat and humidity. Preferably this should be done with one of the transparent semi-rigid plastics. Concrete is better avoided for the floor surface unless the house is naturally a very wet one. Ash floors will retain water and provide humidity.

Which orchids to grow?

This depends not only on personal preference, but on the average temperature of one's greenhouse, particularly the winter temperature. While an occasional drop in temperature during severe winter conditions will do no harm, particularly if the house is kept on the dry side, there is no point in attempting to grow orchids at temperatures consistently below the optimum. Of the commoner genera, *Cymbidium* will do well at winter temperatures of 10−12.8°C (50−55°F), *Odontoglossum* at similar temperatures, *Cattleyas* and *Paphiopedilumn* at 12.8−15.6°C (55−60°F) and *Phalaenopsis* and *Vanda* at 18.3−21.1°C (65−70°F). With one of these as the main crop there are innumerable species available for each temperature range to provide variety.

General cultivation

The conditions required for growing orchids may be summarized as follows: adequate heating; shading from April to September, the amount depending on which orchids are grown and preferably provided by blinds; adequate fresh air combined with air circulation such as may be provided by an electric fan; a relative humidity of from 65 to 85% day and night, provided by watering the greenhouse by watering can, hose, or automatic mist spray system.

Watering is the key success factor in orchid growing. Many orchids require much water during the growing season and infrequent watering during the rest of the year. Much water with any orchid means pouring water through the compost until it is wet, then no more water until the plants require it—this is largely a matter of experience. It does *not* mean dribbling water every day until the compost becomes waterlogged and the orchid roots die. Since in fact orchids in a humid atmosphere require less frequent watering than most other plants, their culture lends itself particularly well to the automatic provision of heat, humidity and ventilation. Even automatic shading is available, although rather expensive.

Potting

Modern potting composts have done away with the principal chore of orchid cultivation. Economy composts were introduced to replace expensive osmunda fibre and have proved to be not only less expensive but easier and quicker to handle and frequently they produce better growth. Bark composts are often used for *Cattleya* and *Vanda*, particularly in the USA, and most genera will do well in equal parts by volume of fibrous, lumpy peat, Perlite or polystyrene granules and sphagnum moss, the aim being to provide a compost which will hold plenty of water but at the same time remain well drained. Where available locally, sphagnum moss alone is quite a useful compost, particularly for *Dendrobium* and newly imported orchids. As economy composts are generally lacking in nutrient, a slow-release fertilizer such as Magamp or Vitax Q4 is generally used. Due to the relatively poor light in Britain, few orchids will respond to as heavy a fertilizing programme as they would in the tropics. Rockwool has now been introduced for orchid culture.

In botanic gardens many orchids are grown on pieces of bark or logs or in open teak or cedar baskets. Orchids may be divided into epiphytic and terrestial plants, the former normally growing on trees, not usually on the bare bark but in association with mosses and other epiphytic plants. Terrestial orchids normally grow on the ground. Most of the popular genera of orchids are epiphytic, but in the open composts mentioned will grow perfectly well in pots and these, if desired, may be hung from the roof of the greenhouse or on the walls. It may seem natural to grow epiphytic orchids without pots but such do require a great deal of attention to watering and spraying.

There are many excellent orchid collections to be seen around this and other countries. Kew, Glasgow and Edinburgh Botanic Gardens are well worth a visit. A little further afield the Eric Young Foundation collection at Victoria Village, Jersey, is one of the best collections in Europe. Gardeners wanting further information on orchids should contact the Royal Horticultural Society, Vincent Square, London SW1P 2PE.

CHAPTER 30
The Alpine House

This romantic sounding name is given to the completely cold greenhouse (no artificial heat whatsoever) utilized for the culture of hardy low-growing rock plants including shrubs. It gives them protection to a certain degree from the extremes of weather and certainly from the ravaging effects of cold winds, enabling them to flower earlier and with more precision than if they were out of doors. It is a form of activity that can occupy an enthusiastic gardener over the winter and early spring months, and of course is a necessity for the rock-gardening enthusiast keen on exhibiting.

Many gardeners automatically think of all rock plants as being extremely hardy and able to withstand very low temperatures because they are indigenous to high alpine valleys on inaccessible rock shelves where, obviously, the average air temperatures are low. They forget, however, that for a major portion of their life many of these alpine plants are protected by a thick insulating blanket of snow which provides an even-temperatured congenial environment. Grown artificially below the snowline in the variable autumn and winter conditions of a temperate climate, rock plants often quickly deteriorate.

Broadly speaking, any type of greenhouse will suffice, provided it is situated in a sunny position and—perhaps more important—provided it is well ventilated with both side and ridge vents to keep temperatures down.

Benches covered with inert gravel or pebbles are desirable and tiering is useful to give effect and better space utilization. Plants are potted up in the summer, using clay pots for preference, and an appropriate compost—broadly speaking one of John Innes No 1 standard with either lime or no lime according to species. Good drainage is essential, using broken crocks or pebbles in the base of the pot. Pots are plunged to the rim in a shady sheltered position and kept moist, and the plants are lifted into the greenhouse in mid-autumn, where they must be kept cool and watered according to temperature, but generally sparingly. Small-flowered spring bulbs are potted in late summer or early autumn and plunged in ashes in a cool shady frame for five or six weeks before being brought into the greenhouse.

It is essential to give continuous air day and night on the top ventilators at least, except during very cold frosty weather, and water very sparingly according to growth. It helps to keep plants moist and at the same time looking attractive if the tops of the pots are dressed with a layer of inert chips of suitable colour, preferably grey, white or red.

Shrubs may be grown in much the same way, using larger pots, and there is obviously a vast range of species to choose from, size being the limiting factor. Full lists of species can be obtained from specialist nurserymen. The following are some of the more popular species grown:

Bulbs
Anemones *A, aspennina, blanda, fulgens* and *stellata*
Miniature daffodils *Narcissus bulbocodium* (hoop petticoat), *cyclamineus* (cyclamen-flowered), *minimus* (with tiny flowers) and *triandrus* (angel's tears)
Fritillarias
Winter-flowering crocuses

Plants

Alyssum	Lewisia
Androsace	Mertensia
Conifers, many dwarf	Omphalodes
varieties	Primula
Draba	Saxifrage
Eritrichium	Sedum
Gentiana verna	Sempervivum
Iberis	Soldanella

CHAPTER 31
Pests & Disorders

Greenhouse cleansing

Whilst routine inspection of the growing plants is helpful in reducing the chances of disease and pest spread, the periodic cleansing of the glasshouse structure is also essential. To do this it is, of course, necessary to move out *all* plants to a suitable environment when a further examination of them can be made. The house should then be thoroughly washed down either with a proprietary cresylic acid solution or with dilute formalin (2%) plus a wetting agent, making sure that cracks and crannies in the structure and on the bench are not neglected, and that old bits of string used for plant supports and remnants of plant material are removed and burnt.

Both formalin and cresylic acid can be applied by brush or by sprayer, but whatever method is used it is advisable to wear an eye-shield or goggles. When formaldehyde is used the structure should be completely closed for 24 hours after treatment, and if possible the temperature should be raised to about 21°C (70°F) during this period. Following this treatment the house should be opened up and thoroughly ventilated until all traces of formaldehyde smell have gone.

In larger glasshouses it may be more convenient to wash down with a proprietary detergent solution and then to fumigate with formaldehyde or with sulphur (provided the main structure of the house is not made of metal). The formaldehyde can be vaporized either by placing the solution in a container over a heater, or by placing crystals of potassium permanganate in a twist of soft paper and dropping it into a *metal* bucket containing the formaldehyde solution. Approximately 5 litre (1 pint) of formalin and 43g (4oz) potassium permanganate are required for each 29m^3 (1,000cu ft) of house. Care should be taken to use a large enough *metal* container for the formalin since the addition of the potassium per-

manganate causes violent bubbling and evolution of heat during which the formalin is vaporized. Allowing a 4.5 litre (1 gallon) container for 1 pint of formalin should be satisfactory. When sulphur is used, it can be placed in small bags 190g per 29m^3 (approx 6$\frac{1}{2}$oz per 1,000cu ft) with wood wool and ignited. Close tightly all the doors and vents in the house; these are subsequently opened after 24 hours (for formaldehyde) or 2−3 days (for sulphur) to allow the fumes to escape.

Safety

Many pesticides are relatively harmless, even when exposure to them is considerable, but some are quite toxic, and a few are *extremely dangerous* both in the concentrated and diluted state. It is, therefore, *essential to treat all pesticides with respect,* and to err on the side of extra care when storing and handling them.

The following points should be constantly borne in mind:

1 Store all pesticides (if possible under lock and key) out of reach of children, in clearly labelled containers. DO NOT TRANSFER CHEMICALS TO SOFT DRINK OR OTHER TYPES OF BOTTLE.

2 Amateur growers should obtain their fungicides and insecticides from the appropriate retail sources. Where possible, use chemicals that carry the seal of approval of the official Agricultural Chemicals Approval Scheme in preference to materials not carrying such approval. All officially approved chemicals have also been cleared for safety under the Pesticides Safety Precautions Scheme (in the UK see *Pesticides 1986*, published by the Ministry of Agriculture, Fisheries and Food. See also the booklet *Garden Chemicals*, available from the British Agrochemical Association, 4 Lincoln Court, Lincoln Road, Peterborough PE1 2RP.

3 Carefully read the instructions on the

pesticide container *and follow them*. Wear rubber gloves when handling pesticide concentrates and also when spraying. Also use a face mask and other protection if so instructed. A face mask should be worn when handling and applying certain dusts.
4 Thoroughly cleanse the spraying equipment after use.
5 Wash hands and face, and all protective clothing after spraying or dusting.
6 Do not eat, drink or smoke when spraying or dusting, nor until protective clothing has been removed and hands and face have been thoroughly washed.

Biological control

Just as the more stable environmental conditions of the greenhouse are favourable for pests they are also extremely suitable for some of the natural enemies of the pests (the parasites and predators). Concern over the hazards and expense of pesticides, together with increasing problems of pest resistance to chemicals, has refocused attention on biological agents. The most notable of the techniques developed at Horticultural Research International, Littlehampton is the use of the predatory mite *Phytoseiulus persimilis* for the control of glasshouse red spider mite *(Tetranychus urticae)* on cucumbers and tomatoes. There are also techniques for the control of aphids and whiteflies on glasshouse crops and other pests and diseases. A full dossier of biological control methods is available from Organic Bodies (see Appendix).

Characteristics and treatment of some disorders and pests of greenhouse plants

In the following pages are described a number of disorders and pests which may affect some of the crops mentioned earlier in the book. It is obviously quite impossible to do more than cover the better-known disorders, and inclusion of particular diseases and pests in the section is based mainly on the likelihood of their occurrence in the greenhouse.

Where a disorder is caused by a pathogenic organism or is of physiological origin, the letters (F), (B), (V) or (Ph) are appended to indicate whether a fungus (F), bacterium (B), virus (V), or physiological feature (Ph) respectively is involved. Pest infestations are indicated by the letter (P). Features marked with a dagger (†) are visible with a magnifying glass ($\times$ 10 magnification).

IMPORTANT NOTE Where a particular chemical is recommended for use against a pest or disease, it is essential (a) strictly to observe the maker's instructions regarding rates and methods of application, (b) to check that the chemical will not damage the variety being treated, and (c) that with an edible crop the stated minimum time should be allowed between the final fungicide or insecticide application before harvest and the picking and eating of the crop.

Plant Disorders and their Treatment*

Name/Disorder/Symptoms	Control
Tomato	
Damping-off root and foot rots *Rhizoctonia solani, Pythium* spp, *Phytophthora* spp etc. (all F) Collapse of seedlings or young plants at soil level. Roots may be rotted	Sterilize seed boxes, pots and compost. Ensure clean water supply. Drench soil surface with zineb★, Cheshunt compound or proprietary copper compound; incorporate various fungicides in compost if *Rhizoctonia* suspected. Sterilize border soil. Do not plant in cold soil (less than 13.9°C/57°F)
Brown root rot and corky root *Pyrenochaeta terrestris* (F) Plants unthrifty and wilt in bright weather. Soft brown rot, outer tissues of root lost. Later, brown uneven cork-like swelling of larger roots. Stem base rot and yellowing and withering of lower leaves	Hygiene and soil sterilization as for stem rot. A stem base drench of various fungicides after planting helps to reduce infection
Grey mould *Botrytis cinerea* (F) Pale brown lesions on stem, with grey fur of fungus (under humid conditions). Fruit may show green rings with pinpoint brown mark at centre (Ghost spots) and grey soft rotting, especially around the calyx	As for stem rot. Also avoid checks to plant growth, and conditions of high humidity (ie ventilate and give a little heat if necessary to create buoyant atmosphere). Spray with benomyl after de-leafing. Tecnazene smokes can be used. Various other sprays are recommended. Avoid physical damage to plants
Stem rot *Didymella lycopersici* (F) Brown, grey or blackish rot of base, or later the upper parts of stem. Dark pimples (fruiting bodies) on lesions may be present. Roots rotted. Dark lesions at flower end of fruit. Easy to confuse with botrytis	Remove and destroy remains of previous tomato crop, including roots, strings and debris. Wash down house with detergent or disinfectant. Fumigate with formalin★ or sulphur★ (not in metal houses). Sterilize canes and boxes. Sterilize soil before planting. Inspect plants during cropping and remove primary infectors. Spray captan★ on stem bases and adjacent soil after planting, and repeat 3 weeks later. A stem base drench of 0.5 litre (1 pint/plant) of benomyl after planting, with subsequent whole plant sprays found to be good
Leaf mould *Cladosporium fulvum* (F) Yellow patches on upper surface of leaves, with corresponding brown or purplish velvety fur of fungus on lower surface often sharply delineated by the veins	Avoid conditions of high humidity (ie ventilate and give a little heat to create buoyant atmosphere). Give reasonable space between plants. Crop hygiene important (see Stem rot). Grow resistant varieties. Spray regularly with benomyl (Benlate) or Dithane 945 (mancozeb)
Blight *Phytophthora infestans* (F) Brown areas on leaves, with dark streaks on stem. Reddish-brown marbled patches on green fruit, which shrivel and die	Spray regularly with potato blight fungicides, such as zineb★, maneb★, or mancozeb, particularly if blight on neighbouring potatoes. Reduce humidity of atmosphere by ventilating and giving some heat
Wilts *Verticillium albo-atrum, V. dahliae, Fusarium oxysporum* f. sp. *lycopersici* and *F. redolens* (all F) Yellowing and/or wilting of leaves, progressively up the plant. Symptoms may be one-sided (especially with *Fusarium*). Wood often discoloured light-, dark-, or reddish-brown. Severely affected plants may die	Hygiene and soil sterilization as for Stem rot. A stem base drench (1 pint/plant) with benomyl after planting may reduce infection. Grow resistant varieties or use plants grafted onto resistant rootstocks
Buck-eye rot *Phytophthora* sp (F) Grey to reddish-brown zonate patches or concentric rings on fruit	Support lower trusses up off ground to prevent fungus splashing from soil on to fruit. Spray soil surface and lower trusses with proprietary copper fungicide to prevent disease

★Not available/legally retailable to amateur gardeners

*VERY IMPORTANT NOTE. The pesticide situation is constantly changing and recent legislation prohibits the use of professional available pesticides by unqualified amateur gardeners. While guidance regarding pesticides is given in these notes, it is vital that there is constant reference to up-to-date literature issued by pesticide suppliers and their products are used strictly according to legal recommendations. Appropriate references are current copies of *Garden Chemicals – A guide to their safe and effective use* available from British Agrochemical Association, 4 Lincoln Court, Lincoln Road, Peterborough PE1 2RP, Tel No 0733 349225 or a current copy of *Pesticides*, published by the Ministry of Agriculture, Fisheries and Food, available at HM Stationery Offices. In the notes which follow products available only for professional users are marked with an asterisk. If in doubt about any product enquire at your local supply centre as some products may only have limited availability. For organic gardeners biological control offers many new opportunities for both pest and disease control. (See Appendix)

Plant Disorders and their Treatment — *continued*

Name/Disorder/Symptoms	Control
Bacterial canker *Corynebacterium michiganense* (B) Small light brown areas on surface of leaves which coalesce and kill the leaf. Raised yellowish-white mealy areas on stem; skin separates easily from wood. 'Birds-eye' spotting (white spot with dark centre) on fruit	Hygiene and soil sterilization as for stem rot. Reduce temperature by ventilation and cease overhead watering. Remove infected plants carefully and spray remaining plants with mild copper fungicide every 3 days until disease under control, then weekly
Tomato mosaic and Streak Tobacco mosaic virus (V) Seedlings are checked and turn purple. On older plants, leaves are mottled light and dark green (Mosaic), with variable distortion. Leaf blades may not form, giving fern-leaf effect. Sometimes grey streaks form on stem and leaf stalks, and bronzing and sunken markings occur on fruit (Streak)	Use virus-treated and tested seed. Hygiene as for stem rot, except that washing down should be done with 3% trisodium phosphate. Fumigate with formalin or sulphur. Sterilization with steam will reduce virus in soil; chemicals ineffective. During growth, handle obviously affected plants last when de-leafing, side shooting etc. Wash hands before handling plants. Maintain well-balanced feeding of plants to minimize effect of virus. If fruit bronzing persistently bad, grow resistant varieties.
Aspermy Tomato aspermy virus (V) Plant appears bushy, with distorted and mottled foliage. Fruits may be small and virtually without seeds	Control aphids which can transmit the virus from neighbouring tomatoes or chrysanthemums which can also harbour the disease
Other virus diseases Spotted wilt virus, cucumber mosaic virus etc Mottling, bronzing, ringspots and distortion. Plants may be stunted or killed	Control aphids and thrips which transmit some of the viruses. Spotted wilt virus is of increasing importance, especially if tomatoes are growing close to many ornamentals
Blossom end rot (Ph) Dark green circular patch at distal end of fruit, later becoming sunken and black	Maintain uniform watering regime, since lack of water in soil can lead to blossom end rot. Do not over-feed as high salt concentration, especially if calcium is low, can also cause the disorder. Avoid excessively vigorous growth and irregular growing conditions
Magnesium deficiency (Ph) Interveinal yellowing and browning of the lower leaves, which later curl and die. Condition progresses up plant	Spray with magnesium salts (Epsom salts). Reduce potash applications temporarily
Iron deficiency (Ph) General yellowish-blanching of leaves with main veins standing out green. Younger growth affected first	Most common under alkaline conditions, so adjust pH to less than 7 before growing tomatoes. To correct condition in growing crop, apply chelated iron to the soil around affected plants. Avoid waterlogging
Manganese toxicity (Ph) Brownish lesions on stems and petioles. Leaves may wither and droop. Condition generally transient	Occurs most frequently in acid soils, particularly after steam sterilization. Check pH of soil before growing the crop: if too low adjust to pH 6–6.5 by addition of suitable form of lime
Calcium deficiency (Ph) Chlorosis or scorch of leaf tips in head of plants, leaves shorter than normal. Failure to transpire freely prevents plants taking up sufficient calcium, even when plenty is present	Ensure adequate transpiration especially in the early stages of growth in dull weather
Dry-set (Ph) Fruit fails to set, or flowers drop off	Since pollination fails if atmosphere too dry or polluted, damp down during morning on sunny days. Use proprietary hormone setting compounds, but avoid excessive application as distorted fruits may occur on lower trusses
Flower abortion (Ph) Although flowers fertilize, flower abortion later occurs and only 'chat' fruits develop. It is thought to be related to light input or day/night temperature relationship, or excessive 24 hour heat producing flowers which are not fully viable	Control propagation regime as much as possible. In poor light areas, use should be made of supplementary lighting or a growing room, ensuring standardization of conditions under which early flower trusses are laid down, this occurring at an early stage and first and second trusses are initiated during the light treatment period

Plant Disorders and their Treatment — *continued*

Name/Disorder/Symptoms	Control
Flower drop (Ph) Flowers drop off at 'knuckle' due to dry atmosphere, lack of moisture at the roots, or a high salt concentration in the soil	Improve environmental control and carefully check the application of water and nutrients
'Missing' flowers (Ph) Flowers do not appear or only open partially although truss has formed. Due to excess of nitrogen and related to low salt content of the soil. Low night/high day temperatures can also contribute, as can high root/low air temperature and excessive vigour	Adjust salt concentration and apply potash to harden growth. Day and night temperatures should be balanced
Greenback (Ph) The shoulder of the fruit stays green. Ailsa Craig and its offspring are susceptible. To avoid this trouble Moneymaker types were developed. Too hard defoliation, lack of potash, or excess sunlight can cause greenback	Do not over-defoliate. Shade in extreme cases when very hot weather persists. Increase the application of potash. Maintain adequate plant density
Blotchy ripening (Ph) Fruit has light patches which do not ripen. Caused by irregular feeding and watering which results in variable salt content of the soil. Those in the 'vigorous' categories tend to be most susceptible	Ensure regular feeding, watering and even temperatures as far as possible. Ensure adequate potash levels
Fruit splitting (Ph) The fruit cracks or splits due to irregular water uptake and sometimes to varying temperatures. More frequent in cold houses when fruit development has taken a long time and the skin has grown tough	Keep temperatures as even as possible and shade if necessary to avoid excessive daytime temperatures. Ensure a regular watering pattern
Bronzing (Ph) A dead layer of cells immediately below the skin due to excessively high daytime temperatures. Virus or boron deficiency can also be the cause	Avoid high daytime temperatures and check for other troubles. The trouble does not usually persist for more than a few trusses
Oedema (Ph) Bumps or blotches on stems or leaves. Transpiration does not take place rapidly enough through the leaves. Due to excess humidity or the application of oil-containing sprays. More common on container-grown systems if excess water is allowed to lie about between troughs or containers	Lower humidity by avoiding excess water. Ensure adequate ventilation, especially at night
Leaf curling (Ph) Leaves curl upwards excessively, especially older leaves, due to a great variation in day/night temperatures, the plant being unable to cope with surplus carbohydrates	Adjust day/night temperature differential
Silvering (Genetical) Foliage turns light in colour on part of the plant and up to half the leaves may be affected. It is thought to be a genetical disorder associated with layers of tissue which may correct itself or persist	
Springtails *Collembola* (P) Seedlings and young plants with pin holes or scraping of surface of foliage. Springtails (minute white or colourless, wingless insects) present in large numbers when soil floated in bucket of water	Apply insecticidal dust or drench to soil using gamma HCH, diazinon*, pirimiphos-methyl or nicotine★

Plant Disorders and their Treatment — *continued*

Name/Disorder/Symptoms	Control
Thrips Mainly *Thrips tabaci* (P) Other species occasionally troublesome Removal of sap causes wilting and scarring of foliage and fruit. Thrips are also important vectors of spotted wilt virus. Minute yellow-brown insect with strap-like wings[†]	Spray foliage with malathion. Two applications at 14 day intervals. Thrips do not really enjoy tomatoes but spread virus if present in quantity
Whitefly *Trialeurodes vaporariorm* (P) Small adults with white wings, larval stage scale-like. Adults fly away in clouds when foliage disturbed. Found in large numbers on young plants and growing point of old plants. Removal of sap causes chlorotic area and sugary waste product (honeydew) induces the growth of black moulds on foliage and fruit	Spray with malathion or permethrin. Resistance to chemicals is a problem. Sticky traps are useful. Biological control possible
Aphids Mostly the glasshouse-potato aphid *Aulacorthum solani* or the peach-potato aphid *Myzus persicae* (P) Removal of sap results in yellowing of foliage. *A. solani* is vector of tomato aspermy virus. Honeydew may spoil fruit. Small (1–1.5mm) dull green or yellowish green insects with or without wings	Many alternative treatments include: on young plants, spray of dimethoate malathion or other insecticides and repeat in 10 days; on mature plants use insecticidal smokes, or sprays of organophosphorus compounds which have systemic action. May develop resistance to certain organophosphorus compounds. Pirimor★ useful commercially
Tomato moth *Laconobia oleracea* (P) Young skeletonize foliage and older larvae eat holes in fruit and stems and strip all leaves from May–July. Adults' wing span dark purple-brown in colour. Caterpillars pale green head with yellow-brown body, dark stripes on back and yellow stripes on side. (Other species may also occur. Control as given.)	Spray with dichlorvos or permethrin at 1 week intervals. Do not spray young plants – try handpicking. Other controls may be tried such as *Bacillus thuringiensis* Berliner
Tomato leafminer *Liriomyza solani* (P) Adults feed on foliage causing pits; larvae tunnel into cotyledons of seedlings often killing them. Small pale orange larvae in tunnels mostly in S. England	Spray soil and seedlings with diazinon★ (care!). Picking off leaflets and overwinter hygiene helps
Red spider mite *Tetranychus urticae* (P) Foliage hard, parchment-like with yellow mottling on upper surface becoming completely yellow. Webs are produced on plants and all stages of pest are visible. Fruit and flowers spoiled by webbing. Mite has small (0.6mm) pear-shaped body with yellow/green or red coloration	Mites come out of hibernation in spring and breed rapidly. Resistance may occur as in aphids and treatment should be varied. Many acaricides are available including: on seedlings, sprays of dimethoate, demeton-S-methyl★ or tetradifon★; on mature plants spray or smoke with malathion or dimethoate. Biological control very effective using predators. Remove old crop immediately after fruit finished to prevent hibernation of mites
Slaters or woodlice *Armadillidium* spp (P) Stems of seedlings chewed through at or below soil level, roots stunted. Occasionally damage foliage by chewing holes. Grey/brown armour plated segmented body with numerous small legs on underside. Nocturnal feeders hiding under pots etc during day	Remove rubbish, boxes etc. Apply gamma-HCH spray or dust to soil. Use slug baits

Plant Disorders and their Treatment — *continued*

Name/Disorder/Symptoms	Control
Symphilids *Scutigerella immaculata* (P) All stages feed on young roots causing wilting and blue discoloration, and encouraging infection by disease organisms. White body (about 6mm) with 12 pairs of legs. Fast moving and prefer moist soil	Control when 10 or more are found at one root system. Drench soil with diazinon or gamma-HCH
Potato–cyst eelworm (PCE) *Globodera (Heterodera) rostochiensis* (P) Dwarf plants with slight purple discoloration and tendency to wilt. Large numbers of fibrous roots near surface of soil. From mid-summer white or golden pinhead cysts visible. †All other stages in life cycle microscopic	Plants may be helped by soiling up and extra water. Efficient soil sterilization should be carried out next winter using steam or chemicals (metham-sodium or Basamid★ (Dazomet★)). This pest is very easily spread by contamination from other Solanaceae, soil, boxes, tools etc
Root-knot eelworms *Meloidogyne* spp (P) Plants with pale lower foliage and severe wilting. Large irregular shaped galls on roots distinguish this pest from PCE above	Take care to purchase clean plants. If soil infested remove damaged plants and roots and steam sterilise or use D-D★ injection. If this is impossible use pot or peat culture methods (using sterilized materials). Grafts on root-stocks are resistant to some species of the pest

Cucumber

Name/Disorder/Symptoms	Control
Black root rot *Phomopsis sclerotioides* (F) Plant wilts and dies. Rotting of stem base and roots. On smaller roots, black spots in outer tissues which slough off easily. Older rotted roots blackened	Sterilize border soil or re-soil, or grow plants on straw bales
Grey mould *Botrytis cinerea* (F) Water-soaked lesions at nodes and at side shoots and leaf scars. Fruits rotted	Remove infected tissue. Reduce humidity. Spray with benomyl
Stem and root rots *Rhizoctonia* sp, *Pythium* sp, *Phytophthora* sp (all F) Light brown *(Rhizoctonia)* or dark brown *(Pythium/Phytophthora)* lesions at stem bases of seedlings or young plants. Rotting of the roots	Sterilize soil in seed boxes and bed. If *Rhizoctonia* occurs, apply quintozene dust★ to surface of bed and rake in. For *Pythium* and *Phytophthora* remove diseased plants and apply copper fungicide to bases of unaffected plants
Black stem rot *Mycosphaerella melonis* (F) Small pale green spots turning brown later on leaves. Edges of leaves water-soaked. Lesions on stems where leaf or side shoot removed. Soft greyish-green rot at distal end of fruit	Thoroughly clean glasshouse and destroy debris. Reduce humidity. Cut out dead or diseased growth. Spray with thiram★ or zineb★ at first sign of disease and then at 14 day intervals, or dust with thiram★
Gummosis *Cladosporium cucumerimum* (F) Grey sunken spots on young fruits exude a sticky liquid. Fruits split open. Green fungal masses on diseased tissue	Destroy affected fruit. Reduce humidity. Avoid low temperatures in house. Spray with zineb★, thiram★ or captan★ at 10 day intervals. Grow resistant varieties
Powdery mildew *Erysiphe cichoracearum* (F) White powdery growth on the leaves	Spray with dinocap★, colloidal sulphur, quinomethionate★ or benomyl at 10–14 day intervals
Mosaic Cucumber mosaic virus (V) Yellow and light green mosaic, with star and ring symptoms and distortion of the leaves and fruits. Symptoms vary according to strain of virus occurring	Destroy young infected plants. Do not handle uninfected plants after infected ones. Spray with insecticide to control aphid vectors

Plant Disorders and their Treatment — *continued*

Name/Disorder/Symptoms	Control
Green mottle Cucumber green mottle virus (V) Inconspicuous light and dark green mottling on the young shoot leaves. No symptoms on older leaves or fruits. Marked loss of crop yield can occur	Disease is seed-borne and easily transmitted by handling. Seed can be free of infection by heating it to 70°C (158°F) for 3 days. Destroy young infected plants by watering pots with disinfectant (eg formalin★ or cresylic acid at 2%) *before* removing. In border, carefully remove and destroy affected plants and adjacent plants to prevent spread. Wash hands and utensils with trisodium phosphate (5%) or strong detergent
Seedling disorders (Ph) Uneven germination, collapse of seedlings and distortion of cotyledons	Use reliable seed. Ensure that uniform watering and fertilizer incorporation are carried out and that temperature for germination is favourable 27°C (80°F). Avoid high salt concentrations (low pC) in seed boxes. Handle seedlings carefully to avoid damage
General plant disorders Causes not fully known (probably Ph) Blindness or fusion (fasciation) of shoots. Marginal and interveinal leaf scorch, with temporary wilting of plant	Avoid damage to shoot tips which causes fasciation
Fruit disorders (Ph) Distortion, or marked failure of fruit to develop. White or pale brown superficial corky scars. Fruit may split	Avoid checks to plant growth. Ensure roots in good condition. Avoid draughts of cold air or sudden general drops in temperature when cucumbers forming
Springtails Collembola (P) See pest in (a). Leaves may be completely skeletonized. Young seedlings only	Drench or dust soil with gamma-HCH. Diazinon★ or pirimiphos-methyl useful
Whitefly *Trialeurodes vaporariorum* (P) See pest in (a).	Spray with diazinon★ or malathion (older plants only). Biological control possible
Aphids *Aphis gossypii* (P) Yellow foliage and distorted fruitlets. Also a vector of cucumber mosaic. Small yellowish-green to black aphid with long feelers[†]	Spray seedlings or young plants with demeton-S-methyl★ or dimethoate. Mature plants are also tolerant to sprays of malathion and insecticidal smokes
Fungus gnats *Sciara* spp (P) Larvae feed on root hairs of seedlings slowing growth or causing collapse. May also feed on foliage causing holes. Larvae 6mm long translucent or white in colour with black heads	Give extra water and drench beds with malathion. Treat soil with diazinon granules★ prior to sowing seed
Bees — domestic and wild (P) Swollen, bitter tasting fruit due to cross pollination	Screen ventilators; or remove male flower/buds. Varieties without male flowers are now available
Red spider mite *Tetranychus urticae* (P) See pest in (a). If not controlled, will kill all young growth	As tomatoes, but do not use tetradifon★ on seedlings and use azobenzene★ or other smokes with caution
French-fly *Tyrophagus dimidiatus* (P) In high temperatures become active and migrate to young plants causing minute holes which enlarge as foliage grows. Severe infestations cause blindness of shoot. NB. These are not flies — but mites visible as creamy-white globular organisms with many large bristles[†]	Mites are brought in on straw and horse manure. Spray with diazinon★ or gamma HCH. Avoid using straw and manure which is infested

Fig. 65 Magnesium deficiency — interveinal yellowing.

a *'Chat' fruit*

b *Greenback*

c *Dry set*

Fig. 66 Tomato — physiological disorders.

d *Split fruit*

Fig. 67 Leafcurling — leaves curl upwards.

Fig. 68 Tomato moth — caterpillar eats away fruit.

Fig. 69 (*a*) Grey mould — shows up on fruits. (*b*) Powdery mildew — powdery white mould on leaf upper surface.

a

b

a

b

Fig. 70 (*a*) Lettuce tipburn — marginal leaf scorch. (*b*) Slug damage — ragged chewed holes.

Fig. 71 Club root on seedlings — swellings on young roots.

267

Plant Disorders and their Treatment — *continued*

Name/Disorder/Symptoms	Control
Millepedes *Oxidus gracilis* (P) Gnawing of stem above soil level destroys plant. Root damage may allow entry of disease. Flattened body 8mm long; brown in colour	Drench soil with gamma-HCH and use sterilized compost for seedlings. Thorough cleaning of house essential after crop lifted
Root-knot eelworm *Meloidogyne hapla* and *M. incognita acrita* (P) See pest in (a)	As tomatoes, but no resistant root-stocks available. Culture on straw bales or in peat reduces incidence

Lettuce

Name/Disorder/Symptoms	Control
Damping-off *Pythium* sp, *Rhizoctonia solani* (both F) Collapse of seedlings at soil level	Sterilize seed boxes and soil for compost. Do not overwater. For *Pythium* remove affected seedlings and water with Cheshunt compound. For *Rhizoctonia* incorporate various fungicides into compost before sowing
Collar rot *Rhizoctonia solani* (F) Brown lesions on stems of older plant at soil level. Extensive rotting results in collapse of plant	Sterilize border soil. Incorporate quintozene* into surface of soil
Grey mould *Botrytis cinerea* (F) Seedlings collapse with water-soaked lesions. On older plants, reddish-brown lesions develop on the stem at soil level. Leaves develop wet brown lesions	Remove debris from glasshouse. Do not allow plants to wilt. Avoid humid atmosphere by ventilating and giving a little warmth. Rake dicloran* dust into surface soil before sowing or planting. Spray or dust plants with thiram*, or spray with benomyl. Use tecnazene* smokes
Downy mildew *Bremia lactucae* (F) Pale green or yellow angular leaf spots, with white fungal growth on underside of leaf	Pick off initially infected leaves. Avoid humid conditions by ventilating and giving a little warmth. Spray with thiram* or zineb*. Try resistant varieties
Mosaic Lettuce mosaic virus (V) Seedlings grown from infected seed are stunted, with mottling of the young leaves. Vein clearing, mottling, blistering and distortion occur on the leaves as the plant grows. Plants are dwarfed	Use mosaic-tested seed (containing less than 0.1% LMV). Spray with insecticide to control aphids which spread the disease
Big vein (believed to be V) Yellow or white vein-banding makes veins appear prominent, especially at base of outer leaves. Distortion and puckering	Efficient sterilization of the soil will kill the fungus (*Olpidium*) which carries the virus. Raising plants in pots of sterile soil before transplanting will delay infection
Tipburn (Ph) Marginal scorching of the leaves	Ensure adequate soil moisture during hot weather. Avoid applying excessive amounts of fertilizer
Springtails *Collembola* (P)	See pest on p. 263

Plant Disorders and their Treatment — *continued*

Name/Disorder/Symptoms	Control
Aphids (P) The lettuce aphid *Nasonovia ribisnigri* The glasshouse-potato aphid *Aulacorthum solani* and several other species Leaves curled or blistered and plant stunted. Honeydew secretion forms sticky layer which holds dust and cast aphid skins on foliage. Some species penetrate to heart and spoil entire lettuce. Several species act as vectors of lettuce mosaic virus and cucumber mosaic virus. Pale or dull green colour, 2–2.5mm long	Inspect regularly. Clear all aphid infested weeds and plant clean seedlings. Raise seedlings away from aphids and spray with demeton-S-methyl★, dimethoate or malathion. Use above-sprays on growing crop giving thorough cover
Symphylids *Scutigerella immaculata* (P)	See pest on p. 265
Slugs and snails (P) (several species) Especially troublesome in frames. Foliage with ragged holes. Roots chewed. Slime trails visible, pests hide under cover during day	High organic matter and humidity encourage slugs. Remove weeds which give food and shelter. Use methiocarb or metaldehyde bait pellets, or spray soil with metaldehyde. May also be trapped under boxes, leaves, pots – then remove and destroy. Slug tapes very useful

Other vegetables

In glasshouse borders such general soil pests as leatherjackets, wireworms, millepedes and slugs attack all vegetables, but are not generally as widespread as they are out of doors.

Name/Disorder/Symptoms		Control
Brassicas (young cauli-flower and Brussels sprout plants raised for outdoor planting)	Clubroot *Plasmodiophora brassicae* (F) Elongated swellings on the roots and/or stem bases of seedlings and young plants	Examine all plants carefully before transplanting and discard and burn any with unevenly thickened or swollen roots. Sterilize soil before using for seed sowing or potting. Ensure boxes and pots clean and free from contamination by the spores
French bean	Foot rot *Fusarium solani* f. sp *sphaseoli* (F) Stem base shrivelled and brown. Leaves yellow progressively up plant	Remove and destroy affected plants. Do not grow beans in soil for several years, or sterilize thoroughly before replanting in following year
	Halo blight *Pseudomonas phaseolicola* (B) Water-soaked spots with surrounding yellow halo on leaves, may coalesce to form brown necrotic area. Pods similarly affected. Affected seeds may show blistering	Do not sow blistered seed. Remove and destroy affected plants. Avoid overhead watering which spreads the bacteria. Spray with liquid copper. Resistant varieties are available
	Aphids Various species (P) Foliage curled or distorted and flowers mis-shaped	Gamma-HCH smoke★, gamma-HCH or malathion sprays. There is a variety of insecticides for Aphid control but follow label recommendations

Plant Disorders and their Treatment — *continued*

Name/Disorder/Symptoms	Control
Silver-Y-moth *Plusia gamma* (P) Holes in foliage and frass granules on lower leaves. Caterpillars in July about 15mm long; green body with dark brown head.	Spray with gamma-HCH
French-fly *Tyrophagus dimidiatus* (P)	See pest on p. 266
Symphylids *Scutigerella immaculata* (P)	See pest on p. 265
Mint Rust *Puccinia menthae* (F) Shoots and leaves thickened and distorted, on which yellow or brown, or, later in the season, black pustules are formed.	Plant runners from healthy bed only. Or spread straw on bed in autumn and burn. Lift runners and wash, then dip in water at 44.4°C (112°F) for 10 minutes. Wash in cold water and plant.
Strawberry eelworm *Aphelenchoides fragariae* (P) Black patches on foliage, distorted brittle shoots.	Try to obtain healthy plants. Runners for forcing can be treated by hot water method (10 minutes at 46.1°C (115°F) followed by rapid cooling).
Cuckoo spit *Cercopis sanguinea* (P) Frothy masses on foliage and roots.	Drench soil with diazinon.
Mustard and Cress Damping-off *Rhizoctonia solani* *Pythium* spp (both F) Dark, water-soaked lesions on stems at soil level. Plants collapse and die.	Sterilize seed boxes and propagating soil. Avoid over-watering, and check water supply for fungal contamination. For *Pythium*, water with Cheshunt compound. For *Rhizoctonia* mix a fungicide with compost.
Rhubarb Grey mould *Botrytis cinerea* (F) Soft brownish rotting of the leaves with grey fur of fungus growth.	Adequate ventilation will reduce the problem. Remove all mature sticks before they rot.
Rosy rustic moth *Hydraecia micacea* (P) Tunnels in stems of mature plants. Foliage eaten.	Destroy plants and obtain new healthy stock.
Vegetable marrow Powdery mildew *Erysiphe cichoracearum* (F)	See disease on p. 265
Grey mould *Botrytis cinerea* (F)	See disease on p. 265
Mosaic Cucumber mosaic virus (V) Pale yellow wavy line or circle mottling on the leaves. Considerable puckering. Shortened internodes. Fruits mottled, with wart-like areas.	See disease on p. 265
Millepede *Oxidus gracillis* (P)	See pest on p. 268
Slugs and snails (P)	See pests on p. 269

Plant Disorders and their Treatment — *continued*

Fruits in pots and border

Because of the protected cropping, at least for the period they are indoors, fruit trees in the greenhouse are probably less likely to contract the diseases which can seriously affect them out of doors. The most common disorder is probably powdery mildew, though grey mould can cause damage under humid stagnant conditions. A wide range of outdoor pests may attack these crops but the ones most likely to be encountered are given in this table.

Name/Disorder/Symptoms	Control
Various fruit trees (and many herbaceous and woody species) — Crown gall *Agrobacterium tumefaciens* (B) More or less rounded growths with rough or smooth surface. Occur on both above- and below-ground parts of plant.	Destroy affected plants. Avoid damaging plants, as bacterium enters through wounds. Take care when grafting, particularly if crown gall present in nursery, by washing down benches with disinfectant and using clean knives etc. Cover graft unions with tape or wax.
Apple — Powdery mildew *Podosphaera leucotricha* (F) Young shoots and leaves covered with white mealy mould. Infected leaves and blossoms wither and drop	If feasible, pick off diseased young shoots in winter, and infected blossoms and buds in spring and summer. Spray with tar oils in Dec-Jan, and with a systemic fungicide, (benomyl) from blossom time at weekly intervals until mid-July
Brown rot and blossom wilt *Sclerotinia fructigena* and *S. laxa* (both F) Cankers on branches. Withered flower trusses and spurs (blossom wilt). Fruits bearing greyish or buff-coloured sporing cushions, often in concentric circles. Fruits later mummified (brown rot)	Cut out cankers and infected spurs during spring or early summer when infection visible. Remove and destroy affected fruit and 'mummies', both on and off the tree. Pre-blossom spray with benomyl or lime sulphur (except on shy varieties) and tar oil winter washes in winter will reduce blossom wilt. Control insects that can cause entry points for fungi
Scab *Venturia inaequalis* (F) Sooty blotches on leaves, and blistering of bark on twigs. Fruits bear dark scabs or spots and surface may be cracked. Sunken black saucer-shaped lesions on fruit in store	Collect and burn fallen leaves. Prune and destroy diseased twigs before bud-burst. Spray with liquid copper or other recommended fungicide at regular intervals from bud burst onwards. Check that varieties are not susceptible before using sprays
Aphids Various spp (P) Yellow or red discoloration, leaf curling or twig distortion and aphids visible	Use tar oil winter washes and spray prior to flowering with demeton-S-methyl★, dimethoate or malathion or any of the number of insecticides available
Common green capsid *Lygus pabulinus* (P) Small holes in foliage which later turns brown. Misshaped fruit with scars	Spray with gamma-HCH
Fruit tree red spider mite *Panonychus ulmi* (P) Yellow specking of leaves later turning brown. Mites' eggs and cast skins visible on underside of leaves. Adult mites small 0.4mm long red or yellow coloured	Use tar oil winter wash and summer sprays (just after petal fall) of demeton-S-methyl★, dimethoate or malathion
Apricot — Leaf curl *Taphrina deformans* (F)	See disease on Peach in this section

Plant Disorders and their Treatment — *continued*

Name/Disorder/Symptoms	*Control*
Brown rot and blossom wilt *Sclerotinia fructigena* and *S. laxa* (both F)	See disease on Apple in this section
Brown scale *Eulecanium corni* (P) Shoots stunted and covered in brown scales (3—6mm long). These scales do not move about on the shoot or twig but in a year or two completely cover the bark	Treat when dormant with tar oil winter wash or try spray of diazinon in growing season
Peach aphid *Appelia schwartzi* (P) Severe leaf curl and leaf fall on young shoots. Globular brown aphids present	After blossom apply spray of demeton-S-methyl★, dimethoate or malathion. Repeat if further infestation occurs
Glasshouse red spider mite *Tetranychus urticae* (P) See pest in (a)	Apply spray of demeton-S-methyl★, malathion or other approved insecticide on an intensive basis
Walnut root-lesion nematode *Pratylenchus vulnus* (P) Stunted plant with leaf chlorosis and poor root system	Remove plant and buy clean stock. Sterilize soil with D-D★, Telone★, or ideally use fresh soil

	Name/Disorder/Symptoms	*Control*
Citrus fruits	Soft scale *Coccus hesperidium* (P)	See pest on Fig in this section
	Palm thrips *Pathenothrips dracaenae* (P) Brown body 1.3mm long with yellow legs. Accumulate on foliage	Spray with diazinon★, malathion or other approved insecticide
Fig	Canker *Phomopsis cinerescens* (F) Canker lesion on branch, with bark roughened at site of infection. Branch may die if canker extensive	Cut off and burn disease branches, ensuring that no snags are left where infection can lodge. Paint wounds with suitable protectant paint.
	Die-back and fruit rot *Botrytis cinerea* (F) Wilt and death of young shoots, and rotting of fruits which may remain mummified on the tree	See Grey mould on p. 276
	Fig cyst nematode *Heterodera fici* (P) Lemon-shaped cysts[†] white to brown in colour protrude from roots	Destroy plant and buy 'clean' replacements
	Soft scale *Coccus hesperidium* (P) Yellow/brown elongate — oval scales on midribs of leaves	Spray with malathion

Plant Disorders and their Treatment — *continued*

Name/Disorder/Symptoms	Control
Grape vine Powdery mildew *Uncinula necator* (F) Grey or purplish areas on the leaves with powdery white patches of fungus both there and on the shoots. Flowers and young fruit may fall, and berries may be cracked	Avoid overcrowding and checks to growth (eg too dry atmosphere or marked changes of temperature). Ensure adequate ventilation without draughts. Spray with dinocap★ or sulphur (i) when laterals are 12–15in long, (ii) just before flowers open, (iii) after berries have set. Spray when temperature not too high
Grey mould *Botrytis cinerea* (F)	See Grey mould on p. 276
Shanking (Ph) Berries at tips of bunches develop spots and later wither. Berry stalks turn rusty colour. Fruits bitter	Remove affected trusses. Ensure adequate moisture and nutrient available to the roots. Do not allow too much fruit to develop, as shanking worst on overladen vines
Scald (Ph) Berries have scorched appearance	Avoid excessive sunlight and high temperature early in the day
Greenhouse mealy bug *Planococcus ciri* (P) Stunted growth foliage covered in stationary scales with mealy wax threads. Underneath many small yellow elliptical eggs[†]	Spray with diazinon before berries swell, otherwise 'bloom' will be spoiled
Wingless weevils *Otiorrhynchus* spp (P) Wilting foliage and damaged roots together with U-shaped notches on foliage. White, crescent-shaped, legless grubs (5mm long) in soil. Adults nocturnal, climb foliage to feed	Drench soil and base of plant with gamma-HCH. Apply gamma-HCH dust to soil around plant
Melon Gummosis *Cladosporium cucumerinum* (F)	See disease on p. 265
Powdery mildew *Erysiphe cichoracearum* (F)	See disease on p. 265
Pests (P)	See pests on p. 266 and 268
Nectarine Leaf curl *Taphrina deformans* (F)	See disease on Peach in this section
Brown rot and blossom wilt *Sclerotinia fructigena* and *S. laxa* (both F)	See disease on Apple in this section
Pests (P)	See pests on Apricot in this section
Peach Leaf curl *Taphrina deformans* (F) Leaves distorted, thickened and yellowed. With tinges of red. Becoming darker red later, then wither and drop. Common outdoors but infrequent in the greenhouse	Pick off affected leaves and gather fallen leaves and burn. Spray before bud burst and after leaf fall with a proprietary copper spray

Plant Disorders and their Treatment — *continued*

Name/Disorder/Symptoms	Control
Powdery mildew *Sphaerotheca pannosa* f. *persicae* (F) Infected shoots stunted with narrow leaves. Powdery growth on leaves and shoots	Spray with sulphur fungicide, dinocap★ or quinomethionate★ at regular intervals
Brown rot and blossom wilt *Sclerotinia fructigena* and *S. laxa* (both F)	See disease on Apple in this section
Pests (P)	See pests on Apricot in this section
Pear Powdery mildew *Podosphaera leucotricha* (F) See disease on Apple in this section.	Spray from petal fall onwards as required with any of the fungicides used against apple mildew
Scab *Venturia pirina* (F) Dark brown velvety patches on leaves. Young shoots and flowers also affected. Similar scabs on fruits which may be misshapen and one-sided	See Scab on Apple in this section
Pests (P)	See pests on Apple in this section
Plum Rust *Puccinia pruni-spinosae* (F) Yellowish spots on upper surface of leaves, and brown spots on lower surface	Pick off initially affected leaves. Spray with a proprietary copper fungicide. Check infection on anemones
Brown rot and blossom wilt *Sclerotinia fructigena* and *S. laxa* (both F)	See disease on Apple in this section See pests on Apple in this section.
Pests (P)	See pests on Apple in the section
Strawberry Powdery mildew *Sphaerotheca macularis* (F) Dark areas on upper surface of leaves, with greyish powdery growth on underside. Leaf margins may curl upwards exposing undersides. Pedicels, flowers and fruits may be affected	Spray with dinocap★, or benomyl at 10–14 day intervals from just before flowering onwards. Do not continue spraying when fruit commences ripening.
Grey mould *Botrytis cinerea* (F) Soft rot of the flowers and fruits, with smoky grey fur of mould	Avoid over-damp conditions around the plants. Spray with benomyl, captan★ or thiram★ at 10 day intervals from early flowering to harvest
Arabis mosaic Arabis mosaic virus (V) In late spring and autumn, yellow spots (bright red in some varieties) or blotches appear on the leaves. Distortion of the leaves, and dwarfing may occur	Destroy affected plants. Kill eelworm vector *(Xiphenema diversicaudatum)* by D-D★ or Telone★ injection in the autumn, or by incorporation of dazomet. Avoid replanting with infected runners

Plant Disorders and their Treatment — *continued*

Name/Disorder/Symptoms	Control
Other virus diseases, including yellow edge and crinkle viruses and green petal virus Various symptoms, including chlorosis, distortion and stunting of the plants. Sepals enlarged, petals dwarfed and green with green petal virus	Distroy affected plants. Control aphids since some of the viruses are aphid-transmitted
Strawberry aphid *Chaetosiphon fragaefolii* Leaves curled and distorted and pale yellow or greenish brown aphids visible	Spray with demeton-S-methyl★, dimethoate or malathion prior to flowering and after picking is complete

Shallot aphid
   Myzus ascalonicus (both P)
 	
Wingless weevils
   Otiorrhynchus spp (P)
	See pest on Grape vine in this section

Glasshouse red spider mite *Tetranychus urticae* (P)	See pest on p. 264
Strawberry mite *Steneotarsonemus pallidus* (P) Very small† colourless mites feed on young folded leaflets causing them to remain small and wrinkled. Other leaves silvery brown	Spray with dicofol★ 3 times at 28 day intervals from first signs of damage. Remove damaged leaves damage. Remove damaged leaves
Stem eelworm *Ditylenchus dipsaci* (P) Leaflets crinkled, margins turned down, midribs underneath puffy and enlarged. Leaf and flower stalks short and swollen	Always buy certified 'SS' or 'A' plants. Treat infested runners in hot water 46°C for 10 minutes (this will also control strawberry mite.) Do not use eelworm infested soil for growing

Leaf and bud eelworms
   Aphelenchoides ritzemabosi,
   A. fragaeriae (P)
Leaflets small and distorted with rough grey/brown areas. Leaves are almost hairless and stalks elongated. Main growth may be killed. Eelworms microscopic
	As for stem eelworm

Bedding plants

A wide variety of disorders affect plants used for bedding purposes, but most of them only occur after the plants have been set out. During the period prior to transplanting, the seedlings, cuttings and young plants are prone to the following diseases and pest infestations:

Disorder

Damping-off, stem and root rots *Pythium* spp, *Rhizoctonia solani, Phytophthora* spp, *Thielaviopsis basicola* (all F)
Water-soaked lesions and shrivelling of tissue of stem at soil level. Plant unthrifty and may wilt, turn yellow and finally wither and die. Roots appear brown or blackened and rotted

Use sterilized soil in seed and potting compost, or use proprietary soilless mixes; ensure composts uniformly mixed. Sterilize seed boxes and pots. Check water supply from static tanks for fungal contamination; sterilize tank with potassium permanganate (1lb in 500gal water). Sow seed thinly to avoid overcrowding. Do not over-water seedlings or allow them to dry out. Raise plants at recommended temperatures. If *Rhizoctonia* suspected, incorporate quintozene★ or other fungicide in compost before sowing. For other fungi, remove infected seedlings and water the remainder with Cheshunt compound or other proprietary copper fungicide. A drench with benomyl may be effective against *Rhizoctonia* and *Thielaviopsis*

Plant Disorders and their Treatment — *continued*

Name/Disorder/Symptoms	Control
Grey mould *Botrytis cinerea* (F) Soft wet rot of seedlings or rotting cuttings with development of smoky grey fur of fungal growth	Avoid overcrowding and delay in pricking-out of seedlings. Remove diseased tissue carefully and destroy. Give adequate ventilation and warmth to create a buoyant atmosphere. Spray or dust with captan or thiram. Spray with benomyl, or use a tecnazene smoke★. Dichlofluanid★ sprays may be useful
Slaters or woodlice, Symphylids Various spp (P)	See pests on p. 264 & 265
Millepedes, Slugs Various spp (P)	See pests on p. 268

Herbaceous plants and shrubs in pots or border

Section I *Diseases which may occur in many plants* **Damping-off and root rots** *Pythium* spp, *Rhizoctonia solani*, *Phytophthora* spp, *Thielaviopsis basicola* (all F)	See Damping-off, stem and root rots on p. 275
Grey mould *Botrytis cinerea* (F) Soft rotting of the tissues, which later become covered with smoky grey fur of fungal growth. Spots may occur on leaves and flowers, which may later rot	Remove diseased, moribund or dead tissue and destroy. Avoid overcrowding. Give adequate ventilation and warmth to create a buoyant atmosphere. Spray or dust with captan or thiram. Spray with benomyl or use tecnazene smoke. Dichlofluanid★ may also be used
Powdery mildews Various species of fungi including *Erysiphe, Sphaerotheca*, etc (F) White powdery growth on shoots and surface of leaves. May cause some distortion and distortion and discoloration of the foliage	Take care with watering to avoid drying out. Remove initially infected leaves. Spray regularly with sulphur, dinocap★, or benomyl. Check for toxicity of chemical to particular crop
Leaf spots Various species of fungi including *Septoria, Cercospora, Phyllosticta* etc (all F) Localized separate spots of dead tissue, sometimes surrounded by a pale green or yellow halo. May coalesce to form larger areas of dead tissue	Remove and burn affected leaves. Protectant sprays with copper or dithiocarbamate★ fungicides may be helpful. Check for any phytotoxicity before using extensively
Springtails, Slaters (woodlice), Symphylids Various spp (P)	See pests on p. 264–5
Millepedes Various spp (P)	See pest on p. 268
Leatherjacket *Tipula* spp (P) Plants wilting or chopped through stem near soil. Large dark grey 25–30mm wrinkled legless grubs present in soil	Spray with gamma-HCH or fenitrothion. Use poison bran baits or pellets
Cutworms Various spp (P) Stem cut through at, or just below, soil level. Large 25–30mm long green-brown caterpillars in soil	Spray or dust with gamma-HCH
Mice (P) Stems and foliage nibbled. Holes visible	Use traps and/or poison baits
Section II *Diseases in specific plants*	

Plant Disorders and their Treatment — *continued*

Name/Disorder/Symptoms		Control
Abutilon	Variegation Abutilon mosaic virus (V) Variegation of the leaf coloration	Since the virus causes the appearance of the desirable variegation feature, no control measures are required!
	Mealy bug *Pseudococcus latipes* (P) Twisted foliage and large colonies of pest	Spray with demeton-S-methyl★ or malathion
Achimenes	Chlorotic leaf spots (Ph) Pale ring-like spots may develop on the leaves	See Saintpaulia chlorotic leaf spots in this section
Aloe	Mealy bug *Rhizoecus elongatus* (P) Small yellow structures on roots of plant covered in white wax. Plant showing poor growth	'Quarantine' plant and treat soil with dilute wash of diazinon. Repeat at 14 days
Antirrhinum	Downy mildew *Peronospora antirrhini* (F) Plants stunted. Leaves curled with grey felty growth on underside	Sterilize seed boxes. Destroy initially infected plants. Avoid cool humid atmosphere by ventilating and giving some warmth. Spray with zineb★, thiram★ or copper fungicide
	Rust *Puccinia antirrhini* (F) Dark brown pustules on leaves	Remove initially infected leaves. Spray with zineb★ or mancozeb
	Peach-potato aphid *Myzus persicae* (P) Stunted plants with pink/yellow aphids (2mm) visible	Spray with demeton-S-methyl★, or malathion
Asparagus plumosus nana and *A. sprengeri*	Basal rot *Pythium* sp (F)	See Damping-off, stem and root rots on p. 275
	Root rot *Eusarium* sp (F) Plant becomes yellow and dry. Basal shoots wither and die	Sterilization of border soil essential, by steaming if possible
	Yellowing (Ph) Tops become yellowed	Often due to over-watering during winter or to an excessive amount of lime
Azalea	Gall *Exobasidium vaccinii* (F) Small hard reddish swellings on leaves and flower buds, later become covered with white bloom of spores	Remove and burn affected parts before the white bloom develops. Spray with copper fungicide
	Grey mould *Botrytis cinerea* (F) Flowers rot and are covered with grey fur of fungus	See Grey mould on p. 276
	Chlorosis Iron deficiency (Ph) Yellowing between the veins, particularly on the younger leaves	Water with chelated iron solution at recommended rate

Plant Disorders and their Treatment – *continued*

Name/Disorder/Symptoms	*Control*
Bud drop (Ph) Flowers drop without opening	Avoid draughts and marked changes of temperature. Ensure adequate but not over-watering
Glasshouse thrips *Heliothrips haemorrhoidalis* (P) Flowers and young leaves show patches or streaks of white. Small adults (1.5mm) brown in colour and yellow larvae found on plant	Gamma-HCH or malathion. Two applications at 14 day intervals
Glasshouse whitefly *Trialeurodes vaporariorum* (P)	See pest on p. 266

Name/Disorder/Symptoms	*Control*
Begonia Grey mould *Botrytis cinerea* (F) Leaves, stems and flowers may be infected	See Grey mould on p. 276
Root and stem rots Various fungi	See Damping-off, stem and root rots on p. 275
Powdery mildew *Oidium begoniae* (F) See Powdery mildew in Table 1 in this section	Care should be taken in the choice of fungicide as some varieties may be slightly damaged
Bacterial blight (on winterflowering vars) *Xanthomonas begonize* (B) Brown spots with yellow translucent margins scattered on the leaves, which may fall prematurely. Stem may be attacked and plant die. Yellow bacterial slime may ooze from petiole when broken	Destroy affected plants and thoroughly cleanse benches and pots. Avoid overhead watering if disease present. Keep pots well spaced. Select cuttings from healthy plants. Spray plants with copper fungicide. Dip cuttings in fungicide
Ringspot Tomato spotted wilt virus (V) Plants weak. Ring markings on leaf	Destroy affected plants. Control thrips, which spread the virus, with insecticide. Cleanse and fumigate the greenhouse
Mosaic Cucumber mosaic virus (V) Yellow areas, with brown spotting, between the veins	Destroy affected plants. Control aphids, which spread the virus, with insecticide. Cleanse and fumigate the greenhouse
Glasshouse whitefly *Trialeurodes vaporariorum* (P)	See pest on p. 266
Broad mite *Hemitarsonemus latus* (P) Young leaves puckered and turned down. Sometimes brittle. Adults† visible in folds of leaves, light brown grey	Repeat sprays of dicofol*, or use weekly light dustings of flowers of sulphur
Greedy scale *Hemiberlesia rapax* (P) Small (2mm) scales with distinct cone on leaves and stem	Spray with malathion

Plant Disorders and their Treatment — *continued*

Name/Disorder/Symptoms	Control

Cacti   Root and stem base rots
    Pythium sp (F)
    Phytophthora spp (F)
	See Damping-off, stem and root rots in (f)

Glassiness (Ph)
 Dark green translucent spots, which later may
    become black. Decay may follow
	Decrease humidity and increase lighting. Note that some
	    species are sensitive to excessive light

Corky scab (Ph)
 Corky spots on stems of many species
    (especially *Opuntia*). Shoots may be so badly
    affected as to be killed. Surface tissues crack
    and curl back
	See Glassiness above

False red spider mites
    Brevipalpus spp (P)
 Damage as red spider mite, but mites very
    small. Grey dry patches on skin
	Apply dicofol★ or other recommended product at 7 day
	    intervals (not Epiphyllums)

Many pests including Scale insects, eg Greedy scale (P) See Begonia in this section	Use demeton-S-methyl★ or other insecticide
Mealy bugs *Pseudococcus citri* and *P. longispimus* (P) Soft oval scales with white wax and filaments	Use several washes of nicotine★ or malathion (if tolerant)
Root mealy bugs *Rhizoecus* spp (P) See Aloe in this section	Diazinon★ wash. (Care!)

Calceolaria   Root rots
    Phytophthora sp, *Thielaviopsis basicola*
    (both F)
	See Damping-off, stem and root rots on p. 275

Spotted wilt
    Tomato spotted wilt virus (V)
 Plants stunted and distorted. Pale irregular
    blotches, or mottling and streaking on
    leaves. Flowers reduced and distorted
	See Begonia ringspot in this section

Glasshouse whitefly *Trialeurodes vaporariorum* (P)	See pest on p. 266
Glasshouse-potato aphid *Aulacorthum solani* (P)	See pest on p. 266 but care with malathion

Callistephus
 (China Aster)   Damping-off, stem and root rots
    Phytophthora spp, *Rhizoctonia solani*,
    Thielaviopsis basicola (all F)
	See Damping-off, stem and root rots on p. 275

Wilt
    Fusarium oxysporum f. sp
    callistephi, *Verticillium*
    albo-atrum (both F)
 Blackening at base of stem with *Fusarium*, but
    much less discoloration with *Verticillium*.
    Plant wilts from base upwards and leaves
    turn yellow
	Ensure adequate sterilization of border soil if diseases suspected

Plant Disorders and their Treatment — *continued*

Name/Disorder/Symptoms	Control
Peach-potato aphid *Myzus persicae* (P)	See Antirrhinum in this section
Camellia — Leaf blotch or spot *Pestalotia guepini* (F) Roundish brown or grey spots or blotches on the leaves	Remove and burn diseased leaves
Bud shedding (Ph) Buds drop off	Avoid sudden changes of growing conditions, eg drought, over-watering, draughts, high or low temperature, or excess nitrogen, etc
Scale insects, Mealy bugs Various spp (P)	See Cacti in this section
Cineraria — Powdery mildew *Oidium* sp (F) See Powdery mildew in Table I of this section	Various fungicidal preparations are available but watch for leaf damage
Wilt *Phytophthora* spp (F) Root and stem base rot, resulting in wilting of the plant	See Damping-off, stem and root rots on p. 275
Grey mould *Botrytis cinerea* (F)	See Grey mould on p. 276
Glasshouse red spider mite *Tetranychus urticae* (P)	See pest on p. 264
Aphids Various (P) Discoloration and honeydew spoilage	Malathion spray
Cissus — Broad mite *Hemitarsonemus latus* (P)	See Begonia in this section
Cyclamen — Grey mould *Botrytis cinerea* (F) Spotting on the flowers	See Grey mould on p. 276
Black root rot *Thielaviopsis basicola* (F) Plants become yellowed and unthrifty. Roots rooted and black	Use sterilized soil for compost. Water with captan★ or benomyl at intervals
Mottled arum aphid *Aulacorthum circumflexum* (P) Flowers and foliage infested with bright green aphid and much honeydew present	Spray with demeton-S-methyl★ or malathion
Vine weevil *Otiorrhynchus sulcatus* (P) Marked stunted growth	See pest on vines on p. 273
Cyclamen mite *Steneotarsonemus pallidus* (P) Outer leaves curled upward. Flower buds rot or wither. Mites very difficult to see†	See pest on strawberry on p. 275

Plant Disorders and their Treatment — *continued*

Name/Disorder/Symptoms	Control
Daphne — Mosaic Cucumber mosaic virus (V) Pale yellow mottle of the foliage, with chlorotic spots, rings and flecks. Plants may be somewhat stunted	Spray with insecticide to control aphid vectors
Dracaena — Leaf spots *Macrophoma draconis* (F)	See Leaf spots on p. 276
Palm thrips *Parthenotrips dracaene* (P) Foliage discoloured with very small (1.3mm) yellow and brown adults visible†	Gamma-HCH★ smokes or dusts, or malathion sprays
Oleander scale *Dynaspidiotus britannicus* (P) Light brown convex scales 2mm diameter	Spray with diazinon at 14 day intervals
Mealy bugs Various spp	See pest on Cacti in this section
Euonymous — Powdery mildew *Oidium euonymi-japonici* (F)	See Powdery mildew in Table I in this section
Bean aphid *Aphis fabae* (P) Black eggs and adults clustered on twigs and foliage	Spray with malathion
Euphorbia (Poinsettia) — Damping-off Various fungi	See Damping-off, stem and root rots on p. 275
Black root rot *Thielaviopsis basicola* (F) See Damping-off, stem and root rots in (f)	A post-planting drench with benomyl in place of the first watering is recommended against this disease
Fuchsia — Grey mould *Botrytis cinerea* (F) Flowers may be rotted under very damp conditions	See Grey mould on p. 276
Gardenia — Stem canker *Phomopsis gardeniae* (F) Brown area on stem near soil level, at first sunken, but later swelling and having a rough cracked surface. Branches also affected. Plant may be stunted or even die	Destroy infected plants. Take cutting from healthy plant. Ensure that rooting medium is sterile. When cutting blooms, do not leave snags where the fungus can enter. A spray with a reliable fungicide may help to prevent infection
Grey mould *Botrytis cinerea* (F)	See Grey mould on p. 276
Chlorosis (Ph) Leaves become yellow	Keep soil on the acid side (less than pH 7) and temperature above 20°C (68°F). If chlorosis due to iron deficiency, apply chelated iron to the soil
Mealy bugs Various spp (P)	See pest on Hippeastrum below
False red spider mites	See pest on Cacti in this section

Plant Disorders and their Treatment — *continued*

Name/Disorder/Symptoms	Control

Gloxinia   Foot rot and corm rot.
    Phytophthora parasitica,
    P. cryptogea (both F)
  Rotting at base of plant spreads into the corm,
    and up into the leaves and flower stalks
	Remove and destroy the affected plants

Hippeastrum   Leaf scorch or tip burn
(amaryllis)   *Stagonospora curtisii* (F)
  Purplish to red spots, or streaks of varying size
    on the leaves. Spotting also on flower stems
    and petioles. Infected bulbs small
	Discard suspected bulbs, or dip in 0.8% formaldehyde* for
	1 hour. Destroy affected parts. Avoid over-watering. Spray at
	shoot emergence, and at first sign of disease with zineb*,
	mancozeb or copper fungicide to prevent spread

Mealybugs
  Planococcus spp (P)
Poor growth pest found in scales of dormant
  bulb and in neck of foliage
	Drench with demeton-S-methyl* or malathion

Hydrangea   Damping-off
    Rhizoctonia solani (F)
  Cuttings liable to collapse under damp
    conditions in infected soil.
	See Damping-off, stem and root rots on p. 275

Grey mould *Botrytis cinerea* (F) Rotting of flower heads	See Grey mould on p. 276
Powdery mildew *Microsphaera polonica* (F)	See Powdery mildew on p. 276
Chlorosis (Ph) Yellowing of the leaves and pale colouring of the flowers	Avoid alkaline conditions. Water with chelated iron to correct induced deficiency

Kalanchoe   Stem rots
    Pythium sp and
    Rhizoctonia sp (F)
  Rotting of stems at soil level
	See Damping-off, stem and root rots on p. 275

Powdery mildew *Erysiphe polyphage* (F)	See Powdery mildew on p. 276
Matthiola Clubroot **(Stock)** *Plasmodiophora brassicae* (F)	See disease on Brassicas on p. 269

Downy mildew
  Peronospora parasitica (F)
Leaves may be distorted, with fungal growth
  on under surface
	Reduce humidity by ventilation and some warmth. Spray with
	zineb*, maneb*, mancozeb, thiram*, or a copper fungicide

Mosaic diseases
  Stock mosaic virus, Turnip mosaic virus,
  Cauliflower mosaic virus (all V)
Mottling of the leaves and 'breaking' of the
  flowers. Plants may be stunted and distorted
	Destroy affected plants. Spray with insecticide to control aphid
	vectors

Plant Disorders and their Treatment — *continued*

Name/Disorder/Symptoms	Control
Pelargonium Rust *Puccinia pelargonii-zonalis* (F) Brown spore masses in concentric rings mainly on lower surface of leaves. Yellowish areas on upper surfaces	Pick off and burn affected leaves. Destroy severely affected plants. Spray at least fortnightly with zineb*, maneb*, mancozeb or thiram*. Grow plants on the dry side. Cuttings can be freed from infection by allowing them to wilt and then putting in a polythene bag at 38°C (100°F) for 48 hours. Remove basal 1in of cutting before striking the cutting
Grey mould *Botrytis cinerea* (F) See p. 276	Spray with dichlofluanid* or benomyl. Reduce humidity
Blackleg *Pythium* spp (F) Soft black rot of stem. Roots also rotted	Take cuttings from healthy stock plants. See Damping-off, stem and root rots on p. 275 for general hygiene
Black root rot *Thielaviopsis basicola* (F) Plants turn yellowish and wilt. Roots show black rotting	See Damping-off, stem and root rots on p. 275. Watering soil with benomyl may control this disease
Bacterial leafspot and stem rot *Xanthomonas pelargonii* (B) Slightly sunken water-soaked, later brown, spots on leaves. Water-soaked lesions near stem apex, spread slowly up and down and darken. Cuttings infected at base appear similar to those infected by blackleg	Check that stock plants healthy before taking cuttings, Ivy-leaved pelargoniums can be symptomless carriers, so keep away from other varieties. See Damping-off, Stem and Root rots on p. 275 for general hygiene
Leaf curl Pelargonium leaf curl virus (V) Small pale green or yellowish spots, sometimes becoming star-shaped, on leaves. Leaves more or less crinkled and distorted. Symptoms most pronounced in spring	Rogue out symptom-bearing plants in spring. Select plants from symptomless stock plants. Give good growing conditions, as starvation and drought will accentuate symptom expression
Ringspot Pelargonium ringspot virus (V) Light green spots and ringspots on the leaves. Plants may be stunted	Same as for Pelargonium leaf curl above
Glasshouse potato aphid *Aulacorthum solani* (P)	See pest on p. 264
Cyclamen mite *Steneotarsonemus pallidus* (P)	See pest on Cyclamen in this section
Peperomia Ringspot Possibly cucumber mosaic virus (V) Plant stunted, with distorted leaves bearing chlorotic or necrotic rings	Discard affected plants. Insecticidal sprays control aphids which may spread the disease
Primula Root rots *Pythium* spp, *Rhizoctonia* spp, *Thielaviopsis basicola* (all F)	See Damping-off, stem and root rots on p. 275

Plant Disorders and their Treatment — *continued*

Name/Disorder/Symptoms	Control
Grey mould *Botrytis cinerea*	See Grey mould on p. 276
Glasshouse whitefly *Trialeurodes vaporariorum* (P) See pest on p. 264	(Don't spray under direct sun or when pots are very dry.)

Bryobia mite
  Bryobia spp (P)
Large numbers of green globular mites with
  hairy bodies
	Spray with malathion, demeton-S-methyl★ or dicofol★

Saintpaulia Grey mould *Botrytis cinerea* (F)	See Grey mould on p. 276

Crown rot
  Pythium ultimum (F)
Leaves wilt and plant becomes soft
	Destroy badly affected plants. Take healthy leaf cuttings. Use
	  sterilized soil for rooting. Do not overcrowd or overwater

Chlorotic leaf spots (Ph)
Irregular yellowish rings and lines on the
  leaves
	Water from below. Avoid overhead watering, particularly with
	  cold water. Shade from bright sun

Cyclamen mite
  Steneotarsonemus pallidus (P)
	See Cyclamen this section, but avoid flowers and do not spray
	  in sunshine

Salvia Glasshouse leaf hopper
  Zygina pallidifrons (P)
White or yellow spots on foliage which may
  extend to form bleached area. Adults (3mm
  long) are slender and angular, pale yellow
  with dark V bands on back
	Gamma-HCH smokes at 14–28 day intervals

Glasshouse whitefly *Trialeurodes vaporariorum* (P)	See pest on p. 264

Zantedeschia
(Arum lily) Leaf spots
  Various fungi (F)
Necrotic spots of various types on leaves,
  petioles, flower stalks or white spathes
	See Leaf spots on p. 276

Soft rot
  Bacterium aroideae and *B. carotovorum* (both B)
Soft rot of rhizome. Plant wilts and dies
	Destroy infected plants. Thoroughly clean and disinfect benches
	  on which plants will stand. Wash down or fumigate
	  greenhouse

Spotted wilt
  Tomato spotted wilt virus (V)
Leaves may be distorted. Whitish, later brown,
  spots and streaks. Flowers mis-shapen.
  Spread by thrips
	Control thrips with insecticide

Zinnia Grey mould
  Botrytis cinerea (F)
Particularly damaging to the flower buds
  and open flowers, causing rotting. Stems
  and leaves also affected
	Remove diseased leaves and flowers regularly. Reduce
	  humidity. Dust with tecnazene★ at regular intervals

Plant Disorders and their Treatment — *continued*

Name/Disorder/Symptoms	Control
Seedling blight *Alternaria zinniae* (F) Dark brown cankers on the stems and somewhat angular reddish-brown spots on the leaves	The fungus is seed-borne, and a seed-dressing with captan★ will reduce infection. Spray seedlings with zineb★ or proprietary copper fungicides

Roses

Name/Disorder/Symptoms	Control
Grey mould *Botrytis cinerea* (F) Brown spotting of the petals and rotting of the blooms under excessively humid conditions	See Grey mould on p. 276. Ensure adequate potash levels in the soil
Powdery mildew *Sphaerotheca pannosa* (F)	See Powdery mildew on p. 276
Black spot *Diplocarpon rosae* (F) Purple or black blotches with ragged margins on upper surface of leaves. Leaves turn yellow and are shed prematurely. Occasional under glass	Pick off and burn initially infected leaves. Spray at first sign of disease (or if disease present previously, after pruning) with captan★, maneb★, mancozeb/zineb★, dichlofluanid★ or Bupirimate formulations. Repeat at fortnightly intervals if disease persists
Rust *Phragmidium mucronatum* (F) *Phragmidium tuberculatum* (F) Orange pustules on the leaves during the summer, with darker brown ones later in the year. Occurs infrequently under glass	Remove and burn infected leaves. Spray regularly with maneb★, mancozeb/zineb★, thiram★, Propiconazole or other fungicide if disease observed. Control rust on nearby outdoor roses, as above, also particularly destroy winter prunings
Stem canker *Leptosphaeria coniothyrium* (F) Red-brown or purplish areas on young green wood of stem, later foming a canker with a rough irregular margin. Darker brown lesions and cankers can also affect the point of grafting	Cut away and burn diseased tissues. Take care when grafting to avoid leaving unprotected wounds through which infection can take place. Use proprietary paint to protect wounds. Fungicide sprays of little use.
Downy mildew *Peronospora sparsa* (F) Irregular yellowish-grey or purple spots on upper surface of leaf, with grey fungus beneath. Flowers and flower stalks may be spotted	Avoid high humidity and condensation at night by giving adequate ventilation and warmth. Collect and burn fallen leaves. Spray at regular intervals with copper sprays, or zineb★
Chlorosis (Ph) General yellowing of the leaves	May be a lime-induced iron deficiency. Soil pH can be lowered by incorporation of sulphur. Water chelated-iron solution onto soil
Scurfy rose scale *Aulacaspis rosae* (P) Stem spotted with white circular and oblong scales (3mm diameter) with red-brown larval skin in the centre	Diazinon or malathion sprays repeated at 21 day intervals
Peach-potato aphid *Myzus persicae* (P) 2mm long green/yellow clusters on foliage	Spray with malathion or demeton-S-methyl★ of dimethoate
Rose aphid *Macrosiphum rosae* (P) 3mmm long pink/green on young buds	Spray with malathion or demeton-S-methyl★ or dimethoate

Plant Disorders and their Treatment — *continued*

Name/Disorder/Symptoms	*Control*
Red spider mite *Tetranychus urticae* (P) See pest in (a)	Spray or smoke on an intensive basis using a variety of insecticides to avoid resistance build-up
Dagger nematodes *Xiphinema* spp (P) Stunting of growth and poor roots with small galls due to pest in soil	Remove affected plants and sterilize or remove soil

Carnations

Methods are now available for detecting the presence of the various bacterial and fungal wilts in carnation cuttings so that only healthy ones are selected for propagation. Similarly, by heat treatment of cuttings and subsequent culture of excised meristem tips, virus-free carnation clones can be established. Since equipment and expertise are required for both these techniques, they should only be considered by the grower of commercial stocks (full details of the methods are given in the MAFF Bulletin No 151, *A Manual of Carnation Production*). The amateur gardener can protect stocks by obtaining cuttings which have been indexed for the above disorders

Stem rots
  Rhizoctonia solani, Fusarium culmorum, Pythium spp,
  Phytophthora spp, *Alternaria dianthi* (all F)
Cutting or newly-rooted plants may be attacked. Lesion at stem base may be pale or dark bown, depending on causal fungus. Stem breaks at a node at or just above soil level with *Rhizoctonia* infection. Orange or pink pustules mayn be present on cutting stems with *Fusarium* infection. Small purple leaf spots, which may enlarge to brown necrotic areas with purple margins, are caused by *Alternaria*
	Ensure thorough soil sterilization. Avoid over-watering. Maintain buoyant atmosphere. Incorporation of quintozene into top 3–4in of border soil before planting will control *Rhizoctonia*. Spray stock plants with captan★ or maneb★ at 7–10 day intervals. Select cuttings from healthy plants and spray or drench with captan during rooting. Spray with zineb★, maneb★, mancozeb or thiram★ against *Alternaria*

Grey mould *Botrytis cinerea* (F) Rotting of stems, with wilting of the shoots. Fluffy fungal growth may be visible. Petals rot and flowers may be destroyed	See Grey mould on p. 276
Powdery mildew *Oidium* sp (F) Whitish powder on the leaves and occasionally on the calyces	See Powdery mildew on p. 276

Wilts
  1 *Phialophora cinerescens* (F)
Rapid, and often initially one-sided wiliting. Plants become greyish-green, with the affected leaves purplishred. Gradually die and become straw-coloured. Vascular tissues brown. Plants do not pull up easily, as roots not rotted
  2 *Fusarium oxysporum* f. sp *dianthi*
  F. redolens (both F)
Plant show slight chlorosis, with affected leaves purplish-red. Effect often one-sided. Vascular tissues brown. Plants pull up easily as roots rotted. Die fairly quickly
  3 Slow wilt
  Erwinia chrysanthemi (B)
Infected plants grow very slowly compared with healthy plants. Wilting gradual and death may take 6—8 months
	Take cuttings from healthy plants or obtain indexed material. Use disinfected cutting boxes and sterilized soil for compost. Sterilize the border soil. Disinfect house if *Fusarium* present previously. If wilt appears in a small area, immediately remove affected plants and those for about 90cm (3ft) around. Remove soil to 60cm (2ft) depth and sterilize with formalin★ drench. Fill with clean soil. For more widespread infections, mark affected area and cultivate deeply after clearance of crop. Sterilize with metham-sodium★ or formalin★, followed if possible by thorough steaming. Soil drenches with Benomyl will usually contain *Fusarium* or *Phialophora* infection

Fig. 72 Apple scab — sooty blotches on fruit.

Fig. 73 Peach leaf curl — Red blisters and curling of leaves.

Fig. 74 Vine weevil — The grub eats away roots on cyclamen.

Fig. 75 (*a*) Geranium rust — brown rings of spores on lower surface of leaves.

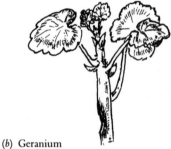

(*b*) Geranium blackleg — black rotting of stem.

Fig. 76 Rose black spot — black blotches on leaves.

Fig. 77 Rose aphids — clusters of aphids on young buds.

287

Plant Disorders and their Treatment — *continued*

Name/Disorder/Symptoms	Control
Rust *Uromyces dianthi* (F) Brown pustules on stems, leaves and flower calyces. Cuttings may be infected	Select cuttings from healthy plants. Destroy badly affected plants and leaves on less severely infected ones. Reduce humidity and overhead watering. Spray at 10–14 day intervals with mancozeb/zineb★, thiram★ or zineb★
Greasy blotch *Zygophiala jamaicensis* (F) Web-like patches on the leaves, may extend to give the surface an oily appearance	Reduce atmospheric humidity
Anther smut *Ustilago violacea* (F) Plants stunted with many weak side shoots, giving a bushy habit. Flower buds short, and calyces tend to split. Flowers have black sooty appearance due to fungus spores replacing pollen	Remove diseased plants before flowering. Take cuttings only from healthy plants, since fungus is systemic in infected plants
Fairy ring spot *Didymellina dianthi* (F) Round or oval brown spots on the leaves and stems. Dark powdery spores produced in concentric rings on the lesions	Reduce atmospheric humidity. Spray with zineb★
Virus diseases Various viruses (V) Symptoms range from slight or moderate mottling to more or less severe necrotic flecks and rings, or streaks of red or yellow on the leaves	Most of the viruses are spread by handling and/or by aphids. Rogue diseased plants, and spray with insecticide to control aphids
Split calyx (Ph) Calyx splits down side, petals spill outwards, so that flower loses its compact shape. Associated with the formation of additional whorls of petals which cannot be contained	Select non-splitting varieties. Control of day and night temperatures, to avoid marked and rapid changes which stimulate production of secondary whorls of petals
Hollow flowers (Ph) Number of petals reduced so that flower appears 'single'	Maintain adequate watering and prevent excessively high temperature by ventilation
Onion thrips *Thrips tabaci* (P)	See pest on p. 264
Glasshouse-potato aphid *Anlacorthum solani* (P)	See pest on p. 264
Peachpotato aphid *Myzus persicae* (P)	See pest on p. 264
Carnation tortrix moth *Cacoecimorpha pronubana* (P) Young shoots and leaves spun together into tents by green caterpillars. Pupa, black, in foliage. Flower buds also attacked	Difficult to control but use repeated spray of gamma-HCH
Red spider mite *Tetranychus cinnabarinus* (P) Small white spots and later leaves become pale. Red/brown mites just visible	Spray with diazinon★, dimethoate, or formothion★

Plant Disorders and their Treatment — *continued*

Name/Disorder/Symptoms	Control
Chrysanthemums	
Root rots *Phytophthora* spp, *Rhizoctonia solani*, *Fusarium* spp, *Thielaviopsis basicola* (all F) Rotting of roots on cuttings and older plants	See Damping-off, stem and root rots on p. 275
Root rot *Phoma* sp (F) Plants stunted, with yellowing of lower leaves. Stem may crack at soil level. Pink flecks on roots which rot	Sterilize border soil thoroughly, or drench with Benomyl before planting. An attack may be contained by drenching the soil with nabam★ at 7–10 day intervals in place of the normal watering. Captan★, zineb★ or Benomyl similarly applied may also be useful in this respect
Stem rot *Sclerotinia sclerotiorum* (F) Light brown lesion on stem becomes covered with whitish fungal growth in which hard black bodies (sclerotia) may be embedded. Sclerotia also present inside stem	Ensure soil is properly sterilized before planting. Destroy affected plants. Incorporating quintozene into the surface soil may help to prevent spread of the disease
Grey mould *Botrytis cinerea* (F) Water-soaked spots on the petals and general rotting of the flowers. Stems and leaves may rot. Cuttings affected	See Grey mould on p. 276
Petal blight *Itersonilia perplexans* (F) Pin-point reddish spots on the petals coalesce to form water- soaked lesions. Tips of outer florets affected first, later spreads to affect whole bloom	Can be largely controlled by reducing humidity with ventilation and warmth. If necessary, spray with zineb★ or general fungicide
Powdery mildew *Oidium chrysanthemi* (F) Powdery white growth on surface of leaves	See Powdery mildew on p. 276
Ray blight *Mycosphaerella ligulicola* (F) Dark lesions on cuttings and on stem and leaves of older plants. Dark brown lesion starting at centre of flower head extends often to affect only one side of bloom	Sterilize border soil to eliminate infected debris. If possible, use steam, as value of chemical sterilization uncertain. Spray regularly with captan★, maneb★, or mancozeb
Rust *Puccinia chrysanthemi* (F) Yellowish-green spots on upper surface of leaves, rusty brown pustules beneath	Reduce humidity. Pick off infected leaves and burn. Destroy severely affected plants. Select cuttings from healthy stocks only. Hot water treatment of stolls against eelworm may reduce rust infection there as well. Spray with zineb★ or thiram★ when the disease first appears, or as a routine if disease occurs commonly. Spray regularly
Wilt *Verticillium albo-atrum, V. dahliae* (F) Lower leaves turn yellow, then brown and wilt. Symptoms spread up the plant. Wood at base of plant may be brown. Bark separates easily from the wood	Sterilize border soil thoroughly. Select cuttings from healthy stocks. If disease appears in isolated patches, remove affected plants, and apply benomyl drench to soil around neighbouring plants
Aspermy. Flower distortion Tomato aspermy virus (V) Flowers smaller than normally, and more or less severely distorted with 'breaking' of the flower colour	Select cuttings from healthy stock plants. Control vector aphids with insecticidal sprays

Plant Disorders and their Treatment — *continued*

Name/Disorder/Symptoms	Control
Stunt Chrysanthemum stunt virus (V) Whole plant miniaturized. In some varieties leaf spotting or flecking occurs, and flowers develop earlier and may be of poor colour and quality	Select cuttings from healthy stock plants. Destroy affected plants
Other virus diseases (V) Various symptoms of mottling or necrosis of the leaves, and discoloration and/or malformation of the flowers may be associated with virus infection	Stocks should be examined regularly and plants bearing symptoms on leaves or flower should be destroyed. Routine insecticidal spraying should be carried out to control possible aphid and thrip virus vectors
Mineral deficiencies (Ph)	Chrysanthemums are sensitive to mineral deficiencies, which are dealt with in general terms in Chapter 12
Earwig Forficula auricularia (P) Flowers and buds ragged and chewed	Spray with gamma HCH and use boards, tiles or sacks as traps
Glasshouse whitefly Trialeurodes vaporariorium (P)	See pest on p. 264
Peach-potato aphid Myzus persicae (P)	See pest on p. 264
Mottled arum aphid Aulacorthum circumflexum (P)	See pest on Cyclamen on p. 280
Bishop bug Lygus rugulipennis (P) Stem, leaves and flowers mis-shapen and distorted	Gamma-HCH spray or smoke
Angleshades moth Phlogophora meticulosa (P) Holes in foliage and buds and flower petals trimmed at outside. Caterpillars dark green-brown with white dorsal stripe and V-shaped grey marks. Nocturnal feeders	Spray with gamma-HCH
Chrysanthemum leafminer Phytomyza syngensiae (P) Fine white spots on foliage (adult feeding marks) followed by the development of silvery white snake-like mines (due to larvae tunnelling)	Spray with gamma-HCH or diazinon
Chrysanthemum gall midge Diarthronomyia chrysanthemi (P) Stems and leaves covered in cone-shaped galls 2mm long where larvae feed	Spray with gamma-HCH or diazinon at 10 day intervals
Glasshouse red spider mite Tetranychus urticae (P)	See pest on p. 264
Leaf and bud eelworm Aphelenchoides ritzemabosi (P) Leaves with yellow-brown blotches which extend and blacken until leaf withers. Buds may turn black	Remove all withered leaves and discard plant after flowering. Take new cuttings from healthy stock and use hot water treatment prior to taking cutting. Remove all infested soil
Sparrows (P) Buds ragged. Petals also ragged and many lying on ground	Net vents and doors and use black thread as extra deterrent

Plant Disorders and their Treatment — *continued*

Name/Disorder/Symptoms	*Control*
Bulbs	
For hot water treatment of rots see MAFF Bulletin NO 201 *Hot Water Treatment of Plant Material*. In addition to bulb disorders clearly associated with pathogen oir pest attack, there are physiological disorders frequently associated with pre-treatment (or preparation) to induce flowering out of normal season. This may result from incorrect preparation or conditions prior to or after treatment (particularly over-heating in transit)	

Name/Disorder/Symptoms	*Control*
Many bulb crops	Grey mould *Botrytis cinerea* (F) Leaves, stems and flowers may rot, with smoky grey fur of spores, under densely grown humid conditions	See Grey mould on p. 276
	Aphids Various spp (P) Foliage and bulb with heavy infestations of greenfly. Distortion of foliage	Spray or drench with malathion
	Glasshouse whitefly *Trialeurodes vaporariorum* (P)	See pest on p. 264

	Large narcissus fly
	    Merodon equestris (P) Small narcissus fly
	    Eumerus tuberculatus and *E. strigatus* (both P)
	Bulbs feel soft and basal plate may be rotted. A longitudinal cut shows a feeding cavity with either one single plump yellow maggot (15mm) or several small (8mm) white maggots. Result: failure to produce a shoot, or production of many adventitious grass-like shoots. Adults resemble blue bottles and house flies
		Nothing can be done after the attack and new infestations on indoor bulbs are unlikely. Buy good quality produce which has been hot water treated

	Bulb mite *Rhizoglyphus echinopus* (P) Large (2mm) creamy white globular mites. Slow moving on lower foliage and bulb scale. Damages is secondary in nature following disease or eelworm activity	Hot water dip for 4 hours at 43.3°C (110°F). *Not* suitable for tulips for forcing
	Bulb scale mite *Steneotarsonemus laticeps* (P) Stored bulbs are very dry with scales sticking close to bulb. If bulb is cut through 6mm below neck small brown pieces of tissue will be seen at tips of scales. Mites microscopic (0.2mm). Ingrowing bulbs — foliage abnormally bright green, distorted and later flecked with yellow. Flower stem with 'saw edge' effect and flower killed or distorted	Buy healthy bulbs. If infestations arise use hot water dip, 4 hours at 43.3°C (110°F) or use insecticide as a bulb dip

Plant Disorders and their Treatment — *continued*

Name/Disorder/Symptoms	Control
Stem eelworm *Ditylenchus dipsaci* Cross-section of bulb shows concentric rings of brown scale. May be white thread like mass of dead eelworms at base of bulb. Growing bulb will eventually die but initial symptoms include yellow swelling (spickels) on foliage, or foliage dwarfed and twisted	Hot water treament 3 hours at 44.4°C (112°F) or dip bulbs in a solution of an insecticide
Freesia and Gladiolus **Fusarium yellows and corm rot** *Fusarium oxysporum* (F) Brown zonate lesions on surface of gladiolus corms. Yellowing of the leaves with reddish-brown discoloration of vascular and surrounding tissue in the corms	Discard diseased corms. Dipping the corms in benomyl suspension before storing in a dry well-ventilated store may be effective. Thoroughly sterilize border soil before planting. A soil drench with benomyl at 4–6 week intervals from the 4-leaf stage reduces disease in freesia crops grown from seed
Core rot *Botrytis gladiolorum* (F) Centre of corm may rot, spreading out to destroy it completely	Discard affected corms. Protect by dusting corms with quintozene★. Sterilize border soil
Dry rot *Sclerotinia gladioli* (F) Small black lesions on flesh of the corm. May extend and destroy the corm. Leaves turn yellow and rot at soil level, leaving a stringy dry rot bearing minute black sclerotia. Sclerotia may also be present on the corms	Discard diseased corms. Sterilize border soil. Primulinus varieties more susceptible than large-flowered varieties
Galdiolus thrips *Taeniothrips simplex* Small dark brown adults (1.5mm) and orange larvae may be visible. Foliage with silvering and stickiness due to leaking of sap	Spray with malathion at 14 day intervals
Hyacinth and Muscari **Black slime** *Sclerotinia bulborum* (F) Leaves turn yellow and collapse. Bulbs decay, with black sclerotia between and within the scales	Remove and destroy affected bulbs. Thoroughly sterilize border soil before replanting
Hyacinth and Tulip **Grey bulb rot** *Sclerotium tuliparum* (F) Shoots may fail to emerge, or may shrivel and die after emergence. Soil sticks to nose of bulb. Rotting, initially at nose portion, spreads and destroys the bulb which is covered with mycelium bearing brown or black sclerotia	Discard diseased bulbs. Sterilize border soil or thoroughly incorporate quintozene★ dust in surface layers of soil
Iris **Ink disease** *Mystrosporium adjustum* Outer scales of bulb discoloured, as if stained with ink. Leaves may bear dark blotches, and turn yellow and die	Discard severely affected bulbs. Less damaged bulbs may be soaked in 2% formalin★ for 1 hour before drying and storing in sand after lifting
Angle shades moth *Phlogophora meticulosa*	See pest on Chrysanthemum on p. 290
Mites Bryobia spp (P)	See pest on Primula on p. 284

Plant Disorders and their Treatment — *continued*

Name/Disorder/Symptoms	Control
Lily — Leaf blight *Botrytis elliptica,* *B. cinerea* (both F) Water-soaked or brownish spots develop on the leaves, flower stalks and buds under humid conditions. Seedlings may be infected and damp off	Discard diseased bulbs. Sterilize soil for compost, or border soil before replanting. Spray affected plants with proprietary sulphur or copper fungicide; benomyl may be used. Destroy old stems and leaves at end of season
Mosaics and mottles Various viruses (V) Leaves distorted and mottled. Flower petals do not open, but remain together at the tips	Destroy affected plants. Spray with insecticide to control insect vectors. Propagate from known healthy stock or from seed
Tulip bulb aphid *Dysaphis tulipae* (P) Grey coloured aphids below outer skin of bulb. Numbers increase rapidly after planting producing stunted growth.l Vector of 'lily-symptomless' and 'tulip break' viruses	15 minute dip in gamma-HCH solution★ (0.01%) or dust with gamma-HCH
Narcissus — Basal rot *Fusarium oxysporum* (F) Bulb initially soft, with rot at base. Chocolate brown rot spreads upwards with white or pinkish mycelium between scales. Infected bulbs either rot away or produce a few stunted chlorotic leaves	Handle bulbs carefully and store in a cool place. Discard any soft bulbs. Inclusion of formalin★ (0.5%) in the hot water treatment against eelworm, controls basal rot infection
Smoulder *Botrytis narcissicola* (F) Bulbs may show small flat black sclerotia under outer scales. Bulbs may rot. Shoots attacked after emergence decay, particularly under humid conditions. Infection less severe under warm dry conditions, but spotting of leaves and flowers may occur	Discard diseased bulbs before planting, and severely affected plants after emergence. Sterilize border soil. Spray plants with zineb★ to prevent spread if disease is severe
Fire *Sclerotinia polyblastis* (F) Small brownish spots on the flowers, and elongate lesions on the leves, which may be killed under very damp conditionis	See Leaf blight of Lily in this table
Stripe Narcissus stripe virus (V) Longitudinal pale green to yellow stripes on the leaves. The surface of the leaves may feel rough to touch in some varieties when infected	Roguing plants during the early growth stages should largely eliminate this problem
Blindness (Ph) No flower emerges, or shoot may be stunted and poorly developed	May be caused by incorrect pre-treatment, or to forcing too soon by grower before bulb adequately developed
Dry set (Ph) Flowers papery and shrivelled	May be caused by incorrect pre-treatment, or to forcing at too high a temperature
Orchids — Virus diseases Various viruses (V) Symptoms of ringspots, mottling and chlorotic or necrotic streaking on the leaves. Colour breaking of the flowers occurs in some instances	Discard diseased stocks

Plant Disorders and their Treatment — *continued*

Name/Disorder/Symptoms	Control
Springtails *Collembola* (P)	See pest on p. 263
Scale insects Various spp (P) See pest in (g), several parts	Use malathion only
Wingless weevils *Ottiorrhynchus* spp (P)	See pest on Vine on p. 273
Fungus gnats *Sciara* spp (P)	See pest on p. 266
Slaters or woodlice *Armadillidium* spp (P)	See pest on p. 264
Tulip Fire *Botrytis tulipae* (F) Sunken circular lesions with raised margins under outer scales on bulb. Black sclerotia present. Shoots may die. Spots on leaves and flowers	Discard obviously affected bulbs. A soak in benomyl after lifting may be effective, or dust the bulbs with quintozene and incorporate dust in the surface soil before planting. Sterilize border soil. Remove any primary infector plants. Spray the plants with captan★, maneb★, zineb★, mancozeb/ or dichlofluanid★ to help prevent spread in cases of severe infections
Shanking *Phytophthora* sp (F) Flower stalk may not emerge or may droop and die. Flowper may fail to open. Growth generally poor. Brownish rot up centre of bulb	Ensure that compost and containers for growing are thoroughly sterilized with steam or formalin
Breaking One or more viruses (V) Marked colour patterns on flowers. Little effect on leaves	To prevent virus spread, keep unbroken stocks separate, and rogue out any infected plants as soon as possible. Spray with insecticide, to control vector aphids
Streak Tobacco necrosis virus (V) Leaves distorted with marked brown streaks, which may coalesce to give larger withered areas. Plants stunted or killed	Rogue out diseased plants. Sterilize soil to kill the fungus which transmits the virus
Chalkiness (Ph) Inner tissues of bulbs become hard and chalky in appearance. Penicillium storage rot and mites are often associated	Avoid damage during handling. Store under best possible conditions, particularly avoiding exposure to hot sunshine after lifting
Topple (Ph) Flower stem kinks and flower falls over	May be associated with conditions during raising and pretreatment of bulbs. Bulb forcers should take care not to force too soon or at too high a temperature. A preventative spray with calcium nitrate may be applied to varieties known to suffer particularly from topple
Hard scale (Ph) Outer skin of bulb very hard, so that roots fail to penetrate and hence grow upwards between outer skin and fleshy scales. Growth poor. Blindness	Cut outer skin before planting
Tulip aphid *Dysaphis tulipae* (P)	See Lily in this section

Appendix

USEFUL ADDRESSES

The following lists do not claim to be exhaustive, nor is any responsibility taken for the information given on the products listed.

Grateful thanks are due to *Amateur Gardening* for their considerable help in compiling these lists.

Greenhouse maintenance

Exmouth Garden Products Ltd, Units 7/8 Salterton Workshops, Budleigh Salterton, Devon EX9 6RJ

Jeyes Fluid, Brunel Way, Thetford, Norfolk

Garden Jack Disinfectant Fluid (now marketed by PBI Ltd), Britannica House, Waltham Cross, Hertfordshire EN8 7DY

Greenhouse staging, shelves etc

(Many greenhouse manufacturers also supply staging)

Exmouth Garden Products Ltd, Units 7/8 Salterton Workshops, Budleigh Salterton, Devon EX9 6RJ

Geeco Products Ltd, Gore Road Industrial Estate, New Milton, Hants BH25 6SE

Halls Garden Products, Church Road, Paddock Wood, Tonbridge, Kent TN12 6EU

Monarch Aluminium Ltd, Manor Road, Cheltenham, Glos GL51 9SQ

Seed trays, pots, propagators, soil warming cables, watering equipment etc

Arcol Ltd, Riverford Road, Pollokshaws, Glasgow G43

Autogrow Products Ltd, North Walsham, Norfolk NR28 0AN

George H Elt Ltd, Eltex Works, Bromyard Road, Worcester WR2 5DN

Erin Marketing Ltd, 33 Bancroft, Hitchin, Herts

Garden Rewards, 104 Branbridges Road, East Peckham, Kent TN12 5HH

Humex MacPenny Ltd (now part of Geeco Products Ltd), Gore Road Industrial Estate, New Milton, Hants BH25 6SE

Jemp Engineering Ltd, Canal Estate, Station Road, Langley, Bucks, SL3 6EG

Langdon (London) Ltd, 5 Worminghall Road, Ockford, Aylesbury, Bucks HP18 9JJ

Richard Sankey & Son Ltd, Bulwell, Nottingham NG6 8PE

Stewart Plastics plc, Purley Way, Croydon, Surrey CR9 4HS

Thermoforce Ltd, Heybridge Works, Maldon, Essex CM9 7NW

Two Wests & Elliott Ltd, Unit 4, Carrwood Road, Sheepbridge Industrial Estate, Chesterfield, Derbyshire S41 9RH

George Ward (Moxley) Ltd, Heathfield Lane, Darleston, Wednesbury, West Midlands WS10 8QZ

Greenhouse heaters – oil, gas and electric

Aeromatic-Barter Ltd, Kynock Road, Eley's Estate, London N18 3BH

J Attwood, Stambermill Industrial Estate, Timmis Road, Lye, Stourbridge, West Midlands

Autogrow Products, Lyngate Road Industrial Estate, North Walsham, Norfolk NR28 0AW

Dimplex Ltd, Millbrook, Southampton, Hants SO9 2DP

George H Elt Ltd, Eltex Works, Bromyard Road, Worcs WR2 5DN

Findlay Irvine Ltd, Bog Road, Penicuik, Midlothian, Scotland

Hotbox Heaters Ltd, Lymington, Hampshire SO41 8JD

Humex MacPenny Ltd (now part of Geeco Products Ltd), Gore Road Industrial Estate, New Milton, Hants BH25 6SE

Parwin Power Heaters, Holme Road, Yaxley, Peterborough PE7 3NA

Shepherd & Norton Ltd, Timmis Road, Lye, Stourbridge, West Midlands

Thermoforce Ltd, Heybridge Works, Maldon, Essex CM9 7NW

Greenhouse insulation

Exmouth Garden Products Ltd, Units 7/8 Salterton Workshops, Budleigh Salterton, Devon EX9 6RJ

Garden Rewards, 104 Branbridges Road, East Peckham, Kent TN12 5HH

A Latter & Co Ltd, 43 South End, Croydon, Surrey

Papronet Propopack Ltd, Wyke Works, Hedon Road, Hull HU9 5NI

Two Wests & Elliott Ltd, Unit 4, Carrwood Road, Sheepbridge Industrial Estate, Chesterfield, Derbyshire S41 9RH

Greenhouses and plastic structures

(Many firms have displays at garden centres)

AGL, Birmingham Road, West Bromwich, West Midlands B71 4JY

Alite Metals (Bristol) Co Ltd, Maze Street, Barton Hill Trading Estate, Bristol

Alitex Ltd, St John's Works, Station Road, Alton, Hants

Alton (see Banbury Compton Ltd)

Banbury Compton Ltd (also Alton), PO Box 17, Banbury, Oxfordshire OX17 3NS

Cambridge Glasshouse Company Ltd, Barton Road, Camberton, Cambs CB3 7BY

Clear Span Ltd, Greenfield, Nr Oldham, Lancs

Cotswold Building Ltd, Cotswold Works, Standlake, Witney, Oxon OX8 7QG

Europa Manor Engineers Ltd, Unit 2, Appletree Road Estate, Chipping Warden, Nr Banbury, Oxfordshire OX17 1LL

Gardenflex Ltd, New Wood Farm, Lathbury, Newport Pagnell, Bucks MK16 8QZ

Garden Rewards, 104 Branbridges Road, East Peckham, Kent TN12 5HH

Halls Garden Products, 44 Church Road, Paddock Wood, Tonbridge, Kent TN12 6EU

Jemp Engineering Ltd, Canal Estate, Station Road, Langley, Berks SL3 6EG (External Roll-shades made from plastic reeds, also pleated shade ideal for conservatory or lean-to-greenhouse)

Pan Britannica Industries Ltd, Britannica House, Waltham Cross, Hertfordshire EN8 7DY (Cooolglass powder)

Pan Products Mallardworth, Unit 8/9 Faraday Road, Bicester Road Industrial Estate, Aylesbury, Bucks (Shade kit made of green uv stabilized fabric)

Two Wests & Elliott Ltd, Unit 4, Carrwood Road, Sheepbridge Industrial Estate, Chesterfield, Derbyshire S41 9RH (various equipment)

A E Headen Ltd, Great North Road, Hatfield, Herts AL9 5SD

LBS, Cottontree, Nr Colne, Lancs

Machin Designs Ltd, Ransome's Dock, Parkgate Road, London SW11 4NP

M D Kidby Buildings Ltd, Kennylands Road, Sonning Common, Reading, Berks RG4 9JP

Norfolk Greenhouses Ltd, PO Box 225, Watton, Norfolk IP25 6PA

Edward Owen Engineering Ltd, C House, Stanhope Road, Camberley, Surrey GU15 3AU

D W Pound, Rock, Kidderminster, Worcestershire

Regal Portable Buildings, Cromford Works, Cromford Road, Langley Mill, Nottinghamshire

Robinsons of Winchester Ltd, Chilcomb Lane, Chilcomb, Winchester, Hants

Rosedale Engineers Ltd, Rosedale Works, 9 Bridlington Road, Hunmanby, Filey, N Yorkshire YO14 9BR

C H Whitehouse Ltd, Buckhurst Works, Frant, Nr Tunbridge Wells, Sussex TN3 9BN

Mist propagators

Access Irrigation Ltd, Crick, Northampton NN6 7XS

Humex MacPenny Ltd (now part of Geeco Products Ltd), Gore Road Industrial Estate, New Milton, Hants BH25 6SE

Thermoforce Ltd, Complete Plantcare Division, Heybridge Works, Maldon, Essex CM9 7NW

Two Wests & Elliott, Unit 4, Carrwood Road, Sheepbridge Industrial Estate, Chesterfield, Derbyshire

Shading applications to glass

Joseph Bentley Ltd, Beck Lane, Barrow on Humber, South Humberside, DN19 7AQ (Shading wash in green or white)

Direct Wire Ties, Wyke Works, Hedon Road, Hull HU9 5NL (Various Equipment)

Exmouth Garden Products Ltd, Units 7/8 Salterton Workshops, Budleigh Salterton, Devon EX9 6RJ

Garden Rewards, 104 Branbridges Road, East Peckham, Kent TN12 5HH

Shading blinds and netting

Exmouth Garden Products Ltd, Units 7/8 Salterton Workshops, Budleigh Salterton, Devon EX9 6RJ

Garden Rewards, 104 Branbridges Road, East Peckham, Kent TN12 5HH

Netlon Ltd, Kelly Street, Blackburn BB2 4PJ (3mm diamond green mesh shading supplied in packs or can be bought off-the-roll at retail outlets)

Nortene Ltd, Linenhall House, 2 Stanley Street, Chester CH1 2LR (Shading available in rolls)

Autovents extractor fans

Bayliss Autovents Ltd, Compton, Ashbourne, Derbyshire

Europa Manor Engineers Ltd, Unit 2, Appletree Road Estate, Chipping Warden, Banbury, Oxon OX17 1LL

Exmouth Garden Products Ltd, Units 7/8 Salterton Workshops, Budleigh Salterton, Devon EX9 6RJ

Halls Garden Products, 44 Church Road, Paddock Wood, Tonbridge, Kent TN12 6EU

Hills Industries Ltd, Pontygwindy Industrial Estate, Caerphilly, Mid-Glamorgan

Humex MacPenny Ltd (now part of Geeco Products Ltd), Gore Road Industrial Estate, New Milton, Hants BH25 6SE

Jemp Engineering Ltd, Canal Estate, Station Road, Langley, Berks SL3 6EG

Thermoforce Ltd, Heybridge Works, Maldon, Essex CM9 7NW

Two Wests & Elliott Ltd, Unit 4, Carrwood Road, Sheepbridge Industrial Estate, Chesterfield, Derbyshire S41 9RH

Conservatories

Alexander Bartholomew Conservatories Ltd, 277 Putney Bridge Road, London SW15 2PT

Amdega Conservatories, Faverdale, Darlington, Co Durham

Anglian Windows Group, PO Box 65, Norwich NR6 6EJ

Banbury Compton Ltd, PO Box 17, Banbury OX17 3NS

Eden Conservatories, Monarch Aluminium Ltd, Manor Road, Swindon Village, Cheltenham GL51 9SQ

Halls Garden Buildings Ltd, Church Road, Paddock Wood, Tonbridge, Kent TN12 6EU

Leofric Conservatories, Leofric Works, Ryton, Coventry CV8 3ED

Robinsons of Winchester Ltd, Chilcomb Lane, Chilcomb, Winchester, Hants

Room outside Conservatories, Goodwood Gardens, Goodwood, W Sussex PO18 0QB

Solardome, Rosedale Engineers Ltd,

9 Bridlington Road, Hunmanby, Filey, Yorks YO14 0LR

Wessex Conservatories, Unit 8, Wyndham Road, Hawksworth Industrial Estate, Swindon SN2 1EJ

Thermometers, lighting etc

S Brannan & Sons Ltd, Cleator Moor, Cumbria CA25 5QE

Diplex Ltd, PO Box 172, Watford, Herts WD1 1BX (SAE for information leaflets)

Jemp Engineering Ltd, Canal Estate, Station Road, Langley, Berks SL3 6EG

Rapitest, Wilson Grimes Products, London Road, Corwen, Clwyd LL21 0DR

Sungro-Lite Ltd, 118 Chatsworth Road, London NW2 5QU

Sunlight Systems, 3 St Mary's Works, Burnmore Street, Leicester LE2 7JJ

Thermoforce Ltd, Camplex Plant Care Division, Heybridge Works, Maldon, Essex CM9 7NW

Commercial Greenhouses

Bridge Greenhouses Ltd, 49 Main Road, Quadring, Spalding, Lincs PE11 4PS

Cambridge Glasshouse Co, Comberton, Cambridge CB3 7BY

HAG Ltd, 16 Spa Industrial Park, Longfield Road, Tunbridge Wells, Kent TN2 3EN

HOK Engineering Ltd, Ottringham Road, Keyingham, nr Hull HU12 9RX

Robinsons of Winchester Ltd, Chilcomb Lane, Chilcomb, Winchester, Hants

Unique Dutch Light Co, Bent Spur Road, Kearsley, Bolton, Lancs

Van der Hoeven, UK Agent: Commercial Greenhouse Sales, Judges Lane, Newent, Glos GL18 1JY

C W Wilco Industries, Ltd, Manchester Street, Hull, North Humberside HU3 4UB

Commercial plastic structures

C A Budd Engineering, Blackfield Farm, The Avenue, West Moors, Wimbourne, Dorset

Clovis Lande Associates Ltd, Branbridges Road, East Peckham, Tonbridge, Kent TN12 5HH

Filclair UK Ltd, Hollyacre, Toddlington Lane, Littlehampton, W Sussex BN17 7PP

Fordingbridge Engineering Ltd, Arundel Road, Fontwell, Arundel, W Sussex BN18 0SD

Glen Heat & Irrigation Ltd, Spalding Road, Pinchbeck, Spalding, Lincs

McGregor Polytunnels Ltd, Soames Lane, Ropley, Alresford, Hants SO24 0ER

Mylan Products Ltd, Squirrels Wood, Reigate Road, Leatherhead, Surrey

Northern Polytunnels, Long Lane, Southport, Merseyside PR9 8EX

Polybuild Ltd, Unit 5C, Tewkesbury Industrial Centre, Green Lane, Tewkesbury, Glos GL20 8HD

Polygrow Designs Ltd, Unit 1, Bactonwood Mill, Spa Common, North Walsham, Norfolk NR28 0QJ

S & W Polytunnel (UK) Ltd, Railway Trading Estate, Martock, Somerset

Composts/soil improvers

Bord na Mona, The Crescent Centre, Temple Way, Bristol BS1 6DZ

Chempak Products, Geddings Road, Hoddesdon, Herts, EN11 0LR

Fisons Ltd, Paper Mill Lane, Bramford, Ipswich, Suffolk IP8 4BZ

ICI Garden Products, Fernhurst, Hazlemere, Surrey G27 3JE

A.W. Maskell & Son Ltd, 72 River Road, Barking, Essex IG11 0DY

Organic Concentrates, Loudhams Wood Lane, Chalfont St. Giles, Bucks

Pan Britannica Industries, Waltham Cross, Herts EN8 7DY

Sinclair Horticulture & Leisure PLC (J. Arthur Bowers), Firth Road, Lincoln LN6 7AH

Vitax Ltd, Owen Street, Coalville, Leicestershire LE6 2DE

Seed suppliers

Booker Seeds Ltd (Hursts), Witham, Essex

J.W. Boyce, Station Road, Soham, Ely, Cambs

D.T. Brown & Co, Ltd, Station Road, Poulton-le-Fylde, Blackpool, Lancs

Carters Seeds, Hele Road, Torquay, Devon.

Chiltern Seeds, Ulverston, Cumbria

S. Dobie & Sons Ltd, Hele Road, Torquay, Devon

Mr. Fothergill's Seeds Ltd, Kentford, Newmarket, Suffolk

Johnsons Seeds Ltd, Stells Lane, Boston, Lincs

Kings Crown Seeds, Coggeshall, Colchester, Essex

Marshalls Seeds, Wisbech, Cambs

W. Robinson & Sons Ltd, Sunny Bank, Forton, nr. Preston, Lancs

Suttons Seeds Ltd, Hele Road, Torquay, Devon

Thompson & Morgan, London Road, Ipswich, Suffolk

Unwins Seeds Ltd, Impington Lane, Histon, Cambs

Organic growing organisations

The Henry Doubleday Research Association, Ryton-on-Dunsmore, Coventry

The Soil Association, 86/88 Colston Street, Bristol

Index

Acknowledgements

The publishers are grateful to the following for granting permission to reproduce the colour photographs: Crittall Warmlife Ltd. [p. *vi* (middle)]; Robinsons of Winchester Ltd. [pp. *i* (top, lower)], *iii* (top)]; Banbury Homes and Gardens Ltd. [pp. *ii* (top, lower), *v* (lower), *vi* (top), *vii* (lower)]; Cambridge Glasshouse Co. Ltd. [pp. *iii*, (lower)], Clovis Lande Associates Ltd. [pp. *iv* (top), *v* (top)]; Serac Ltd [pp. *iv* (lower)]; Rosedale Engineers Ltd. [pp. *vi* (lower)]; Frank Fawkes [pp. *vii* (top)), *ix*, *x* (lower), *xix* (lower), *xxii* (top)]; Sungro-Lite Ltd. [pp. *viii* (lower)]; Suttons Seeds Ltd. [pp. *xi*, *xii*, *xv* (lower), *xvi* (top right, lower right), *xvii*, *xviii*, *xix* (top left, top right), *xx*]; Ronald Menage [pp. *xvi* (top left), *xxiv* (top)]; National Chrysanthemum Society [(p. *xxi* (lower)]; Clive Innes, [(p. *xxii* (top right)]. The photographs on pp. *viii* (top), *x* (top), *xiv* (top), *xv* (top), *xvi* (lower left), *xxi* (top), *xxii* (lower), *xxiii*,

and *xxiv* (lower) are by Bob Challinor.

The publishers are also grateful to the following for providing locations for the following photographs: Arthur Billitt of Clack's Farm [pp. *xiv* (top), *xv* (top), *xvi* (lower left) and *xxi* (top)]; the Royal Horticultural Society's Garden, Wisley, Surrey [pp. *xxii* (lower), *xxiii* and *xxiv* (lower)]; and Alan Titchmarsh [p. *x* (top)].

The publishers also wish to thank Clovis Lande Associates Ltd. for permission to reproduce the black and white photographs on p. 37 and Jemp Engineering Ltd. for those on pp. 56, 72, 73 and 99 (top).

The following drawings were prepared by Frank Hardy: Figs. 2–8, 12–17, 23, 25, 26, 31, 34, 37–39, 42–44, 48–51, 8–61a, 62 and 64–77. Fig. 18 is by Nils Solberg.